Jebel al-Mutawwaq

LEMA III
STUDIES IN THE ARCHAEOLOGY & HISTORY OF THE LEVANT & EASTERN MEDITERRANEAN

General Editor

Hermann Genz, *American University, Beirut*
Marc Lebeau, *European Centre for Upper Mesopotamian Studies*

Editorial Board

Frank Braemer, *CNRS, UMR 7264, Nice*; Isabella Caneva, *Università del Salento, Lecce*
Peter M. Fischer, *University of Gothenburg*; Raphael Greenberg, *Tel Aviv University*
Eric Gubel, *Royal Museums of Art & History, Brussels*; Maria Iacovou, *University of Cyprus, Nicosia*
Karin Kopetzky, *Austrian Academy of Sciences, Vienna*; Ourania Kouka, *University of Cyprus, Nicosia*
Michel al-Maqdissi, *Institut d'études avancées de Paris*; Pierre de Miroschedji, *CNRS, UMR 7041, Nanterre*
Mirko Novák, *Universität Bern*; John K. Papadopoulos, *Cotsen Institute of Archaeology, UCLA, Los Angeles*
Vasıf Şahoğlu, *Ankara Üniversitesi*; Karin Sowada, *Macquarie University, Sydney*; Aslihan Yener, *(Emerita) University of Chicago / Koç Üniversitesi, Istanbul*; Sireen El-Zaatari, *Eberhard-Karls-University, Tübingen*

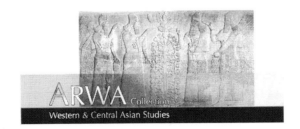

Cover image: Dolmen 535 of Jebel al-Mutawwaq at sunset, southern necropolis, from east.

Volumes published in this series are listed at the back of the book.

VOLUME 3

Jebel al-Mutawwaq

A Fourth Millennium BCE Village and Dolmen Field
Six Years of Spanish-Italian Excavations
(2012–2018)

Edited by

Andrea Polcaro, Juan Ramon Muñiz & Alessandra Caselli

BREPOLS

Keywords: Archaeology of Jordan, Transjordan Highlands, Dolmens, Jebel Mutawwaq, River Zarqa, Early Bronze Age.

British Library Cataloguing in Publication Data

A catalogue record for this book is available from the British Library.

All images unless otherwise indicated are copyright of the Italian-Spanish Expedition to Jebel al-Mutawwaq and reproduced with permission.

© 2024, Brepols Publishers n.v., Turnhout, Belgium

All rights reserved. No part of this publication may be reproduced, stored in a retrieval system, or transmitted, in any form or by any means, electronic, mechanical, photocopying, recording, or otherwise, without the prior permission of the publisher.

D/2024/0095/15
ISBN: 978-2-503-60939-3
e-ISBN: 978-2-503-60940-9
DOI: 10.1484/M.LEMA-EB.5.135808

Printed in the EU on acid-free paper

TABLE OF CONTENTS

List of Illustrations vii

ANDREA POLCARO & JUAN RAMON MUÑIZ
    An Introduction to the Volume 1

JUAN RAMON MUÑIZ
    1. Jebel Al-Mutawwaq: History of Investigations 7

ANDREA POLCARO
    2. The Historical Framework: EB I in Jordan 15

ANDREA POLCARO & JUAN RAMON MUÑIZ
    3. The Site of Jebel al-Mutawwaq: Architecture, Settlement Planning, and Space Organization 25

ELOISA CASADEI & JOAQUIM DEL RIO
    4. The Pottery: Function and Typologies 97

ALESSANDRA CASELLI
    5. The Lithics: Function and Typologies 179

**CHIARA PANICUCCI, SARA SILVESTRINI, GIORGIO GRUPPIONI,
DONATA LUISELLI, ELISABETTA CILLI & PATRIZIA SERVENTI**
    6. Biomolecular Archaeology: Preliminary DNA Analysis of Skeletal Remains from Jebel
    al-Mutawwaq 221

ALESSIA D'AURIA & GAETANO DI PASQUALE
    7. The Development of Olive Growing at the Jebel al-Mutawwaq Site: Preliminary Data 233

ANDREA POLCARO
    8. Conclusions: The Importance of the Jebel al-Mutawwaq Settlement at the Beginning of the
    First Urbanization in the Southern Levant 237

Works Cited 243

LIST OF ILLUSTRATIONS

An Introduction to the Volume — *Andrea Polcaro & Juan Ramon Muñiz*

Figure 0.1 General view of Jebel al-Mutawwaq from the east. All images reproduced in this volume are, unless otherwise indicated, copyright of the Italian-Spanish Expedition to Jebel al-Mutawwaq and are reproduced with permission. 2

1. Jebel Al-Mutawwaq: History of Investigations — *Juan Ramon Muñiz*

Figure 1.1 Juan Antonio Fernández-Tresguerres during a visit in Jordan, 1992. 8

Figure 1.2 Juan Antonio Fernández-Tresguerres. 10

Figure 1.3 Juan Antonio Fernández-Tresguerres on the site of Jebel al-Mutawwaq. 13

2. The Historical Framework: EB I in Jordan — *Andrea Polcaro*

Figure 2.1 The main EB I settlements in the Transjordan area mentioned in the text. 16

3. The Site of Jebel al-Mutawwaq: Architecture, Settlement Planning, and Space Organization — *Andrea Polcaro & Juan Ramon Muñiz*

Figure 3.1 The landscape of the Wadi az-Zarqa Valley in front of Jebel al-Mutawwaq. 26

Figure 3.2 The Hanbury-Tenison Door, in 2015, from the east. 27

Figure 3.3 The southern part of the settlement wall in the Central Sector, from the south. The two stone jambs of the Southern Gate are visible on the left. 28

Figure 3.4 The south-eastern corner of the settlement wall, Area A, from the south. 29

Figure 3.5 General view of the Central Sector, photographed in 2019 from the Temple of the Serpent toward the west. The megalithic entrance of the Great Enclosure is visible in the background. 30

Figure 3.6 The Southern Gate from the north. In the background it is possible to see the pathway descending downstream, now cut by the modern iron fence surrounding the site. 31

Figure 3.7 Plan of the south-eastern corner of the Eastern Sector of Jebel al-Mutawwaq. It is possible to observe the orientation of the houses along the east–west street crossing the village. 32

Figure 3.8 The south-eastern entrance of the settlement wall excavated in Area A, from the west. 33

Figure 3.9 Photogrammetry of House 152 of Jebel al Mutawwaq, north of the Central Sector. 34

Figure 3.10 General view of House 76, from the north. 37

Figure 3.11 The deep conical cup mark in House 76. 38

Figure 3.12 One of the jars with serpent appliques discovered in House 76 of the Temple of the Serpent, now kept in the Department of Antiquities of Jordan storeroom of Zarqa district. 39

Figure 3.13 General view of the Great Enclosure from west, the standing stone in the centre is visible in the foreground. 41

Figure 3.14	Inner side of the northern segment of the wall of the Great Enclosure, from the south.	42
Figure 3.15	Photogrammetry of the Great Enclosure's doorway and the eastern side of the wall W. 102.	43
Figure 3.16	Frontal view of the Great Enclosure's doorway during excavations, from the west.	43
Figure 3.17	Photogrammetry of the Great Enclosure north excavation trench, between the standing stone and W. 102.	44
Figure 3.18	The northern trench of the Great Enclosure after the end of the excavations. In the foreground the long channel naturally carved in the bedrock can be seen.	45
Figure 3.19	The jar discovered behind the standing stone of the Great Enclosure, with the sheep bones preserved on the bottom.	46
Figure 3.20	Photogrammetry of the round structure, possibly a tower tomb, sealing the entry of the Great Enclosure.	47
Figure 3.21	The two large platforms (I. 158 and I. 159) discovered in the southern part of Building 131, from the north.	48
Figure 3.23	Installation I.65, where the base of a jar was discovered in situ in L. 51.	49
Figure 3.22	Detail of the cup mark discovered in Building 131.	49
Figure 3.24	Plan of the second phase of Building 131.	50
Figure 3.25	The copper object recovered in Building 131.	51
Figure 3.26	The cluster of Dolmens 317, 321, and 316 in Area B, from the north.	52
Figure 3.27	Dolmen 228 after excavations, from the north.	54
Figure 3.28	Dolmen 232 after excavations, from the west.	55
Figure 3.29	Dolmen 317 with intact tumulus, before the opening of the funerary chamber, from the north-east.	57
Figure 3.30	Skull of inhumation B. 25, discovered in the burial chamber of Dolmen 317. On the right: detail of the cranium, with the triangular section wound.	58
Figure 3.31	Dolmen 321 after excavations, before the opening of the funerary chamber, from the north-west.	58
Figure 3.32	The entrance corridor of Dolmen 534, from the north-east.	60
Figure 3.33	Copper arrowheads discovered in Dolmen 534: a) rhomboidal arrowhead associated with Burial B. 702; b) foil-shaped arrowhead discovered in secondary context outside the funerary chamber.	60
Figure 3.34	Later view of Dolmen 535, from the west.	61
Figure 3.35	Inner view of the burial chamber of Dolmen 535, from the south. In the foreground the two parallel grooves carved on the later slabs are visible.	62
Figure 3.36	Photogrammetry of Dolmen 535 and of the shaft leading toward Cave 1012, located in front of the entrance to the megalithic monument.	63
Figure 3.37	The bone piles discovered inside Cave 1012, partially crushed by the fall of the hypogeum roof. Amid the human bones two of the miniature vessels are visible.	64
Figure 3.38	The bowl discovered on the bottom of Cave 1012, close to the hearth, before the start of the human depositions in the cave.	64

LIST OF ILLUSTRATIONS

Plate 3.0	Topographical map of Jebel al-Mutawwaq.	65
Plate 3.1a	Eastern façade of the settlement wall, in Area A.	66
Plate 3.1b	Western façade of the settlement wall, in Area A.	66
Plate 3.2a	The south-eastern settlement door, in Area A.	67
Plate 3.2b	Plan of the south-eastern settlement wall and door, in Area A.	67
Plate 3.3	Plan of the southern settlement door and associated structures.	68
Plate 3.4a	Plan of Tower A, in the Western Sector of the settlement.	69
Plate 3.4b	Plan of Tower B, in the Western Sector of the settlement.	69
Plate 3.5	Plan of one of the houses of the Central Sector (2019 Survey BC1).	70
Plate 3.6a	Plan of one of the houses of the Eastern Sector (2019 Survey BE1).	71
Plate 3.6b	Plan of one of the houses of the Eastern Sector (2019 Survey BE2).	72
Plate 3.7a	Plan of one of the houses of the Eastern Sector (2019 Survey BE3).	73
Plate 3.7b	Plan of one of the houses of the Eastern Sector (2019 Survey BE4).	74
Plate 3.8	Plan of one of the houses of the Western Sector (2019 Survey BW2).	75
Plate 3.9a	Plan of one of the houses of the Western Sector (2019 Survey BW3).	76
Plate 3.9b	Plan of one of the houses of the Western Sector (2019 Survey BW4).	77
Plate 3.10a	Plan of one of the houses of the Western Sector (2019 Survey BW5).	78
Plate 3.10b	Plan of House 81, excavated by the Spanish expedition leaded by J. A. Tresguerres Velasco.	79
Plate 3.11a	Plan of one of the houses visible outside the settlement wall (2019 Survey B_Ext1).	80
Plate 3.11b	Plan of one of the houses visible outside the settlement wall (2019 Survey B_Ext2).	81
Plate 3.12	Plan of the Temple of the Serpents, excavated by the Spanish expedition led by J. A. Tresguerres Velasco.	82
Plate 3.13a	Plan of the Great Enclosure, in Area C.	83
Plate 3.13b	Western façade of the eastern wall (W. 101) of the Great Enclosure, in Area C.	83
Plate 3.14	Plan of the small enclosure in the Western Sector (2019 Survey Platform 2).	84
Plate 3.15	Plan of Building 131 with Courtyard L. 51, in Area C.	85
Plate 3.16	Plan of a round isolated platform in the Western Sector (2019 Survey Platform 1).	86
Plate 3.17	a) Plan and b) southern façade of Dolmen 232.	87
Plate 3.18	a) Plan and b) north-western façade of Dolmen 228.	88
Plate 3.19	a) Plan and b) façade of Dolmen 318.	89
Plate 3.20	a) Plan and b) northern façade of Dolmen 317.	90
Plate 3.21	a) Plan and b) northern façade of Dolmen 321.	91
Plate 3.22	Northern façade of Dolmen 535.	92

Plate 3.23	Plan of Dolmen 535 phase I.	93
Plate 3.24	Plan of Dolmen 535 phase II.	94
Plate 3.25	North–south section of Dolmen 535 and Cave C. 1012.	95
Plate 3.26	Plan of Cave C. 1012.	96

4. The Pottery: Function and Typologies —*Eloisa Casadei & Joaquim Del Rio*

Figure 4.1	Mesoscale photographs of the sections of Production Group 1, fine (PG1.1, left), medium (PG1.2, centre), and coarse (PG1.3, right). Pictures taken by the author with a © CanoScan LiDE 110.	109
Figure 4.2	Mesoscale photographs of the sections of Production Group 2. Picture taken by the author with a © CanoScan LiDE 110.	109
Figure 4.4	Examples of manufacturing techniques shown by macro-traces. String-cut disc base indicating the use of wheel (JM.18.CSUD.W.1013/1). Orientation of voids indicating the different coils and the joint points (JM.18.CSUD.415/19, JM.18.CSUD.417/18). Joint between the base and the first coil of the wall indicating by the Y-shape fissure and U-shaped fracture (JM.18.CSUD.418/11, left and right); fissures are visible on the inner surfaces, indicating the different coils (JM.18.CSUD.418/11, centre).	110
Figure 4.3	Storage jar base JM.03.H76.I.291. The base is made by pressing the clay on a mat (lower picture), and then the first coil of the wall is added, leaving a Y-shaped fissure (upper picture).	110
Figure 4.5	Dish fragment JM.16.CSUD.406/14. Example of volcanic mineral inclusions visible on the inner surface, where the burnished slip is not preserved (upper picture). Horizontal and vertical fracture could indicate the use of wheel (lower picture).	111
Figure 4.6	Results of the XRF analysis.	112
Figure 4.7	Analysis of thin section. a) Sample 15/14, surface treatment with calcareous concretions. First petrographic group, with dark reddish rounded grains, x60. b) Sample 15/14, first group with reddish rounded grains. Thin section (TS) x60. With surface treatment. c) Sample 10/14. Thin section (TS) x60. d) Sample 24/15 (TS) x200. e) Sample 8/15 (TS) x60. f) Sample 2/14 (TS) x60. g) Sample 3/15 (TS) x200. h) Sample 22/15 (TS) x60. i) Sample 6/15 (TS) x60. j) Sample 7/15 (TS) x60. k) Sample 5/14 (TS) x60. Sediment with fossils and calcareous rock.	113
Figure 4.8	Production Group 1.	115
Figure 4.9	Production Group 1 (continued).	116
Figure 4.10	Production Group 2.	116
Figure 4.11	Distribution of the parallels of types C.b, B.A.2–6, H.B.3.	119
Figure 4.12	Distribution of the parallels JB.A.3, NJ.B, WNJ.B.2.	120
Figure 4.13	Distribution of the parallels of types B.D.1, W.NJ.A, H.B.12.	121
Figure 4.14	Distribution of the parallels of types JB.A.2, H.B.9, H.B.10, H.B.11, H.B.4.	122
Figure 4.15	Distribution of the parallels of types B.B.2, B.B.3, B.C, JB.C, JB.A.1, H.B.5, H.B.7, H.A, LSJ.C, LSJ.A, N.A.2, NJ.A.3, NJ.A.4, LSJ.C.3, LSJ.D.	123
Figure 4.16	Net painted jug from the Temple of the Serpent (Fernández-Tresguerres 2005a, fig. 18).	124

Graph 4.1	Quantity of diagnostic sherds. Total number of diagnostic sherds per area (left); percentage of diagnostic sherds per contexts (right): public/production = Area CW, CC; domestic = A, survey area; cultic = House 75, House 76, temple court (including Rooms 1 to 5); funerary = Area B, Area CC Dolmen 534, Area CS Dolmen 535; other = the Great Circle in Area CE.	98
Graph 4.2	Quantitative analysis of the decorations.	107
Graph 4.3	Quantitative analysis of production groups.	115
Graph 4.4	Distribution of the types per area.	117
Plate 4.1	Types C.A.1, C.A.2, C.B.1a, C.B.1b, C.B.2.	129
Plate 4.2	Types C.C.1, C.C.2, C.C.3, C.C.4.	131
Plate 4.3	Types B.A.1, B.A.2, B.A.3, B.A.4, B.A.5, B.A.6, B.A.7.	135
Plate 4.4	Types B.B.1, B.B.2, B.B.3, B.C.1, B.C.2, B.D.1, D.A.1.	137
Plate 4.5	Types JB.A.1, JB.A.2, JB.A.3.	141
Plate 4.6	Types JB.B.1, JB.B.2, JB.B.3, JB.B.4, JB.C.1, JB.C.2, JB.C.3.	143
Plate 4.7	Types NJ.A.1, NJ.A.2, NJ.A.3, NJ.A.4.	147
Plate 4.8	Types NJ.B.1, NJ.B.2, NJ.B.3.	149
Plate 4.9	Types NJ.C.1, NJ.C.2, NJ.C.3, NJ.C.4, NJ.D.1, NJ.D.2, NJ.D.3, NJ.D.4.	151
Plate 4.10	Types WNJ.A.1, WNJ.A.2, WNJ.A.3, WNJ.B.1, WNJ.B.2.	153
Plate 4.11	Types OJ.A.1, OJ.B.1, OJ.C.1, LSJ.A.1, LSJ.A.2, LSJ.A.3, LSJ.B.1, LSJ.B.2, LSJ.B.3, LSJ.B.4, LSJ.C.1, LSJ.C.2.	155
Plate 4.12	Types LSJ.C.3, LSJ.D.1.	157
Plate 4.13	Types LSJ.D.2, LSJ.D.3, H.A.1.	159
Plate 4.14	Types H.A.2, H.A.3, H.A.4, H.A.5.	161
Plate 4.15	Types H.B.1.	163
Plate 4.16	Types H.B.2, H.B.3.	165
Plate 4.17	Types H.B.4, H.B.5.	167
Plate 4.18	Types H.B.6, H.B.7, H.B.8.	169
Plate 4.19	Types H.B.9, H.B.10, H.B.11, H.B.12.	171
Plate 4.20	Bases.	173
Plate 4.21	Decorations.	175
Plate 4.22	Decorations (continued).	177
Plate 4.23	Miniature and Production Group 2 jugs.	179
Table 4.1	Procedure of the typological classification adopted in the present analysis.	99

5. The Lithics: Function and Typologies — *Alessandra Caselli*

Figure 5.1	An example of a Canaanean blade with glossy surface found in the Temple area (JM.17.O.113).	183

Figure 5.2	The tabular scrapers found as grave goods of the burial B. 25 inside Dolmen 317. JM.13.0.70 on the right, JM.13.0.69 on the left.	185
Figure 5.3	The flint tools found gathered in L. 51, Area C West.	187
Figure 5.4	The Neolithic point found in L. 51, Area C West (JM.14.0.57).	188
Figure 5.5	Limestone grinding slab JM.18.0.37.	190
Figure 5.6	The intact limestone loom weight/spindle whorl found in Building 151 (JM.17.0.34).	193
Figure 5.7	Some examples of mace-heads from Jebel al-Mutawwaq: 1 (JM.14.0.74) and 2 (JM.14.0.73) were found in Area C East; 3 (JM.17.0.31) and 4 (JM.17.0.32) were found inside Building 151.	196
Figure 5.8	The stone disc (JM.18.0.36) found in Area C South.	197
Graph 5.1	The distribution of the chipped stone tools throughout the site of Jebel al-Mutawwaq.	199
Graph 5.2	The distribution of the worked stone tools throughout the site of Jebel al-Mutawwaq.	200
Plate 5.1	Canaanean and non-Canaanean blades.	203
Plate 5.2	Non-Canaanean blades.	205
Plate 5.3	Scrapers.	207
Plate 5.4	Tabular scrapers.	209
Plate 5.5	Tabular scrapers.	211
Plate 5.6	Borers.	213
Plate 5.7	Points.	215
Plate 5.8	Grinding slab.	216
Plate 5.9	Grinding slabs.	217
Plate 5.10	Handstones.	218
Plate 5.11	Pestles and loom weights.	219
Plate 5.12	Mortars.	220
Plate 5.13	Mace-heads.	221
Plate 5.14	Stone vessels.	222
Table 5.1	Distribution of the typologies of the chipped stone tools.	182
Table 5.2	Details about the tabular scrapers found at Jebel al-Mutawwaq.	186
Table 5.3	Distribution of the worked stone tools throughout the site of Jebel al-Mutawwaq.	189
Table 5.4	Details of the grinding slabs found at Jebel al-Mutawwaq.	190
Table 5.5	Details of the handstones and pestles found at Jebel al-Mutawwaq.	191
Table 5.6	Details of the mortars found at Jebel al-Mutawwaq.	193
Table 5.7	Details of the textile production tools found at Jebel al-Mutawwaq.	194
Table 5.8	Details of the mace-heads found at Jebel al-Mutawwaq.	196

Table 5.9	Details of the stone vessels found at Jebel al-Mutawwaq.	198

6. Biomolecular Archaeology: Preliminary DNA Analysis of Skeletal Remains from Jebel al-Mutawwaq — *Chiara Panicucci, Sara Silvestrini, Giorgio Gruppioni, Donata Luiselli, Elisabetta Cilli & Patrizia Serventi*

Figure 6.2	Skull detail of the individual B. 25.	227
Figure 6.1	Skeletal remains of the individual B. 25 discovered in archaeological campaign of 2013.	227
Figure 6.3	The several steps of analysis, from the petrous bone collection, to DNA extraction (A–F). In particular, this procedure consists of different phases: digestion (A–B), binding to the silica matrix (C–D), washing (E), and final elution (F).	229
Table 6.1	HVS-I motifs of the researchers who had been in contact with the ancient samples during the archaeological excavation and the laboratory work. * Overall quality: 1–0.9 the haplogroup assignment is quite reliable.	231
Table 6.2	Qubit® quantification and PCR amplification results.	232
Table 6.3	DNA quantification analysis of LER samples using Quantifiler® trio kit. This sample was extracted twice (LER1a and LER 1b) and each extraction was amplified in two replicas.	233
Table 6.4	mtDNA results of samples from Jebel al-Mutawwaq site. [1] sample MU3 shows ambiguous results for haplogroup assignments based only this portion of mtDNA. * Overall Quality: 1–0.9 the haplogroup assignment is quite reliable.	233

7. The Development of Olive Growing at the Jebel al-Mutawwaq Site: Preliminary Data — *Alessia D'Auria & Gaetano Di Pasquale*

Figure 7.1	Whole olive stone from the archaeological site of Jebel al Mutawwaq.	236
Table 7.1	Archaeobotanical data of *Olea europaea* referred to the Levantine area (Neolithic–Early Bronze Age).	237

8. Conclusions: The Importance of the Jebel al-Mutawwaq Settlement at the Beginning of the First Urbanization in the Southern Levant — *Andrea Polcaro*

Figure 8.1	Dolmen 534 in the southern necropolis, with its external 'stone box' shape well preserved.	241

An Introduction to the Volume

Andrea Polcaro & Juan Ramon Muñiz

Jebel al-Mutawwaq is an archaeological site located in the Zarqa region, Jordan. Geographically, it is located in the so-called 'Transjordanian Highlands', along the Middle Wadi az-Zarqa Valley, around seven kilometres south-east of Jerash.

The name of the site in Arabic literally means 'the mountain surrounded' or 'the rounded mountain'. Effectively, looking from the satellite images, the high hill of Mutawwaq appears as a circular relief surrounded by water at least on two sides: on the southern side by the Wadi az-Zarqa and to the western one by Wadi Quneye. Both the western stream and the southern river, together with two active springs — the biggest one called Ain Qreysan — are still used as water sources by the local villages like Quneye (Polcaro & Muñiz 2017). This rich water landscape was much more suitable during the fourth millennium BCE, when, at the end of the Late Chalcolithic (3800–3700 BCE) a dry period began in the southern Levant.[1] For this reason between the 3500 and 3100 BCE the local communities of the region started to permanently settle on the top and on the southern side of Jebel al-Mutawwaq, building a large village of around twenty hectares, reaching several hundred inhabitants at the end of the fourth millennium. Living with a mixed agro-pastoral economy, they started to shape this naturally well-defended high place with a megalithic monumental architecture. Located along the main river of the central Transjordan Highlands, at the fringe of the eastern desert, Jebel al Mutawwaq occupied a strategic position, controlling the east–west route for pastoral movements and commercial exchange toward the fertile Jordan Valley. The megalithic construction programme of this Transjordanian population at the beginning of the Bronze Age, involved the erection of thousands of dolmens covered by stone tumuli and sometimes provided with a sort of monumental entrance (*dromos*). Organized in clusters along the slopes of the mountain of Mutawwaq and the neighbouring hills, these huge megalithic structures surrounded the village of Mutawwaq and, as shown by the following chapters, aimed at the creation of an anthropic landscape, changing and transforming forever the natural view of the Wadi az-Zarqa Valley, in a strong and impressive way, striking the imagination of the people arriving in this region over the centuries: ancient Egyptian and Romans, as well as Arabs and Europeans.

The Discovery

There are no written source mentioning Jebel al-Mutawwaq, and we have no idea of the ancient name of this settlement. This area, clearly characterized by the high concentration of megalithic monuments, was noticed not very early in the history of the Near

---

[1] This is supported by the palaeo-climatic data, showing wetter climate conditions in the southern Levant during the fifth millennium BCE, starting to change in the first half of the fourth millennium BCE (see Clarke et al. 2015, 10–15).

Andrea Polcaro (andrea.polcaro@unipg.it) is an Associate Professor in Near Eastern Archaeology at Perugia University (Italy).

Juan Ramon Muñiz (juanramunhiz@gmail.com) is a Professor and Researcher in Near Eastern Archaeology at Pontificia Facultad de San Esteban de Salamanca (Spain).

Figure 0.1: General view of Jebel al-Mutawwaq from the east. All images reproduced in this volume are, unless otherwise indicated, copyright of the Italian-Spanish Expedition to Jebel al-Mutawwaq and are reproduced with permission.

Eastern exploration surveys in Jordan by the British army.

Nelson Glueck was the first to identify the site during his survey of eastern Palestine between 1932 and 1947, but he misnamed the site as Tell Mughaniyeh (Glueck 1951, 73). Nevertheless, in the 1980s, Jack W. Hanbury-Tenison was the first explorer who recognized the real historical value of Jebel al-Mutawwaq, identifying it as an important Early Bronze Age I site (Hanbury-Tenison 1986, 137). He began his archaeological survey in the Jerash region, already famous for the impressive remains of one of the largest Roman cities in Jordan, then descended toward the Wadi az-Zarqa Valley with the aim of mapping the presence of fourth-millennium BCE sites. In particular, he looked at the presence of pottery sherds on the surface as well as other materials and features defining the passage between the Late Chalcolithic and the Early Bronze Age. This was and still is, as we will see in Chapter 2, one of the main archaeological topics for the study of the beginning of the urbanization process in the southern Levant.

Hanbury-Tenison immediately understood the importance of Jebel al-Mutawwaq and he came back for a brief excavation campaign and a more accurate survey of the site (Hanbury-Tenison 1989), creating the first topographical map. He was the first to recognize the three main features of the ancient settlement: 1. Dimensions: it is the largest Early Bronze Age I site in the central Jordanian Highlands (comparable only with Tell Umm Hammad in the Jordan Valley and Jawa in the Badia Eastern Desert); 2. Presence of a surrounding stone wall, such as in Jawa; 3. Circular domestic architecture, usually related to the very early beginning of the Bronze Age (Early Bronze Age IA).

The Following Archaeological Expeditions

The architectural and topographic characteristics of the site immediately proved the great historical importance of Jebel al-Mutawwaq, a site still visible on the surface, well preserved, in appearance without significant superimposition of later structures. It is thus a perfect place to study an example of a large fourth-millennium BCE village community at the beginning of the social transformations leading toward the future mature urbanization process. After the Hanbury-Tenison preliminary investigation, the site began to be excavated by a Spanish expedition of Oviedo University led by J. A. Fernández-Tresguerres Velasco (see Chapter 1). The Spanish expedition worked on the site for twenty years, discovering several important buildings dated to the main phase of use of the Early Bronze Age I village, such as the Temple of the Serpent (Fernández-Tresguerres 2008a), a large sacred area located in the centre of the village and characterized by the presence of a precinct including not only a main broadroom for the cult, but also five smaller rooms for productive activities, proving centralized organization of at least part of the village economy. The excavation to the Temple of the Serpent had also provided a corpus of C14 data of the settlement proving that the main period of the life of the village was effectively the Early Bronze Age I.[2]

Another contribution provided by the Oviedo's archaeological expedition to the site was the definitive identification of the village organization already proposed by Hanbury-Tenison, with the clear recognition of the three main sectors of the settlement, called the Eastern, Central, and Western Sectors. This organization is no longer easily recognizable due to disturbances by modern agricultural activity that have erased the upper part of the site, where the majority of the stone alignments originally identifiable on the field was lost. However, the difference in the architecture and the inner spatial organization of the dwellings and the buildings inside these sectors is still evident and, together with the discovery of the Temple of the Serpent is one of the several proofs, later highlighted in Chapters 2 and 3, that the Early Bronze Age I village of Jebel al-Mutawwaq was becoming a real city at the end of the fourth millennium BCE and that it was abandoned before it could complete a full urbanization process of the living community. Finally, the historical importance of the site is very high and connected with a delicate moment of human history: the passage from the life of the village to the life of the city, which involved a revolution in the economy, social organization, and religion of the Levantine population. A following extension of the excavation in Jebel al-Mutawwaq was extremely important to clarify this historical passage from the Late Chalcolithic to the urban periods of Early Bronze Age II and III, in order to interpret the function and the meaning of the unique extended megalithic monumental necropolis and the complexity of the settlement and of several large public structures already identified by past surveys and excavations, but whose investigation was not completed.

This is the main reason which lead Juan Ramon Muñiz Alvarez and Andrea Polcaro to restart the excavation at the site with a new joint Spanish-Italian Project, after more than twenty years of excavations by the Spanish expedition of Oviedo University headed by J. A. Fernández-Tresguerres Velasco (see Chapter 1). The Spanish-Italian Project started in 2012 and, after ten years, it is still working, aiming at a deeper comprehension of the site.

Structure of the Volume

The volume summarizes the results of the first six seasons of excavations (2012–2018) at Jebel al-Mutawwaq, showing the characteristics of the architecture and of the material culture typical of the site. After the first Chapter (1) summarizing the work undertaken by the old Spanish expedition headed by J. A. Fernández-Tresguerres, the second Chapter (2) will set the site in its historical framework, looking at the still open issues and debates on chronology, social complexity, and settlement typology in the southern Levant and, in particular, in the Transjordanian Highland.

The third Chapter (3) is dedicated to the planning and architecture of the site, both village and necropolis. In particular, concerning the settlement, the domestic architecture will be read looking at the general organization of the village space, together with the peculiar features of some public buildings, indicating a high level of internal social and political organization. The peculiar characteristic of the wall surrounding the settlement, representing one of the oldest 'fortification' walls in the history of Jordan together with the walls of Jawa, will also be analysed. Concerning the megalithic necropolis, the general characteristics of architecture and the location of the dolmens will be analysed, together with the findings recovered, with the aim of trying to delineate the organization of the Early Bronze I society in Jebel al-Mutawwaq. At the end of Chapter 3 a group of dolmens discovered and excavated on the southern slope of the village, some of them *intra moenia*, will be presented.

---

2 More precisely, analysis has been performed on carbonized olive seeds giving 3250–3000 BCE (Muñiz & Polcaro 2016) and on animal bones giving 5290–5040 BP = 3340–3090 BCE (Beta Analytic 194526) and 5270–5170 BP = 3320–3220 BCE (Beta Analytic 194527), see Polcaro et al. 2014. See also Chapter 3.

This group of dolmens pertains to the last phase of occupation of the site (Early Bronze Age IB) as suggested by the pottery repertoire and confirmed by the C14 analysis performed, presented in Chapter 3.[3]

The fourth and the fifth Chapters (4 and 5) are dedicated to the analysis of the pottery assemblage and the small finds (lithic). These chapters aim to give a general view of the findings recovered by the Spanish-Italian Expedition and some of those discovered in the last seasons of the Spanish expedition (excavations to the Temple of the Serpents), establishing the first typological and functional classification of the pottery and of the lithic tools of Jebel al-Mutawwaq. Moreover, in Chapter 4, the study of the pottery sherds is enriched with optical X-ray diffraction analysis to reconstruct the mineralogical context.

The sixth Chapter (6) is dedicated to the ancient DNA analysis performed on some human bone samples recovered in the megalithic necropolis, in one of the groups located in the south-eastern cliff of the mountain. This analysis aims to give more information about the population which lived in the large Early Bronze Age I village of Jebel al-Mutawwaq.

Finally, the seventh Chapter (7) is dedicated to the analysis of the olive seeds found during the excavations in distinct archaeological contexts, such as funerary and domestic settings. The presence of several olive seeds is consistent with the development of olive growing occurring since the beginning of the Early Bronze Age.

The volume ends with a conclusion by the editors, summarizing all the available data about the settlement and the necropolis, in order to present a coherent historical picture of the site in the framework of the Early Bronze Age I Transjordan Highlands and, mostly, its importance for the studies about the beginning of urbanization in the southern Levant.

Methodology

The data presented in this book coming from archaeological excavations performed by the Spanish-Italian expedition to Jebel al-Mutawwaq mostly in the Central and Eastern Sectors of the village and in the southern megalithic necropolis. The excavations have been performed using stratigraphical methods, registering every layer as a stratigraphical unit by the acronym 'SU' followed by a progressive number, and the term of 'locus' for the structures and architectonical features, labelled using a capital letter followed by a number. Thus the acronyms used for the locus are 'L' for floors, 'W' for walls, 'D' for doors, 'B' for burials, 'P' for pits or wells, 'I' for installations like ovens or platforms, 'C' for caves, and 'S' for slabs. Concerning the stratigraphical units, it must be taken into account that generally the stratigraphy, in particular along the central-southern topographical areas of the settlement, is low and poorly preserved. An exception seems to be the southern slope of the mountain and the upper part of the settlement, where a different morphology of the bedrock allows a higher stratigraphy compared to the other parts of the site with a consequent better state of preservation of the archaeological structures. The megalithic tombs of the large necropolis extending around the walled settlement of the Early Bronze Age I, mostly of the classical trilithon dolmen typology, are called simple 'Dolmen' followed by a number corresponding to the one given by the past Spanish expedition of Oviedo University during their general assessment survey of the funerary structures preserved at the site in 2010.

During the Spanish-Italian archaeological excavations all the findings recovered in the field have been registered. The core of the data presented in the book in Chapters 4 and 5 comes from a database, where not only the drawings and the counting of the sherds and of the flints, but also all the information about the typologies and morphological characteristics of vessels and tools identified have been collected. The terminology used for the identification of pottery sherds is an acronym composed by two initial capital letters of the site (JM), the last two numbers of the year of excavation (such as 15), the area where the sherd was found (such as CEST), the stratigraphical unit where it was discovered (such as 102) and, finally, after a slash sign in lower case the progressive letter of the sherd (such as /5), for example JM.15.CEST.102/5. The terminology used for objects, both lithic tools and other materials, is an acronym composed by two initial capital letters of the site (JM), the last two numbers of the year of excavation (such as 17), followed by the capital letter 'O' and a progressive number given at the end of the excavations such as (O.32), for example JM.17.O.32.

Acknowledgements

The directors of the Spanish-Italian Expedition to Jebel al-Mutawwaq, J. R. Muñiz and A. Polcaro want to thank the Italian 'Ministero degli Affari Esteri

---

3 For the chronology of the Early Bronze Age I of the southern Levant the editors have chosen the last classification based on the C14 dates from Jericho/Tell es-Sultan (Nigro et al. 2019).

AN INTRODUCTION TO THE VOLUME

e della Cooperazione Internazionale', the Spanish 'Ministerio De Educatión, Cultura y Deporte', the Italian Embassy in Amman, the Spanish Embassy in Amman, the 'Università degli Studi di Perugia', the 'Pontificia Facultad San Esteban' and the Centre of Excellence Studies and Archaeological Research of Rome for their constant help and support. In particular, from the Italian Embassy, we want to thank the excellencies former Italian Ambassadors H. E. Giovanni Brauzzi and H. E. Fabio Cassese and the current Italian Ambassador H. E. Luciano Pezzotti, the former Cultural Attachés Dr Marco Marzeddu and Dr Federico Vidic and the current Cultural Attaché Dr Emilio Fralleone, together with the First Secretary and Consul Valeria Romare, for kindly sustaining our work with great interest and passion of which we are proud. We want to thank also our friends and colleagues of the Department of Antiquities of Jordan, working hard with us on the field every time, first of all the former General Directors of the Department of Antiquities of Jordan H. E. Mother Jamhawi, H. E. Yazid Elayan, H. E. Ahmad Ashami, H. E. Hisham al-Abadi, the current General Director of the Department of Antiquities of Jordan H. E. Fadi Bala'awi, the former Director of Excavations and Surveys of the Department of Antiquities of Jordan Mr Khalil Hamdan, and the current Director of Excavations and Surveys of the Department of Antiquities of Jordan Mr Aktham Oweidi, the former Directors of the Zarqa Region area of the Department of Antiquities of Jordan Mr Romel Grayb and Mr Aref Naar, and the current Director of the Zarqa Region area of the Department of Antiquities of Jordan Mr Akram. We want to deeply thank all the authors and contributors to this volume for their work, and particularly Dr Alessandra Caselli (vice-director of the Italian team, who wrote Chapter 5 and is one of the editors of this volume) and Dr Eloisa Casadei (who wrote Chapter 4), both skilled area supervisors for several years and responsible for the fieldwork laboratories organizing students for hard, constant, and precious work. Moreover, we want to thank the Italian and Spanish archaeologists who have contributed in the past to the archaeological expedition with their expertise as area supervisors and consultants, such as Prof. Sara Pizzimenti (Università degli Studi di Pisa) and Prof. Marta D'Andrea (Sapienza Università di Roma); Ann Anderson for the precious help in the fieldwork; Dr Valentin Alvarez, for technical work; Dr Silvia Mogliazza and Dr Chiara Panicucci for anthropological analysis; and Dr Martin Monik and Dr Zuzana Lendakowa for the geophysical analysis. Finally, a deep acknowledgement goes to the numerous Italian and Spanish students of archaeology who worked with the Spanish-Italian Expedition at Jebel al-Mutawwaq over the last seven years of field research in Jordan.

1. Jebel Al-Mutawwaq: History of Investigations

Juan Ramon Muñiz

The Spanish Expedition and the History of Explorations between the 1989 and the 2011

It is important to know the reason why Spanish archaeological teams are present in Jordan and their origin. To explain this fact, we must go back to the first Spanish archaeological excavation in Jordan, which took place in 1960. Spain has historically had an important gap with archaeology that was developed in the Holy Land, including in this definition the territories of Palestine, Syria, and Jordan. While European governments began to create research institutions in these lands since the late nineteenth century (the British Palestine Exploration Fund was created in 1865, the German Deutscher Verein zur Erforschung Palästinas in 1877, and the École Biblique et Archéologique Française in 1890, for example), Spain continued to direct its cultural efforts towards Latin America and to a lesser extent North Africa. In an isolated way, and carried by the fashion trend, in 1871 the National Archaeological Museum of Spain had sent an expedition to the Middle East in search of finds for its collection, without major research significance.

The geopolitical reasons for this distancing are many, such as the lack of economic or political interests in the Middle East — since the nationals were in the former colonies — or the distance at a religious and cultural level from the peoples of the Mediterranean east. Whatever they were, Spain did not have its own research institution in the Holy Land until 1956, when after years of negotiation the Spanish Biblical and Archaeological Institute of Jerusalem was inaugurated, known as Casa de Santiago, founded by Monsignor Maximino Romero. Until that time, Spaniards who wished to investigate or deepen their knowledge of history, archaeology, or the Holy Scriptures had to go to the centres of study of religious orders or to academic institutions in other countries such as the French École Biblique.

The activity of Spanish archaeology in Jordan began in 1960, when Joaquín González Echegaray, then Director of the Spanish Biblical and Archaeological Institute of Jerusalem, directed the excavation of Mogaret Dalal in the Zarqa River basin.[1] That expedition was promoted by the Chargé d'Affaires of the Spanish Embassy in Amman, Mr José Antonio Varela, and was aimed at studying this cave with the aim of finding prehistoric levels in it (Sánchez Caro & Calvo Gómez (eds) 2015, 166–80).

Although the objective pursued by Spanish archaeologists was half achieved — the site had been partially destroyed in the Middle Ages for the construction of a monastery — that first excavation was an example of scientific rigour and quality for the Jordanian administration and that was how the successive rulers of Jordan opened and responded to requests for cultural collaboration between the two countries.[2]

Juan Ramon Muñiz (juanramunhiz@gmail.com) is a Professor and Researcher in Near Eastern Archaeology at Pontificia Facultad de San Esteban de Salamanca (Spain).

1 The results of the works were published in the review *Ampurias* 31–32 of 1969.

2 With this memory I wanted to introduce several data to understand the presence of Juan A. Fernández-Tresguerres in Jordan. The existence of the Spanish Biblical and Archaeological Institute of Jerusalem, under the Spanish Episcopal Conference, is the reason why most of the first excavation directors were priests. The second is the close relationship of the Spanish Embassy in Amman

Figure 1.1: Juan Antonio Fernández-Tresguerres during a visit in Jordan, 1992.

This new bridge laid by the House of Santiago facilitated the entry into Jordan of other researchers such as Emilio Olávarri. Its first excavation in the Transjordan was the Iron Age site of Ḥirbet 'Ara'ir or Arair, which is located in the central area of Jordan, 3 km north of Arnón and near Dibón. He had previously excavated in Jerusalem and other parts of Palestine. Emilio Olávarri was preparing his campaigns from Jerusalem — then on the border between Jordan and the state of Israel — with a team composed of students from the House of Santiago and the Seminary of Oviedo, as well as the labour staff working in Jerusalem.[3] These excavations of Olávarri in Aroer were brief in duration, three campaigns between 1964 and 1966, since the Six Day War in 1967 meant the departure of the Spanish community that resided in the House of Santiago and with them the investigations they had opened (Sánchez Caro & Calvo Gómez (eds) 2015, 265).

From the seventies, this archaeological collaboration between Jordan and Spain was strengthened with the financing line opened by the Directorate General for Cultural and Scientific Relations of the Ministry of Foreign Affairs of Spain that allowed the arrival of Martín Almagro Basch and his team in 1971 to undertake the restoration of Qsair Amra, in the province of Zarqa. Thus the first Spanish Archaeological Mission in Jordan was starting, and from that moment also led the restoration work of the Omeya Palace and the Citadel of Amman, the excavation of the Agora of Gerasa (Jerash) since 1981, and the Tell Abu Swwan 1982 expedition of Mario Menendez. For its part, the House of Santiago also maintained the works of Olávarri in Khirbet Medeineh (or Medeinet al-Ma'arradjeh) in 1976 and 1982.[4] This Spanish archaeological effervescence that became available to two research institutions (La Casa de Santiago and the Spanish Archaeological Mission in Jordan) that also collaborated with each other, stopped around 1983 with the loss of the line of financing that had sustained the work and diplomatic issues related to the Directorates General. Thus began a period of six years with hardly any Spanish archaeological expeditions in the country.

From 1989 the works were resumed in the Citadel of Amman, now directed by Antonio Almagro Gorbea, with the involvement in the project of the School of Arab Studies of the CSIC and the Centre of Arab and Archaeological Studies 'Ibn 'Arabi' of Murcia. That year the first excavation permit was also requested for Jebel Mutawwaq, in Zarqa, under the direction of Professor Juan Antonio Fernández-Tresguerres who led these works until his death in 2011 (Fig. 1.1).

The first campaigns in Mutawwaq focused on the downstream Neolithic settlement,[5] the detailed exploration of the site (the Neolithic settlement, the Early Bronze Age settlement, the Bronze Age terrace, the burial mounds and dolmens), and the first measurements, with the participation of the first students and graduates of the University of Oviedo. These outstanding students already were focusing their careers on archaeology or prehistory and were directing their thesis or thesis studies taking advantage of their presence on the site. The results and the support that the expedition

---

with archaeology, and finally, I wanted to expressly quote Joaquín González Echegaray, the priest and archaeologist who invited Juan Fernández-Tresguerres to learn about the archaeology of the Holy Land in 1981.

3 José Manuel Legazpi, then a seminarian in Oviedo, or Ángel Miranda Tamargo are some of them.

---

4 Mario Menéndez was part of the team of Emilio Olávarri, who promoted this expedition in the tell located in the city of Gerasa in 1982.

5 The site, called Kheraysin, is currently under investigation by another Spanish team, see Ibañez et al. 2016.

had with the creation of the Archaeological Mission in 1992 facilitated the incorporation of numerous teams of Spanish students with French archaeologists from IFAPO, a collaboration that was maintained over the next decade.

As of 1998 the investigation underwent an unpleasant adjustment for the first time lacking public funds to continue the excavation. Since 1999 the teams were reduced from the dozens of students in the previous five years to teams of three or four students plus the director, which was the number of people who could travel to Jordan on the meagre budget. The excavation campaigns were balanced with long periods of material processing at the residence and the Institute, aimed at the systematic publication of the results. In the 2001 campaign, the aim of the work was also extended by excavating Al Hawetan, near Wadi Hmeid (Fernández-Tresguerres 2002; 2010 and 2011), while in 2002 it was decided not to travel to the site in order to process and publish the material studied — such as children's burials in vessels — and due to the lack of budgetary certainty for the expedition.

In the next stage of work, initiated in 2003, the Temple of the Serpents was discovered, Fernández-Tresguerres's most cited contribution to Jordanian archaeology. During the following years the ritual complex located in the central portion of the Early Bronze Age I village was completely excavated, and it consisted of a main room with an annexed courtyard where a series of complementary structures of the main building had been built.[6] In these years of work, during which students of the University of Oviedo and former students of Fernández-Tresguerres who already worked as professional archaeologists collaborated, it was possible to document the decorative and formal programme of ceramics, flint tools, quartzite, and bone related to this temple. The ritual complex linked forms of sacred Chalcolithic buildings (such as Ein Gedi) with the techniques and materials of the new era, the Early Bronze Age. The dates provided by the C14 confirmed these theories.

Since 2007, funds were obtained to carry out a photographic flight over the site and to restore some of the most outstanding pieces of the excavated complex. And from the following year the renovation of the Mutawwaq dolmens inventory and its surroundings was undertaken, separating the work into two campaigns: one summer campaign with the students of the University of Oviedo and another autumnal campaign with the professional archaeologists who carried out this inventory. This approach was complemented by a complete renovation of the general planimetry, after several years of work on local systems and partial topographies.

This work was suddenly interrupted in 2011 by the unexpected death of Juan A. Fernández-Tresguerres, who in 2010 had not been able to attend his annual appointment with Jordan. This unwanted change meant that the scientific direction of the project was taken by Josefa Sanz Fuentes in the 2011 campaign to finish the work of Fernández-Tresguerres and, later, by Ángel Martínez Casado OP of the Pontifical Faculty of San Esteban de Salamanca who assumed all his technical team.

Juan Antonio Fernández-Tresguerres Velasco: A Life for Archaeology

The life of Juan Antonio Fernández-Tresguerres was dedicated to study, continuing education, and the pleasure of discovering, reading, and thinking. Fernández-Tresguerres studied history, when he was already a Dominican friar. His first career, that of theology, had been completed in 1968 at the Pontifical Faculty of San Esteban de Salamanca. He later moved to Valladolid where he graduated in history in 1973.

He immediately began his career as an archaeologist because that same year, and in a conversation in Ribadesella, Martín Almagro Basch commissioned him to direct the work in the Cave of Los Azules, in Cangas de Onís. This circumstance, which he always described as a lucky hit by Almagro who ordered him and insisted that he go to Los Azules, marked the most important change in his archaeological career. That same year he taught for the first time at the University of Oviedo.

This opportunity to excavate the Cave of Los Azules opened the way for the prehistoric Cantabrian investigation, which culminated in his doctoral thesis 'El Aziliense en las provincias de Asturias y Santander', read in 1980 and for which he obtained the note of Outstanding cum laude.

Juan A. Fernández-Tresguerres and his Work in Spain

The first works and archaeological publications of Fernández-Tresguerres focused on the Castilian plateau, where he toured the territory in his student days

---

6 See Chapter 3.

Figure 1.2: Juan Antonio Fernández-Tresguerres.

in the company of Germán Delibes or Pedro Rodríguez Oliva, locating remains of archaeological interest for his research lines.

However, his most important contribution was the study of the Cantabrian Aziliense from the excavations in the Cave of Los Azules, in Asturias. Through thirty-five publications in Spanish, French, German, and English, he deepened several research topics of the prehistoric period, setting the first criteria for the study of art, sepulchral behaviour, chronostratigraphy, industry, and habitat of the time in the Cantabrian region. In addition, to complete his doctoral thesis, he included data and remains from the same period in the Caves of La Paloma, La Riera, Balmori, Coberizas, Collubil, Cueto de La Mina, Dark Cave of Ania, Dark Cave of Perán, El Pindal, La Lloseta and Sofoxó in Asturias and La Paloma Cave, La Riera Cave, Morín Cave, Pendo Cave, and Valle Cave in Cantabria. Furthermore, on the theoretical level, he made contributions on the Epipaleolithic in the Cantabrian region.

His ability to understand this period of prehistory made him participate in a timely manner in collective works, manuals, or dictionaries of archaeology, history, and art related to Asturias, in which he provided definitions, citations, or encyclopaedic entries (Fig. 1.2).

Finally, due to his skills in graphic representation, he produced a lot of drawings later used by several authors.

After receiving the Extraordinary Doctorate Award from the University of Valladolid in 1981, he made his first trip to Jerusalem, encouraged by Joaquín González Echegaray, where he began his research on biblical archaeology supported by the House of Santiago and the École Biblique de Jerusalem.

His Experience in the Near East

Juan Antonio Fernández-Tresguerres established a professional and personal relationship with archaeologists of various nationalities who marked his 'Jordanian life'. Even then, he thought about moving permanently to Jerusalem. In those early years he studied materials from Tell El-Farah, the site that Roland de Vaux (École Biblique) excavated and is today investigated by Juan

Luis Montero Fenollós (University of La Coruña). The beginning of this new line of research coincided with his reinstatement in 1983 to university teaching in Oviedo.

Following his stays in Palestine, he began an archaeological collaboration with Jean Baptiste Humbert and the École Biblique that facilitated his passage to Jordan, where he finally developed his career in the Middle East. In 1987 he joined the team that Jean Baptiste led in Khirbet Samra, and even that corner of Jordan took his students and collaborators. In that first time his main work was the search for engravings and remains of human presence in prehistoric times (Fernández-Tresguerres 1987; 1991), which was his specialty. There in Samra he contacted the French archaeologist Jean Sapin who played a very important role for the location of the site in this part of Jordan, as it was already advanced. He himself guided Juan Tresguerres, Jean Baptiste, and his collaborators on the 1988 excursion, where they recognized in the slope of the new road that connected Zarqa with Jerash through Sukhna and Quneya, the remains of a Neolithic village located at the foot of Jebel Mutawwaq.[7] The following year he began his excavation in Jebel Al Mutawwaq, in the same area where Glueck, Thorpe, Edwards, Hanbury-Tenison, and Jean Sapin had located the Neolithic and Bronze Age remains that we are currently studying.

The Spanish Mutawwaq team continued to stay in Samra, with the French expedition that welcomed him from the beginning, in the former Ottoman houses that had been briefly rehabilitated by the Dominicans of the École Biblique. This residence was austere and uncomfortable for researchers and students, as they themselves remember and attest. There, a heterogeneous group of students met, professors and archaeologists of various nationalities and institutions that were the germ of the Jebel Mutawwaq expedition. The visit to Samra of the Swiss ambassador, Dr Dino Sciolli, was important for the Spanish embassy to determine the accommodation of the team in a residence of its own.[8]

The Attempt of a Spanish Archaeological Mission in Amman 1992–2014

As we saw in the previous section, the presence of the Spanish archaeological teams in Jordan did not have the stability granted by a research centre, but instead responded to personal efforts and the conjuncture in the field of cultural policy in Spain. With the impetus for Spanish archaeology in Jordan that led to the opening of the Mutawwaq excavation, the Ministry of Culture developed, from 1991, a project to equip these teams with a Spanish Institute in Jordan that centralized and facilitated these efforts, to the time it served as a stable residence for researchers. This assignment was made personally to Juan A. Fernández-Tresguerres who knew other research centres and who could take that reference for the new institution he intended to create.[9]

In 1992, the headquarters of the Spanish Archaeological Mission was opened in a building on the current Ibrahim Al-Muweyleh Street, in the former offices of the Spanish Foreign Ministry and Consulate in Jordan. The residence of archaeologists was also opened in the neighbouring building, owned by Abu Sam, on the floor that had hosted the Spanish Cultural Centre. In this way, he tried to shape the archaeological centre integrated in the Project of Spanish Academies abroad (Requejo Pagés 2012, 375), a project that also did not have the necessary endowment to establish itself in time.

The residence of archaeologists was closed in the winter of the year 2000, centralizing all the research activity and residence of archaeologists in the former Chancellery. The activity was reduced to the temporary stays of the team of Jebel Mutawwaq during the summers. The definitive closure of the headquarters took place in 2014, returning to the awkward situation of the teams that lack a stable base, residence, or warehouses for their technical teams. This is also the end of Juan A. Fernández-Tresguerres's attempt to place Spanish archaeological research at the level of other research centres in Western countries.

Juan A. Fernández-Tresguerres and his Work in the Near East

As already quoted, Juan Tresguerres's first contact with the East took place in 1981, when Joaquín González

---

7 In these first campaigns the team was integrated by Fernando Junceda, Mario Menéndez or Pablo Arias as collaborators.

8 A daughter of Ambassador D. Dino Sciolli was part of the Mutawwaq excavation team. The ambassador's visit alerted the Spanish authorities to the discomfort and inconvenience of the residence in Samra, which at the latter's recommendation sought more comfortable accommodation in the capital. Dino Sciolli himself gave the first equipment and furniture for the residence of archaeologists in Amman.

9 Copies of the letters, faxes, and texts related to this attempted foundation are preserved. In the archive of the Convent of Santo Domingo de Oviedo, a copy of the draft Regulations of the Spanish Academies abroad is maintained, which should govern the function and use of this institution.

Echegaray invited him to spend time at the House of Santiago in Jerusalem. The close relationship of the Spanish Institute with the École Biblique, the status of Dominican, and Professor Tresguerres's ease handling the French language facilitated his integration into the world that opened for him. There he met Jean Baptiste Humbert and, through him, other collaborators and friends such as Jean Sapin, Jean Michel de Tarragon, and Alain Desremaux who were his support in his new line of research. In the House of Santiago he also had the fortune to meet Emilio Olávarri, whom he already knew previously because they were both priests and archaeologists resident in Oviedo, and that generated a very comfortable environment for Fernández-Tresguerres, who was integrated into a very heterogeneous group of researchers with whom he had many points in common.

In those first years resident in Jerusalem, he published a brief communication made at the 1982 Spanish Bible Symposium on Neolithization in Palestine and the study he conducted on the lithic pieces of Tell El-Far'ah (Fernández-Tresguerres 1987), whose drawings had impressed Jean Baptiste Humbert. These were followed by the series of four publications made on Khirbet Samra, three in Spanish (the most important ones are Fernández-Tresguerres 1987 and Fernández-Tresguerres & Junceda 1991), one in French in collaboration with Alain Desreumaux and Jean Baptiste Humbert (1989).

Since the 1990s, the Spanish archaeological presence in Jordan can be reduced to the great project of the Citadel of Amman and to the excavation of Jebel Mutawwaq, which in that decade consolidated its project and began publishing its important findings in the field of Early Bronze Age Jordan. This systematic and meticulous work of Juan A. Fernández-Tresguerres served to place Jebel Mutawwaq as the reference site for that very specific period of the transition from the Chalcolithic to the Bronze Age in the Levant. The analysis of dozens of publications and communications offered in this regard are a minimal portion of Mutawwaq's potential (Fig. 1.3).

In the first stage of studies, he published three articles in Spanish aimed at presenting both the site and the potential of its resources. These articles were signed with his collaborators Fernando Junceda, to whom he directed his thesis on the dolmens of Mutawwaq, and Mario Menéndez, also a collaborator of the Olávarri team. In those first teams, students very interested in archaeology were integrated who ended up making archaeology their profession in the academic world (Mario Menéndez and Pablo Arias) or in professional archaeology (Alicia García, Otilia Requejo, Leonardo Martínez, Santiago Calleja). These three articles between 1991 and 1993 are a synthesis of these emerging works published in the field of Spanish Bible studies: 'Jebel Mutawwaq (Jordania). Campañas 1989–1991'; 'Jebel Mutawwaq. Los inicios de la Edad del Bronce en la zona de Wadi Zarqa (Jordania)'; 'Los dólmenes de Jebel Mutawwaq (1990–1992)'.[10]

The second stage of publications on the Middle East began in 1998 with an article on the book of Genesis and archaeology in the *Biblical Review* magazine. The text relates the way of life of human groups in the prehistory of the Middle East and its documentation through archaeological works in the Negev, Sinai, in the Black Desert, Jordan Valley, Mutawwaq and in urban centres of Hazor, Meggido, and Shechem. An approach similar was used in its 2010 publication 'Bible and Archaeology', which raises the revision of the history of the Middle East through biblical archaeology, with the advances that had taken place in those years.

As for the articles dedicated to general approaches and the description of the Mutawwaq site, these began with the contribution 'Jebel Mutawwaq, a Town of the Early Bronze IA in the Jordanian Steppe' for the tribute to Emilio Olávarri, published in Salamanca in 1999. In 2001, a presentation of Mutawwaq was published in its geographical framework under the title: 'The Northern Jordanian Plateau at the End of the Fourth Millennium', in *ERIDU* no. 1 of Barcelona. He continued with the one raised in the review *Bienes culturales: revista del Instituto del Patrimonio Histórico Español*, in 2004 and the monographic publication of the catalogue of *La aventura española en Oriente (1166–2006)*. The last general description of the site and its state of excavation was presented in the proceedings of *I Jornadas de Arqueología en Asturias* (April–May 2005), which was the first time he was invited to speak at his own university about his work in Jordan.

Among his works, two articles were dedicated to burials and anthropological studies. The first was 'La casa 81 y enterramientos de niños en jarras en el Bronce Antiguo I de Jebel Mutawwaq (Jordania)', published in Zaragoza in 2004, where he reviews the infants found in the 2000 campaign in the perimeter corridor of that house. That same year, in collaboration with Teresa Cabellos and María Dolores Garralda, an anthropological study on the human remains that had been studied in Spain also appeared.

---

10 See Fernández-Tresguerres 1992.

Figure 1.3: Juan Antonio Fernández-Tresguerres on the site of Jebel al-Mutawwaq.

For the book tribute to Victoria Cabrera in 2006, Fernández-Tresguerres chose the theme of the architecture of the village of Jebel al-Mutawwaq (Jordan) that followed the line started the previous year with the publication of 'El "Templo de Las Serpientes". Un santuario del Bronce Antiguo I en el poblado del Jebel al-Mutawwaq (Jordania)' in the number that *ISIMU* dedicated to Paolo Matthiae. This topic was deepened in the article 'La Casa 77 dentro del conjunto del "Templo de las Serpientes" de Jebel al-Mutawwaq (Jordania)' published in Zaragoza that same year. The temple continued to be studied and published in summaries of campaigns and works.

Finally, Fernández-Tresguerres gave several contributions to the magazine, *Report and Works*, of the Institute of Cultural Heritage of Spain, where communications are sent about the excavations financed by the Archaeological Excavations Abroad programme. These articles summarize work campaigns in Mutawwaq, showing the degree of progress made each year. Fernández-Tresguerres thus showed the excavations and complementary works of Mutawwaq in numbers 1, 3, and 5 of this yearbook.

As for their publications in English, they were limited to articles related to the Department of Antiquities of Jordan in the years 2001, 2005, and 2008 and translations of catalogues of exhibitions held in Madrid: *The Spanish Near Eastern Adventure, 1166–2006: Travellers, Museums and Scholars in the History of the Rediscovering of the Ancient Near East in 2006* and *Viatge a l'Orient Bíblic* published in Barcelona by the Institut Europeu de la Mediterrania in 2011, this one would see light posthumously.

The last publication that it is important to highlight was also published after his death: 'Pierres dressées dans la región de Mutawwaq, al-Hawettan and Hmeid (Jordanie) region', published by the former collaborator and specialist in ancient bronze Tara Steimer, under the general title: *Pierres dressées et statues anthropomorphes*, BAR International Series 2317.

It is important to mention the first exhibition that was organized on the excavations in Jebel-Al-Mutawwaq. This took place in the exhibition hall of the Historic Building of the University of Oviedo and the inauguration conference on 18 June 2009. It was the last communication made by Fernández-Tresguerres about the Jordanian site.

2. The Historical Framework: EB I in Jordan

Andrea Polcaro

History of the Study of Early Bronze Age I in the Southern Levant

Early Bronze Age I (3800–2900 BCE) is a long, crucial period in the studies focused on the passage between the proto-urban communities of the Late Chalcolithic and the fully urbanized settlements of Early Bronze Age II–III (2900–2300 BCE).[1] This is particularly important in the southern Levant, a wide region where urbanization is generally considered as a 'secondary process', not self-generated as in Mesopotamia or Egypt, but caused by external pressures or contacts. EB I was for a long time considered as a 'transitional' or even 'dark' period, especially its first part, characterized by a return to an agro-pastoral society with a high degree of mobility in the landscape and, consequently, a low degree of internal social complexity. According to this view the first social structures created by the elites of the Ghassulian culture quickly disappear at the beginning of the fourth millennium BCE,[2] with a return to the organization of the territory on the basis of tribes or chiefdoms, this situation changing only seven centuries later — at the end of the period in around 3100 BCE. This is a crucial date for the southern Levant, because in this moment several attestations of the *Serekh* of Narmer, the first Pharaoh of Egypt (Dynasty 0), start to appear in the south-western regions.[3] This presence seems connected to the expansion of the economic interests of the first territorial state of the region, in particular related to the need for raw materials, like copper from the Feinan mines and for special products for the Egyptian elites, such as olive oil and wine produced in the fertile valleys of Canaan.[4] Moreover, only in this last phase of the EB I period do archaeologists usually recognize settlement features clearly related to a newly structured organized and centralized society able to build, first of all, fortification systems and secondly, in Early Bronze Age II–III during the third millennium BCE, public buildings such as granaries, temples, and even palaces at the end, the final proof of a fully urbanized society.

The period was first established by G. E. Wright (1937), thanks to the identification of Grey Burnished Ware,[5] but was the following the work of Kathleen Kenyon at Jericho (1960), which clearly recognized its 'proto-urban' characteristics. Then, Early Bronze Age I began to be investigated deeply, both in the

---

[1] Concerning the periodization of the Early Bronze Age I several different proposals have been offered by scholars, developing with ongoing fieldwork research and with the growth of available C14 data. See for the more recent debate about the Early Bronze Age chronology of the southern Levant: Regev et al. 2012 for the so-called 'high chronology' and the recent work of Nigro et al. 2019, for the 'low chronology'. In this book we follow the second.

[2] In Jordan, this is related to the abandonment of the Tuleilat al-Ghassul sacred area (see the following section).

Andrea Polcaro (andrea.polcaro@unipg.it) is an Associate Professor in Near Eastern Archaeology at Perugia University (Italy).

[3] See on this topic Braun 2009.

[4] Amiran & Gophna 1992; Brandl 1992; Levy & van den Brink 2002; Gophna 2002; Braun 2011a; Polcaro 2018.

[5] This type of pottery, considered an imitation of the Late Chalcolithic stone vessels, was recognized first by Wright (1937) and is widespread in the southern Levant, specifically the area west of the Jordan River: see Philip & Baird (eds) 2000; Braun 2012; Braun & Roux 2013.

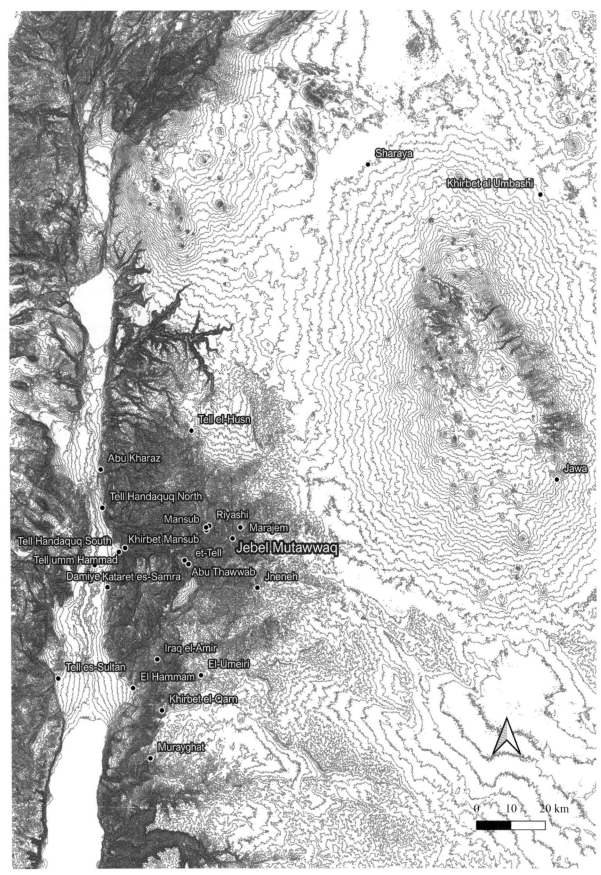

Figure 2.1: The main EB I settlements in the Transjordan area mentioned in the text.

Cisjordan (e.g. Megiddo / Tell el-Mutesellim)[6] and in the Transjordan area (e.g. Bad edh Dhra).[7] Despite the long extent of the period, between the collapse of the Late Chalcolithic around 3800 BCE, and the beginning of EB II, dated to 2900 BCE, and the fact that the various regions of the southern Levant had different developments, EB I has been traditionally divided into two phases: an earlier phase, Early Bronze Age IA, and a later phase, Early Bronze Age IB. This division is marked by distinctions in pottery manufacture and architectural traditions, such as the passage from a circular to a rectangular plan in domestic buildings. Some peculiar pottery shapes, surface treatments, and decorations on vessels do not appear in many regions before 3300/3100 BCE.[8] These changes in pottery production and in the architectural traditions are spread all over the southern Levant, including the Transjordan Highlands, albeit with several differences in the main productions and manufactures between the different regions of the area.

Despite the strong 'regionalized' situation and the aforementioned differences between the absolute chronologies of the sites investigated in the whole southern Levant, several recent studies proved that EB I was in general similar in the area when it comes to its main characteristics. Moreover, it becomes clear with continuing research on the subject that EB I was a formative period for most of the ideologies, subsistence strategies, typologies of landscape, and settlement organization of the future urban periods.[9] During the first long phase (EB IA), starting from around 3500 BCE, the settlements show a slow but constant growth in social and economic complexity.[10] Then, in some areas around 3300 BCE, elsewhere around 3100 BCE, a brief phase (EB IB) starts with a quick growth in social complexity and the internal stratification of society, leading to the future mature urbanization process of EB II. During recent decades, several archaeological excavations in EB I sites of the Transjordan area of the southern Levant, particularly those without further superimposition of later Early Bronze Age settlements, such as Tell Murayghat,[11] Jawa,[12] or Jebel al-Mutawwaq,[13] are revealing further data that allows us to support and better clarify this picture[14] (Fig. 2.1).

EB IA in Jordan: The Beginning of the Bronze Age and the End of the Chalcolithic Period

In the first two centuries of the fourth millennium BCE the site of Tuleilat al Ghassul in Jordan, located in a fertile zone close to the northernmost shore of the Dead Sea in the south Jordan Valley, was still a heavily populated settlement.[15] The priests of the huge village, probably living in a dedicated domestic complex of the settlement,[16] exercised their cult in a temple area delimited by a sacred precinct, where possibly they also organized the community and at least part of its economic activity.[17] The Ghassulian culture was widespread all over the southern Levant, with the same distinctive material culture discovered in several Cisjordanian sites.[18] Here, on the western side of the Jordan Valley, the large sanctuaries of Gilat and Ein Gedi probably worked in a similar way for the organization of the communities.[19] This system of landscape organization, with

---

6 Identified mainly on the eastern slope of the tell, see Braun (ed.) 2013.

7 See Rast & Schaub 2003; Schaub & Rast 1989.

8 The C14 analysis performed on samples coming from sites located in different regions of the southern Levant, in particular between north and south, indicate chronological differences in the appearance of these features marking the starting point of the EB IB, that oscillate between 3400/3300 and 3100/3000 BCE (compare Regev et al. 2012 with Nigro et al. 2019).

9 G. Philip (2003; 2008, 209–10; 2011, 203) proposed a radical change between the Chalcolithic and the Early Bronze Age in the replacement of portable artefacts as sources of power by agricultural products, connecting the role of the new EB IA elites with control of land, water, and labour. This fits with the idea of the birth of kinship, constructed through funerary ideology in EB I, stressed by M. S. Chesson (2001; 2007) for the large number of secondary interments discovered at Bab edh-Dhra.

10 See on this topic also Wilkinson et al. 2014.

11 Kerner 2019.

12 Müller-Neuhof 2020.

13 Polcaro & Muñiz 2019; 2021.

14 See also for a recent re-analysis of the period: Polcaro 2021.

15 The site was excavated first by the Pontifical Biblical Institute in the 1930s (Mallon et al. 1934; 1940) and later in the 1970s by an archaeological mission of the University of Sidney (Hennessy 1977; Bourke 2001).

16 In some specific buildings of these areas the plastered walls were continuously painted with pictures on cultic and religious themes (see Cameron 1981).

17 Seaton 2008.

18 As such as the famous 'cornets', elongated pointed cups, often painted with red bands on the upper part of the vessel (Seaton 2008, 42–43) and widespread, at least in southern regions, also in the Cisjordan area (Rowan & Golden 2009, 57).

19 Concerning the differences and similarities of the Chalcolithic cult in the macro-regions of the southern Levant and its role in the organization of the landscape and of the human communities see: Rowan & Ilan 2007; Rowan & Golden 2009; Lovell 2010; Ilan & Rowan 2012.

the tentative establishment of the first social complexity, ended in 3800 BCE when the sacred area of Ghassul was abandoned.[20] In the following three hundred years new sites appeared in the Transjordan area, discovered by the archaeological surveys of the last century.[21] The characteristics of some of them, small and apparently semi-permanent settlements, led the scholars to see a complete collapse of Ghassulian society and economy, with a sharp decline of agriculture in favour of the establishment of a fully pastoral society.[22] Regarding Jordan, this picture was strengthened by the explorations of the Bad edh Dhra Cemetery in southern Jordan by E. Lapp in 1965–1967 and of the EB I village of Tell Umm Hammad along the Jordan Valley by S. W. Helms in 1982–1984. In Bab edh Dhra a large EB IA cemetery of shaft tombs without a permanent settlement in the vicinity was discovered,[23] while in Tell Umm Hammad only domestic structures with a characteristic oval plan were investigated, without the presence of any kind of public building to attest to a centralized institution.[24] The circular architecture recognized at Tell Umm Hammad is a typical feature of the EB IA in the whole southern Levant and is found in both the eastern and western Jordan Valley.[25] The oval or round shape, mostly comprising walls of one course of raw stones, can suggest low crumbling structures, more like huts than real houses, suitable for a village settlement without real urban planning.

However, it must be considered that Bad edh Dhra is a site located in the Southern Ghor, a very dry semi-desert area in southern Jordan, probably more affected than the northern area of Jordan at the end of the Late Chalcolithic period by the Rapid Climate Change that started around 3800 BCE, possibly one of the causes of the collapse of the Ghassulian society.[26] On the other side the excavations at Tell Umm Hammad were able to expose only a small part of the settlement, which was mostly bulldozed before the fieldwork, and a large part of the site is unknown. Slightly earlier, the site of Jawa was discovered in the Black Desert (the *Harrar*), in the Northern Badia region of Jordan.[27] Here, the surveys and excavations bring to light an EB IA site, organized in clusters of domestic buildings, with a huge public cistern suggesting centralized organization of the settlement. Even if a 'temple' or 'palace' were not identified, or any other proof of a central authority, Jawa shows itself to be in any case a large, complex settlement, permanent and well organized in a mostly pastoral society with at least part of the population possessing a high degree of mobility. Surveys on the ground have revealed the presence of enclosures with 'standing-stones' possibly used as open-air sanctuaries,[28] agricultural terraces,[29] and finally a settlement wall.[30] The latter was partially excavated, displaying a system of fortification of the gates which clearly demonstrate a defensive function, even if the chronology was long debated.[31] The excavations of S. W. Helms at the site (1973–1975) didn't discover clear proof of social stratification; however, the features noted imply a kind of central institution, able to organize labour, economic activities, and settlement defence.

This first discoveries of huge sites of the EB IA also bring to light another peculiarity of the period, the differences in material culture, which appear strongly regionalized. The Jawa Ware, widespread throughout

---

20 For the C14 absolute dates from the Tuleilat al-Ghassul temple area see Bourke & Lovell 2004; Seaton 2008, 65.

21 Glueck 1951; Hanbury-Tenison 1986.

22 Esse 1989. However, several recent studies highlight continuity and discontinuity between the Chalcolithic and EB I, particularly in material culture, and the collapse of the Chalcolithic societies could also be interpreted as a consequence of new choices in settlement strategies and social organization following strong changes in the environment due partly to climate change and partly to the action of human communities (Joffe 2022).

23 The cemeteries are not connected to a permanent settlement, and the main town of Bab edh-Dhraꞌ was not settled before EB IB-EB IIA. Moreover, the shaft-tombs of EB IA contained only secondary burials. This has suggested the idea of several semi-nomadic pastoral groups with a high degree of mobility (Schaub & Rast 1989).

24 Helms 1984; Betts (ed.) 1992.

25 See on this topic: Sebag 2005; Braun 2020.

26 Arid episode clusters in southern Levant happened in 5600–5800 BCE, 4700–4900 BCE, 3600–3800 BCE, 3100–3300 BCE, and 2200–2600 BCE (Clarke et al. 2015).

27 Betts & Helms (ed.) 1991.

28 Müller-Neuhof et al. 2013.

29 Recent studies by Müller-Neuhof proved that in the Jawa area during EB I agriculture was also practised in the desert, thanks to the use of advanced water systems; moreover, he discovered a system of hill forts around Jawa in the *Harrar* Desert, and almost every fortified site had agricultural terraces associated with the structures, clearly pointing to planning in the exploitation of the landscape (Müller-Neuhof 2020).

30 The wall is still partly preserved up to a height of *c.* 4 m, and has a width of up to *c.* 5 m (Müller-Neuhof 2020).

31 Betts & Helms 1991, 34–35. Despite its disputed chronology between EB IA, EB IB, and EB II, the fortification wall of Jawa seems to pertain to the oldest phase of the site, now dated through new C14 analysis between 3500 and 3350 BCE (Müller-Neuhof 2015). Following the so-called 'high chronology' (Regev et al. 2012) this period fits in the EB IB, but following the more recent re-analysis of southern Levantine chronology of the Bronze Age (Nigro et al. 2019) it pertains to the EB IA.

the region of northern Jordan, was different from the southern productions of Bad edh Dhra. Moreover, the Grey Burnished Ware, typical of EB IA in Cisjordan, is totally absent in Transjordan, apart from a few finds in the northern Jordan Valley. In this regard, the northern and southern regions of the southern Levant, much as the western and eastern regions, have not necessarily evolved according to the same historical dynamics.[32] Differences in the pottery horizons between the macro-regions of the southern Levant point to a strongly regionalized cultural panorama distinguishing the fertile Cisjordan hills from the semi-arid Transjordan Highlands, or the southern desert area of Judaea and the eastern Arabic desert fringes from the fertile plains.[33]

Another important characteristic of the EB IA is the birth and spread of the dolmen phenomenon, in particular along the River Jordan and in the Transjordan Highlands.[34] In the past, it has also been related to the notion of large pastoralist societies.[35] Thus, the EB IA cave tombs with multiple interments in the Palestinian and Israeli areas, such as Megiddo, Tell el-Fara, and Arad, have been connected to farming villagers tentatively connected to small societies with small-scale economies, very different from the old mature and highly specialized Ghassulian society.[36] This reading has completely changed in recent years, after the extended excavation of dolmen fields and necropoleis, often connected to permanent settlements, in the whole southern Levant, showing that this megalithic funerary tradition is in fact generally related to a growth in relationship stability between the human community and the landscape.[37] The dolmen phenomenon is linked to the organization of an organized agro-pastoral territory, well established and fixed, even if with heterarchical relationships, connecting people to their land through the visibility of their ancestors.[38] Moreover, it must be considered that dolmens are not the only type of tomb in the EB IA southern Levant in general and in Jordan in particular. Apart from the quoted example of the shaft tombs of Bad edh Dhra, both hypogea and stone-built tombs are known in the different geological macro-region of Jordan, in the form of cairns, stone cists, rock-cut tombs, cave tombs, and some rare pit- and jar-burials.[39]

Together with new excavations in cemeteries and dolmen fields, other explorations of EB IA settlements have in the last thirty years changed the conception of the beginning of the Early Bronze Age as a 'dark period', particularly its first phase. The Spanish excavations headed by J. A. Fernández-Tresguerres in Jebel al-Mutawwaq (1991–2010) brought to light a large village, well organized, with different kinds of public structures and at least one temple area.[40] The settlement was clearly permanent and arose in the centre of an organized landscape, characterized by a mixed agro-pastoral economy. The site of Jebel al-Mutawwaq was probably similar to Jawa and Tell Umm Hammad, large settlements (over ten hectares), located in different key economic zones, able to attract a huge population from the countryside. Jebel al-Mutawwaq was located at the fringe of the eastern desert, close to two springs, on top of a hill overlooking the Wadi az-Zarqa.[41] In that place the river, running from south to north, turns west to flow toward the Jordan Valley. From one side, it is a natural meeting point for the shepherds following the river between east and west with the herds during the transhumance seasons. From the other, it is one of the best points along the valley for a seasonal agriculture of vegetables and wheat. Jawa is

---

32 Braun & Roux 2013.

33 Casadei 2018.

34 Polcaro 2013.

35 See Gilead 1968; Yassine 1985; Prag 1995.

36 Ilan 2002; Polcaro 2006.

37 Regarding the connections between dolmen and landscape, already stressed by T. Steimer-Herbert (2004), a recent analysis by J. Fraser (2018) proposed a new 'geological' approach to the motivation behind the huge megalithic construction programme in Transjordan and in the southern Levant during EB I. Starting from the analysis of data coming from the extended survey of the megalithic landscape of the Wadi ar-Rayyan in northern Jordan in 2008–2009, first surveyed by Palumbo in 1989, Fraser proves that it is not possible to date to the same period all the megalithic structures in the valley and that dolmens must be seen both as funerary monuments within a short time perspective and as enduring visible agents in the landscape that influenced the ideologies of people in the region for millennia. From the analysis of the architecture and finds discovered in the surveyed dolmens of Tall er-Ras, containing the disarticulated bones of several individuals interred in different multiple events, compared to the data coming from the EB I Bab edh-Dhraᶜ cemeteries, Fraser argues that the dolmen-building communities in the area were structured as heterarchically organized kin groups (Fraser 2018, 250).

38 Polcaro 2019a; 2021.

39 Apart from the numerous shaft-tombs of Bab edh Dhraᶜ, the cobble-lined cist tombs of Feifa and some isolated dolmens, there are few intact burials of the fourth millennium BCE that have been properly excavated in Jordan. The larger corpus of data for the funerary traditions of this period comes from the cemeteries of Bab edh-Dhraᶜ (Schaub & Rast 1989).

40 Jebel al-Mutawwaq had at least two attested sacred areas used during the EB IA: the Great Enclosure and the Temple of the Serpent (see Chapter 3).

41 Polcaro & Muñiz 2017.

located far north in the Black Desert, but at a crossing point of the transhumance shepherds moving between the Southern Hauran and the Northern Badia regions from north to south.[42] Finally, Tell Um Hammad was located far to the west, at the confluence of the Wadi az-Zarqa and the River Jordan, another important crossing point between the Transjordan Highlands and the fertile Cisjordan hills to the west. These huge sites emerge at key points, suitable for agro-pastoral societies that are reorganizing themselves in new relationships with the landscape and with other communities after recovering from the arid period which saw the end of the Ghassulian culture. This kind of reassessment of the landscape and of the social relationships between the communities probably set in train the historical dynamics leading to a new complex centralized economy. Recent explorations of the Jawa region by German archaeologists have brought to light several sites, apparently with different functions, spread all around the main EB I site in the North-Eastern Badia region.[43] The presence of fortified sites dedicated to agricultural production as well as more complex sites,[44] like Tulul al-Ghusayn, where early contacts with the Uruk culture of the Euphrates Valley have also been identified,[45] led the archaeologists to advance the hypothesis of heterarchically organized communities in the region, among which Jawa should have had a central role.[46]

The degree of social and economic complexity reached by the EB IA communities was surely different between the central Jordanian Highlands, the Southern Ghor region, and the western shores of the Dead Sea, as well as in the Northern Badia desert area. However, everywhere in Jordan it is possible to discern an increase in the complexity of the internal organization of the settlements and in the relationship with the surrounding landscape, as for example in the improvement in subsistence activities, particularly concerning agriculture, herding, and the establishment of new commercial and trade routes. The new landscape conditions of the second half of the fourth millennium BCE probably favoured the implementation of a mixed agro-pastoral economy, which required greater territorial organization and permitted an increase in the accumulation capacity of food resources. Thus, EB IA was a period of growth in social and economic complexity and settlement planning. Another case in Jordan is that of the Madaba region. Much more fertile than the eastern shores of the Dead Sea, the Madaba Plain had a flourishing megalithic funerary tradition, with several attested dolmen fields. Danish expeditions in the region during recent years have in two cases connected these cemeteries with sites dedicated to the organization of the agro-pastoral landscape. The first is with the so-called 'Conder's Circle', close to the Wadi Jedideh dolmen field.[47] This is a large stone circular structure with rooms dedicated to the production, storage, and protection of the food resources of the surrounding villages.[48] The second case, investigated by a Copenhagen University expedition, is Tell Murayghat. The site, previously known solely for its dolmen field,[49] is going to reveal a huge amount of data about public economic production activities in the site and the complex organization of the landscape resources reached during the EB IA in the Madaba region.[50]

EB IB in Jordan: The End of Early Bronze I and the Beginning of Urbanization

The *Serekh* of Narmer does not appear in the Transjordan Highlands of around 3100 BCE, and evidence of direct contacts with Egypt is completely absent till EB II–III. However, in that moment something changes in the

---

42 Moreover, the region of northern Jordan is clearly culturally connected with the area of southern Syria in this period. In particular, the sites of Khirbet Embassy and Sharaya, in the Leja geographical area, show many similarities with Jawa, both in cultural material and domestic architecture; Sharaya, larger than Jawa and even Mutawwaq with an extension of eighty-four hectares and more than five hundred houses and possibly around four thousand inhabitants, has a general urban plan very close to these two Jordanian sites, divided into sectors and encircled by a settlement wall (see Nicolle & Braemer 2012).

43 Müller-Neuhof et al. 2013.

44 Müller-Neuhof 2017.

45 Particularly interesting is the astonishing discovery in a building of Tulul al-Ghusayn of an Uruk jar, with other stone tools, all of the Uruk culture, with very good comparisons with the Habuba Kebira horizon and very probably fabricated along the River Euphrates (Müller-Neuhof 2021).

46 Müller-Neuhof 2020. See also about the settlement organization in northern Jordan and the possible connection with the region of southern Syria: Bradbury et al. 2014.

---

47 Conder 1989.

48 The excavations of I. Thuesen within the site have identified a number of spaces to process and store food, apparently protected by the imposing circular wall that surrounds the area, which seems in effect a huge fortification system, 110 m wide, with a platform surrounded by a rampart (still 8 m high) and one or two large stone walls on top (Thuesen 2009).

49 Savage 2010.

50 Kerner 2019.

complexity of the societies and in the organization of the settlements and also, in a minor way, in the material culture. The first new feature is the spread of fortification systems. At the present state of the excavation and of published C14 results, following the 'lower chronology' of the southern Levant, the settlement walls appear independently during the EB IA (between 3500 and 3300 BCE) in Jawa in the Northern Badia region, in Jebel al-Mutawwaq in the middle of the Transjordan Highlands, and, perhaps, in Tell Handaquq North in the Jordan Valley.[51] The first typologies of settlement walls are different from each other. The Jawa walls seems to be quite advanced, with complex gates and towers, even if more excavation is needed to determine the evolution of the wall between EB IA and EB IB. Jebel al-Mutawwaq's walls are apparently more simple, without fortified gates and probably lower than those of Jawa, and they seem to be in use also in the EB IB.[52] As at Jawa, the settlement walls of Tell Handaquq North have gates and, moreover, regular rectangular watch towers along the curtain.[53] The walls of Jawa and of Tell Handaquq, more similar to each other than the walls of Mutawwaq, nevertheless retain strong differences and seem to belong to different traditions. In these three sites, the settlement walls, even if built during the EB IA, continued to be used during EB IB. During EB IB, between 3100 and 2900 BCE, other settlements provide themselves with fortification walls, in particular those along the Jordan Valley, continuing the tradition of the walls of Tell Handaquq: thus, organized fortification systems with huge, wide stone wall foundations and watch towers. An example of these new settlement walls is Tell Abu Kharaz: this site, its settlement begun between 3150 and 3000 BCE,[54] presents a huge Early Bronze Age fortification wall, at least 4.2 m wide, with stone foundations and an elevation in mud brick.[55] However, the settlement wall was found to be mostly obliterated by the structures of later periods and its final form could pertain to the Phase IIA–B, thus probably the early beginning of EB II.[56] Effectively, there are no new settlement walls of the EB IB in Jordan away from the Jordan Valley; the first walled towns in the eastern highlands, like Khirbet al Batrawy on the Wadi az-Zarqa,[57] and those in the south, like Tell el-Umeyri in the Madaba Plain, or even the Bad edh-Dhra walled settlement, date to the beginning of EB II.[58] These later fortification systems are very similar to each other, indicating a much more effective defensive tradition during the mature urban period of the third millennium BCE.

The debate about the starting date of the fortification walls in the southern Levant is very important, since they are clearly connected with a rise in conflict between communities. Moreover, the appearance of strife between the communities of Transjordan, before the inception of Egyptian pressure on Cisjordan, is an indication of a change in internal dynamics uninfluenced by external stimuli. At the present state of art, it seems that the defensive needs of the settlements and their human and economical resources originated during the EB IA in only a few areas, where large settlements located at key strategic points perhaps assume a new role in the organization of the surrounding landscape. In these places different traditions are taken into account for the construction of the walls, one along the Jordan Valley (Tell Handaquq), connected with the western Levantine and perhaps Egyptian traditions, one in the desert Badia region, possibly connected with a northern Syro-Mesopotamian tradition, and finally in the Transjordan Highlands (Jebel al-Mutawwaq), showing a more local 'megalithic' tradition, apparently without any external influences.[59] The 'Jordan Valley' tradition continues in EB IB, leading to the strong evolution of the fortification system in the EB II, when settlement walls became common for every small or larger town of the southern Levant, Jordan included. This panorama reflects rising conflict between human communities of the Levant during the Early Bronze Age, but also the growth of central authorities and institutions which appeared during EB IA, rose in EB IB, and establish themselves in a new political relational city-states

---

51 Even if the phase of the walled settlement at Tell Handaquq North is probably related to EB IB, the C14 data from the charcoal collected from the dams point to a construction during the last half of the fourth millennium BCE, around 3500 (Mabry 1995, 124), thus EB IA for the 'lower chronology'.

52 See the next Chapter 3 for a description of the Jebel al-Mutawwaq settlement wall.

53 Mabry 1989.

54 Fischer 2008, 31, 325, tab. 73.

55 Fischer 2008, 175–76.

56 The EB settlement wall is also obliterated by Late Bronze and Iron Age structures, so much so that entrance gates relevant to the most ancient phase have not been identified by archaeological excavation (see Fischer 2008, 162–65, 345).

57 Nigro 2013.

58 Stratum III of Bab edh-Dhra. However, the major implementation of the defensive systems of gates and towers dates to Stratum II of the Early Bronze Age city (see Rast & Schaub 2003, 264–86).

59 See Chapter 3.

system in the EB II. In fact, the construction of fortification walls during the EB I, and their improvement in EB II and III, is an indication of the beginning of the end of the EB I as an institution able to organize both the work and security of the communities, with the growth instead of a military elite to replace the old 'cultic' elites of the Late Chalcolithic and EB IA.[60]

Concerning the material culture, there are no strong changes in EB IB, at least for the simple ware shapes, though some peculiar pottery shapes (e.g. spouted jars, dishes, and amphoriskoi) and surface treatments and decorations on vessels appeared, such as red burnished, line-painted, band slip, and grain wash decoration.[61] Despite these general changes, the EB IB continues to show several regional differences in the pottery fabric and typologies for the Jordanian macro areas. By contrast, the whole southern Levant during EB IB is characterized by the return of rectangular architecture, both in domestic and public buildings. This feature, that sometimes also sees the appearance of an 'apsidal' shape as an intermediate phase of the plan,[62] seems to be much more widespread as a characteristic of the period. However, in this case, too, Jordan exhibits more differences than the other regions of the southern Levant: the architecture changes quickly along the rift valley, both along the shores of the Dead Seas and the River Jordan, while it seems to go slowly in the Transjordan Highlands, at sites like Jebel al-Mutawwaq. The shift from a circular to a rectangular plan in domestic architecture doesn't necessarily require a high degree of sedentarism or internal organization, which as we have already shown, had probably already been reached by the communities of the southern Levant. On the contrary, it clearly implies a higher degree of urban planning in the settlements.[63]

Furthermore, a general change in the economy of the sites is recognized all over Jordan and the southern Levant, in particular regarding a strong implementation of oliviculture and the production of olive oil. This kind of product, surely known before the Early Bronze Age, has a strong growth in EB I, particularly during EB IB.[64] Oliviculture needs a very organized and controlled landscape, due to the delicate nature of plants that need constant care and protection to be productive. This fits well with the characteristics of the period previously quoted. The question of the reason for the growth in demand for this product, and the eventual implications of the birth of the neighbouring pharaonic state of Egypt, remains an open question.[65]

Concerning funerary customs, in some regions of Jordan, such as the Southern Ghor along the Dead Sea, hand-in-hand with the first sedentarization and urbanization process,[66] it is possible to see a marked change in the funerary architecture, with the appearance of the first charnel houses instead of shaft tombs.[67] However, in

---

60 Also for Tell Abu Kharaz, P. M. Fischer (2008, 97) advances the hypothesis that the large variety of specialized objects were not only essential for the survival and thriving of the community but also provides proof of far-reaching contacts and seems to be the result of a centralized administration.

61 Already identified by R. K. Amiran (1969) as late EB I, these kinds of decorations appear widespread between Cisjordan (Tel Erani) and the Jordan Valley (Tell Abu Kharaz) as well as in the Transjordan regions (Bab edh-Dhra, Tell el-Umeyri: see for comparisons Philip & Baird (eds) 2000). However, in Transjordan it is possible to see a general division between the northern 'band slip' ware and the 'line group' and red-slipped wares in the south (Richard 2014, 461).

62 A stage between oval and rectangular-shaped buildings, featuring a passage of apsidal shape, is attested between EB IA and EB IB in Jericho, Tell es-Sultan (Phase Sultan IIIa2): see Nigro (ed.) 2006, 122–26. See also Nigro (2019) for the periodization of Jericho in the 'lower chronology'.

63 The development of the rectangular plans of the EB IB in the future 'broadroom' classical buildings was also important for the birth of larger public complexes in the following EB II–III cities (Nur el-Din 2000; de Miroshedji 1989).

64 Oliviculture and the production of olive oil, at least for domestic use, is securely documented in the Levant from the Chalcolithic period on (Sabatini 2019). Domesticated around the beginning of the fifth millennium BCE, it was also proposed that it was the hunt for better uplands for horticultural crops like olive which pushed human communities to move from the valleys up to the highlands during the passage from the Late Chalcolithic to the Early Bronze Age IA (Lovell 2002). Finally, palynological analysis at Lake Kinneret proved the high implementation of the presence of *Olea europea* in EB IB (Sabatini 2019, fig. 7, 258). It must be considered that olive cultivation and olive oil production in the Transjordanian Highlands remained one of the main important economic activities for all the Early Bronze Age, till the end of the period, as the latest excavations of J. Fraser at Khirbat Umm al-Ghuzlan have shown (Fraser et al. 2021). See also Chapter 7.

65 Finkelstein & Gophna 1993; Lovell 2002; Polcaro 2018; Sabatini 2019.

66 In Bab edh Dhra the first permanent village at the site was settled in EB IB (Stratum IV: see Rast & Schaub 2003, 102–30), the first temple, and the first settlement wall, seems to be dated to the EB II (Stratum III: see Rast & Schaub 2003, 156–66), while the full evolution of the city with the construction of the gates and towers occurred at the beginning of EB III (Stratum II: see Rast & Schaub 2003, 264–86).

67 The first charnel houses of Bab edh Dhra, dated to the EB IB, like Tomb A 53 (Schaub & Rast 1989, 209–33), are of circular shape, with walls made of mud brick; they are characterized by the appearance of the first primary burials, instead of the diffused secondary burials

other regions, like the Transjordan Highlands, the eastern side of the Jordan Valley, and the Madaba Plain, dolmens continued to be used as the main tombs. However, almost everywhere the dolmens of EB IB seem to be larger than those of EB IA and, moreover, continued to be used to host mostly multiple burials in secondary position.[68] Further, different forms of rituals connected to this kind of dolmen emerge, together with a diversification in the funerary gifts.[69] In this framework, the archaeological excavations at Jebel al-Mutawwaq have given more results for the interpretation of these later EB IB dolmens, helping to clarify the social changes at the end of Early Bronze Age I. At the moment, it seems that the same process happened in the southern regions of Jordan with different burial traditions, as at Bab edh Dhra in the Southern Ghor. Here, the evolution of the mortuary practices of EB IA, based on secondary burials in the shaft tombs, first developed a system of 'structured agency',[70] with a new system of belief perfect for heterarchically organized kin groups. Then, in the EB IB, this heterarchically structured organization of society clearly started to change, with the rising importance of some families or clans above others, taking upon themselves in the EB II specific prerogatives in relation to the defence of the settlement, the organization of worship, and the management of economic activities.[71]

This evolution, begun during the second half of the fourth millennium BCE, probably experienced a drastic acceleration at the end of the EB I period. Moreover, apparently this didn't occur anywhere else at the same time in Jordan or the whole southern Levant. This is perhaps the reason why, looking at different sites or regions, different periodization proposals have been advanced in the last twenty years, shifting the beginning of EB IB, a period which continues to be considered by the whole scientific community as the starting point for the formation of the future kinship lines of the EB II–III city-states of the southern Levant.

---

of the EB IA shaft tombs. This custom starts to appear also in the later shaft tombs, which, like Tomb A4, continued to be constructed till the EB IB or early beginning of EB II.4 (Schaub & Rast 1989, 319–24).

68 One example is the dolmen of Tell el Umeyri, a site in the Madaba Plain, in Field K01 (Dubis & Dabrowsky 2002).

69 As an example, activities connected with the production of food for festivities related to the ancestor cult, at least for some families, seem to be attested at Jebel al-Mutawwaq (see the next Chapter 3).

70 Chesson 2007.

71 Concerning the different theoretical approaches to the Early Bronze Age urbanization process in Transjordan and the several possible dynamics of the internal organization of the communities see: Richard 2014, 454–58.

3. The Site of Jebel al-Mutawwaq: Architecture, Settlement Planning, and Space Organization

Andrea Polcaro & Juan Ramon Muñiz

The Village of Jebel al Mutawwaq

First surveyed by Hanbury-Tenison, the EB I settlement of Jebel al-Mutawwaq was identified at the south-western edge of the hill of Mutawwaq, close to the modern village of Quneye along the Middle Wadi az-Zarqa Valley. From a topographical point of view, the site is well positioned to control the valley of the River Zarqa (at a height of between 500 and 550 m above sea level), at a key point between the eastern desert area and the fertile western hills of the Transjordan Highlands, descending toward the Jordan Valley (Fig. 3.1).

The clearest feature on the ground was the settlement wall, enclosing a space of about thirteen hectares (880 m from west to east and 260 m north to south), within which hundreds of stone-built buildings were still visible. Hanbury-Tenison identified two types of building. The first and more numerous was the 'oval' or 'double-apsidal' domestic building, typical of the EB IA, which the British archaeologist recognized in several sites along the Wadi az-Zarqa Valley. The other one was the circular or 'semicircular' enclosure, another feature already identified in sites of the beginning of the Early Bronze Age. Hanbury-Tenison also noticed the presence of long inner walls, dividing the space of the settlement into different areas or neighbourhoods. This characteristic, together with differences in the topographical features of the areas of the settlement, suggests the presence of three sectors, called the Western, Central, and Eastern.[1] The best-preserved inner wall at that time was the easternmost, nowadays almost disappeared. It was also marked by an entrance, called the 'Hanbury-Tenison Door'. This is characterized, as at all the other entrances to the sites, by two huge megalithic jambs, still standing (Fig. 3.2). The width of the doorway (1.5 m) is greater than that of all the others in the domestic structures identified up to now on the site and its dimensions are comparable with the 'Southern Gate', identified by Hanbury-Tenison along the southern settlement wall. This and the 'Western Gate' are the only entrances to the village identified on the ground by the archaeologist.[2] Finally, Hanbury-Tenison noticed the huge megalithic necropolis extended all around the settlement wall, which in the 1980s numbered almost a thousand dolmens.

The Spanish Oviedo University expedition first surveyed the whole site (Pl. 3.0), gaining a better understanding of the inner divisions of the settlement space. Since then, the excavations have been concentrated on the domestic buildings, identifying the main architectonic characteristics of the houses and the main construction features of the settlement wall in its southern part. Moreover, the Spanish expedition clearly identified the main enclosure of the site, the so-called *Gran*

Andrea Polcaro (andrea.polcaro@unipg.it) is an Associate Professor in Near Eastern Archaeology at Perugia University (Italy).

Juan Ramon Muñiz (juanramunhiz@gmail.com) is a Professor and Researcher in Near Eastern Archaeology at Pontificia Facultad de San Esteban de Salamanca (Spain).

1 Muñiz et al. 2013.

2 Hanbury-Tenison (1989, fig. 4) calls both the gates 'south'; this is because the 'Western Gate' is located on the south-western corner of the settlement.

Figure 3.1: The landscape of the Wadi az-Zarqa Valley in front of Jebel al-Mutawwaq.

Cercado or Great Enclosure, characterized by the presence of a standing stone in the middle. Finally, the Spanish archaeologists identified the so-called Temple of the Serpents, one of the main sacred structures of the EB I village. Further, the Oviedo University expedition mapped all the dolmens still visible on the ground, clearly identifying three main clusters of megalithic monuments; the most numerous group is located to the east of the settlement, another is to the west of the village, and the last, the smallest, to the south, close to the settlement wall. Their work also permitted the documentation of the constant destruction of the dolmens due to the extension of the agricultural fields on the slopes of the hill of Mutawwaq towards the top, counting at least three hundred monuments lost in less than twenty years.

After 2012, the join Spanish-Italian expedition of Perugia University and the Pontificia Facultad San Esteban of Salamanca restarted the excavations in a different part of the site. The first seasons were centred on the easternmost part of the settlement (Area A), where the south-eastern corner of the settlement wall was excavated, and the closest part of the eastern megalithic necropolis (Area B), where six dolmens were investigated. From the third season, due to problems related to land ownership, the fieldwork had to move west, inside the land purchased by the Department of Antiquities of Jordan. Thus, several excavation trenches were opened in Area C, a large open area at the eastern limit of the Central Sector of the Jebel al Mutawwaq EB I village. In this area excavations were concentrated in Area C West and Area C Centre,[3] were several structures and one intramural dolmen have been excavated, in Area C East,[4] where the Great Enclosure already discovered by the previous Spanish expedition was thoroughly investigated in its northernmost limit, and in Area C South,[5] where another large, extramural, isolated dolmen has been excavated. This dolmen, the first one discovered in connection with a cave (used as a hypogean ossuary chamber), was part of the so-called southern necropolis. This funerary area was composed of at least four iso-

---

3 In the following chapters sometimes abbreviated as Area CW and Area CC.

4 In the following chapters sometimes abbreviated as Area CE.

5 In the following chapters sometimes abbreviated as Area CS.

Figure 3.2: The Hanbury-Tenison Door, in 2015, from the east.

lated monumental dolmens located at about 30 m from each other along the southern settlement wall, following the natural slope of the mountain from the Great Enclosure toward the Temple of the Serpents. A second dolmen of this cluster was excavated in 2019–2021 in Area EE, 15 m west from the dolmen of Area C South. Other excavation areas opened by the Spanish-Italian Archaeological Expedition to Jebel al-Mutawwaq are Areas D and E, on the northern part of the site. At the beginning of the explorations, these areas seemed badly affected by modern agricultural works, particularly the presence of long terrace walls crossing the site from west to east. These walls were made of the collapsed stones of the ancient structures of the EB I settlement, taken from the site and reused by people from the nearby modern villages. However, geophysical analysis performed in 2018 demonstrates the presence of intact stone structures under the surface, particularly in Area D, where a well-preserved domestic/productive structure has been under excavation since 2019.

Ten years into the resumed excavations at the site, it is now possible to assert that the Jebel al-Mutawwaq settlement had at least two main phases of use: one in the Early Bronze Age IA, between 3500 and 3300 BCE, then a second phase of urban expansion in the Early Bronze Age IB, between 3200 and 2900 BCE.[6] Concerning the necropolis, analysis shows that the southern cluster of dolmens, close to the southern settlement wall, belongs to the second phase (EB IB), as such as the few intramural dolmens in the Central Sector, while the larger eastern megalithic necropolis probably started being built during the first phase of settling at the site (EB IA) and continued to be used in the second phase.

The Internal Organization of Space in the Village of Jebel al-Mutawwaq: The Three Sectors and the Settlement Wall

Considering the general aspect of the Jebel al-Mutawwaq EB I village, some features clearly indicate a complex organization of the space, completely unusual

---

6 This chronology is now confirmed from the available C14 data from the site, with older results obtained in the Great Enclosure and the more recent from Area D of the settlement (see the following sections).

Figure 3.3: The southern part of the settlement wall in the Central Sector, from the south. The two stone jambs of the Southern Gate are visible on the left.

compared to other sites of the beginning of the period (EB IA) already excavated in the Transjordan region. Some of these features, such as the settlement wall, point to a strong correlation with Jawa, strengthened by the similarities of some pottery types. However, the shape of the settlement wall seems to be slightly different: no fortified gates have been discovered up to now and, mostly, the Jebel al-Mutawwaq wall is different in construction techniques. The settlement wall was first traced by Hanbury-Tenison, who clearly identified the western, southern, and eastern limits. The northern line of the wall was identified only for a small distance in the north-west, but in the northern and north-eastern sectors had already disappeared and nowadays is completely under modern buildings constructed on the top of the mountain. The first investigations of the settlement wall were performed by the former Spanish expedition,[7] mostly on its southern stretch. The wall is constructed directly on the bedrock, following the natural slope of the mountain (Fig. 3.3). The lower part of the wall is formed of huge, squared stone blocks, the upper part by stones of smaller dimensions, roughly worked; other small stones and pebbles are used between the larger blocks to sustain the wall.[8] This type of construction seems to be similar for the whole western and southern sides of the settlement wall.

While it is impossible to reconstruct the building technique of the northern circuit of the wall, the lower part of the eastern side is still preserved. With this in mind, excavations were undertaken in 2013 in Area A and the south-eastern corner of the settlement wall investigated (Fig. 3.4). This segment of the wall appears quite different from the western and southern ones; the lower part of the wall is composed of large standing stones, one beside the other in a single line, with no evidence of further elevation.

This suggests that the height of the settlement wall in this part was not more than 1.5 m, by contrast with

---

[7] Excavations were performed by J. A. Fernández-Tresguerres (2008b, 40, fig. 1).

[8] Muñiz et al. 2013, 82.

3. THE SITE OF JEBEL AL-MUTAWWAQ: ARCHITECTURE, SETTLEMENT PLANNING, AND SPACE ORGANIZATION

Figure 3.4: The south-eastern corner of the settlement wall, Area A, from the south.

Figure 3.5: General view of the Central Sector, photographed in 2019 from the Temple of the Serpent toward the west. The megalithic entrance of the Great Enclosure is visible in the background.

the southern and western lengths, which could have reached at least 2–3 m high. Due to the slope of the mountain following the north–south axis of the site, the eastern segment of the settlement wall was constructed using small stones and pebbles to level the bedrock and set up the standing stone blocks (Pl. 3.1a–b). These characteristics, also visible in the northernmost part of the eastern side of the wall, persuaded J. A Fernández-Tresguerres that the settlement wall of Jebel al-Mutawwaq could not have had a defensive purpose, but only defines the boundary of the urban space, separating it from the megalithic necropolis; moreover, it was useful to keep the herds and domestic animals inside the village.[9] However, an important factor must be considered: the presence along the western edge of the settlement wall of at least one tower,[10] already identified by the Spanish surveys. The tower is preserved only in its foundations, consisting of a stone platform (Pl. 3.4a). It has a circular shape, 5 m in diameter, with a perimeter wall built of large square stone blocks, infilled with small stones and rubble; it is clearly connected with the settlement wall. During a survey undertaken in the 2018–2019 seasons another possible tower, less well preserved, was identified about 20 m to the north (Pl. 3.4b). The shape and dimensions of this second round structure are very similar to the first: 5 m diameter and a circular perimeter wall made of large squared stone blocks. Unfortunately, both the structures are now located outside the recently built fence delimiting the land owned by the Department of Antiquities of Jordan; thus, it will be impossible to further investigate

---

9 See Fernández-Tresguerres 2005b; 2008b; Muñiz et al. 2013, 82.

10 See Nicolle 2012, 435–36; Polcaro & Muñiz 2017, 20. It must be considered in any case that later fortification towers in the Transjordan area are usually of rectangular shape, as appeared from the late EB IB period in fortification walls at, for example, Tell Handaquq North (Mabry 1995, 123–24), and became a typical feature in the EB II–III fortification systems, like in Khirbet al-Batrawy (Nigro 2013, 195–97; 2016, 138). Furthermore, the towers attested in the EB I at Jawa and in the sites of Eastern Badia are more or less rectangular (Müller-Neuhof et al. 2013, 130), such as the EB III tower at Bab edh-Dhra in southern Jordan (Rast & Schaub 2003, 254, fig. 10.2). Different is the case of the EB II Arad fortification system in Cisjordan, which features semicircular towers (Amiran & Ilan 1996).

Figure 3.6: The Southern Gate from the north. In the background it is possible to see the pathway descending downstream, now cut by the modern iron fence surrounding the site.

it in the following years. However, the connection of the two towers with the western part of the settlement wall, close to the Western Gate, suggests one should not exclude a priori the hypothesis of their defensive function. Consequently, it is also possible the wall may have been conceived as part of a fortification system of the settlement, at least in its last phase of use.

Looking to the three sectors of the EB settlement, it is possible to note that the first internal division is naturally caused by the course of the natural soil. In particular, the Western and the Central Sectors are located at different altitudes. No certain dividing wall between these two sectors has been recognized by the surveys performed on the site and the typologies and orientation of the structures seem to be similar in the two areas. In the Western Sector, extending 400 m east–west and 190 m north–south, at least eighty-four domestic buildings, some with and some without courtyards, have been recognized on the ground.[11] Together with these kinds of structures, a circular platform (Pl. 3.16) and one enclosure (Pl. 3.14) have also been discovered, but never yet excavated.[12] The Central Sector, extending 286 m east–west and 156 m north–south, occupies a saddle of the mountain between two promontories, delimiting one sector on the west, where the Temple of the Serpent was constructed, and one on the east, where the Great Enclosure was built (Fig. 3.5).

Between the two promontories several domestic buildings were recognized on the ground.[13] There is at least a clear pathway crossing the Western Sector reaching the Central Sector, where a southern entrance to the settlement is located. This is the Southern Gate (Pl. 3.3) already identified by Hanbury-Tenison, a simple portal with two still-standing stone jambs and an opening of about 1.5 m. It led toward a road, partially excavated in the bedrock descending to the river valley at the point of the Qreisan Spring, an important fresh water source

---

11 Muñiz et al. 2013, 91.

12 See later in this Chapter.

13 Muñiz et al. 2013, 92.

Figure 3.7: Plan of the south-eastern corner of the Eastern Sector of Jebel al-Mutawwaq. It is possible to observe the orientation of the houses along the east-west street crossing the village.

still used today by the local villagers (Fig. 3.6). Just outside the Southern Gate at least two water cisterns excavated in the bedrock are still visible. Here, the Spanish-Italian expedition started to deepen the investigation in 2019 to explore other cavities that are possibly part of a complex water system. The Central Sector ends a few metres east of the eastern limit of the Great Enclosure, where the Hanbury-Tenison Door is located. Here a long dividing wall was still visible in the 1990s and it is possible, also due to the dimensions of the door, that it was originally the eastern limit of the settlement, before a second phase of expansion and enlargement of the settlement wall. Thus, the Western and the Central Sectors could be contemporary, with the Eastern Sector probably a late addition to the site. If this is so, the eastern part of the settlement wall could pertain to a second eastward phase of expansion of the settlement and this could explain the difference in construction technique compared to the southern and western parts of the wall.

Looking to the Eastern Sector, it appears smaller compared to the other two, extending 209 m east-west and 175 m north-south; here several buildings have been recovered.[14] The orientation of the buildings is always parallel to the slope of the mountain in an east-west direction, built on the northern and southern sides of a main road crossing the southern part of the site and close to the settlement wall (Fig. 3.7). There are no houses oriented north-south, as in the other two sectors, and it seems that the buildings are without courtyards and built in a slightly different way from the houses of the other sectors.[15] The only entrance identi-

---

14 Muñiz et al. 2013, 92.

15 J. Fernández-Tresguerres suggested from the shape and the disposition of the houses that they could be structures used not

Figure 3.8: The south-eastern entrance of the settlement wall excavated in Area A, from the west.

fied so far in the eastern settlement wall is in the south-eastern corner, excavated in Area A in 2013 (Pl. 3.2b). It is smaller than the Southern Gate and the Hanbury-Tenison Door, about 0.80 m (Pl. 3.2a), and comparable with the doors of the private dwellings. It gives access to an external road leading toward the eastern megalithic necropolis, connecting this part of the settlement with the dolmens excavated in Area B (Fig. 3.8).[16]

Finally, it is very interesting to note the presence of domestic structures outside the settlement wall (Pl. 11a–b). These are organized in three clusters, quite different to each other. The first is located in the Western Sector, where a few isolated houses are built close to the external facade of the settlement wall. The second is located in the southern part of the Central Sector, along the pathway descending toward the Qreisan Spring. Here, at least ten dwellings are built close to one another, some parallel and some perpendicular to the slope of the mountain, about 5 and 10 m from the settlement wall.[17] The extramural dwellings of the Western and Central Sectors do not have courtyards; they are built in a similar way to the houses of the Eastern Sector, and thus might represent additions to the original nucleus of the settlement. Finally, the third cluster is located north of the Central Sector and is comprised of at least seven houses,[18] built apparently isolated but close to a huge standing stone, similar to the one inside the Great Enclosure.[19] One of these houses (no. 152) excavated by

---

as dwellings but as working places for activities connected to agriculture. This was indicated by the presence of several basalt saddle grinding stones for cereals recovered inside the structures (Muñiz et al. 2013, 92).

16 For a detailed description of the street see Polcaro et al. 2014.

17 One of these structures has been under excavation in Area EE since 2021. The C14 analysis performed on carbon sampled in the filling layers of the house gave a date of 3243–3102 BCE (Calibrated Beta Analytic n. 624947).

18 Muñiz et al. 2013, 92.

19 In Jebel al-Mutawwaq EB I society the standing stones clearly have a religious purpose, connected both to the settlement cult and to the funerary cult. See Chapter 3 for the standing stone of the Temple of the Serpents and for the description of the standing stone of the Great Enclosure. During the 2019 and 2021 seasons of excavations

Figure 3.9: Photogrammetry of House 152 of Jebel al Mutawwaq, north of the Central Sector.

the previous Spanish expedition has particular features, such as a cave, possibly used as a storeroom, accessible from the courtyard of the house (Fig. 3.9). Some findings discovered inside the building, like a small zoomorphically shaped stone pestle and a stone mortar, could suggest cultic activities or the production of special aliments used during rituals.[20] The possibility that this cluster could represent an extramural sanctuary is still open and has to be explored by future excavations.

The surveys performed in the 1990s clearly distinguished 186 structures on the ground at Jebel al-Mutawwaq. Considering the geophysical analysis performed in Area D during the 2018 season, the number of the dwellings at the maximum expansion of the site during the EB IB reached at least two hundred.[21] This data suggests a population of the huge walled village of around 1500 people at the end of the fourth millennium BCE on the top of the mountain looking down the Wadi az-Zarqa Valley.

The Domestic Architecture

The data on the EB I private dwellings comes from Spanish excavation soundings made in twelve houses between the Western, Central, and Eastern Sectors. The majority of the structures have an oval or 'double-apsidal' plan, and average dimensions of 10.62 m long and 4.21 m wide, for a living area of 44.19 m² (Pl. 3.5).[22] In the Western and Central Sectors,[23] the foundation of the houses is made by levelling the bedrock, often using small stones, rubble, and pebbles to obtain a flat surface, on which one layer of stones of larger size (up to 1 m long) is placed (see Pls 3.8; 3.9; 3.10a). The foundation wall is generally low, about 0.5 m tall. By contrast, in the Eastern Sector the foundation wall is placed directly on the bedrock without levelling rubble layers, with a first course of huge stone blocks, sometimes reaching 1 m high. The elevation of the walls, which has almost always completely disappeared, had to be constituted by smaller stones (average width 0.70–0.35 m and 0.20–0.40 m high), recovered collapsed during excavations in the filling layers.[24] The stone architecture was of dry typology, without use of mortar, and the stability of the wall is ensured, as with the megalithic architecture, by the insertion of smaller stones and rubble inside the voids between the larger blocks. No sign of further elevation of the wall made by mud-bricks or *pisé* was ever detected in the excavations, thus it is probable that houses had low flat ceilings, perhaps placed directly on the last stone course of the wall and built with perishable materials such as reeds, shrubs, and leaves or textiles/fabrics. The floors of the houses are obtained usually directly through the bedrock, levelling it where possible and necessary, sometimes with the use of layers of pebbles, or of beaten earth. The doors of the dwellings are made, as in the entrances of the settlement, by two megalithic door jambs, often still in place. The height of the stone jambs is between 1.10 and 1.40 m, the width of the entrance is generally narrow, between 0.75 and 0.85 m. In a few cases the entrances of the dwellings present a stone threshold and a door ring carved in the bedrock, suggesting the presence of a wooden door,[25] but mostly there is no sign of these features in private dwellings. In these cases, it is also possible to imagine the use of simpler door closing systems, such as curtains or woven reeds. The lintels were made of huge stone slabs, in a very few cases recovered collapsed in situ beside the doorway; in a single case, the Great Enclosure, the lintel was found in its original position.[26] The sole entrance of a typical house of Jebel al-Mutawwaq is located in the middle of one of the long sides of the building,[27] often towards the courtyard, if there is one. Concerning the courtyards, they are irregular in shape, evidently adapting to the availability of urban space.[28] They are delimited by walls

---

in Area EE a standing stone connected to a dolmen in the southern megalithic necropolis was investigated (see Polcaro & Muñiz 2023).

20 The basalt pestle was discovered in House 151, close to House 152 in the same complex, together with a basalt mortar; the object is decorated on the upper part with a mouth and possibly two feline-shape heads (see Fernández-Tresguerres 2011c, 218, fig. 6).

21 One of the houses under excavation since 2019 in Area D, located intramurally in the northern part of the Central Sector, is dated from C14 analysis performed on carbonized fragments of olive seeds to 3115–2921 BCE (Calibrated, Beta Analytic n. 576900).

22 Fernández-Tresguerres 2008b, 41.

23 See for examples of houses of the Eastern Sector Pls 3.6a–b; 3.7a–b.

24 Muñiz et al. 2013, 85.

25 See for example the case of Building 131 in Area C (Chapter 3). Between the domestic buildings the earlier Spanish expedition observed this characteristic in Houses 117 and 109 (see Muñiz et al. 2013, 84, 85, fig. 4).

26 See Chapter 3.

27 Only public buildings or buildings with a special function seem to have two entrances, always on the long side of the double-apsidal broadroom, as in the cases of the Temple of the Serpents and of Building 131 (Chapter 3).

28 It must be borne in mind that the data about the domestic spaces comes from just four houses completely excavated by the

made of a single row of stones, roughly squared, usually smaller in dimension than the construction stones used for the house walls. This suggests a low elevation of the courtyard's delimiting walls, possibly encircling open-air spaces. The presence of storage ware in the pottery assemblages discovered in the courtyards, especially in the case of the long and narrow ones like House 81 (Pl. 3.10b) suggests a storage purpose for the space, possibly to preserve food resources. However, it is also possible to advance the hypothesis of use as an animal pen, for sheep or pigs, in the case of the larger, ovoidal or trapezoidal courtyards. The discovery of two child jar burials in the courtyard of House 81 also suggests a function of the courtyard as funerary space for infants.[29]

An understanding of the internal organization of the living space inside the dwellings can be gained by observing the arrangement of the findings. Usually there is a concentration of functional lithic materials, especially grinding stones, together with pottery, in a corner of the house, while the opposite side, often occupied by hearths (circular stone platforms usually covered by traces of ash layers),[30] contains less lithic and pottery material. This suggests a functional differentiation of the inner space of the house, with a zone dedicated to the productive activities and another one to commensality and resting.[31] In some cases the two areas are separated by an inner wall, made by a single row of small stones, thinner than that of the perimeter walls of the house.

Finally, from the surveys carried out on the ground at Jebel al-Mutawwaq, it is possible to note that some dwellings don't have the typical double-apsidal plan. In a few cases a circular shape was recognized,[32] as well as rectangular or squared plans.[33] In at least three cases, both in the Western and Central Sectors, houses of apsidal plan with two right angles and a single apsis on one side have been identified. They are all connected to another structure of double-apsidal plan through a courtyard. The only structure of this last typology so far excavated is Building 131 in Area C, which didn't have a domestic function.[34] Without future extensive investigations in the settlement area it is not possible at the present to be sure whether the differences in the shape of some intramural structures of Jebel al-Mutawwaq are due to chronological or functional differences. However, the data coming from the excavations of the Great Enclosure and of Building 131 do not preclude the possibility that both explanations could be valid. In fact, during the expansion of the settlement between EB IA and EB IB, some structures with specific functions fell out of use and other structures of different typologies were built for other purposes, reflecting the new mature proto-urban society of Jebel al-Mutawwaq.

All the houses excavated so far were quickly abandoned at the end of their use, due to an event of probably around 2900 BCE. Most of the vessels and tools were left inside and the doors were carefully walled up with rough stone walls. No destruction layers have been recognized by excavation inside the houses or the other types of building. This could suggest a natural cause for the site abandonment.

The Temple of the Serpents

The 'Temple of the Serpents', excavated by the Spanish expedition of Oviedo University between 2003 and 2006, is a complex of buildings, recognized as one of the main sacred areas of the Jebel al-Mutawwaq settlement (Pl. 3.12). Located at the western limit of the Central Sector, on the top of one of the highest points of the site, it has a wide-open view toward the valley of River Zarqa. The complex consists of a main 'broadroom type' building used for cult (House 76),[35] another apsidal building (House 75), and a unique small five-roomed building (Rooms 1–5), encircled by a sacred precinct with a central courtyard. Another elongated building outside the *temenos* (House 77), close to the main broadroom, must also be included in the temple complex. The plan of the temple is closely comparable with the sanctuaries of the Late Chalcolithic period of the southern Levant, such as Gilat, En Gedi, or Tuleilat al-Ghassul, a

---

former Spanish expedition, number 20, 81, 151, and 152 (Muñiz et al. 2013, 86).

29 Fernández-Tresguerres 2004b, 270–71.

30 Muñiz et al. 2013, 86, fig. 5.

31 Muñiz et al. 2013, 87.

32 One circular house, more properly a 'hut', is visible on the ground close to a later tumulus or 'tower tomb' visible between the Western and the Central Sectors.

33 One squared structure of about 15 m on each side called Building C1 was identified on the surface in the necropolis, close to the dolmens of Area B, but the lack of excavation in the structure means its function cannot be established, not even if it was an open-air courtyard connected with funerary rituals performed outside dolmens (see Polcaro et al. 2014, 4, fig. 3).

34 See Chapter 3.

35 The buildings pertaining to the Temple of the Serpents were originally called 'houses' by the Spanish expedition of Oviedo University, like all the other single-room buildings of Jebel al-Mutawwaq, in part because their public nature was recognized only at the end of the excavations.

Figure 3.10: General view of House 76, from the north.

series of room with a central open courtyard, and also to the later EB II–III temples of the urbanized settlements of Transjordan, such as Khirbet ez-Zeraqun.[36] However, the Temple of the Serpent of Jebel al-Mutawwaq is one of the few cases where working areas, possibly dedicated to food production activities, were clearly identified from the features and finds discovered inside the complex. All the complex is built following the natural slope of the mountain, descending from north (where the main entrance to the courtyard is located) to south, with a difference in elevation from the top to the bottom (end of House 75) of more than three metres.

The structure most affected by this strong inclination of the ground is the main House 76 (Fig. 3.10). This building is in fact oriented north–south, perpendicular to the slope; it is 12.67 m long and 3.30 m wide, built with huge and regularly cut stone blocks at the base of the wall. As for the other houses of the settlement, the elevation is built with smaller stones without the use of mortar. The building had two entrances on the long sides, one to the west and one to the east (not in axis), a characteristic never identified in the private dwellings. The floor is formed by the natural bedrock, where several particular features have been identified. Against the northern apse of House 76, partially excavated in the bedrock, a shaft (1.75 m long, 0.55 m wide, and 0.50 m deep) was discovered, together with a stone table (1.40 × 0.55 m), set up on small stones, interpreted as an 'altar'.[37] South of the altar a deep cup mark has been discovered. The cup mark (0.24 m of diameter and 0.20 m deep) has its edges slightly raised (Fig. 3.11). This last characteristic could also suggest a function of the cup mark as mortar, even if the lack of intense rubbing marks, its deep and its conical shape, ending in a narrow point, could also suggest a support function for a wooden post. Fernández-Tresguerres proposed its interpretation as a posthole to support the roof;[38] however, it is located close to the northern part of the building, not in a central position, and could thus hold only a light roof covering only part of the northern apse of the building. It is also possible that it supported a wooden pole for ritual or cultic purposes,[39] due to the function of this room and the nearby presence of the altar and of the sacred pit.

---

36 See for an analysis of the architecture of Levantine temples from the Chalcolithic to the Early Bronze Age III period: Sala 2008.

37 Fernández-Tresguerres 2008a, 24, fig. 3.

38 Fernández-Tresguerres 2008a, 25.

39 It is noteworthy that a similar deep cup mark of conical shape has been discovered in the Great Enclosure. See the following Chapter 3.

Figure 3.11: The deep conical cup mark in House 76.

The majority of the cultic vessels decorated with applied figures of serpents have been discovered in House 76 (Fig. 3.12).[40] The sherds belong mostly to large storage jars with ledge handles, probably used to hold a precious or sacred liquid or aliment for the rituals kept in this broadroom, clearly dedicated to perform specific rituals. Moreover, the connection of the symbol of the serpent with that of the ear of barley incised on the shoulder of some vessels, could also suggest the consumption of a sort of fermented beverage used during the cult.[41] The serpent figures applied on these large vessels gave the name to the temple, clearly dedicated to a sort of chthonic deity. The possible connection with the underworld of the cult carried out in the temple is also given by the presence of a standing stone, close to the northern apse of House 76 and included in the precinct wall delimiting the sacred area.[42] The standing stones (single and isolated or in rows) are a typical feature of cult in the Protohistoric Levant. They are well attested from the beginning of the Neolithic period in the Cisjordan and Transjordan regions and there are many examples of standing stones in connection with sacred areas and megalithic necropoleis. The ancient

---

40 Some sherds with serpent appliques are shown in Chapter 4 (Pl. 4.21).

41 These vessels are usually recovered in temples or sacred areas and are a typical feature of the Levantine Canaanean cult from the Late Chalcolithic period to the end of the Early Bronze Age (see on this topic Polcaro 2019b; Ajlouny et al. 2022).

42 Fernández-Tresguerres 2008a, 25, fig. 4. Due to the damage inflicted on the site during the past twenty years, the megalith is no longer standing. Moreover, the southern half of the temple area is now outside the fence enclosing the land owned by the Department of Antiquities of Jordan; the modern fence unfortunately bisected the structure of House 76, today strongly affected by its construction.

Figure 3.12: One of the jars with serpent appliques discovered in House 76 of the Temple of the Serpent, now kept in the Department of Antiquities of Jordan storeroom of Zarqa district.

religious traditions of the Levant clearly connected this kind of monument to the veneration of the ancestors.[43]

The courtyard of the temple was delimited by a wall made of a single row of stones (average size, 0.50 m) preserved only on the northern and western sides. The entrance, on the north-east, was marked as usual by two huge stone jambs, each 1.5 m high, while a second smaller shaft carved in the bedrock was discovered close to the doorway.[44] From this point, it was possible to descend toward the second building clearly connected with House 76 through the courtyard. This building, of roughly square plan, is built through the juxtaposition of five rooms, to which a long stepped corridor gives access on the western side. The more interesting feature of this five-roomed building is that each room is distinctive, so that it is possible to advance the hypothesis that each one had a particular function, all related to sacrifices and the production of different kinds of food, possibly consumed during religious festivities and daily rituals. Room 1 (4.10 m long and 2.48 m wide), where the stepped corridor leads, represents the entrance of the structure. No particular features have been discovered inside this room, just part of a painted jug, decorated with a row and incomplete net and line red paintings, typical of EB IB ware.[45] The northern rooms of the complex, Room 3 on the west and 2 on the east are connected with each other through a door and both gave access to the southern rooms of the complex, the larger Room 5 and the smaller circular Room 4. Access from one room to the other was obtained through the construction of the typical doors of Jebel al-Mutawwaq, with two stone jambs and a stone lintel, found in situ only once (in Room 3); moreover, the doors of this complex always have a stone threshold, with a step leading to the southern lower room and often a door socket carved in the bedrock beside the entrance, possibly indicating easy-to-lock wooden doors. In Room 3 (2.56 m wide and 3.47 m long) a cut-stone cist (0.97 × 0.95 m), squared and lined with stone slabs has been discovered;[46] the purpose of the cist is not clear, but it has to be connected with some productive or cultic activity. The nearby Room 2 (2.92 long and 1.96 m wide) had a long bench, probably a seat, carefully carved directly on the bedrock against its northern side.[47] Room 5 was the larger (4.75 m long and 3.15 m wide); but no particular features have been recognized inside. However, a complete globular jar with short neck and small, flat vertical handles was found within; this jar, with its red burnished surface decoration (also dated to EB IB),[48] is very important. It presents some stamps on the shoulders that have been identified as possible seal impressions.[49] The presence of a jar with seal impressions in the complex is indicative of a storage function for this larger room and of an organized and centralized institution involved in the cult of the settlement and in its social and economical organization.[50] Finally, the western Room 4 has a circular plan (2.64 × 2.76 m), without particular features or finds helping in the interpretation of its function; interesting is the mention of a few scattered human bones discovered close to this room in the patio, that might suggest a cultic function also connected to possible funerary rituals in the temple.

---

43 These monuments, simply roughly worked large stone blocks set up in the ground standing toward the sky, are common features in southern Levant; their tradition is well attested in ritual contexts of the Early Bronze Age I, such as in the Hartuv temple (Mazar et al. 1996), and lead to the later Iron Age tradition of the *masseboth*, the stele of the ancestors, referred to in the Old Testament texts.

44 Fernández-Tresguerres 2008a, 25–26.

45 Other appliques on the shoulders of the vessel can be interpreted always as small animals like serpents or worms rising up the vessel toward the mouth (Polcaro 2019b); concerning the decoration and chronology see also Chapter 4, Fig. 4.16).

46 Fernández-Tresguerres 2008a, 28, fig. 10.

47 Fernández-Tresguerres 2008a, 27, fig. 8.

48 See also Chapter 4.

49 Fernández-Tresguerres 2008a, 31–32, fig. 14.

50 The presence of seal impressions on Early Bronze Age southern Levantine pottery is generally well attested only from EB II (see Greenberg 2001).

South of these rooms, another building, House 75, was built against the wall of the previously mentioned five-room complex. This building has an irregular apsidal shape: the northern wall of the structure is straight, while the parallel southern wall is slightly curvilinear, the apsis is on the eastern side. The inner space was divided in two by a wall made of a single row of stones. The western room of House 75 (2.41 × 3.52 m) might have been dedicated to cooking activities, possibly indicated by the presence of a fireplace in the northern corner. The eastern room (3.55 × 3.87 m) had in the centre a flat stone,[51] intentionally placed on the bedrock and fixed with smaller stones, a table of stone similar to the altar of House 76. In this case, it has been interpreted as a working table, based in part on the presence of flint scrapers and blades nearby.[52] The last building which can be connected with the temple complex is House 77, located just two metres from the eastern side of House 76.[53] The plan is very similar to House 75: the building (8.50 m long and 3.30 m wide) has an irregular apsidal plan: the northern wall of the structure is straight, while the parallel southern wall is slightly curvilinear, the apse is on the western side of the building. The inner space is divided into two rooms by a stone wall, larger (at least two rows of stones) and better built than that inside House 75, with a doorway on its southern edge. The eastern room (1.50 m wide and 3 m long) had a lower stone-paved platform in its southern part, located directly on the bedrock and formed of large flat limestones.[54] The western room (3.50 m wide and 6.75 m long) had another two stone platforms, made by large flat limestones, located against the apse.[55] Another interesting detail is that the rocky ledge on which the western part of the building is built had a deep crack which may have been due to a earthquake.[56] The huge number of fragmented jars discovered inside the eastern room of House 77 led J. A. Fernández-Tresguerres to hypothesize a storage function for this building, connected to the activities performed in the temple area.[57]

The aspect of production is very important concerning the interpretation of the space functionality in the temple of Jebel al-Mutawwaq. Several animal bones have been recovered inside the pits or close to the installations identified in the area; these bones, mostly belonging to sheep, could represent the remains of animal sacrifices and banquets performed inside the sacred precinct.[58] Connected with the sizeable presence of sheep bones in the palaeofauna of the site is the discovery of several tabular scrapers between Rooms 1–5 and mostly House 75. Among their possible functions could be ones related to wool shearing activities and their presence in a public context outside a domestic area could indicate centralized production. Several olive seeds (*Olea oleaster*) have also been recovered in Houses 76 and 75; some of them were carbonized, so possibly used as fuel, but others were discovered intact or crushed but not burned. Together with other data coming from Area C, this could be a clue that oliviculture, and possibly the production of olive oil, was an important new component of the Jebel al-Mutawwaq economy. The concentration of these seeds in the temple area could again suggest in this case the beginning of centralized production, or at least a central role for the temple in the organization of this economic activity. The presence of oliviculture fits well in the historical framework of the passage between the EB IA and EB IB and both the materials and the C14 analysis point to this chronology, giving the Temple of the Serpent a date of around 3200 BCE.[59]

Thus, the Temple of the Serpents was built in the middle of the life of the settlement, as the village of Jebel al-Mutawwaq grew in the last centuries of the fourth millennium BCE. In the same period it was probably equipped with city walls and partially changed its internal organization, as is clearly shown by the excavations in Area C.

[AP, JRM]

The Great Enclosure and Area C

Area C is located in the southern area of the Central Sector of the settlement, close to its eastern edge. The excavations here between 2014 and 2018 (and still ongoing) brought to light the Great Enclosure (Area C East) and other structures located on the west, in particular Building 131 (Area C Centre) and Courtyard 51 (Area C

---

51 Fernández-Tresguerres 2008a, 26, fig. 6.
52 Fernández-Tresguerres 2008a, 32, fig. 15.
53 Fernández-Tresguerres 2005b; 2008a, 47–48.
54 Fernández-Tresguerres 2008a, 29, fig. 11.
55 Fernández-Tresguerres 2008a, 30, fig. 12.
56 Fernández-Tresguerres 2008a, 30, fig. 12.
57 Fernández-Tresguerres 2005b; 2008b, 48; 2008a, 29–30.

58 The slaughtering of sheep and the cooking of their meat for food offering is attested from the recent excavation of Area C, season 2019 (see Chapter 3).
59 5290–5040 BP = 3340–3090 BCE (Beta Analytic 194526) and 5270–5170 BP = 3320–3220 BCE (Beta Analytic 194527), see Fernández-Tresguerres 2008b, 33; Polcaro et al. 2014. See also, regarding the debate and historical importance of oliviculture Chapter 7.

Figure 3.13: General view of the Great Enclosure from west, the standing stone in the centre is visible in the foreground.

West). Finally, in the same area, an intramural dolmen (no. 534), possibly connected with Building 131, has also been excavated. Measuring about 30 m north–south and 80 m east–west, the area presents the most interesting data to investigate the passage between Early Bronze Age IA and Early Bronze Age IB.

The Great Enclosure (Pl. 3.13a)

The Great Enclosure is a large open-air structure of semi-circular shape, about 60 m in diameter, delimited by a huge stone wall, called W. 102. It is located along the southern edge of the settlement on the top of a promontory looking toward the Temple of the Serpent, sited on the opposite side of the Central Sector to the west. It is a very good location with great visibility over the entire river valley, as noted also in the case of the temple complex. The large semicircular structure is open toward the valley and its perimeter wall stands directly on the edge of the mountain cliff. At this point the settlement wall seems not to be present. The whole structure is built following the slope toward the cliff, cutting the bedrock to make a stepped floor from the north to the south. In the centre of the enclosure, close to the northern limit, at 2 m from W. 102, there is a standing stone (Fig. 3.13), wider than it is high, very similar to the extramural standing stone already mentioned close to the group of seven houses north of the Central Sector. Excavations were concentrated along the western limit of the structure and on the northern half of the enclosure, from its western to its eastern limit.

The construction technique of the wall presents some peculiarities. Large stone squared blocks (1–2 m long, 0.5–1 m wide), were used to build its lower part. At some points, such as the northern segment, this lower part of the wall is preserved to a height of almost two metres (Fig. 3.14). The excavation trenches opened along the western part of the wall indicate a similar style of foundations for the settlement wall in its western and eastern segments. Due to the steep slope of the bedrock from north to south, the jumps in altitude from one rock terrace to another are filled with a layer of pebbles and small stones before the laying of the first row of large stone blocks (Pl. 3.13b). The elevation of the wall was made everywhere with two rows of more roughly worked stones of lesser dimensions compared to the blocks of the lower part — average size 0.30 m long and 0.5 m wide — whose collapse was recognized during the excavations. Between

Figure 3.14: Inner side of the northern segment of the wall of the Great Enclosure, from the south.

both the larger lower blocks and the stones of the upper part small stones and rubble were embedded in the voids. Wall W. 102 seems to have been built in one construction stage in its western and northern segments, with a single curvilinear line. By contrast, the eastern side of the wall was built or, more probably, rebuilt in a second phase, because its foundation stones lean against the end of the northern part of the wall to the east. It is not strange that such a huge perimeter wall, at least 2 m high, had to be continuously restored, easily suffering collapse, especially in a region of seismic risk like Transjordan.

Thus far, it seems that the Great Enclosure had only one entrance, in its western perimeter wall (Fig. 3.15). It took the form of a megalithic portal (1 m wide) called D. 1110, formed by two regular, well-cut stone jambs 1.2 m high, a flat stone as threshold, and a huge stone lintel still in place (2.5 m long, 1.2 m wide, 0.80 m high). The incredible state of preservation of this door is due to the sealing undertaken at the end of the first use of the Great Enclosure, when it was filled with stones (Fig. 3.16). Later a large circular structure,[60] now preserved only in its lower part, was built at this point of the enclosure, including the entrance, no longer in use.[61] The presence of a single, not particularly wide, portal points to a slow flow of people, or animals, inside this large encircled open space. The possibility that this structure could serve as a sort of communal animal pen for the villagers has to be excluded because of its peculiar semicircular shape, without a southern delimiting wall. Thus, the Great Enclosure was an open space which descended directly down toward the cliff, and, even if there were a wooden fence, it would have been a very risky place to keep herds. Another hypothesis involves the use of this space for public activities related to the herd's exploitation, such as the wool cycle, due to the discovery of some tabular scrapers and fragmented loom weights in the area.[62]

---

60 Possibly a 'tower tomb', see later in this section.

61 Polcaro & Muñiz 2021; 2023.

62 See the scraper recovered outside of the western side of Building 131, later in this section; see also Chapter 5 for descriptions of the tabular scrapers (Chapter 5, Pls 5.4–5.5) and loom weights (Chapter 5, Pl. 5.11). Some of the objects recovered in the western side of the Great Enclosure include fragmentary mace-heads (see Chapter 5, Pl. 5.13).

Figure 3.15: Photogrammetry of the Great Enclosure's doorway and the eastern side of the wall W. 102.

Figure 3.16: Frontal view of the Great Enclosure's doorway during excavations, from the west.

However, the presence of the standing stone in the central position of the enclosure also suggests a probable cultic function for this large open space. Excavations in the northern part of the Great Enclosure, against the inner facade of the W. 102, just behind the standing stone, have revealed the presence of ritual depositions of vessels with food offerings, located in a large and long natural channel carved in the bedrock (Fig. 3.17). This channel comes from north of the Great Enclosure and crosses it just behind the stele, curving toward the east

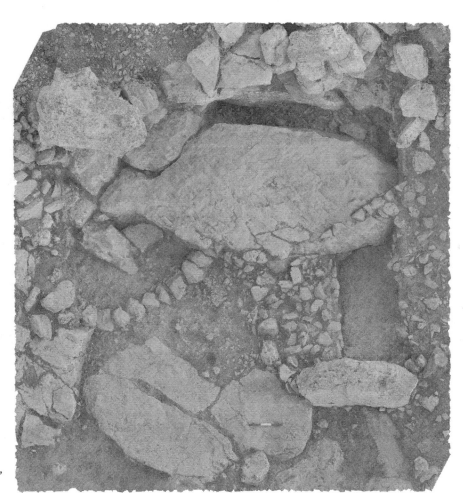

Figure 3.17: Photogrammetry of the Great Enclosure north excavation trench, between the standing stone and W. 102.

and then going south-east to the middle of the eastern wall of the structure. The 1–2 m high channel appears to be natural and follows the change in height between the limestone rock platforms descending toward the southern cliff of the mountain (Fig. 3.18). The channel was intentionally closed when the northern wall of the enclosure was built. It was covered first with a hard layer of red clay and white gypsum and then filled with layers of small stones and pebbles, almost till the top. In the northern part of the channel, behind the stele and in front of the W. 102, the upper part of the channel bed dug into the rock was used to set up jars inside small stone circles. The number of jars, broken one on top of the other in a single place, indicates frequent repeated depositions. The last layer of depositions was dated thanks to charcoal discovered inside the last jar located in the place. The bottom of the jar still also contains the bones of a sheep (Fig. 3.19).[63] The C14 analysis suggests a date of about 3300 BCE for the last use of the space to locate ritual depositions behind the stele.[64] It may be that this was the date when the portal of the Great Enclosure was blocked. With the possible interpretation of the Great Enclosure as an open-air sanctuary in mind, we should note the deep cup mark identified in the lower southern part of the enclosure, on a flat rock terrace close to the cliff boundary, which offers probably the best view over the whole river valley. The cut is perfectly circular, 21 cm in diameter, and 20 cm deep, almost identical to the one in House 76 of the Temple of the Serpents. The conical shape and the pointed bottom suggest, as for the temple, the purpose of holding a pole, but in this case it could be difficult to imagine it sustaining a roof and it might be more realistic to envisage the presence of a standing pole for cultic purposes.

Summarizing the data as things now stand, it is possible to advance the hypothesis that the Great Enclosure

---

63 The choice of the joints of meat, in particular the shoulder and pelvis, indicates the bones are food remains, probably related to a sort of stew of lamb. This interpretation was confirmed by the presence of clear signs of butchery on the bones (see Polcaro & Muñiz 2023).

64 3521–3367 BCE, Beta Analytic — 576901 (see Polcaro & Muñiz 2023).

Figure 3.18: The northern trench of the Great Enclosure after the end of the excavations. In the foreground the long channel naturally carved in the bedrock can be seen.

was originally an ancient open-air sanctuary of the EB IA, with a standing stone in the centre, representing the *sancta sanctorum* of the temple area, with a wide courtyard to bring together a large number of people with a perfect view of the underlying valley of the River Zarqa. The huge standing structure of the Great Enclosure was then reused in the following centuries and millennia, both during the evolution of the village in the Early Bronze Age IB and later, after the final abandonment of the site, possibly by shepherds, passing soldiers, and local people. Several other features have been identified by the excavations in this area. However, due to the scarcity of the findings and the shallow stratigraphy of the excavation trenches opened inside the structure, it is not always easy to attribute a precise chronology to these features. On the eastern side of the northern part of the enclosure, at least two small rectangular rooms (3 × 2 m) were built, one parallel to the other, against the eastern wall of the Great Enclosure. They are formed of thin walls of just one row of small stones. A high chronology of the EB IB is suggested by the few pottery finds inside the rooms, and by a small miniaturist vessel discovered close by. On the opposite side other small structures built against the western wall of the enclosure were discovered. One of these rooms is perfectly circular (5 m in diameter) and lies against a single wall perpendicular to W. 102, roughly preserved.[65] The circular room is made by a thin wall of one row of small stones; it had its entrance on the west and a stone installation inside, perhaps used as a base of a fireplace. No dating sherds have been recovered in the area, apart from a later Islamic sherd possibly indicating that this circular structure was the base for a later small hut built inside the ruins of the enclosure, long after its abandonment.

Concerning the closing and possible repurposing of the Great Enclosure during EB IB, it may be worth noting the huge perfectly circular 8 m-diameter structure built over the entrance to the Great Enclosure. The structure was completely excavated in the 2019 season, and identified as the base of a sort of huge cairn, possibly a 'tower tomb' (Fig. 3.20), similar to those recently studied by

---

65 Polcaro & Muñiz 2019, 94, fig. 19.

Figure 3.19: The jar discovered behind the standing stone of the Great Enclosure, with the sheep bones preserved on the bottom.

Tara Steimer-Herbet at Menjez.[66] It is characterized, like the tower tombs surveyed and excavated in other sites of the Levant, by the presence of a central ovoidal cist lined with stones. The elevation of the structure is completely lost above its foundation, formed by a circular perimeter wall of well-cut regular rectangular stones (average size 1 m long, 0.5 m wide) and several other concentrical walls, filled with stones in between. This kind of monumental tomb, that on Syrian sites is sometimes dated to the same period as the dolmens built in the same areas (end of the fourth millennium BCE), could in this case represent a new typology of individual funerary monument. Unfortunately, the cist of the 'tower tomb' in Area C East of Jebel al-Mutawwaq was found emptied, probably by later robbers, and thus the excavations have not identified enough diagnostic pottery sherds to securely date the structure to this period. However, it is interesting that there is in the same area (Area C Centre) a dolmen (no. 534), also dated to the end of EB IB,[67] built against the southern wall of Building 131, a few metres west of the tower tomb. These data suggest that during the EB IB this part of the Central Sector of the site changed its main function. The Great Enclosure was no longer used to perform rituals connected to the deposition of food offerings behind the stele from approximately 3300 BCE, when the Temple of the Serpent probably started to be used. The Great Enclosure and the neighbouring zone shift their use toward being an intramural funerary area, perhaps dedicated to special families or members of the new society of Jebel al-Mutawwaq.

It may be interesting to mention the only other structure comparable to the Great Enclosure, the Small Enclosure identified in the Western Sector (Pl. 3.14). It also had a megalithic entrance, less well preserved, and a later rounded structure, mostly damaged by bulldozing activities, added to one side close to its entrance. Even with the Small Enclosure's poor state of conservation, future investigations in the area could allow us to understand if similar repurposing of some urban areas happened in the Western Sector too between the EB IA and EB IB.

Building 131 and Courtyard L. 51 (Pl. 3.15)

About 10 m west of the Great Enclosure, along the southern edge of the settlement, is another structure excavated between 2014 and 2016: Building 131 (10 m long, 4 m wide). The plan, oriented north–south, is apsidal, with the rectangular side on the south and the apse on the north. The building had two doorways, one leading east toward the Great Enclosure, close to its entrance, and one leading west to Courtyard L. 51, an open-air courtyard of rectangular shape enclosing an area of about 150 m². Due to the absence of structures between Building 131 and the Great Enclosure it is possible to imagine an open space between the two structures,

---

66 See Steimer-Herbet 2013; Steimer-Herbet et al. 2020.

67 See Chapter 3.

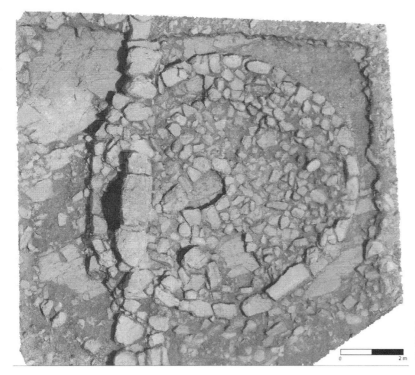

Figure 3.20: Photogrammetry of the round structure, possibly a tower tomb, sealing the entry of the Great Enclosure.

apparently unenclosed by walls. The western entrance of Building 131 had to be a wooden structure, due to the presence of a door socket carved in a stone close to the entrance. The features discovered inside the building, particularly in its southern part, suggest a food production function for this structure. In fact, there were two large platforms (I. 158 and I. 159) of 1.8 m diameter, 20 cm high, built against the southern wall, occupying almost one third of the inner space of the building (Fig. 3.21). The two circular installations are stone-lined and filled with levelled layers of small white pieces of rubble.[68] Close to the eastern circular platform I. 159 a cup mark (19 cm diameter, 6.5 cm deep) has been discovered (Fig. 3.22). The cup mark is different from the two described hitherto and identified in the Temple of the Serpent and the Great Enclosure: the shape is more similar to a cup, with only one side of the rim raised and, at that point, intense rubbing marks inside. This data suggests the cup mark acted as a mortar for grinding, perhaps with a wooden stick or a stone pestle, seeds or any kind of hard vegetal element. The two large circular installations with the mortar indicate that Building 131 had a role in the production of large quantities of food, not so far identified due to the scarcity of botanical remains. This function could explain the unusually large doors of the building (around 1.5 m), wide enough to allow the passage of a discrete flow of people. It is also possible that the aliments produced in Building 131 would be then stored in the nearby western courtyard (L. 51). Close to the northern border of Courtyard L. 51, the natural bedrock rises in elevation; here the rock was carved in order to create small circular installations (I. 65 and I. 66), in which almost complete large storage jars have been discovered. Moreover, in installation I. 65 the base of a jar was found in situ directly above the bedrock, demonstrating the use of the natural rock as the main surface of the courtyard (Fig. 3.23). Thus, it seems that at least this part of the open courtyard was used as a storage area. In the southern part of the courtyard some flint tools were discovered during the excavations. These, scrapers and blades, perhaps indicate other kinds of production activities performed in the area.[69] Courtyard L. 51 was connected to another building to its west (Building C), parallel to Building 131, resembling the typical double apsidal dwellings of the village but narrower (10 m long and only 2.5 m wide). The northern apse is completely lost and the excavations of the interior of the structure are not yet complete. However, its connection with Courtyard L. 51 and Building 131 is clear, repeating a pattern already noted in other parts of the village in the Western Sector.[70] In front of the only visible entrance, toward the courtyard in the middle of its eastern wall, this building had a stone platform, built

---

68 See Polcaro & Muñiz 2019, 91, fig. 11; Casado et al. 2016, 285, fig. 8.

69 See Chapter 5 (Fig. 5.3) for their description.

70 See later in this chapter.

Figure 3.21: The two large platforms (I. 158 and I. 159) discovered in the southern part of Building 131, from the north.

against the two still upright stone jambs of the door, directly above the bedrock. The stone platform (I. 57) has a circular shape (2 m wide) and could be considered another indication of the use of the courtyard for productive activities. By contrast, thus far any possibility of interpreting the circular platform as an altar for cultic activities cannot be confirmed by the area's finds.[71]

Concerning the chronology of the complex of Building 131 and Courtyard L. 51, few diagnostic sherds have been discovered, mostly from large storage jars which in Jebel al-Mutawwaq do not show the main morphological changes between EB IA and EB IB.[72] Its apsidal shape could suggest its dating at least to the end of the EB IA, like the complex of the Temple of the Serpents, where apsidal buildings were also present. A later date could be suggested by the connection of Building 131 with the intramural Dolmen 534, dated to the end of EB IB by the finds. This dolmen was built directly against the southern wall of the building, but its entrance was clearly conceived in order to respect its integrity. We can thus hypothesize that Building 131 was built during the last phase of the life of the Great Enclosure as an open sanctuary, or after its sealing, when the zone was repurposed as a funerary area. In any case, in distinction from the Great Enclosure, Building 131 seems to have maintained its function, although reduced in its production capacity. In fact, in a second phase, perhaps during the construction of the dolmen, the interior of the structure was modified. The inner space of the build-

---

71 On the basis of the comparison with the famous altar of the EBA Megiddo temple in Cisjordan, the circular stone platforms and installations located in courtyards are usually interpreted as open-air altars in the Early Bronze Age II archaeological contexts in Jordan: see e.g. Bāb adh-Dhrāʿ (Rast & Schaub 2003, 157–66, fig. 10.57) and Khirbat al-Batrawy (Nigro 2013, figs 4–5). Nevertheless, these features are usually located some metres from the main broadroom building (the *sancta sanctorum* of the temple) and not placed against its wall. Moreover, usually their dimensions are much greater. In this regard, the only comparison with a similar structure in Jebel al-Mutawwaq is the 'stone platform' identified by the survey in the Western Sector (Pl. 3.16), although it has not yet been investigated and its connection with a sacred or temple area remains unproved.

72 See Chapter 4 (pottery types: NJ.B.3; NJ.C.1–3; WNJ.B.1; OJ.C.1; H.A.1; LSJ.C.3).

Figure 3.22: Detail of the cup mark discovered in Building 131.

Figure 3.23: Installation I.65, where the base of a jar was discovered in situ in L. 51.

ing was reduced: in the northern part, wall W. 172 was built, forming a small room (L. 174), just as in the southeastern corner of the building through another wall, obliterating the second platform, which was clearly no longer in use (Fig. 3.24). Moreover, a semicircular shallow pit (P. 155), lined with stones, was joined to the eastern external facade of Building 131. Here, some animal bones and a tabular scraper have been discovered in a secondary context.[73] Finally, it is interesting to note that

this complex, used for food production activities, was built in this part of the Central Sector during its repurposing as an intramural cemetery area, or at least, it maintained the same function later, possibly related to funerary rituals performed in connection with Dolmen 534.

Another find recovered inside Building 131 connects the structure with the adjoining funerary monument. Between platform I. 158 and the southern wall of Building 131 a fragmentary copper object has been discovered. It was first interpreted as the remains of

---

73 See Chapter 5 (Pl. 5.4: 4).

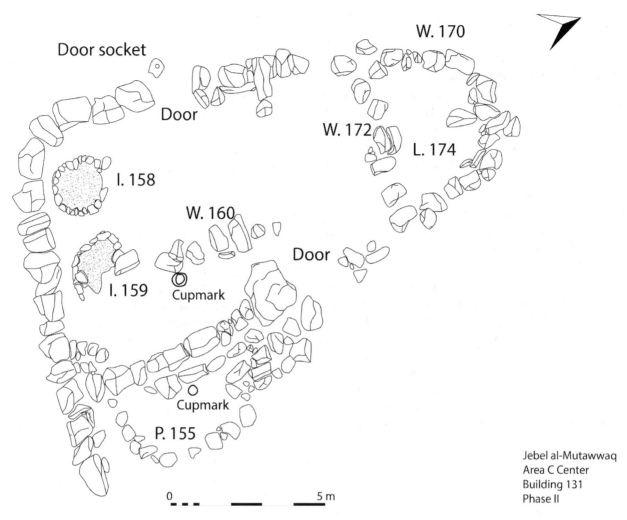

Figure 3.24: Plan of the second phase of Building 131.

an ingot, shaped like a chisel, because of its thickness and flat termination.[74] However, it must be considered that it represents just the head of an artefact; in fact the elongated object, terminating on one edge with a slight fan retrospicient blade, is just 5 cm long (Fig. 3.25). Comparing the object with the copper weapons typical of the Early Bronze Age, it seems close to some kinds of copper axes common in the EB I–II southern Levant, usually 15 cm long.[75] Due to the presence of copper weapons within the funerary gifts of the inhumation excavated in Dolmen 534,[76] and the intense robbing of this area in later periods, it is possible that the copper axe discovered in Building 131 originally belonged to the funerary assemblages of the funerary chamber of the dolmen.

[AP]

The Megalithic Necropolis of Jebel al-Mutawwaq

Jebel al-Mutawwaq in the 1980s was completely covered by almost one thousand dolmens, extending all over the mountain. As already mentioned, modern agricultural and building activities strongly affected the conservation status of the necropolis. The surveys carried out by the Spanish expedition in the 1990s showed that more than three hundred dolmens had been destroyed. The reason for this destruction is that the land owned by the Department Antiquities includes only part of the set-

---

74 See Casado et al. 2016, 283–84, fig. 7.

75 The type is the retrospicient single blade, see for comparisons Montanari 2020, 61, fig. 3.6; 337, pl. XIX:14, 339, pl. XX: 21, 40; 347, pl. XXIV:15. These last examples are also comparable for the section thickness and not just for the shape of the fan blade.

76 See later in this chapter.

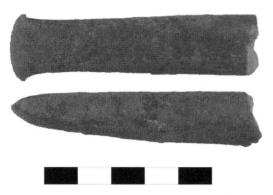

Figure 3.25: The copper object recovered in Building 131.

tlement, leaving outside almost all the funerary areas, located extramurally. Due to the absence of further threats, like the stone quarries that affected a lot of dolmen fields in Jordan, such as Daymie in the Jordan Valley or Tell Murayghat in the Madaba region, the large dolmen field of Jebel al-Mutawwaq was still during the first twenty years of this century the best-preserved megalithic cemetery in the whole country. Unfortunately, new construction work begun in 2020 on the top of the mountain began to change this picture, and, at best, probably more than two thirds of these monuments will completely disappear in the coming two or three years.

General Description of the Necropolis and Dolmen Typologies

The dolmens of Jebel al-Mutawwaq, made up of local limestone slabs, were organized, as already mentioned, in three large cemetery areas. The first was on its eastern slopes, covering a large space of 1.5 km north–south by 700 m west–east, extending from the eastern settlement wall toward the bed of an ancient wadi, nowadays completely dried up, delimiting the mountain to the east. This eastern necropolis extends not only on the south-eastern and eastern slopes but also on the top of the eastern and northern plateaus of the mountain, probably representing the most intensive use of a funerary area in Jebel al-Mutawwaq. The second megalithic cemetery was located on the opposite side of the mountain, on its south-western and western slope. It once covered an area of at least 500 m east–west by 1 km north–south, but today only the south-western part of this necropolis survives. The disposition of the dolmens between the western and the eastern necropoleis is similar: they are organized in clusters of two or three dolmens, close to each other (Fig. 3.26). The clusters usually are at least 5 m apart from each other. The prevailing architecture of the dolmens in the western and eastern necropoleis is the simple *trilithon* structure, forming the skeleton of the megalithic above-ground funerary chamber. This is closed by a back stone slab and by a usually huge and heavy capstone. The lateral megalithic slabs of the *trilithon* structure, are sometimes prolonged by two other long stones, standing in front of the entrance of the funerary chamber, to create a short corridor to reach the floor slab, also in the form of a huge flat megalithic stone. Sometimes, due to the orientation of the dolmens, built with the entrance toward the north against the natural slope of the mountain, the floor slab is at a lower elevation than the entrance of the corridor. Thus, the corridor is stepped, with two or three flat stones used to make the steps descending into the funerary chamber like a *dromos*. In these cases the capstone is normally longer, or made of two slabs, to cover the entire length of the monument from the back of the chamber to the beginning of the front corridor. The entrance of the funerary chamber was generally closed by another stone slab, or by a stone wall, while the corridor was generally sealed with stone and earth at the end of its use. All the dolmens and their front corridors were covered originally by 'tumuli' or 'cairns' made by stones and rubbles.[77] The tumulus has always almost completely disappeared and the only trace recovered on the ground is usually the circular, apsidal, or rectangular retaining wall, made by a single or double row of stones, like the one used for the wall of the dwelling. The walls around the dolmens were sometimes used as platforms or perimeter walls for the funerary space of the monument, but in at least two cases during the Jebel al-Mutawwaq excavations of Area B,[78] the tumulus was recovered intact, with the elevation preserved covering all the dolmen as far as the capstone, the only megalithic slab that was originally visible from outside.[79] These kinds of dolmens have an inner funerary space of around 1 m^2; thus, they are suitable to host

---

[77] In this volume we chose the term 'tumulus' instead of 'cairn' to indicate a stone superstructure, of different plans, covering the whole dolmen structure, which only represents the funerary chamber of the monument, but not always its external shape.

[78] See later in this chapter.

[79] The method of construction of the dolmens of Jebel al-Mutawwaq, as reconstructed by the excavation data is as follows: the two lateral slabs, which also set the orientation of the entrance, were the first to be erected, after the bedrock had been levelled. The back slab, door slab, and lateral slabs of the entrance corridor were then positioned. Finally, the surrounding apsidal wall was constructed and the empty space filled with small stones. The last stage of construction was the placement of a thin covering slab over the corridor, followed by the positioning of the main capstone on the top of the dolmen, which also covered the *dromos*. The tumulus heaped up around the lateral slabs would have also been used as a ramp by

Figure 3.26: The cluster of Dolmens 317, 321, and 316 in Area B, from the north.

a maximum of just one or two complete human bodies lying on the floor slab. From the excavation of Dolmen 317,[80] it seems that the funerary ritual sees the body first deposited lying on the floor slab, but, after the decomposition of the soft tissues, the bones were rearranged and pushed to the back of the chamber, if not completely removed to be located in another secondary location, to host new inhumations inside.

Another typology of dolmens visible in only a few cases in the eastern necropolis, but representing the prevalent typology of the southern necropolis, is much more monumental. Usually the chamber is built with a higher lateral slab (more than 1.4 m), creating a larger funerary chamber, sometimes divided into two separate spaces by a horizontal slab. This upper floor was never found in situ, so it was probably made of a perishable material, like wood.[81] Thus, in these cases the dolmen had two funerary chambers one on top of the other, Dolmen 535 probably being an example. In at least two other cases in the eastern necropolis, this type of dolmen had two parallel funerary chambers, with the inner space being divided through a further standing megalithic slab. All the megalithic slabs of the *trilithon* structure of these dolmens are more regularly cut. The tumulus was made of large stone blocks (up to 1 m long, 0.50 wide, and 0.30 m high), resting one on the top of the other, lying against the lateral slabs of the monument up to the capstone; its shape is more apsidal than circular and the retaining walls are made of the same squared stone blocks as in dolmens nos 534 and 535.[82]

As for the organization of this type of dolmen in the southern necropolis, we can say that they are not organized in clusters, but in single monuments isolated from each other by at least 30 m in the case of Dolmens 534 and 535. Dolmens of this necropolis are found following the southern settlement wall, running along the

---

means of which the heavy capstone could have been raised to the tops of the lateral slabs.

80 See later in this chapter.

81 However, it is possible to recognize the two parallel grooves carved on the middle of the inner side of the lateral slabs of the

dolmen, such as in the case of Dolmen 535, described later in this Chapter.

82 See later in this chapter.

southern border of the Central Sector, from the Great Enclosure to the Temple of the Serpent. In at least two cases they are divided by the settlement wall, as in the case of the last two mentioned, located one intramurally (Dolmen 534) and one extramurally (Dolmen 535). Moreover, each of the dolmens investigated in the southern necropolis is connected to nearby features, to the circular installation and Cave 1012 for Dolmen 535 and to Building 131 for Dolmen 534.[83] These features could be related to special rituals performed by the families which owned these huge megalithic monuments located south of the Central Sector of the settlement. Considering the chronology of these monuments, all dated to the EB IB (between 3100 and 2900 BCE) and the peculiar characteristics of their unique funerary assemblages,[84] it is probable that they have to be connected to the birth of exclusive funerary rituals dedicated to selected families or members of the new society of Jebel al-Mutawwaq. It is noticeable that all these dolmens of the southern necropolis are located following the main pathway which starts from the Southern Gate of the settlement, descending toward the River Zarqa and reaching the Qreisan Spring, located downstream. Thus, they are pointing out what was probably the main and most important road to the walled village of the EB IB.[85]

The Excavated Dolmens of the Eastern Necropolis (228, 232, 318; 316, 317, 321)

In the 2012–2013 season of excavations of the Spanish-Italian expedition, six dolmens have been investigated in the eastern necropolis, in its western edge, close to the limit of the settlement wall. At least three of these dolmens could have been connected with the eastern portal of the settlement wall, leading to the Eastern Sector of the walled village.[86] However, at the present state of knowledge, due to the difficulty in establishing a clear chronology for these dolmens, it is not possible to be sure of their dating to the first phase of the settlement, whether during the Early Bronze Age IA or later in Early Bronze Age IB. The absence of any pottery wares clearly dating to the mature EB IB,[87] the lithic tools recovered in the funerary assemblages of the inhumation discovered intact inside Dolmen 317,[88] and their connection with the Eastern Sector of the settlement, suggests a date around the end of the EB IA, almost contemporary with, or slightly earlier than, the construction of the Temple of the Serpents. As with most of the monuments of the eastern necropolis, the dolmens of Area B are divided into two clusters, the first comprised of Dolmens 228, 232, and 318, excavated in the 2012 season, and the second of Dolmens 316, 317, and 321, excavated in the 2013 season. The dolmens of the first cluster are more distant from each other (about 10 m) than the dolmens of the second group. In the second cluster, Dolmen 316 is located just 1 m south from the other two dolmens, while Dolmen 321 is built directly against the tumulus of Dolmen 317. Unfortunately, ancient DNA analysis can be performed only on the bones of Dolmen 317,[89] so it is not possible to establish with certainty the family ties between the inhumed inside the dolmens of the same cluster. An important consideration is that, apart from Dolmen 317, most of the dolmens were recovered already emptied at the end of their use or violated in antiquity.

Dolmen 228 (Pls 3.18; 3.19)

Dolmen 228 was built close to the southern cliff of the mountain, following the natural slope of the bedrock (Fig. 3.27). Its entrance faces to the north, while its back slab is positioned against the southern cliff face.[90] It has an apsidal surrounding wall, made by one row of large stones at the front and two at the back (each one almost 1 m long by 1 m wide). The dolmen entrance was sealed with another large stone and had a 2.5 m long *dromos*, consisting of two further lateral slabs (1 m high).[91] The roof of the dolmen and its corridor was made by two capstones lying one on top of another. The corridor had two steps made of large flat stones leading into the funerary

---

83 Moreover, in the recent excavations of Area EE, located close to the Southern Gate of the settlement, another dolmen was investigated between 2019 and 2021: Dolmen 11, located a few metres south-east from the water cistern identified by Hanbury-Tenison in his survey (Hanbury-Tenison 1986, fig. 37; 1989, fig. 4). This dolmen, not included in the present book, was connected to a standing stone, a small open-air food production area with a stone bench and a cup mark used as a mortar. Another cave, possibly related to the dolmen, has been also discovered. C14 calibrated dates from human bones discovered scattered inside the dolmen gave 3031–2907 BCE (Beta Analytic — 576899), so also EB IB. See for Dolmen 11 Polcaro & Muñiz 2023.

84 See later in this chapter.

85 See later in this chapter.

86 See Polcaro et al. 2014, 8–9, figs 8–9.

87 As in the dolmens of the southern necropolis: see Chapter 4.

88 See later in this section, and Chapter 5 (Fig. 5.2) for their detailed description.

89 See Chapter 6.

90 Alvarez et al. 2013, 412, fig. 6.

91 Alvarez et al. 2013, 411–13.

Figure 3.27: Dolmen 228 after excavations, from the north.

chamber, which was completely emptied before it was filled with layers of stones and rubbles, like the frontal corridor, and finally closed with a large squared stone. The dolmen's use as a funerary chamber is witnessed only by a few pottery sherds and scattered fragmentary human bones discovered in the layer just above the floor slab. The presence of a tumulus covering the monument is testified by its huge surrounding wall (5 m long, 4 m wide, of apsidal shape) and by the layers of small stones and compact earth that completely fill the space between the surrounding wall and the lateral slabs of the dolmen and *dromos* on both the eastern and western sides. The tumulus had to cover most of the structure, save for the capstone of the dolmen, which remained in view.[92] This means that the surrounding apsidal wall should be interpreted not as the border of a platform, but as the retaining wall of the tumulus. The corridor might have remained clear, being sealed with a large stone so that it could be reopened for new depositions. It was only in the last phase of use that the *dromos* and funerary chamber were emptied of their contents and filled in.

Dolmen 232 (Pl. 3.17)

Dolmen 232 is located on a ledge on the southern cliff, west of Dolmen 228 and south of the settlement wall (Fig. 3.28).[93] It has its entrance oriented to the north; it also has a circular surrounding wall consisting of a single row of large stones (roughly worked, from 0.30 to 0.50 m of diameter), one of which is missing. The dolmen is constructed of two lateral slabs (0.9 m high), a back slab, a capstone, and a floor slab. There is no evidence for a *dromos* in front of the entrance; a squared stone, not in situ, was found near the entrance and probably functioned as a door. The surrounding circular wall is smaller than that of Dolmen 228 (3 m long; 3.5 m wide) and there is less space between it and the slabs. However, a layer of rubble and stones, discovered filling the space between the surrounding wall and the eastern slab of the megalithic chamber, probably repre-

---

92 As proved in the cases of Dolmens 317 and 321 (see later in this section).

93 See also Muñiz et al. 2016, 480, fig. 3.

Figure 3.28: Dolmen 232 after excavations, from the west.

sents the remnants of the tumulus that in this case, too, originally covered the monument.[94]

The funerary chamber was clearly violated in antiquity. This is proved by two fragments of a Geometric Painted Ware jar with brown painted spiral motifs on a white slip found just over the floor slab, which clearly dates the intrusion into the megalithic monument to the Mamluk period.[95] Interestingly, the violators of the dolmen during the Islamic period resealed the funeral chamber with material derived from the original emptying and sealing phases of the Early Bronze Age. The original chronology of the first use of the dolmen is difficult to reconstruct. However, a fragment of a miniature bowl with a pierced loop handle discovered at the back of the funerary chamber could be related to the original inhumations in the tomb,[96] putting it between EB IA and EB IB.

---

[94] Alvarez et al. 2013, 414–17.

[95] Alvarez et al. 2013, 417, fig. 12.

[96] Miniature bowls were also discovered in Cave 1012: see Chapter 4, Pl. 4.23.

Dolmen 318 (Pl. 3.19)

Dolmen 318 is located at the southern rock cliff of the mountain, following the natural slope of the bedrock, and is close to the other two dolmens excavated during the same season further up the mountainside. The main architectural elements of the dolmen are the same as the other two previously mentioned, a megalithic *trilithon* burial chamber with an access corridor. The burial chamber is smaller than those of nearby dolmens. The narrow access corridor was constructed with double parallel rows of stones. It was built as a stepped *dromos* in order to deal with the natural slope. A slab was placed at the entrance to the chamber, partially sealing it. An interesting feature is that the covering tumulus differs from the others of this cluster. It was built above an artificial platform of apsidal shape providing both a foundation for it and perimeter around the monument. It was constructed with three straight walls of stone slabs, placed directly against the lateral slabs of the dolmen and preserved to a height of three courses of large, rectangular stone blocks. As with Dolmen 232, some sherds recovered scattered on the floor slab of the dolmen point to a chronology between the late EB IA and the beginning of the EB IB; even if two fragmentary flat dishes could also suggest a late date in EB IB.[97]

Dolmen 316

Dolmen 316 is the larger of the second cluster of Area B, with a megalithic funerary chamber 2 m long and 1.7 m wide. Unfortunately it was discovered violated in antiquity and completely emptied. The only interesting feature is the external tumulus, with its apsidal surrounding wall badly preserved. It seems similar to that of Dolmen 228, made up of large stones (some reaching 1.5 m in length and 1 m width), especially on the back of the dolmen, lined directly against the back slab.

Dolmen 317 (Pl. 3.20)

Dolmen 317 is the most interesting dolmen of Area B, particularly for its very good state of preservation, due to the natural depositional layers which buried the monument almost completely till the capstone (Fig. 3.29). The dolmen was recovered perfectly intact, with the tumulus (4 m long, 2.8 m wide, 1.5 m high) still in place and the front slab closing the door of the corridor well sealed. Due to the slope in this part of the mountain, the builders levelled the bedrock under the dolmen with layers of small stones, upon which the door slab was laid. The entrance was on the north and had a *dromos* comprising two stone steps leading toward the floor slab of the burial chamber, measuring 2 m². The entrance of the burial chamber was discovered sealed with a frontal stone slab. Inside the chamber, below the usual filling layers of stones and earth and above the original door slab, another layer of compact earth, human and animal bones was found.[98] In this layer, two concentrations of human bones were discovered and were identified as two different burials. The first, designated B. 25, is a single burial, placed close to the entrance of the burial chamber. It consists of an ordered pile of long bones, an intact human skull, and other small human bones probably from the same individual. The presence of ribs, vertebrae, and especially finger bones and other small bones pertaining to the same inhumation suggests that the corpse decomposed inside the burial chamber and was then rearranged in a ritual position in the same place. With this burial, animal bones and two flint tools were also discovered (O. 69, O. 70).[99] A second burial, designated B. 26, is a multiple secondary burial of at least four individuals pushed against the back slab of the dolmen, in the south-eastern corner of the chamber.[100] Concerning the secondary disposition of the bones inside the burial chamber, this arrangement is very similar to that with the bones discovered in secondary deposition inside the shaft tombs of Bab edh Dhra, particularly during the EB IA.[101] The main difference is that the bone pile in the centre of the burial chamber comes from the bones of only one individual and is not mixed with the long bones of the other people of B. 26 at the back of the chamber. Concerning the funeral assemblages recovered with the inhumation of Dolmen 317, few pieces of pottery were recovered inside the burial chamber and it seem that no pottery vessel was buried with B. 25 or with B. 26, unless, when the other burials inside Dolmen 317 were removed, all the vessels were carried away. However, the last burial located in the tomb, B. 25, the only complete burial left in the chamber, had just two flint tools as funerary gifts. These flints were two large tabular scrapers, one of fan and the other of elongated shape, very well worked; they are a couple of tools that have been associated both with wool shearing and with meat butchering, discovered in working areas but also in a sacred context.[102] These tools are sometimes associated with burials in southern Levantine contexts: the same pair of objects was discovered in the EB IB burial Cave F-55 of

---

97 Alvarez et al. 2013, 421, fig. 16:b. See comparison with the dishes discovered outside Dolmen 535, later in this section and in Chapter 4 (Pottery Type D.A.1).

98 See also Polcaro et al. 2014.

99 See Chapter 5, fig. 5.2, pl. 5.4:1–2.

100 It consists of small human bones, including finger bones, ribs, and teeth, without a skull or long bone (see Polcaro et al. 2014).

101 See e.g. the bone pile of Tomb A 69: Schaub & Rast 1989, 109, fig. 61. The fusion of the long bones of the dead could be interpreted as a way to highlight the family ties between the group, only the skulls representing the individuality after death (concerning the connection between secondary burials, megalithic tradition, and ancestor cult see Polcaro 2008; 2013). See also on the topic of the ancestor cult in EB Bab edh-Dhra: Chesson 2001; 2007.

102 So far, tabular scrapers of Jebel al-Mutawwaq have been discovered only in public or funerary contexts (see Chapter 5). They were also recovered at different southern Levantine sites in Early Bronze temple contexts and sacred areas, as at Bab adh-Dhraᶜ and Megiddo (Rosen 1997, 74–75; 2011, 252). At Bad edh-Dhra, Field XII, at least eight fan scrapers were discovered. Analysis of the scrapers suggests they were used not as scraping utensils alone but also as butchering knives (see McConaughy 1980). This kind of utensil has also been recovered from Ghassulian period sites, and the association between them and votive deposits in Late Chalcolithic sites strengthens the interpretation of these tools as ritual butchering objects (see Elliott 1977). See also Chapter 5 for comparison.

Figure 3.29: Dolmen 317 with intact tumulus, before the opening of the funerary chamber, from the north-east.

Nesher-Ramla Quarry in Cisjordan.[103] Their presence in the funerary assemblages of inhumation B. 25 could be a clue for identifying the social role of the dead deposed in Dolmen 317. The possible association of these scrapers with the work of slaughtering animals or processing wool points to a connection between the dead and the world of the shepherd, even if the very high manufactures of the flint tools could indicate some important role in life. Some animal bones have been identified in association with B. 25: amid the remains was the bone of a piglet.[104] The presence of a pig, an animal usually connected to a sedentary life typical of a mixed agro-pastoral society, fits well in a funerary context, due to the high symbolic value of this animal in the funerary ideology of the whole Near East. A preliminary anthropological analysis made of the human bones of the burial B. 25 recognized the absence of stress pathologies, suggesting that in life she was a person who never carried heavy weights, nor did she use her teeth for housework. Behind the skull a clear wound, very precise, has been identified. It is a triangular-shaped hole measuring 8–9 mm, which ends in a very small opening only 1 mm in size inside the cranium. Due to the absence of cranial bone growth around it, this 'wound' can be interpreted as perimortem or post-mortem (Fig. 3.30). This means that the person inhumed in Dolmen 317 may have been killed with a sharp blow to the back of the head. The new genetic analysis performed on the bones of B. 25 confirms the first impression obtained from the bones that the person was surely a woman of about forty years, a very old age for the beginning of the Early Bronze Age.[105] It remains unknown why, unlike the bones of all the other individuals buried in the burial chamber, those of this woman were left and not removed at the end of the monument's use.

---

103 See Avrutis 2012, 215, fig. 7.3:C; 214, fig. 7.2:B.

104 See Polcaro et al. 2014. Other bones of pigs or boars were recovered also in the village of Jebel al-Mutawwaq in the private houses (Fernández-Tresguerres 1999, 325).

105 See Chapter 6.

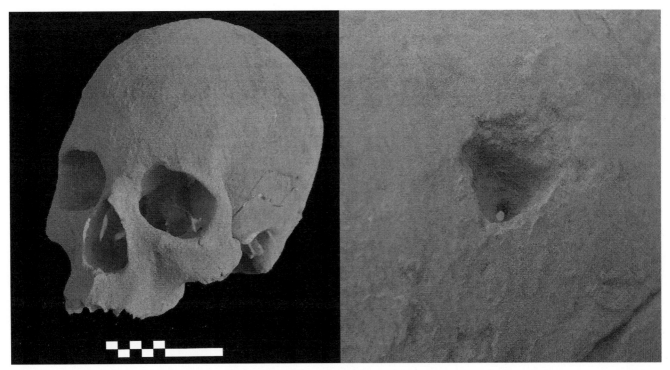

Figure 3.30: Skull of inhumation B. 25, discovered in the burial chamber of Dolmen 317. On the right: detail of the cranium, with the triangular section wound.

Figure 3.31: Dolmen 321 after excavations, before the opening of the funerary chamber, from the north-west.

Dolmen 321 (Pl. 3.21)

The last dolmen excavated in Area B was clearly built in connection with Dolmen 317. In particular, the surrounding tumulus of Dolmen 321, of perfect rectangular shape,[106] abuts the western curvilinear wall of the tumulus of Dolmen 317 (Fig. 3.31). Moreover, the monument bisects the street that from the south-eastern entrance of the settlement points toward Dolmen 317. It is smaller and was also recovered intact, with the tumulus sealed and not violated. The external dimensions of the tumulus are width 2.5 m, length 3.7 m. Dolmen 321, like Dolmen 317, had three stone steps in the frontal corridor leading down toward the floor slab of the burial chamber, measuring only 0.8 m². The dolmen was carefully emptied at the end of its use, then was completely filled with stones and compacted earth, before being permanently closed with a large slab sealing the entrance of the *dromos*. The burial chamber revealed no sign of human bones, pottery sherds, or flints, indicating that the people who used it for burials took away all their bones and funerary assemblages before leaving the site. However, its connection with Dolmens no. 317 and no. 316 could indicate some relationship with the other individuals deposited nearby. Even without C14 data, or diagnostic pottery analysis from the architectonic stratigraphy, it is clear that this was the last dolmen built in this second cluster of Area B and possibly it belongs to a more mature phase of the EB IB.

The Excavated Dolmens of the Southern Necropolis (534, 535, and Cave 1012)

As already mentioned at the beginning of the chapter, the southern necropolis had a prominent position, clearly connected with the urban evolution of the settlement during the second phase of expansion (EB IB). The funerary monuments of this area are connected with the external pathway going along the southern settlement wall in the Central Sector and also with the main street going from the Southern Gate of the village downstream at the Qreisan Spring. The two dolmens of this group excavated in 2015–2019 are the intramural Dolmen 534 and extramural Dolmen 535. Both are connected with the Great Enclosure, with Building 131 and with the whole Area C, repurposed between the end of the EB IA and the beginning of EB IB. The connection of Dolmen 535 with an underground hypogeum chamber, discovered intact and sealed, hidden in front of the monument, brings to light the funeral rituals performed by the people of the village in the last century of the fourth millennium BCE.

Dolmen 534

Dolmen 534 was built directly against the southern wall of Building 131. It faces north, and is characterized by a unique angular corridor, which bends to the east following the course of the wall of the nearby building (Fig. 3.32). The dolmen had a tumulus, which covered an area measuring approximately 3 × 4 m, constructed of large square limestone blocks, which was very different from those associated with the dolmens in Area B.[107] The rectangular stone blocks were positioned one above the other, forming a stone box around the dolmen which originally exceeded the height of the capstone. The burial chamber (1 m long, 0.90 m wide, 1.10 m high), had the two lateral slabs and the large capstone of the chamber carefully smoothed on the inner surfaces, while the two back slabs were also perfectly square in shape. The entrance corridor to the chamber, around 2 m long and 0.6 m wide,[108] had three stone steps leading down toward the burial chamber. The regular lateral stone blocks were rectangular in shape and very different to the large, unworked stones used to build the dolmens of the eastern necropolis. In addition, the way in which the corridor and the burial chamber were sealed was also different from that seen in the case of the other dolmens. This usually consisted of a single large stone, but in the case of Dolmen 534 access to the chamber was restricted at the entrance of the *dromos* by a wall of stones and earth.

Unfortunately the tomb had been extensively disturbed by grave robbers, probably quite recently. The robbers had entered from the rear, causing significant damage to the slab which formed the back of the chamber and, in doing so, disturbed the upper layer of burials (which probably represented the final phase of the tomb's use), with the result that the bones lay scattered partly inside and partly outside the chamber. Two partially preserved burials were identified close to the front of the chamber, lying immediately adjacent to the inner side of the wall which sealed the entrance to the chamber from the corridor. Unfortunately, the looting of the chamber had also damaged the lower layer of burials and the human bones had been partially removed. Only a jawbone and a number of long bones had sur-

---

106 This is the only surrounding rectangular tumulus covering a dolmen since identified in the eastern necropolis.

107 Polcaro & Muñiz 2018.

108 See Polcaro & Muñiz 2018.

Figure 3.32: The entrance corridor of Dolmen 534, from the north-east.

Figure 3.33: Copper arrowheads discovered in Dolmen 534: a) rhomboidal arrowhead associated with Burial B. 702; b) foil-shaped arrowhead discovered in secondary context outside the funerary chamber.

vived the looting, belonging to two inhumations, one adult and one juvenile (B. 701, 702). Two jugs with loop handles and red burnished decoration on the external surfaces were recovered from the same layer, close to the human bones. These, although broken, were largely complete.[109] The vessels, which were almost certainly part of the funerary assemblages, were found lying against the northern wall of the chamber, between the inhumations and the front wall. Their shape and the surface treatment suggest that they can be compared to examples from Phase II of Tell Abu al-Kharaz in the Jordan Valley,[110] placed between 3050 and 3000 BCE.[111] These parallels date the inhumation to the end of Early Bronze Age IB. In addition to these offerings, other finds were also recovered from above the floor of the chamber. These included fragments of bronze, probably from some sort of dress accessory and an unusual copper arrowhead with a 2.5 cm long square-sectioned tang and a blade (4 cm long and almost 2 cm wide) with a distinctive rhomboidal shape, sharply bent close to the point (Fig. 3.33a). The arrowhead lacks any parallel in the southern Levant, although this may be because arrowheads are, in general, very rare amongst the weapons discovered in the Early Bronze Age I–III funerary contexts and only become more common in the burials of the Middle Bronze Age.[112] In the Early Bronze Age IB cave burial on the Coastal Plain at Nesher-Ramla Quarry a copper weapon has been discovered, albeit very different in form: it is a copper tanged and socketed spearhead of elongated shape. The same tomb also contained a jug similar to the ones from Dolmen 534.[113] A further parallel might be an arrowhead with a square-sectioned tang and a triangular-shape blade, discovered in Tomb 1101B at Megiddo, in this case in a context dating to the Early Bronze Age II–III.[114]

---

109 See Chapter 4, Pl. 4.23:13–14.

110 Fischer 2000, fig. 12.7.

111 Fischer 2008, 381.

112 Philip 1989. See also Montanari 2020, 132–34; 614, pl. CLVIII.

113 See Avrutis 2010, fig. 2.2.

114 See Guy 1938, pl. 86.1. See also a comparison of the EB IB in Montanari 2020, 614, pl. CLVIII:343.

Figure 3.34: Later view of Dolmen 535, from the west.

The excavation of the dump of compacted earth at the rear of Dolmen 534 which originated with the activities of the looters, produced an additional find alongside fragmentary human bones. This was a second copper arrowhead with a foil-shaped, ribbed blade, 7.5 cm long and 3 cm wide and a square-sectioned tang (Fig. 3.33b). The foil shape is very common in the southern Levant amongst weapons of the second millennium BCE.[115] If the weapon from Mutawwaq can be dated to the Middle Bronze Age, this could indicate a second phase of burial inside the chamber of Dolmen 534 dating to the same period. However, this hypothesis cannot be confirmed as no sherds of pottery dating to the Middle Bronze Age have been recovered either in the area around the dolmen or in the burial chamber.

Nevertheless, considering that the fragmentary copper axe found in Building 131 could originally belong to the same burial (B. 702) in Dolmen 534, the discovery of weapons in the funerary assemblages of this tomb is very important. It connects the inhumation of this family group to the specific role of defence of the settlement, during the EB IB, when the settlement wall was probably built. The intramural location of the dolmen also suggests an important role for this family, and a probable higher status than other clans using extramural funerary monuments. Moreover, the important status of the deceased buried in Dolmen 534 can also be demonstrated by the precise construction techniques, particularly in the case of the access corridor, noticeably larger than those identified in the other dolmens

---

115 In particular, examples with longer blades and socketed tangs, interpreted as spearheads, are common in the Middle Bronze Age II tombs at Megiddo, including, for example, Tomb 9011D (Guy 1938, pl. 122.7). Similar examples of copper arrowheads, also with square-sectioned tangs, were discovered in funerary contexts inside the dolmens of the Golan region which date to the Middle Bronze Age I period. Examples include Dolmens 13 and 14 in the Deir Sras field (Epstein 1985, 44).

of the necropolis. A wider and much more monumental entrance has to be connected with a more frequent opening of the tomb. This might suggest the periodic enactment of funerary rituals connected with the memory of the ancestors. It is thus possible that, at least in its second phase of use, Building 131, even if reduced in the inner space, could have been used to produce food supplies for special rituals and festivities dedicated to the memory of the ancestors of this important family group within Jebel al-Mutawwaq society, whose role may have been the protection and defence of the settlement.

Dolmen 535

Located just 4.50 m south of the natural upper rocky terraces where the Great Enclosure is built, and about 30 m to the south of Dolmen 534, Dolmen 535 has been recognized as one of the largest on this part of the mountain (Pl. 3.22). The dolmen was unfortunately looted from behind. The back slab was not in place and the inner chamber of the megalithic structure had been almost completely emptied. The dolmen was surrounded by a huge stone tumulus (4.40 m wide, 5.50 m long) of apsidal shape, preserved to a height of three layers of squared stone blocks (Fig. 3.34). The typology of the large stones used for this tumulus more closely resembles Dolmen 534 than the dolmens of the eastern necropolis. The inner chamber of the dolmen is the largest discovered to date on Jabal al-Muṭawwaq, with a height of 2.27 m, length of 2.33 m, and width of 0.80 m. Moreover, two parallel lines are carved bisecting the two lateral slabs equally; as already observed,[116] these are usually interpreted as mountings for a second floor of a perishable material such as wood, which would divide the vertical space of the burial chamber in two (Fig. 3.35). This feature indicates that in the funerary chamber at least two, or even four complete bodies can be located at the same time lying on the two floors of the chamber.

Outside the entrance there were two high stone steps leading from the outside to the inner chamber. In front of the dolmen a beaten-earth floor (L. 1007) was discovered (Pl. 3.24). Associated with the floor, on the left side of the dolmen's entrance, a small circular installation was also recognized (I. 1006). This was built of medium-sized stones and measured about 1.18 m in diameter. It was filled with a compacted layer of earth and rubble, quite similar to the construction method of the two platforms discovered inside Building 131. However, an explanation of its function for the purpose of producing food cannot be advanced with certainty. An inverted rim platter and a small bowl with a disc base, both with red-burnished decoration on the inner and outer sides, have been discovered in connection with the beaten-earth floor and the circular installation.[117] These wares could be dated to the final EB IB and represent the last phase of use of the monument, almost contemporary with the use of Dolmen 534. Only a few fragmented human bones have been discovered on the lower floor slab of the burial chamber of Dolmen 535. Most of the bones originally located in the dolmen were discovered relocated inside

Figure 3.35: Inner view of the burial chamber of Dolmen 535, from the south. In the foreground the two parallel grooves carved on the later slabs are visible.

---

116 See Chapter 2.

117 These sherds were characterized by black basalt and white limestone grits in the red-orange coloured fabric, this being very different to the EB IA or Early EB IB pottery fabric of Jebal al-Muṭawwaq village and could represent a later phase of the EB IB (see Chapter 4, Pottery Production Group 2).

Cave 1012, in front of the megalithic monument, under the earth beaten floor which hides a well-cut oval hole in the bedrock (Pl. 3.23).

Cave 1012

The opening in the bedrock discovered just in front of the short *dromos* of Dolmen 535, close to the cliff and 15 m south of the Great Enclosure, was the entrance to a vertical shaft excavated in the limestone rock of the mountain (Pl. 3.25). The shaft, almost 3 m deep and 1.5 m wide, leads to an underground cave, artificially cut in the rock (Fig. 3.36). The entrance of the cave at the bottom of the shaft was found to be blocked by a stone wall (W. 1014). In front of the wall that sealed the cave, a complete hemispherical bowl of red fabric with basalt and limestone grits was discovered,[118] perhaps testifying a rite associated with the final closure of the cave, before the construction of the upper floor sealing the shaft entrance. Inside cave C. 1012 several secondary burials were discovered, their original position partly broken up by the ancient collapse of the roof (Pl. 3.26). At least three main burial groups were discovered (B. 1020, B. 1023, and B. 1024). The inhumations were clearly in secondary deposition, with long bones arranged in piles and a few vertebrae and other small bones scattered on the floor of the cave. At the back of the hypogeum chamber, against its northern wall and mostly at the corners, a minimum of five skulls were recognized. Unfortunately, the collapse of the limestone roof had crushed most of the skulls and scattered parts of the bone piles. However, a first anthropological analysis performed on the bones distinguishes at least ten individuals buried in the cave — infants, juveniles, and adults. The adult bones show signs of wear compatible with a working life: agriculture would be a good fit. Moreover, the first morphological analysis of the human bones discovered in Cave 1012 points to a severe protein/vitamin deficiency, indicating a diet mostly based on cereals and vegetables, possibly with fish as a complement, but without frequent consumption of meat. Finally, some bones present signs of burning, compatible with a swift cremation of the body when the corpse was not completely decomposed. This is usually a common practice in secondary burial rituals, when the incompletely decomposed body has to be moved to its final location, so fire is used both as a practical instru-

Figure 3.36: Photogrammetry of Dolmen 535 and of the shaft leading toward Cave 1012, located in front of the entrance to the megalithic monument.

ment to remove the remaining flesh and to 'purify' the human remains.[119]

Among the bone piles, a miniature cup and miniature *amphoriskoi* were discovered, for a total of six vessels; two more miniature jars were discovered amongst the skulls (Fig. 3.37). All of these vessels could be dated to EB IB.[120] The dating of the cave burials to the beginning of the EB IB was confirmed by C14 analysis, giving a calibrated time span of 3241–3104 BCE.[121] The exclusive presence of miniature vessels — without any other pottery types — might suggest that, rather than being funerary assemblages for the dead, the pottery from the C. 1012 burial layer was associated with funerary rites connected with secondary deposition. It is noteworthy that they are vessels which usually contain oils and unguents, so they could be linked to the role of the fam-

---

118 The type of fabric and nature of the grits are perfectly comparable with pottery discovered on upper floor L. 1007 in front of Dolmen 535 (see Chapter 4, Pl. 4.19, Pottery Type C.A.1).

119 Anthropological and ancient DNA analysis on the human remains discovered in Cave 1012 is ongoing.

120 See Chapter 4.

121 Beta Analytic no. 561343. See also the conclusive chapter for a resume of the carbon data from Jebel al-Mutawwaq.

Figure 3.37: The bone piles discovered inside Cave 1012, partially crushed by the fall of the hypogeum roof. Amid the human bones two of the miniature vessels are visible.

Figure 3.38: The bowl discovered on the bottom of Cave 1012, close to the hearth, before the start of the human depositions in the cave.

ily or clan owning the burial cave and the frontal megalithic monument, connected to these products. The evidence of the human bones, this last consideration, and the presence of olive seeds also discovered in the cave,[122] could point to oliviculture and olive oil production as one of the main activities of the human group deposited in the cave. However, in the absence of further data from the bones or from the pottery assemblages of Cave 1012 this hypothesis remains merely speculative.

Finally, it is interesting to note that the cave was used before its repurposing as a funerary chamber to perform some rituals. In the lower layer under the burials, above the bedrock representing the floor of the cave, the remains of a hearth have been identified. Close to the hearth a complete bowl has been discovered (Fig. 3.38), together with several sherds of large storage vessels with ledge handles, olive seeds, and some animal bones. A stone disc, probably a circular chopper, was also discovered in the lower layers representing the first use of the cave, before the inhumations began to be relocated inside.[123] This phase of use could also be related to the repurposing of the cave as a hypogeum ossuary when Dolmen 535 was built.

[AP]

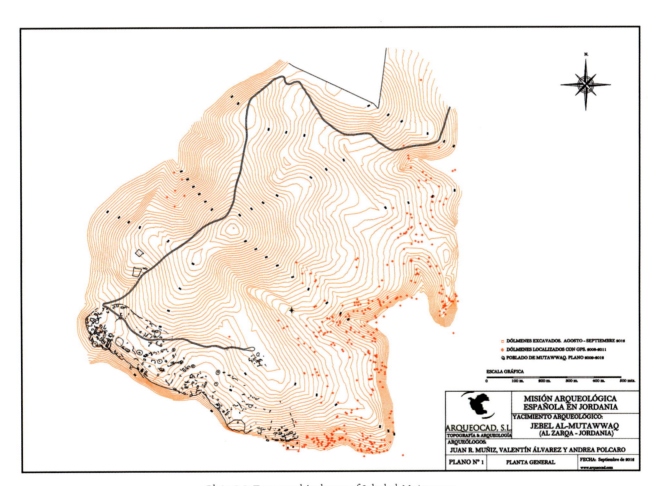

Plate 3.0: Topographical map of Jebel al-Mutawwaq.

---

122 See Chapter 7.
123 See Chapter 5, Fig. 5.8.

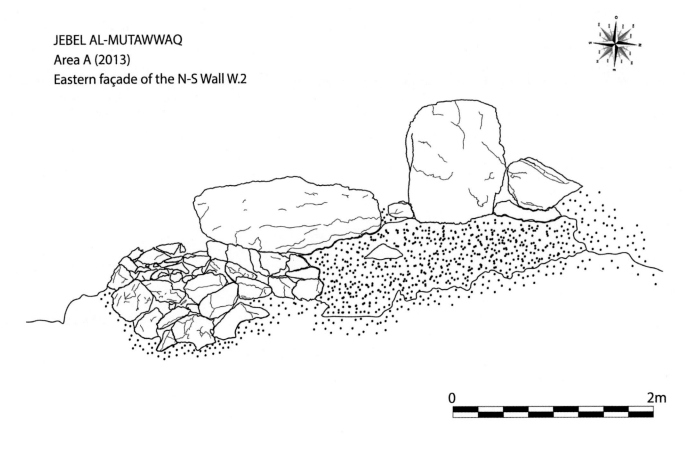

Plate 3.1a: Eastern façade of the settlement wall, in Area A.

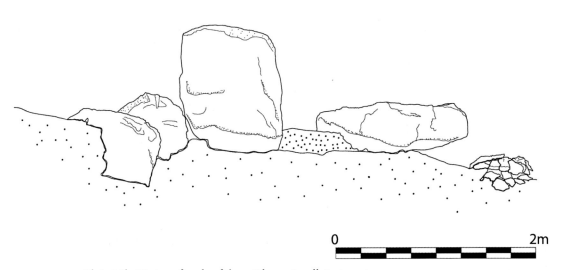

Plate 3.1b: Western façade of the settlement wall, in Area A.

3. THE SITE OF JEBEL AL-MUTAWWAQ: ARCHITECTURE, SETTLEMENT PLANNING, AND SPACE ORGANIZATION

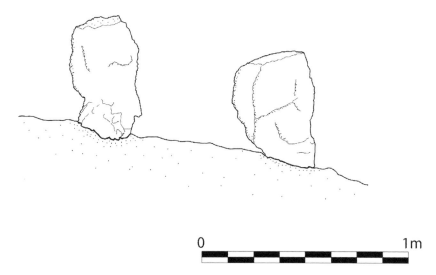

Plate 3.2a: The south-eastern settlement door, in Area A.

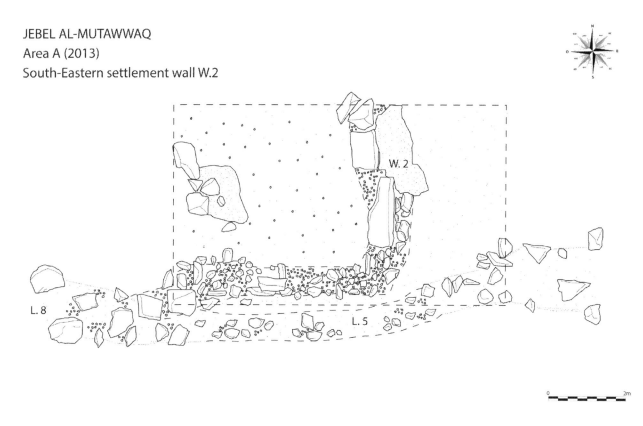

Plate 3.2b: Plan of the south-eastern settlement wall and door, in Area A.

JEBEL AL-MUTAWWAQ
Central Sector (2019)
Southern Door and Settlement Wall

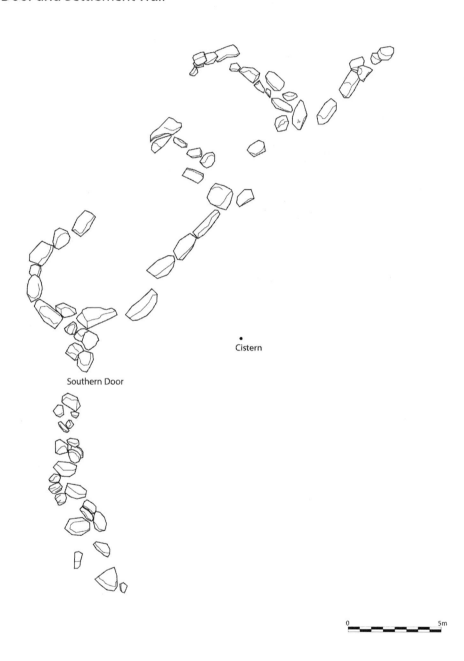

Plate 3.3: Plan of the southern settlement door and associated structures.

3. THE SITE OF JEBEL AL-MUTAWWAQ: ARCHITECTURE, SETTLEMENT PLANNING, AND SPACE ORGANIZATION 69

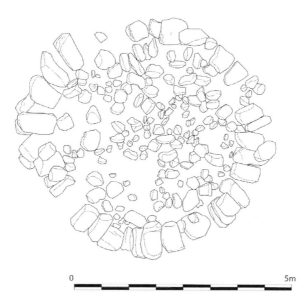

Plate 3.4a: Plan of Tower A, in the Western Sector of the settlement.

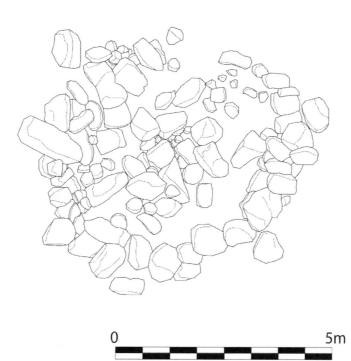

Plate 3.4b: Plan of Tower B, in the Western Sector of the settlement.

Plate 3.5: Plan of one of the houses of the Central Sector (2019 Survey BC1).

3. THE SITE OF JEBEL AL-MUTAWWAQ: ARCHITECTURE, SETTLEMENT PLANNING, AND SPACE ORGANIZATION

JEBEL AL-MUTAWWAQ
Eastern Sector (2019)
Survey B_E_1

Plate 3.6a: Plan of one of the houses of the Eastern Sector (2019 Survey BE1).

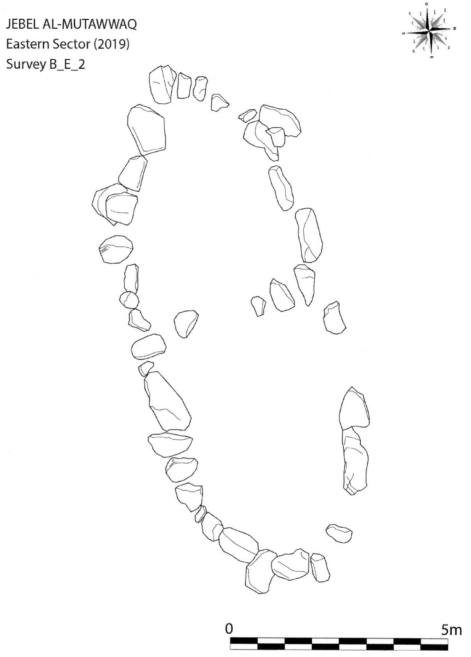

Plate 3.6b: Plan of one of the houses of the Eastern Sector (2019 Survey BE2).

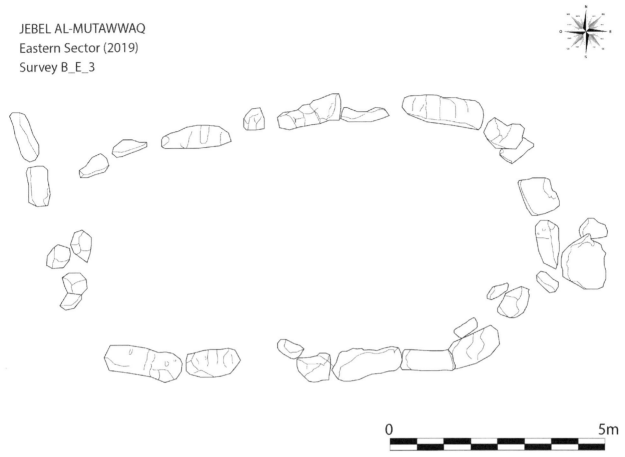

Plate 3.7a: Plan of one of the houses of the Eastern Sector (2019 Survey BE3).

Plate 3.7b: Plan of one of the houses of the Eastern Sector (2019 Survey BE4).

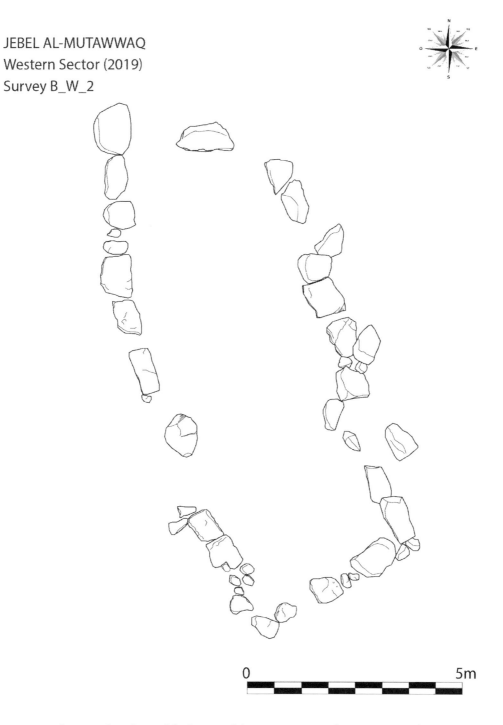

Plate 3.8: Plan of one of the houses of the Western Sector (2019 Survey BW2).

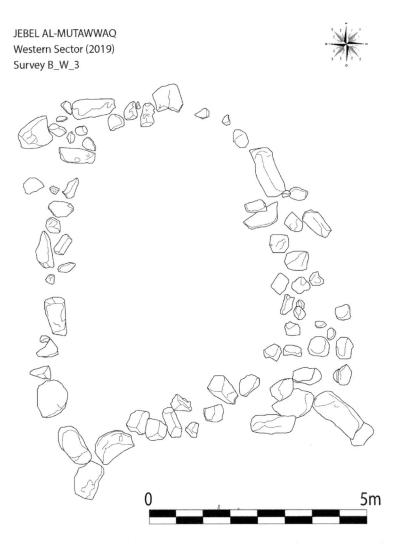

Plate 3.9a: Plan of one of the houses of the Western Sector (2019 Survey BW3).

JEBEL AL-MUTAWWAQ
Western Sector (2019)
Survey B_W_4

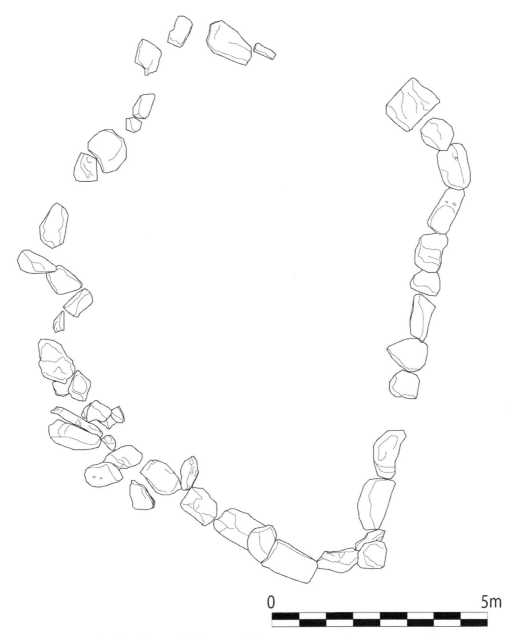

Plate 3.9b: Plan of one of the houses of the Western Sector (2019 Survey BW4).

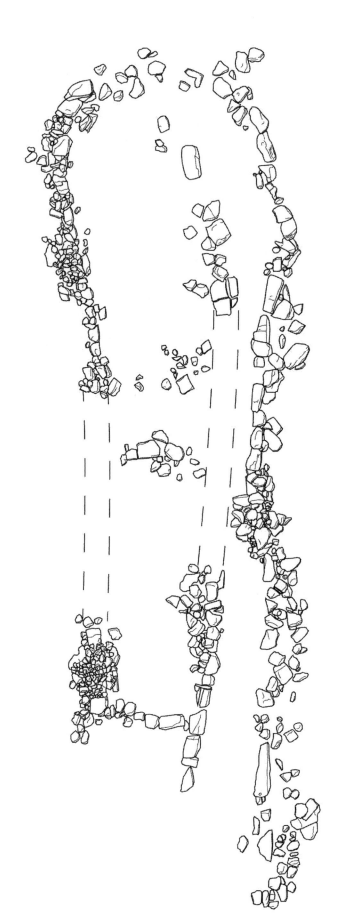

Plate 3.10a: Plan of one of the houses of the Western Sector (2019 Survey BW5).

3. THE SITE OF JEBEL AL-MUTAWWAQ: ARCHITECTURE, SETTLEMENT PLANNING, AND SPACE ORGANIZATION 79

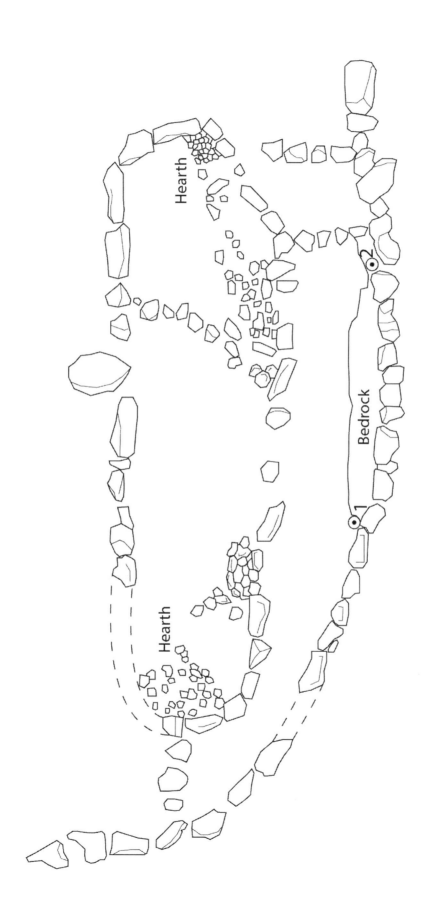

Plate 3.10b: Plan of House 81, excavated by the Spanish expedition leaded by J. A. Tresguerres Velasco.

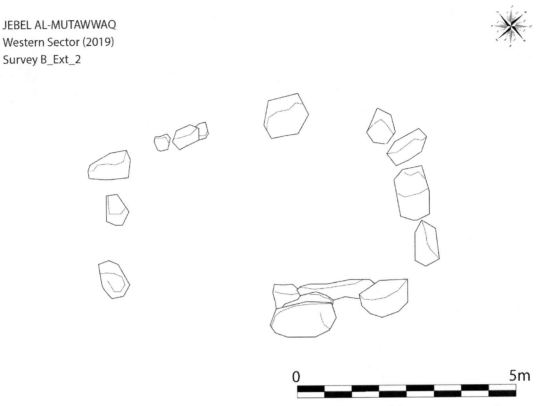

Plate 3.11a: Plan of one of the houses visible outside the settlement wall (2019 Survey B_Ext1).

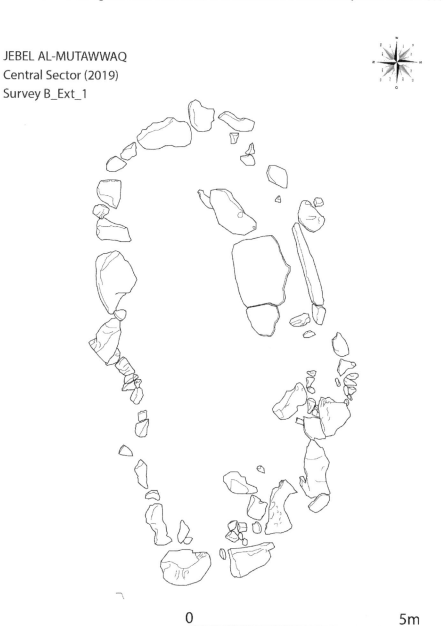

Plate 3.11b: Plan of one of the houses visible outside the settlement wall (2019 Survey B_Ext2).

JEBEL AL-MUTAWWAQ
Temple of the Serpents

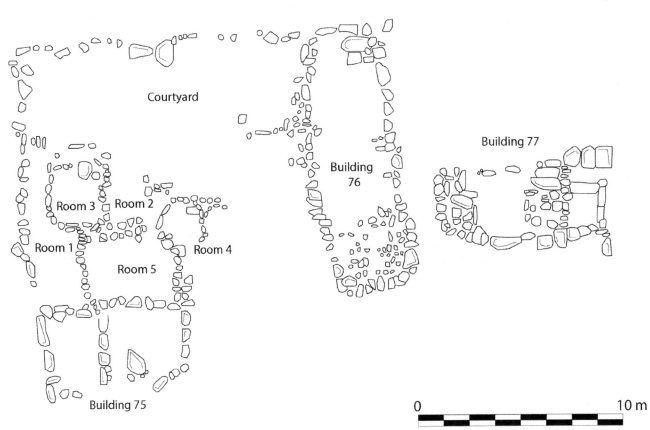

Plate 3.12: Plan of the Temple of the Serpents, excavated by the Spanish expedition led by J. A. Tresguerres Velasco.

3. THE SITE OF JEBEL AL-MUTAWWAQ: ARCHITECTURE, SETTLEMENT PLANNING, AND SPACE ORGANIZATION   83

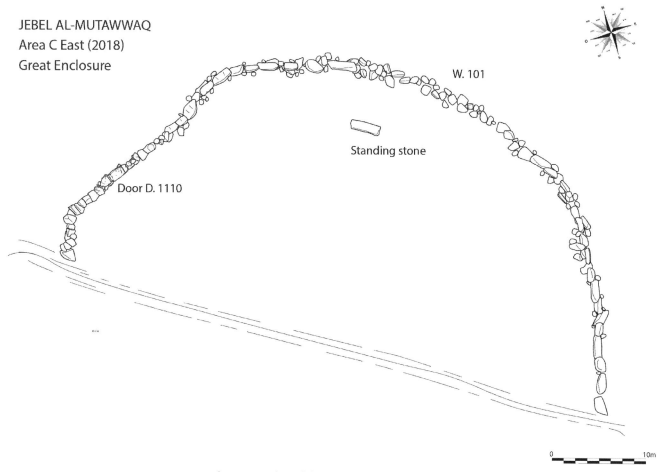

Plate 3.13a: Plan of the Great Enclosure, in Area C.

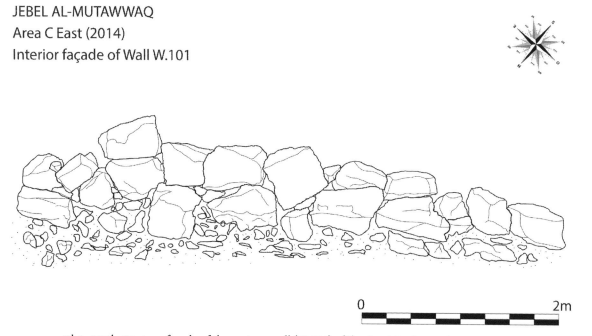

Plate 3.13b: Western façade of the eastern wall (W. 101) of the Great Enclosure, in Area C.

JEBEL AL-MUTAWWAQ
Western Sector (2019)
Survey Platform_2

Plate 3.14: Plan of the small enclosure in the Western Sector (2019 Survey Platform 2).

3. THE SITE OF JEBEL AL-MUTAWWAQ: ARCHITECTURE, SETTLEMENT PLANNING, AND SPACE ORGANIZATION 85

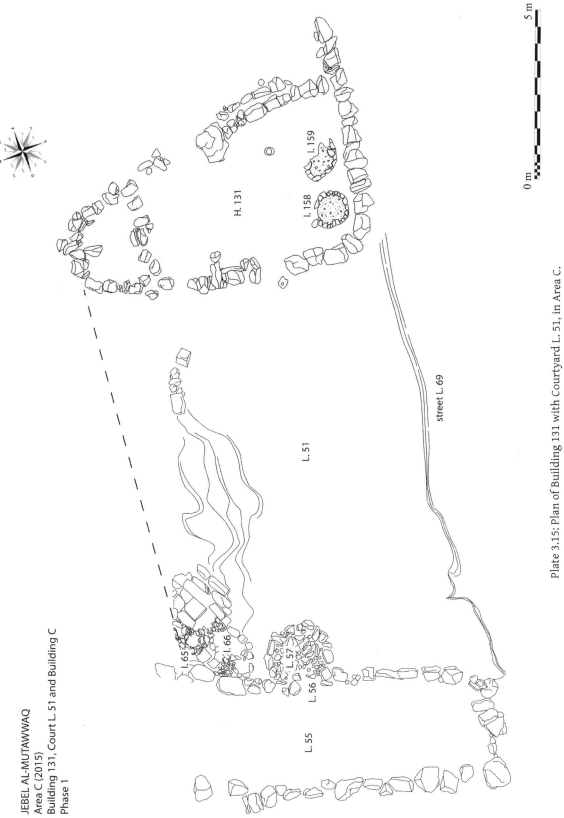

Plate 3.15: Plan of Building 131 with Courtyard L. 51, in Area C.

JEBEL AL-MUTAWWAQ
Western Sector (2019)
Survey Platform_1

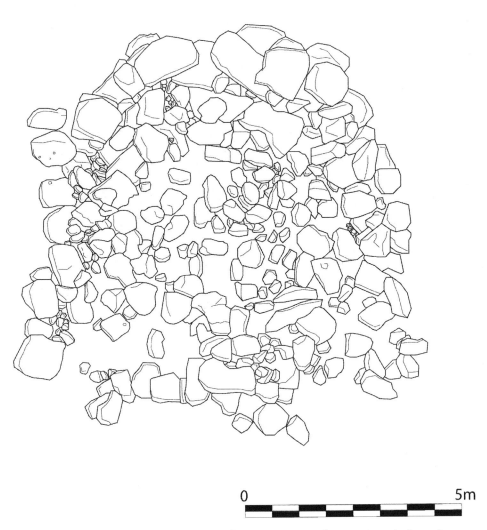

Plate 3.16: Plan of a round isolated platform in the Western Sector (2019 Survey Platform 1).

JEBEL AL-MUTAWWAQ
Area B (2012)
Do. 232

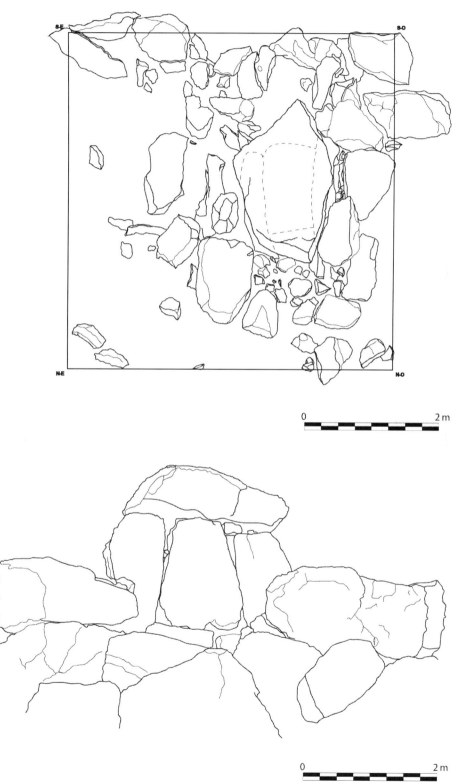

Plate 3.17: a) Plan and b) southern façade of Dolmen 232.

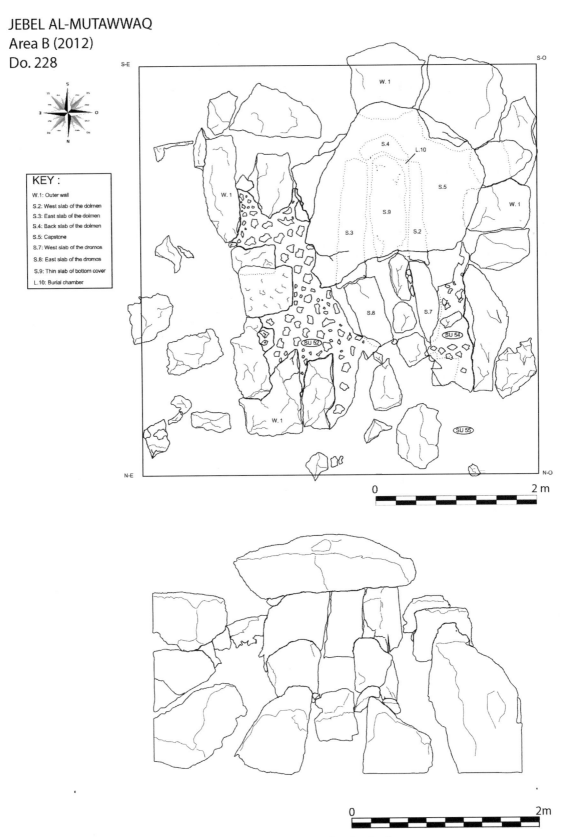

Plate 3.18: a) Plan and b) north-western façade of Dolmen 228.

JEBEL AL-MUTAWWAQ
Area B (2012)
Do. 318

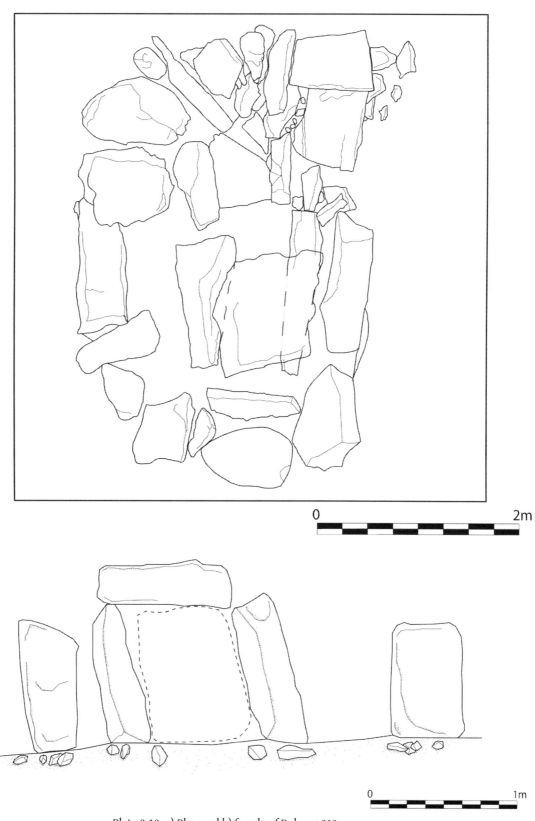

Plate 3.19: a) Plan and b) façade of Dolmen 318.

JEBEL AL-MUTAWWAQ
Area B (2013)
Do. 317

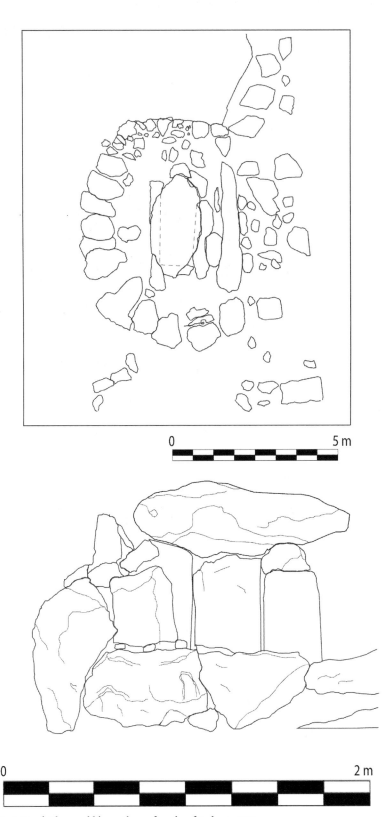

Plate 3.20: a) Plan and b) northern façade of Dolmen 317.

JEBEL AL-MUTAWWAQ
Area B (2013)
Do. 321

Plate 3.21: a) Plan and b) northern façade of Dolmen 321.

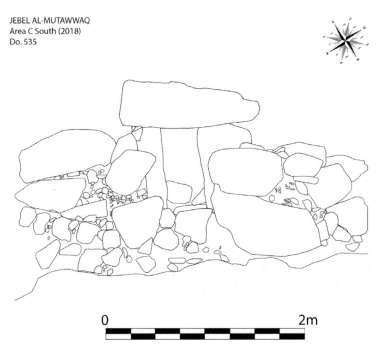

Plate 3.22: Northern façade of Dolmen 535.

3. THE SITE OF JEBEL AL-MUTAWWAQ: ARCHITECTURE, SETTLEMENT PLANNING, AND SPACE ORGANIZATION

JEBEL AL-MUTAWWAQ
Area C South (2018)
Do. 535
Phase I

Plate 3.23: Plan of Dolmen 535 phase I.

Jebel al-Mutawwaq
Area C South
Phase II

Plate 3.24: Plan of Dolmen 535 phase II.

JEBEL AL-MUTAWWAQ
Area C South (2018)
Section Do. 535 and C. 1012

■ Pottery

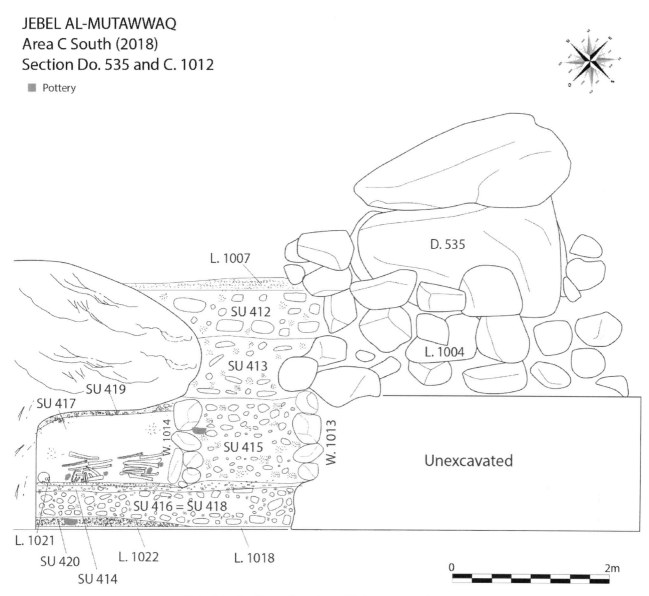

Plate 3.25: North–south section of Dolmen 535 and Cave C. 1012.

JEBEL AL-MUTAWWAQ
Area C South (2018)
C. 1012

s: skull

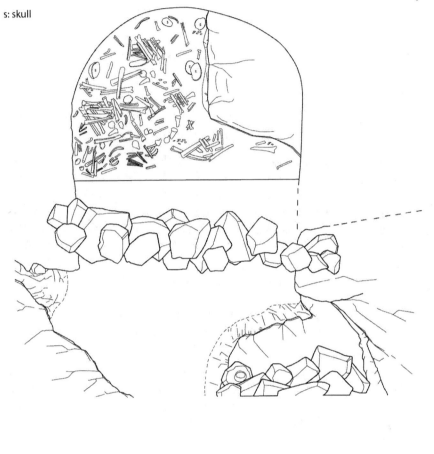

Plate 3.26: Plan of Cave C. 1012.

4. The Pottery: Function and Typologies

Eloisa Casadei & Joaquim Del Rio

General Description and Provenance of the Pottery Repertoire

The present study focuses on the pottery from the new Spanish-Italian joint project, including assemblages from Areas A, B, C, and the survey. Moreover, a re-examination of the pottery from the old excavations is still in progress. Sherds collected in the court, the cella (House 76), and the adjacent rooms (Rooms 1–5 of the Temple of the Serpents and Buildings 75 and 77) have been catalogued.[1] Thanks to the long-lasting activity on the site, different kinds of contexts have been excavated, domestic (Area A and survey), public/production-related (Area CW and CC), funerary (dolmens from Areas B and C), and cultic (temple area).[2] The Graph 4.1 shows that the majority of the diagnostic sherds come from the temple area, especially from the main room of House 76 (302), followed by the public/production contexts in Area CW+CC (218) and funerary contexts (104). The Great Circle could have served different purposes, and it has been isolated on the right in Graph 4.1 (see Chapter 3).

During the excavations of the Spanish-Italian expedition, all the sherds were collected, photographed, and described. A database including all the diagnostic sherds, drawings, and detailed pictures has been compiled during the field campaigns, and the information is detailed in the catalogue. Moreover, a group of twenty-seven pottery samples was selected in 2015 for archaeometric analysis.

The study of pottery is based mainly on macroscopic observation of the fabric, manufacturing process, and morpho-functional seriation of the diagnostic sherds. The last allowed the organization of the whole assemblage into a typology based on shapes, families, types, and decorations, with a chronological, economic, and social perspective. The study of the manufacturing processes sheds new light on the organization of the pottery production at the site. The chemical analysis on fabrics allows the identification of petrographic groups matched with soil samples taken from the site and nearby.

The combination of morpho-functional, stylistic, and technological aspects identified two main groups, Production Group 1 (PG1) and Production Group 2 (PG2). The first one is locally made and encompasses the great majority of shapes (PG1). The second one is less attested and related only to the funerary contexts of Area C (PG2). The two groups were considered together in the morpho-functional and technological analyses and they are described separately in the concluding section (see below).

[EC]

---

1 Fernández-Tresguerres Velasco 2005a: 24; Polcaro et al. 2014, 4–7. At present, the repertoire from House 77 is still under study.

2 A separate consideration is needed about the Great Circle. Its structural peculiarity impacts an immediate interpretation of the building as cultic or productive place (Chapter 3).

Eloisa Casadei (eloisacasadei@gmail.com), PhD in Near Eastern Archaeology at Sapienza University, was collaborator of the Spanish-Italian Archaeological Expedition to Jebel al-Mutawwaq (Italy).

Joaquim Del Rio (quimrio1@gmail.com) was a collaborator of the Spanish-Italian Archaeological Expedition to Jebel al-Mutawwaq (Spain).

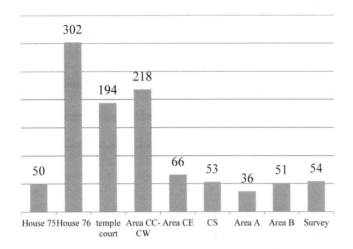
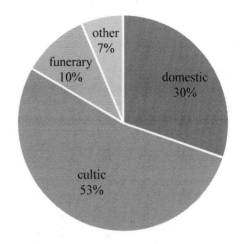

Graph 4.1: Quantity of diagnostic sherds. Total number of diagnostic sherds per area (left); percentage of diagnostic sherds per contexts (right): public/production = Area CW, CC; domestic = A, survey area; cultic = House 75, House 76, temple court (including Rooms 1 to 5); funerary = Area B, Area CC Dolmen 534, Area CS Dolmen 535; other = the Great Circle in Area CE.

Shapes and Typology

A total of 1024 diagnostic sherds are considered in the present study, 141 from the Western Sector (Areas A, B, and survey), 337 from Area C, and 546 from the temple area (Graph 4.1). All the diagnostic sherds have been seriated according to the morphological variation of attributes that characterize the profile, to create a sound typology of the Mutawwaq repertoire.[3] The idea of type intends a practical realization of an ideal model that materializes a shared conceptual system developed in a social context of interaction and, for that, it undergoes constant change through time and space.[4] From this insight, the type interprets at the same time functional and cultural needs, expressed — on the one hand — by the employment of the different shapes in everyday life activities and — on the other hand — by the free choice of morphological details characterizing the different parts of the vessels.

Nevertheless, two factors have to be pointed out that affected the creation of the present morphological typology, the state of preservation of the pottery sherds and the primarily domestic, non-specialized level of production. The bad state of preservation of the sherds, and the absence of large, well-stratified repertoires coming from closed and culturally related sites, often impacts the proper attribution of the sherd to a complete known shape. The handmade production on a domestic scale provoked a non-standardized high variability in profiles. This impacts the creation of a straight morphological seriation, and each type is represented by several slightly morphological varieties.

The typology is based on three subsequent subdivisions: shapes, genres, and types.[5] The first stage of the classification is based on shapes, namely the intuitive function of the complete vessel: cups, bowls, dishes, jugs/bottles, short and high-necked jars, and holemouth jars.[6] As was already pointed out, because almost all the repertoire is composed of sherds, the definition of shapes is sometimes difficult, and depends on parallels from other sites. In some cases, the range of size and diameter is determinant in distinguishing dimensional varieties. Of course, because the food tradition of preparing and consuming food during the EB I period is not yet understood, our intuitive functional distinction must be taken with caution, and the definitions proposed for the description of different shapes is more related to the modern parameters.[7] In fact, as suggested by many scholars, the direct link between shape and function has more to do with the concrete possibility that the profile of a vessel offers, and geometric parameters are associated with different practices in daily

---

3 Rice (2015, 223–24) highlights well the role of the morphological attributes in the construction of a pottery typology, and how to select them according to the historical-archaeological questions.

4 Read 2007, 86; Vacca 2014, 56.

5 This classification is taken from the well-established method elaborated by Peroni in prehistoric archaeology (see Peroni 1998). For its application in the EBA Levanitne tradition see D'Andrea 2014, 169.

6 See Rice 2015.

7 For a discussion about commensality during the EBA see Joffe 2018.

4. THE POTTERY: FUNCTION AND TYPOLOGIES

Table 4.1: Procedure of the typological classification adopted in the present analysis.

SHAPE			Related exclusively to intuitive function	
	FAMILY		Profile of the body	Indicates the manner of manufacture and style
		TYPE	Profile of the rim	Indicates preference in the appearance of the vessel
		SUBTYPE	Profile of the lip	

activities.[8] The Mutawwaq's assemblage can be well subdivided into open, closed-necked, and holemouth shapes. Among the open shapes, cups are distinguished by bowls according to the general ratio between deepness and diameter. Closed-necked shapes represent the most variable group in size and general morphology, ranging from high and clearly distinguished necks to short and sinuous or slightly incurved and not distinguished from the shoulder. The holemouth shapes are easily recognizable as vessels with the opening simply at the highest point of the shoulder, and they are very distinctive shapes of the Chalcolithic and Early Bronze Age southern Levant.

The morphological typology of the different shapes is based on the profiles, subdivided into genres, types, and subtypes (Table 4.1). This distinction identifies specific preferences both in production and in the final products. Because of the state of preservation of the sherds, the subdivision is based almost exclusively on the neck, rim, and lip variations. The genre is determined by the profile of the body (for the open shapes), the neck, and the shoulder (for the closed shapes), and it can indicate the different ways of production of a specific shape. The rim profile determines the type, and the type can be divided into subtypes according to the different lips. In most cases, the same type or subtype is attested in two dimensional categories, small and large. This classification method intends types in a strictly morphological sense, according to slight variation. A clear separation of the different morphological variations can be helpful both in a chronological and geographical sense and in the socio-cultural determination of the variability in pottery production. In this way, types and subtypes indicate specific preferences in the style or appearance of the vessel. As described in the following section, all the vessels from the site are handmade, so the internal variability of families, types, and subtypes is relatively consistent.

In the catalogue, the nomenclature adopted is the following:

- Shape → first letter of the noun of the shape, in capitals (e.g. C for cups, JB for jugs/bottles, HJ for holemouth jars, etc.)
- Family → capital letter in alphabetical order, divided per shape (e.g. the shape cup, C, has three families: C.A, C.B, and C.C)
- Type → Arabic numeral, in ascending order, divided by shapes (the family C.A has two types, C.A.1 and C.A.2, while the family C.C has three types: C.C.1, C.C.2, and C.C.3)
- Subtypes → lower case letter, in the same manner as family and type
- Dimensional subtypes → when two different sizes are attested for the same type, dimensions determine the subtype or variant, and in this case, this is indicated by the symbols -s (small) and -L (large).

Cups

The cups (C) are represented by a small open shape, with the rim diameter of less than 15 cm and a general deepness similar to the rim diameter. They are supposed to be used for drinking, even if some were also used as lamps, as shown by traces of burning on the rim. They are divided into three genres according to the profile of the body: hemispherical, sinuous, and conical.

C.A — Hemispherical cups represent a homogeneous group, with rim diameters varying from 8 to 12 cm. They are divided between two types, one with vertical rim (C.A.1) and pointed lip, internally bevelled in some cases, and the other with incurved rim (C.A.2) and sharp lip. In one case (Pl. 4.1:10), the vertical rim is slightly profiled outside and has plain round lips. Only one sherd in the C.A genre is painted outside (Pl. 4.1:7).

Parallels — The hemispherical cup is a common genre, well attested in the southern Levant during the

---
8 Cocchi-Genick 2012.

Early Bronze Age. Type C.A.1 was found at Jericho, in Sultan IIIa1–2, according to Nigro's periodization, at 'Ai, in tombs G ('Ai Pl. VI) and C ('Ai Pl. XIII), at Arad level IV (Arad Pl. 7:3), and in the funerary context of Dolmen 7 at Tell el-Umairy. Types C.A.2 was found in contemporary contexts at Jericho, Sultan IIIa-2,[9] Arad level IV (Arad Pl. 7:4, 7, 19), 'Ai, tombs G and C. This family is also attested in later EB IB contexts such as Tell Abu Kharaz, but here most of them are red burnished and wheel made.[10]

C.B — The sinuous profiled cups are characterized by a higher variety, probably because of the manufacturing process. In fact, while C.A family is modelled in mould, C.B sherds seem to be totally handmade. Two types are attested, the out-flared (C.B.1) and incurved (C.B.2) profile. Among the first type, cups can have a thick (C.B.1a, Pl. 4.1:15–20) or thin (C.B.1b, Pl. 4.1:21–23) section. The lip is always pointed, except in one case (Pl. 4.1:20) where a round, slightly thickened rim is attested. Only three exemplars represent type C.B.2. Only one of this family (Pl. 4.1:22) is decorated with a knob on the upper external wall.

Parallels — The sinuous profiled cups are attested in smaller quantities than the previous group, but they are nevertheless well documented in the same contexts. Notably, the four C.B.2 type exemplars found perfect parallels among the grave goods of Dolmen 7 at Tell el-Umairy.[11]

C.C — The conical cups are deeper than the other two families, with incurved or straight bodies. Four types are attested according to the rim orientation. The type with incurved walls, vertical rim, and rounded thinned lip (C.C.1) is attested both in small and large subtypes, the first having the rim diameter of 7 cm large (C.C.1-s), while the second ranges from 12 to 15 cm (C.C.1-L). Type C.C.2 has again the incurved wall, but inturned, and plain or pointed lip, again attested in small (rim diam. 9–10 cm) and large (rim diam. 14–15 cm) subtypes. One of the most prominent examples presents an inner bevelled lip (Pl. 4.2:17). Types C.C.3 and C.C.4 have straight walls. C.C.3 is a small, homogeneous group with a bent rim. C.C.4 is a simple small conical cup until now attested by a single sherd (Pl. 4.2:18).

---

9 See Kenyon square E III–IV, phases Q-M; trench II levels XIII–XIV.

10 The vessels from Abu Kharaz (Fischer 2008, fig. 104:9–10) have the same base as Pl. 4.1:9, and also the same fabric, at least as described macroscopically.

11 Dubis & Dabrowski 2002, fig. 8.3:2.

Parallels — Again, Dolmen 7 at Tell el-Umairy returned a parallel with Pl. 4.2:1, type C.C.1. Other parallels for this type (mainly with Pl. 4.2:3) come from Jericho.[12] The larger variant of C.C.2 could possibly be related to the large grain wash bowl from Abu Kharaz, phase IB.[13] Type C.C.3 is most common, and it finds parallels with Jericho Sultan IIIa2, Arad phase IV (Arad Pl. 7:21), and Tell esh-Shuna level 10.

Bowls

The bowls (B) are intended as open shapes with a rim diameter larger than the general height and usually larger than 15 cm. Because of the homogeneity in the body profile, two families are recognized according to the thickness of the wall.

B.A — Thin, incurving walled bowls are the most frequent family of bowls and are attested in various dimensions and morphological characters. B.A.1 is a type with incurving walls, with a slight depression on the outer side of the rim, probably resulting from the manufacturing process. It is attested in two dimensional variants, the small one with 12 cm diameter and the large one with the diameter ranging from 16 to 20 cm. One (Pl. 4.3:1) presents two bands of red paint on the outer surface, while another (Pl. 4.3:2) has a small knob attached to the rim. Pl. 4.3:4 is a variant of this type, with a flat bent rim and flat lip. Type B.A.2 has a vertical rim, with the inner part of the rim slightly thickened, probably again a fact deriving from the manufacturing process. The rim diameter ranges between 12 and 17 cm. One sherd (Pl. 4.3:5) has a small triangular knob. Types B.A.3 and B.A.4 are represented respectively by one single sherd. B.A.3 has a vertical rim starting from a sub-carination at the middle point of its high and internal bevelled lip. B.A.4 has a vertical termination starting from a sub-carination in the lower part of the body. The lip is bevelled externally.

Type B.A.5 has a body similar to B.A.4 but a pointed lip. Type B.A.6 is represented by open shallow bowls, known in two variants: pointed lip (B.A.6-a) and round lip (B.A.6-b). Variant -a is attested in two dimensions, small (rim diam. 4–7 cm) and large (rim diam. 12 cm). One small bowl (Pl. 4.3:12) has a painted dot inside. A subtype is represented by bowls with thickened walls, round lips, and a red burnished surface, all from Area C South. A variant (Pl. 4.3:17) has thin walls and an inner thickened (almost

---

12 Kenyon & Holland 1982, fig. 34:10, type C.II — square E levs III-IV, DD-R.

13 Fischer 2008, fig. 258:25.

bead-shaped) rim. Another variant has an expanded, flat lip (Pl. 4.3:18). Finally, B.A.7 is a large deep bowl with an oblique plain rim, attested for only one sherd.

Parallels — This family is represented by a high variety of types that can be associated with manufacturing techniques and functional and stylistic criteria. B.A.1 has parallels at Arad, level IV (Pl. 7:6, 20), the larger subtype is also attested in Tomb G at 'Ai, and the variant Pl. 4.3:4 was also found at Jericho.[14] B.A.2 is a widespread type, with parallels from Arad level IV (Arad Pl. 7:5), 'Ai Tomb G, and Jericho Sultan IIIa2. Another sherd with thick wall like Pl. 4.3:6 was found at Jericho, Kenyon's excavation (trench III level XV — from the apse). Both B.A.3 and B.A.4 find parallels at Jawa,[15] 'Ai,[16] and Jericho.[17] B.A.5 is again very common, with parallels at Jericho Sultan IIIa1 and Tell esh-Shuna 2a. The type B.A.6 is well represented in the southern Levant during the EB period, both in plain, painted, and red burnished variants. Pl. 4.3:11 matches perfectly with sherds from Kenyon's excavation at Jericho (square E III–IV, DD-R and trench II, levs XIII–XIV) and Shuna.[18] Red burnished B.A.6 vessels are particularly well attested starting from the EB IB period, e.g. Abu Kharaz phase II–III,[19] Jericho (CIT), Bet Shean (CIT). From the same site is a parallel with B.A.6 variant Pl. 3:18.[20]

B.B — Small (B.B.1, B.B.2) and large (B.B.3) bowls with a thickened wall. The only difference between B.B.1 and B.B.2 is the swelling orientation of the rim. It is possible that this genre performed some specific function, given the unusual thickness of the walls.

Parallels — This genre is rare in the published assemblage. B.B.2 finds a parallel at Jericho,[21] while the larger B.B.3 is also attested at Umm Hammad,[22] and Shuna.[23]

B.C — Large conical bowls or basins with thick straight walls. Just like family B.B, B.C is also rare, and they both could be related to some specific function, as possibly testified by the hole in Pl. 4.4:6. B.C.1, attested in the small (diam. 12 cm) and large (diam. 17 cm) versions, has an inner thickened rim. B.C.2 is a large vessel with a rim diameter of 22 cm and an outer thickened rim.

Parallels — This genre is rare. The large B.C.1 sherd has a parallel at Shuna (12b), while B.C.2 was found at Shuna (10) and Jericho, Sultan IIIa1–2.

Dishes

Only one half-complete sherd pertained to the carinated dish (D), a shape that spread in the southern Levant from late EB IB until the EB IIIB (see Joffe 2018). The rim's orientation, the burnishing pattern, and the rim diameter of around 28 cm indicate a type similar to the earlier examples dated to the late EB IB (Pl. 4.4).

Parallels — In the following only the closest parallels to the D.A.1 from Mutawwaq are cited, in order to better point out the exact chronological span of the sherd. From Tell Abu al-Kharaz, the straight oblique rim is attested from phases IA to IIIA.[24] The same characteristics are attested at Arad,[25] Umm Hammad,[26] Jericho,[27] Beth Shean,[28] and Tell el-Far'ah N.[29]

Jugs and Bottles

These two shapes (JB) and the small jars are considered part of the table repertoire because of their hypothesized function in the consuming process, for keeping and serving liquids. Nevertheless, because of the highly fragmented state of the sherds, there is a robust morphological relationship between jugs, bottles, and jars. The difference between the three shapes depends on the dimensions. Even if such a category is not always taken as a typological parameter, the present study considers the ratio between the rim diameter and the neck height an important role in classification. The jugs/bottles are represented by closed necked shapes with a rim diameter around 10 cm or less, with the small mouth of the vessel helpful in maintaining the right temperature and pouring liquids. The wall thickness does not exceed

---

14 Kenyon square E III level IV, DD-R.
15 Betts & Helms 1991, fig. 146:495–96; fig. 146:489.
16 Callaway 1964, pl. V:768; pl. III:10; pl. V:857a.
17 Kenyon & Holland 1982, fig. 34:29, type F.I; fig. 54:8, type F.II; fig. 54:11–16, type F.II.b.
18 Gustavson-Gaube 1985, perhaps fig. 30:1.
19 Fischer 2008, fig. 259:6, 12–14; 260:1–2.
20 Fischer 2008, fig. 258:19–20.
21 Kenyon & Holland 1983, fig. 17:20.
22 Betts 1992, fig. 233:6.
23 Gustavson-Gaube 1985, fig. 9:5, 14c, 20.

24 Fischer 2008, fig. 261:2, 6; fig. 262:3; fig. 263:4; fig. 256:3.
25 Amiran et al. 1978, pl. 13:38.
26 Betts 1992, fig. 228:8–13.
27 Kenyon & Holland 1982, fig. 49: 27, type A.II.c.
28 Rotem 2012, pl. 2:18; pl. 16:2–7; pl. 19:8–9.
29 de Vaux 1955, fig. 13:15, 17, 20.

0.7 cm to maintain a general low weight. There are three genres recognized according to the neck profiles, while the variation of the rims determines the types.

JB.A — Jugs/bottles with out-flared necks are more numerous and present high variability in the rim profiles. The first type, JB.A.1, is characterized by a flaring rim almost horizontal, with a typical groove on the lip. The shape of the lip determines the three subtypes, which can be round (Pl. 4.5:1–2), band (Pl. 4.5:3–5), and thickened shaped (Pl. 4.5:6–10). A bent rim characterizes type JB.A.2, and it is attested in three different dimensions, miniature (Pl. 4.5:11), small (Pl. 4.5:13, 15), and medium (Pl. 4.5:12, 14, 16). Almost all the rims are bevelled, except one (Pl. 4.5:15) that is round and thin. The third type, JB.A.3, is represented by simple, slightly flaring rims and different lip profiles, plain (Pl. 4.5:17–18, 22), bent (Pl. 4.5:19, 21), and thinned (Pl. 4.5:20–23). Only one sherd (Pl. 4.5:23) is bigger than the others, with a diameter of 15 cm. One sherd (Pl. 4.5:18) has a layer of white slip on the outer surface.

Parallels — Because of the bad state of preservation of the sherds, the parallels mentioned are related exclusively to the rim and neck profiles. At the same time, it is impossible to recognize the original shape of the bodies. Type JB.A.1 is exclusive to the middle Zarqa region, being found only in the Hanbury-Tenison survey.[30] Some parallels are known for JB.A.2, from Arad level IV,[31] Abu Kharaz,[32] Umm Hammad,[33] 'Ai,[34] Jericho.[35] It is also attested at Jawa[36] and as far south as Bab edh-Dhra.[37] The small variant of this type, Pl. 4.5:11, has a parallel from Shuna.[38] Type JB.A.3 is more common, and parallels were found at Shuna[39] and 'Ai Tomb G.[40] Pl. 4.5:18 has a parallel from level IV at Arad,[41] Abu Kharaz,[42] and many from Jericho, Sultan IIIa2.

JB.B — The second group, less numerous, is characterized by a straight oblique neck. JB.B.1 has an outside-oriented straight neck with an outer bevelled lip, and it is attested in sizes small (diam. 4 cm) and medium (diam. 8 cm). JB.B.2 has a vertical neck and broad out-flared rim, with the same variation in rim diameter as JB.B.1 (small and medium variants). One complete vessel of this type was found in the temple area, inside Room 1 (Polcaro et al. 2014, fig. 5). JB.B.3 is represented by only one miniature vessel, with a vertical wall and outer bevelled lip and decorated with a short rope-like application on the neck. Finally, JB.B.4 is represented by one single sherd from Area C South and shows a different manufacturing technique (made in PG2, see below).

Parallels — This family is less represented. Some parallels have been found from Abu Kharaz, phase I[43] and II,[44] and from Bab edh-Drah.[45]

JB.C — The third genre of jugs/bottles is represented by incurved necks. Type JB.C.1 has a long incurved neck and out-flared rim. Among the JB.C.1, one (Pl. 4.6:11) is larger than the others (rim diam. 13 cm), has a rather inturned neck, and is decorated with paint. Type JB.C.2 has a shorter neck, with apparently higher and larger shoulders, and the lip is shortly expanded on the outside. Type JB.C.3 is represented by a single sherd with a different manufacturing technique (made in PG2, see below).

Parallels — One globular-shaped bottle is attested at Abu Kharaz in phase II.[46] Type JB.C.1 was found during the survey in the Jerash region,[47] and in the funerary context from Tell el-Far'ah N.[48] Type JB.C.2 was found at Umm Hammad,[49] Jericho,[50] and Tell el-Far'ah N.[51]

Jars

In the macro-category of the jars, four different groups have been intended as different shapes according to the different sizes and types of necks: the necked jars, jars

---

30 Hanbury-Tenison 1986, fig. 9:8.
31 Amiran et al. 1978, pl. 12:5 — here pl. 5:12.
32 Fischer 2008, fig. 268:3, 6; fig. 269:2, 15.
33 Betts 1992, fig. 205:14.
34 Callaway 1964, pl. XIX: 44.
35 Kenyon & Holland 1982, fig. 58:28, type D.I.a; fig. 59:8–10, type E.II.
36 Betts & Helms 1991, fig. 144:464.
37 Rast & Schaub 2003, fig. 7.2:8.
38 Gustav-Gaube 1986, fig. 16:64, with red slip.
39 Gustav-Gaube 1986, pl. 16:65.
40 Callaway 1964, pl. IX:954–13.B.42.2.
41 Amiran et al. 1978, pl. 10:3.
42 Fischer 2008, figs 1, 4–5; fig. 269:7–11; fig. 270:2.

43 Fischer 2008, fig. 269:12.
44 Fischer 2008, fig. 270:2.
45 Schaub & Rast 1989, type 0274.
46 Fischer 2008, fig. 270:6.
47 Hanbury-Tenison 1986, fig. 6:12.
48 de Vaux 1955, fig. 13:19.
49 Betts 1992, fig. 205:2.
50 Kenyon & Holland 1982, fig. 45: 4, type D.2.
51 de Vaux 1955, fig. 1:20; fig. 14:7, 23.

4. THE POTTERY: FUNCTION AND TYPOLOGIES

with a short neck, and the holemouth jars. They have been treated separately because the marked difference in the neck shape strongly correlates with the vessels' intuitive function.

Necked Jars

This shape (NJ) is strongly correlated with the jug/bottle shapes already analysed, so it is possible to hypothesize a correlation with liquids (Pls 4.7–4.9). As already mentioned, the distinction between jugs/bottles and necked jars is determined mainly (and in some instances only) by the rim diameter and the thickness of the walls, that in the case of jars can indicate a bigger capacity. In some cases, small variants (but bigger than the jug/bottle shape) are integrated with the NJ shape because of the morphological similarity with larger examples. This criterion is fundamental in a functional sphere, considering the ability to transport and move the full vessels and the ease of using it during mealtimes (as a serving vessel).

This shape is the most numerous in Mutawwaq's repertoire, and three genres can be recognized according to the neck profile. Morphological details of the rim determine the types; for each type, dimensional criteria determine subtypes. This choice highlights the manufacturing process and finishing of the vessel more than its intrinsic function. The bad state of preservation impacts a more functional reconstruction of the sherds.

NJ.A — This genre comprises jars with straight, cylindrical necks and everted rims. The rim diameters vary from 8 to 18 cm, but no dimensional categories can be easily recognized. The slight variation of the rim and lip determines four different types. NJ.A.1 has a bent flaring rim with a plain lip. NJ.A.2 has a bent rim again, but the sherds have thicker walls than NJ.A.1, which is 1 cm or more. One sherd (Pl. 4.7:11) shows painted decoration inside, on the rim, and outside the neck. Type NJ.A.3 has a flaring rim and thickened lip, with thin walls at the neck (c. 0.5–0.7 cm). Type NJ.A.4 has an everted rim bevelled on the inner side and flat lip.

Parallels — The necked jars are a common feature in the EB I repertoire at Bab edh-Dhrah and other contemporary sites in the southern Levant. NJ.A.1 was found at Jericho, in Kenyon's excavations (square E III–IV, Q–M), at Arad, level IV (Arad Pl. 12:1), at Shuna (58), and in Dolmen 7 at Umayri. NJ.A.2 has parallels at Shuna (60), Arad, level IV (Arad Pl. 10:13), and maybe V (Pl. 6:11, Arad Pl. 4:3). Jars with cylindrical neck and large high shoulder are attested at Abu Kharaz.[52]

NJ.B — The second genre of the necked jars is represented by sherds with a slightly incurved neck. The neck walls are thinner than NJ.A, never exceeding 0.8 cm. The diameter at the rim follows the same variation, but some dimensional distinctions can be recognized between the types. NJ.B.1 has an out-flared thinned rim, almost pointed, and rim diam. around 8 cm, being the smaller NJ type. A variant (Pl. 4.8:4) has an out-flared rim, almost horizontal, with a round lip. Type NJ.B.2 is quite numerous, and is characterized by a bent flared termination of the neck and everted slightly thickened triangular-shaped rim. Rim diameter varies consistently from 10 to 20 cm, as well as the ratio between wall thickness and neck diameter (see, e.g. Pl. 4.8:5 and 11). This fact could suggest a wide range of functions. Type NJ.B.3 has a bent flaring rectangular-shaped rim and externally bevelled lip. All the sherds have a wall thickness of more than 1 cm. A variant of this type (Pl. 4.8:13) has a bead-shaped rim and a less evident break between rim and neck.

Parallels — Storage jars of NJ.B.1 type are attested at Abu Kharaz,[53] Umm Hammad,[54] Jericho,[55] Tell el-Far'ah N.[56] NJ.B.2 and NJ.B.3 are attested at Jawa,[57] and they have been found during the Jerash survey.[58]

NJ.C — This family is composed of necked jars with a straight but flared neck, and it is quite rare compared to the two previous families NJ.A and NJ.B. Dimensions are more homogenous, rim diameter between 13 and 20 cm, and wall thickness around 1 cm. The rims are shaped in three different ways, bead-shaped (NJ.C.1), squared (NJ.C.2), slightly thickened (NJ.C.3), and everted and round (NJ.C.4).

Parallels — Type NJ.C.1 is similar to exemplars from 'Ai.[59] Also NJ.C.2 has a parallel from the same site.[60] Both

---

52 Fischer 2008, fig. 276:1–7; fig. 278:2, 4–5; fig. 279:7, 10.
53 Fischer 2008, fig. 278:1; fig. 279:10.
54 Betts 1992, fig. 210:9; fig. 205:10–13.
55 Kenyon & Holland 1982, fig. 59:1, type E.I.a.
56 de Vaux 1955, fig. 13:3, 14; fig. 14:21.
57 Betts & Helms 1991, fig. 126:200–03; 1991, fig. 127:211.
58 Hanbury-Tenison 1986, fig. 6:50; fig. 7:44.
59 Callaway 1964, pl. XV:380; pl. XVIII:103, 35; pl. XIX:97, 1192.
60 Callaway 1964, pl. XII:741.

NJ.C.2 and NJ.C.3 were found during the Jerash survey.[61] Storage jars related to type NJ.C.4 have parallels from Shuna (60 and 63), Abu Kharaz.[62]

NJ.D — This genre is a heterogenous group comprised of strongly flaring necked jars, almost horizontally oriented. Each of the four exemplars has a different rim, thickened, thinner, squared, expanded, and triangular shaped.

Parallels — Similar flaring necked jars are attested in the Jerash region,[63] at Jericho,[64] and at Tell el-Far'ah N.[65]

Wide-Mouthed Necked Jars

The wide-mouthed necked jars (WNJ) represent one of the largest categories of vessels attested in Mutawwaq's repertoire, with a diameter ranging from 25 to 40 cm. Nevertheless, the wall thickness is similar to those of the other necked jars. The rims are all different from each other, indicating a non-specialized production. Two genres can be distinguished according to the neck profile, cylindrical and flaring.

WNJ.A — The sherds of the first genre are large storage jars with cylindrical necks. As happened in other large jars, no clear typology of the rim shape is visible, creating a high variety of the morphological type: all of them have everted rim, two (Pl. 4.10:1–2) with a shallow groove on the lip, and one has a thinned lip (Pl. 4.10:3), and one has a plain round lip (Pl. 4.10:4).

WNJ.B — Large jars with an incurving neck. Two types are distinguishable for this genre. The first, WNJ.B.1, is represented by one single sherd with an expanded rim. The second, WNJ.B.2, is represented by a flaring rim and round lip. A half complete vessel of this type has a down-turned stripe handle, the type most frequent at Mutawwaq, and a short rope-like applique with a circular thumb impression, again quite common at the site and in other contemporary sites of the Transjordanian area (see below).

Parallels — Both WNJ.A and WNJ.B have a limited regional diffusion, being attested only at Jawa,[66] Abu Tawwab,[67] and Umm Hammad.[68] Type WNJ.B.2 is also attested at Jericho.[69]

Ovoid Jars

This shape (OJ) is represented by a few vessels with short everted neck and a prominent shoulder. This shape could have originally been a globular body from some parallels with complete vessels found in other contemporary sites.

OJ.A — Two sherds of small jars are characterized by a short, everted neck, high, prominent shoulder, and small size, being the rim diameter around 9 cm and the maximum diameter at shoulder only c. 16 cm. For these peculiarities, they have been separated into a specific genre. Two types are attested, bead-shaped everted rim (OJ.A.1) and vertical rim, slightly thickened on the outside, with pointed lip (OJ.A.2).

OJ.B — One sherd (OJ.B.1) is related to a small vessel with a slightly everted neck and thickened rim. It can probably be related to the whole preserved jar from Room 2 of the Temple of the Serpents, with a high prominent shoulder and small base (Fernández-Tresguerres Velasco 2005a, fig. 17).

OJ.C — This genre is represented by only one sherd, with no clear break between rim and neck. It terminates with a vertical, plain rim and round lip.

Parallels — Genre OJ.A is particularly well attested in the southern Levant, finding parallels at Arad,[70] Umm Hammad,[71] 'Ai,[72] in the Jerash region,[73] Umayri Dolmen 7,[74] Jericho,[75] and Tell el-Far'ah N.[76] Type OJ.C is known from Arad[77] and Tell el-Far'ah N.[78]

---

61 Hanbury-Tenison 1986, fig. 5:41; fig. 7:17.
62 Fischer 2008, fig. 276:1, 4, 7; fig. 278:6–7; fig. 279:13.
63 Hanbury-Tenison 1986, fig. 6:8.
64 Kenyon & Holland 1983, fig. 121:6, 13–14; Kenyon & Holland 1982, fig. 59:11–12, type E.II.
65 De Vaux 1955, fig. 4:10.
66 Betts & Helms 1991, fig. 126:193, 195; fig. 126:194; fig. 123:197; fig. 127:209; fig. 124: 180–81; fig. 125:182–87; fig. 126:200–03.
67 Douglas & Kafafi 2000, fig. 6.4:1.
68 Betts 1992, fig. 196:4, 8; fig. 185:1; fig. 178:4–6.
69 Kenyon & Holland 1983, fig. 19:1; fig. 113:22, 26.
70 Amiran et al. 1978, pl. 9:7.
71 Betts 1992, fig. 193:16.
72 Callaway 1964, pl. III:16.
73 Hanbury-Tenison 1986, fig. 5:44.
74 Dubis & Dabrowski 2002, fig. 8.4:2.
75 Kenyon & Holland 1982, fig. 37:4, type A.I.d.
76 de Vaux 1955, fig. 13:5.
77 Amiran et al. 1978, pl. 12:13.
78 de Vaux 1955, fig. 11:22; fig. 1:18.

Jars with Low Shoulder

A large group of jars of different sizes is characterized by a marked neck, that can run everted or straight, and low shoulder (LSJ). Thanks to parallels from other sites, it is known that the body these vessels is biconical. Two genres can be distinguished according to the neck, that can be incurved or vertical.

LSJ.A — This genre is characterized by a short, incurved neck and low shoulder, while the rims are represented by a considerable variety of types. The first type (LSJ.A.1, Pl. 4.11:5) is characterized by one single complete vessel, small in size, with short straight oblique neck and plain rim, and a rather globular body attached to it with a visible over-thickness at the joint. It is also finished with a thin layer of red burnished slip (PG2). The second type (LSJ.A.2) is attested by two sherds with flaring rim and pointed lip, one small (rim diam. 12 cm) and the other large (rim diam. 18 cm). Type LSJ.A.3 has flaring rim similar to the previous, but it has thickened walls and round lip. LSJ.A.2 and LSJ.A.3 could be also considered two varieties of the same type.

Parallels — LSJ.A is quite common in contemporaneous contexts. Parallels were found at Umm Hammad,[79] Shuna,[80] Abu Tawwab,[81] and Tel el-Far'ah N.[82]

LSJ.B — this group is rather heterogenous, and it is comprised of small jars with vertical rim and thick walls. The smallest type is represented by one single sherd with straight oblique neck hard bevelled on the inner side (LSJ.B.2, Pl. 4.11:10). It also has a marked junction between neck and shoulder. Such a trace is quite rare in the Mutawwaq repertoire (PG2). The second type (LSJ.B.3) is represented by two sherds of small jars with round expanded lip (almost bead-like). They are very badly preserved and their entire shape is only hypothetical.

LSJ.C — This genre has a short, everted rim that vary in the general shape, being round (LSJ.C.1, Pl. 4.11:14–15), expanded (LSJ.C.2, Pl. 4.11:16), and bead-shaped (LSJ.C.3, Pl. 4.12:1–3). This last type is bigger than the others. One sherd of the last types (Pl. 4.12:3) has a rope decoration with circular impressions.

Parallels — Up to now, this genre is rare, and parallels were found only at Shuna[83] and Umm Hammad.[84] The larger type LSJ.C.3 is also attested at Jerash[85] and Jericho.[86]

LSJ.D — The third group of short-necked jars is characterized by a total absence of separation between neck and rim, presenting a vertical termination. On the other hand, when preserved, the shoulder is directly joined to the rim and it is easily recognizable by a marked change in orientation. This character separates the LSJ.B family from the H.A family, where it is difficult to recognize changes between rim, neck, and shoulder. Rims can be simple round (LSJ.D.1), squared with horizontal flat lip (LSJ.D.2), or slightly thickened on the inner side (LSJ.D.3). Among the LSJ.D.1, a half complete vessel has a triangular knob on the upper part of the body. The third type, LSJ.D.3, is known from three sherds, one of which has red painted decoration on the outer surface of the neck (Pl. 4.13:6) and another sherd with paint decoration and a serpent-like vertical applique starting from the mouth of the vessel (Pl. 4.13:7).

Parallels — The distribution of this genre is still restricted. Type LSJ.D.1 is attested only at Umm Hammad,[87] Jericho,[88] and in the Jerash region.[89] Type LSJ.D.2 is only known from one sherd from the Jerash survey.[90] Type LSJ.D.3 is restricted to the northern part of the Jordan Valley, at Umm Hammad,[91] and Shuna.[92]

Holemouth Jars

This shape (H) is a hallmark of the Early Bronze period in the southern Levant, even if at present it is not possible to determine a precise chronological or geographical definition of the high variability of the lip nor the different orientations of the rim. At Mutawwaq, two groups of holemouth have been recognized, according to the rim orientation.

---

79 Betts 1992, fig. 201:4.
80 Gustavson-Gaube 1985, type 51d.
81 Douglas & Kafafi 2000, fig. 6.4:4.
82 de Vaux 1955, fig. 6:11; 1:6, 17.
83 Gustavson-Gaube 1985, type 48h.
84 Betts 1992, fig. 180:5.
85 Hanbury-Tenison 1986, fig. 7:1.
86 Kenyon & Holland 1982, fig. 37:8, type A.III.
87 Betts 1992, fig. 177:3.
88 Kenyon & Holland 1982, fig. 38:28, type B.II.b.
89 Hanbury-Tenison 1986, fig. 7:49.
90 Hanbury-Tenison 1986, fig. 6:47.
91 Betts 1992, fig. 177:6–7.
92 Gustavson-Gaube 1985, type 56c-d.

H.A — Holemouth jars with vertical or inclined rims and low shoulders are less frequent and follow the Late Chalcolithic tradition. In some cases they are very close to LSJ.D genre, because of the almost vertical rim, but the two groups can be recognized by the joint point between the shoulder and the neck, absent in H.A. They are represented by high variability of rim types, indicating less care in rim manufacturing, and for this reason, types are indicated by lip variation more than rims. The type with a vertical upturned lip is the most common of this group (H.A.1) and is attested in different sizes. The other three types are less common, and they are characterized by a plain lip (H.A.2), lip flattened on top (H.A.3), and sliced lip (H.A.4).

Parallels — Parallels for H.A were found at Shuna[93] and Jericho,[94] in the Jerash region,[95] Umm Hammad,[96] and Tawwab.[97]

H.B — The holemouth jars with horizontal rim are more numerous and usually they are decorated with short rope, or lines of dots, and present a high variability of types, according to the lip:

- Swollen lip on the inner side (H.B.1);
- Folded lip (H.B.2);
- Type with no distinction between shoulder and lip (H.B.3), that can be slightly round (H.B.3a) or squared (H.B.3b);
- Sliced lip, usually (but not always) thickened (H.B.4);
- Grooved lip (H.B.5);
- Pointed lip (H.B.6);
- Type with lip flattened on top (H.B.7);
- Seed-like lip (H.B.8);
- Broad rim (H.B.9).

Parallels — This group represents one of the most distinct genres of the EBA. Types H.B.1, H.B.3, H.B.4, H.B.5, H.B.9, H.B.10 are the most common, and it spread in the region in almost all the contemporaneous levels. H.B.2 is less attested, with parallels at Jawa[98] and Jericho.[99] H.B.6 and H.B.8 are attested only at Jericho.[100] Type H.B.7 is again less attested, and some parallels have been found at 'Ai,[101] Jericho,[102] and Tell el-Far'ah N.[103] Type H.B.11 and H.B.12 are attested only along the Wadi Zarqa, from Jawa[104] and Umm Hammad.[105]

Decorations

On the total amount of diagnostic sherds (1024), 30 per cent show decorations, of which 73 per cent are applied (rope, knob, or snake-like), 22 per cent are impressed, 12 per cent are painted (Graph 4.2).

Among the painted decorated sherds, only a few have a recognizable geometric pattern. Some of the sherds have wavy horizontal short lines divided by a single, straight vertical line, and are described by Fernández-Tresguerres Velasco as 'tree motifs', found exclusively in the temple area.[106] Wavy painted decorations are attested elsewhere,[107] but they are closer to each other and less regular. Another type is the 'net' pattern, composed of crossing bands of red paint, of which the complete jug from the Temple of the Serpents constitutes the best example.[108] In other examples (Pl. 4.21:3–4), the bands are quite thick (0.5 to 1 cm) and the design is crude, more similar to those found in simple and storage ware vessels and already attested in the Chalcolithic period.[109] A sherd (Pl. 4.21:2) has a single thick red band on the outer side and a series of six red circles spreading in a random pattern on the inner side. This type of pattern has a perfect parallel with an EB IB sherd from Bab edh-Drah',[110] and a small sherd from Jawa.[111] Braun (2012) associates this pattern from Arad level II to the

---

93 Gustavson-Gaube 1985, type 54 and KH.

94 Kenyon & Holland 1983, fig. 12:20; fig. 13:30; fig. 121:30.

95 Hanbury-Tenison 1986, fig. 5:43; fig. 5:42.

96 Betts 1992, fig. 141:1–5.

97 Douglas & Kafafi 2000, fig. 6.2:2.

98 Betts & Helms 1991, fig. 117:88.

99 Kenyon & Holland 1982, fig. 39:5, 8–10, type A.I.c, A.II.

100 Kenyon & Holland 1982, fig. 64: 9–10, type A.II.a; fig. 65:28, type D.I.d.

101 Callaway 1964, pl. XIX: 2269.

102 Kenyon & Holland 1982, fig. 39:19, type B.I.b.

103 De Vaux 1955, fig. 4:7.

104 Betts & Helms 1991, fig. 120:137–40; fig. 114:56–58.

105 Betts 1992, fig. 145:9.

106 Pl. 4.21:1; Fernández-Tresguerres Velasco 2005a, figs 12–14.

107 Dated at the Proto-Urban period at Jericho, Kenyon & Holland 1982, fig. 34:4.5.

108 Pocaro et al. 2014, fig. 5.

109 Kenyon & Holland 1982, fig. 34:28; fig. 59:23; Amiran et al. 1978, pl. 11:12–16. See e.g. the Late Chalcolithic repertoire from Arad (Amiran et al. 1978, pl. 4:5–6, 10).

110 Schaub & Rast 1989, fig. 75:3.

111 Betts & Helms 1991, fig. 149, 546.

4. THE POTTERY: FUNCTION AND TYPOLOGIES

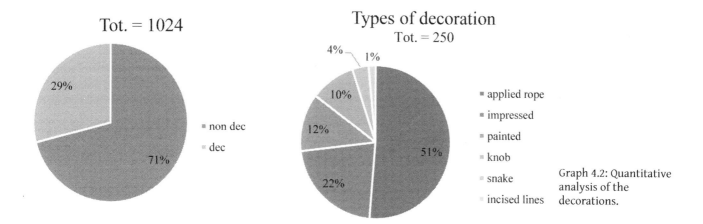

Graph 4.2: Quantitative analysis of the decorations.

Light Faced Painted Ware of the EB II.[112] Decoration with painted dots seems to be rare but definitely attested in the southern Levant at the earlier stages of the EB, known from Jericho (Proto-Urban period).[113] Properly net painted decoration characteristic of the EB IB at Jericho[114] and along the Jordan Valley[115] are almost unknown at Mutawwaq, except for a loop handle probably related to amphoriskoi. Finally, trickle paint from the rim is attested in a limited number of cases, usually of necked jars and bottles from the domestic sectors (Pls 4.6:11; 4.7:11; 4.13:6–7).

The impressed decorations are represented almost exclusively by the horizontal line of small dots typical of the holemouth Jawa type (Pl. 4.15:3.5; Pl. 4.16:8–9; 4.17:3, 6; 4.18:7–11, 17; 4.19:1, 7; 4.22:9, 12). As already pointed out in the previous section, the holemouth Jawa type are easily recognizable thanks to the typical decoration, with a horizontal line of small impressed dots (c. 3 mm in diam.) and sometimes four knobs are applied immediately under it. At Mutawwaq, this kind of decoration is attested only on the holemouth shape (Pl. 4.15:8, 10; 4.16:3; 4.18:14). Some of them present a rope-like impression instead of the line of dots, and it is not clear if this type could also be associated with Jawa type decoration or if it is closer to later examples (Pl. 4.15:2, 6, 15, 17).[116]

In one case, the lower part of a medium-size storage vessel shows a mat impression on the base and a double thick loop handle located at the middle point of the body (Pl. 4.22:12). Here, at least one knob and three intermittent lines of dots are preserved, one on the knob and two that run parallel on the handle. In other rare cases, small dots are arranged differently, in groups (Pl. 4.22:8, 10) or in geometric patterns of horizontal and vertical short lines close to the rim (Pl. 4.16:4–5) or in two cases close to and on a spout (Pls 4.16:6; 4.22:11).

Finally, a complete vessel from Room 5 of the temple area show a line of oval-shaped impressions modelled like 'grapes', as defined by Fernández-Tresguerres Velasco (2005a, 19, fig. 17). This motif is known from Jawa to Umm Hammad and Betts called it 'seal impressions',[117] showing a distribution along the Zarqa Valley and at its confluence with the Jordan River.[118]

The applied decorations are the most represented group, and they have a high variety of types. Rope decorations are the most attested type. It consists in usually horizontal lines of applied clay decorated with circular or thumb impressions, giving the appearance of a rope (Pls 4.12:3; 4.16:10; 4.22:2–7). This kind of decoration is very common in the southern Levantine horizon, known from the Chalcolithic to the MB I period. A second type consists simply in a rope-like applique, but short and modelled squashing the two ending points (Pls 4.6:6; 4.10:8; 4.13:7; 4.15:9, 18; 4.17:4–5; 4.19:15; 4.21:8–9). The upper part is decorated with small circular or oblique impressions made by a stick or similar tool. In one case, this applique appears on a storage vessel handle (Pl. 4.21:10). A variant of this type is the serpent-like applique, consisting of a long ribbon of clay, circular in

---

112 Amiran et al. 1978, pl. 28:2, 7; pl. 29:4; pl. 30:5; pl. 56–65; Braun 2012.
113 Kenyon & Holland 1982, fig. 48:3; Tomb D 12, Kenyon & Holland 1982, fig. 93:5.
114 Kenyon & Holland 1982, fig. 48:7–8 dated to the Proto-Urban period.
115 See examples at Arad, Amiran et al. 1978, pl. 9:8–9.
116 The sherds at Pl. 4.18:12 could be better associated with the Jawa type for the presence of a knob. For the chronology of the decorations see below.

117 Betts & Helms 1991, 111, figs 160–63, 166.
118 Betts & Helms 1991, 115.

session, applied wavy, usually from the bottom to the top of the vessel. The 'body' of the snake is decorated with small circular impressions, while the head, when preserved, is decorated with two small circles as eyes.[119] At present, these decorations are exclusively attested on medium-sized closed vessels: JB.B, WNJ.B, LSJ.C, LSJ.D, H.B. Only one miniaturistic sherd was found with short serpent-like applied decoration (Pl. 4.6:6).

Finally, separated knobs are attested in a variety of shapes, from triangular to elongated (Pls 4.1:24; 4.3:3, 5; 4.11:3; 4.12:9; 4.13:11; 4.18:16; 4.22:1).

[EC]

Manufacturing before the Wheel: Analysis of the Pottery Production

The study of the pottery production of the Mutawwaq repertoire comprehends the macro-analysis of fabrics and manufacturing traces. Moreover, the Geology Laboratory of the Universitat de Girona analysed a small sample (twenty-seven sherds and three soil samples) from the site.

Manufacturing Process

The autoptic observation of the sherds allows some remarks regarding the manufacturing process of the ceramic production at Jebel al-Mutawwaq. Following are some tentative considerations about the way-of-doing of the different pottery families and types, which aim to shed new light on the manufacturing processes. As pointed out recently by Roux (2019, 140), identifying unambiguous elements indicating precise manufacturing technique is rare, and a set of experiments should be conducted to understand the visible traces. Unfortunately, no experiments have been conducted until now to fix the macro-traces of the Mutawwaq ceramic assemblage, and the results described here must be taken as preliminary considerations.[120]

Starting from the preparation of the raw materials, it is possible to distinguish between three different kinds of inclusions: mineral, vegetal, and grog. Mineral inclusions can be naturally present in the clay sediment or intentionally added (temper) by the potters (Rice 2015, 85–86). At Mutawwaq, the shape and high range of inclusions indicate a process of crushing the mineral rock before adding it to the clay. However, the high size variability could indicate the presence of both natural mineral elements and tempers (Figs 4.1; 4.2). The chemical analysis of fabrics identified two origins for the mineral temper, metamorphic (limestone) and volcanic (basalt or hematite). The two rocks are processed in two different ways. The limestone inclusions are represented by small to large grits, and they are mainly characterized by larger irregular shapes. The volcanic mineral tempers are smaller, and their frequency is higher than the metamorphic ones. They are characteristics of small consuming and serving vessels (Fig. 4.2). This differentiation could be interpreted as the presence of two different ways of preparing clays.

About the metamorphic mineral tempered fabric, thanks to the rough finishing techniques, the shaping of the vessels has left some visible traces both in fracture and on the surface, particularly evident in larger storage vessels. Flat bases are usually created separately, and then a slab or coil of clay is added (Fig. 4.4: JM.18.CSUD.418/11). Some larger bases have mat impressions on the lower part. This feature usually is considered characteristic of the Late Chalcolithic period (Fig. 4.3). In some cases, the orientation of the vacuoles along the wall of larger closed vessels marks the presence of coils (Fig. 4.4: JM.18.CSUD.415/19, JM.CSUD.417/18, JM.18.CSUD.418/11). The rims are modelled by hand, and they are usually quite irregular, leaving some traces on the external surface immediately below the rim. The tableware is usually finer, so traces are more difficult to read. Small concave bases could have been modelled into a mould, and then walls were added to them at a second stage. No indication of coils or joints has been recognized until now, but the irregular topography of some open vessels could indicate shaping by pinching. The use of moulds for manufacturing cups C.B and C.C and bowls is highly improbable because of the high variability of the dimensions of the body.

When the volcanic tempers are attested, the manufacturing process is also different. Only a small group of serving vessels are produced with this particular fabric. The small hemispherical cups have string-cut disc bases, indicating that a wheel was used to finish the surfaces (Fig. 4.4: JM.18.CSUD.W1013/1). Also, for this fabric, coils are visible in the sections of the vessels. Still, the horizontal direction of the fractures of the dish

---

119 Pl. 4.21:6–7; Treguerres-Velasco 2005a, figs 14–16; Polcaro et al. 2014, fig. 7.

120 For the identification and interpretation of the macro-traces, the main reference taken is the parameter grid elaborated by Roux (2019, tab. 3.1). When used, other references are given case by case.

4. THE POTTERY: FUNCTION AND TYPOLOGIES

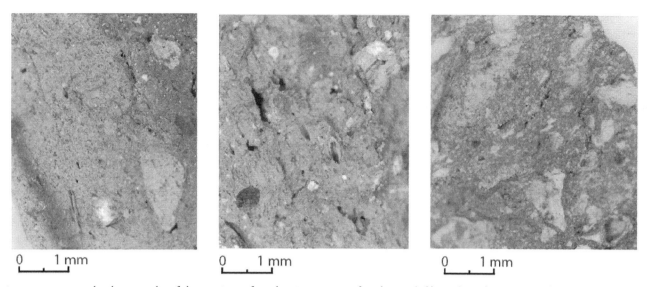

Figure 4.1: Mesoscale photographs of the sections of Production Group 1, fine (PG1.1, left), medium (PG1.2, centre), and coarse (PG1.3, right). Pictures taken by the author with a © CanoScan LiDE 110.

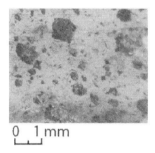

Figure 4.2: Mesoscale photographs of the sections of Production Group 2. Picture taken by the author with a © CanoScan LiDE 110.

could indicate wheel-finishing (Fig. 4.5). A double mode of production is visible in two sherds of small, closed shape (Pl. 4.11:5, 10) where a string of clay marks the join between neck and shoulder.

Archaeometric Analysis: Some Preliminary Remarks

Besides autoptic analysis on the sherds during the excavations, DRX analysis on thirty samples, three soil samples, and twenty-seven pottery samples was conducted. The selection of samples has been made in the attempt to cover different shapes (large vessels, pitchers, bowls, drinking cups, etc.).

The Raw Materials: Archaeometric Analysis on Clays and Tempers

The study of the clays and the tempers was possible thanks to the archaeometric analysis conducted in 2015. Thin sections of the pottery samples were prepared in the Thin Section Preparation Laboratory at the Autonomous University of Barcelona. The petrographic characterization was performed in the Geology Laboratory of the Universitat de Girona with a Leitz Orthoplan petrographic microscope.

The mineralogical content of the samples was determined by powder x-ray diffraction (XRD) measurements. For this purpose, the samples were air-dried and pulverized with an agate mortar to obtain randomly oriented powders. XRD scans were collected between 4º and 60º in 2θ, with 0.035º per step, by using a Bruker D8-A25 diffractometer equipped with a Cu X-ray source (Cu Kα radiation, λ = 1.5418 Å) working at 40 kV and 40 mA. The scans were acquired with a LynxEye position-sensitive detector (total integration time of 192 s per step), using a nickel filter to remove the Kβ contribution. The identification of the crystalline phases was carried out with the DIFFRAC.EVA software, together with the Powder Diffraction File PDF-2 and the Crystallography Open Database (COD). The XRD Analyses have been carried out in conjunction with the XRD Department of the Jaume Almera Earth Sciences Institute of the Council of Scientific Research (CSIC). The ICP-MS geochemical analyses are still under study.

Despite a lack of other edaphological studies, we have some initial X-ray diffraction (DRX) analyses of the mineralogical composition of three soil samples. Two are from the Temple of the Serpents, and one is from inside Dolmen 534 (Fig. 4.6). The three soil samples analysed featured high contents of calcite, quartz, and dolomite. In smaller quantities: albite, palygorskite, microcline, and kaolinite. Illite, nontronite, and ferropargasite are

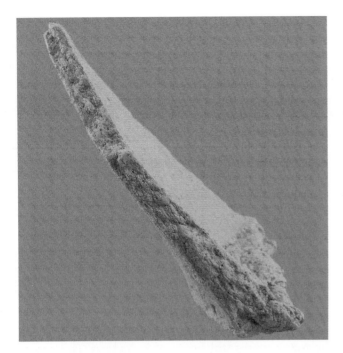

Figure 4.3: Storage jar base JM.03.H76.I.291. The base is made by pressing the clay on a mat (lower picture), and then the first coil of the wall is added, leaving a Y-shaped fissure (upper picture).

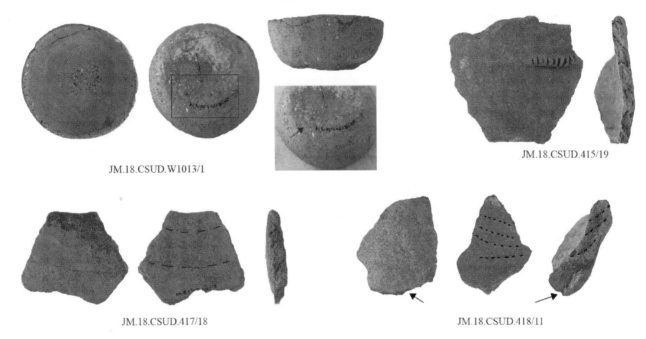

Figure 4.4: Examples of manufacturing techniques shown by macro-traces. String-cut disc base indicating the use of wheel (JM.18.CSUD.W.1013/1). Orientation of voids indicating the different coils and the joint points (JM.18.CSUD.415/19, JM.18.CSUD.417/18). Joint between the base and the first coil of the wall indicating by the Y-shape fissure and U-shaped fracture (JM.18.CSUD.418/11, left and right); fissures are visible on the inner surfaces, indicating the different coils (JM.18.CSUD.418/11, centre).

present in the two samples from the temple area but not in the one from inside the dolmen. Hematite has been found in one of the samples from the temple (Fig. 4.6:b).

Mineralogical Composition of the Ceramics

The minerals present in the ceramics can be classified into:

– Primary: Contents in the raw materials. They may have accompanied the clay when it was sourced or been added as degreasers. In the Mutawwaq repertoire, while kaolinite and illite-smectite were detected in three analyses, clays from the illite-smectite group were detected in eight of the ceramics. XRD did not detect any clays from this

4. THE POTTERY: FUNCTION AND TYPOLOGIES

Figure 4.5: Dish fragment JM.16.CSUD.406/14. Example of volcanic mineral inclusions visible on the inner surface, where the burnished slip is not preserved (upper picture). Horizontal and vertical fracture could indicate the use of wheel (lower picture).

group in five samples. Calcite and quartz appeared in high quantities in all the samples.

- Firing: Minerals that could have formed during the firing were detected in all ceramic sherds. Gehlenite, sanidine, plagioclase, diopside, and hematite. Although some of these minerals are already present in the site sediment, the abundant presence of gehlenite indicates equivalent firing temperatures of around 950 ºC. (Rice 1987; Rasmussen et al. 2012).
- Secondary: This is the name given to minerals secondary to those produced by use and depositional alterations. Calcite appears in high quantities in all the samples. Even if the firing temperature causes a reduction of part of the calcite, much remains present in the matrix, as a degreaser, calcareous rocks, or fossils, or due to post-depositional processes, in which the secondary calcite penetrates into the fissures and pores of the ceramics (Buxeda i Garrigós 1995).

A first look at the surface treatments has been possible on the selected samples. Numerous samples were detected to have reddish, well-finished surface treatment, although they were profusely covered by calcareous concretions (Fig. 4.7:a, b). The DRX analysis of surface treatments, which we scratched from the surface of two drinking cups, indicates the presence of compounds with iron, such as maghemite (M10/14) or magnetite and magnesioferrite (M15/14) (Fig. 4.6, see Fig. 4.4:JM.18.CSUD.418/11).

The Study on Fabrics: The Archaeometric Analyses and the Identification of Petrofabric according to Inclusions

Analysis of the twenty-seven thin sections allows us to establish groupings based on degreasers. This is because the matrix is common to all the samples, and it is made up of carbonates and quartz and marked by a high presence of foraminifera.

- Group one: Large, rounded, reddish grains (iron oxides). This group has the lowest representation and was found in just two samples, M14/14 and M15/14 (which could belong to the same single ceramic). Very rounded, very uniform reddish grains ranging from 0.2 to 0.4 mm in diameter were observed in the thin section. They could be hematite. Under direct observation, these grains have a dark colour. They are not magnetic. In both samples, quartz was detected as a degreaser. It presents wind impacts. Its origin was metamorphic, as it has undulated extinction (Fig. 4.7: a, b). XRD analysis of the two samples indicates the presence of palygorskite and microcline.
- Group two: Characterized by grains of mafic igneous rock (plagioclase + pyroxene) of volcanic origin, with four samples. Additionally, they all present limestone fragments (Fig. 4.7: c, d, e). There are grains of potassium feldspar and opaque minerals mixed in the plagioclase. Some shells appear in two samples; in others, quartz crystals and quartzite clasts were detected. In another, iron oxide and marl fragments were found. Last, another sample was found to have biotite layers. XRD analyses revealed the presence of nontronite and analcime.
- Group three: Shell fossils. This is represented by nine samples. Although shells also occasionally appear in other samples, they were clearly selected as the main and very extensive degreaser in these nine. They are shell fossils carefully separated from the rest of the sediment, though in some cases, sediment still adhered to them. It is possible that most of the shells were from oysters. Some of these shells have been found in the two sediment

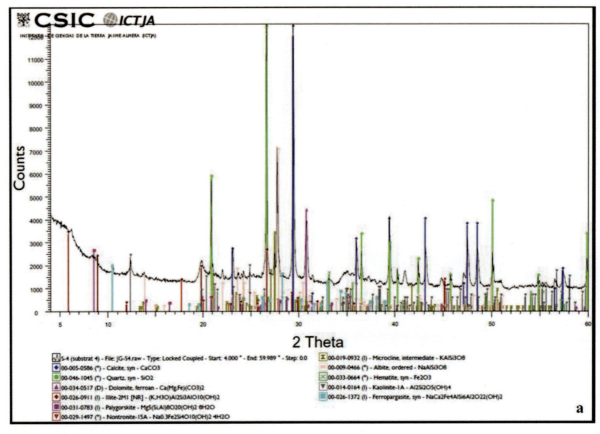
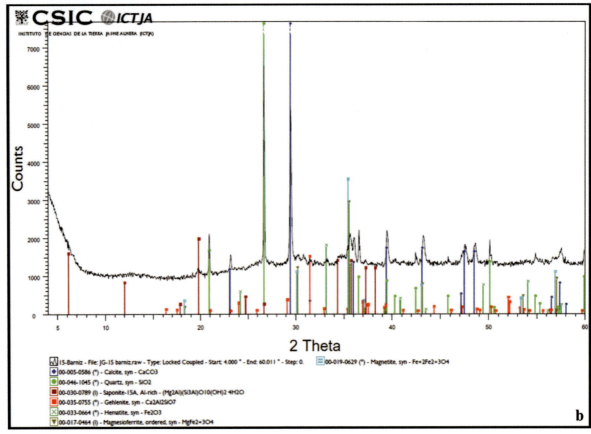

Figure 4.6: Results of the XRF analysis.

4. THE POTTERY: FUNCTION AND TYPOLOGIES

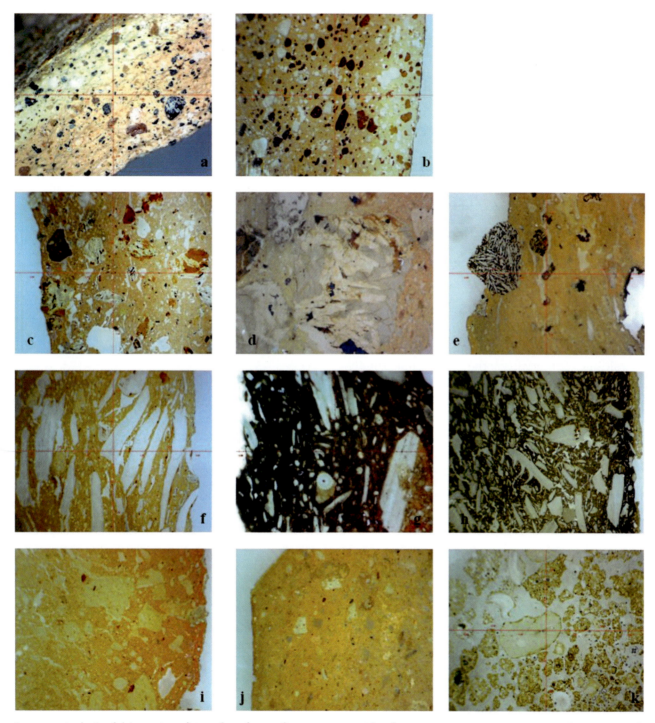

Figure 4.7: Analysis of thin section. a) Sample 15/14, surface treatment with calcareous concretions. First petrographic group, with dark reddish rounded grains, x60. b) Sample 15/14, first group with reddish rounded grains. Thin section (TS) x60. With surface treatment. c) Sample 10/14. Thin section (TS) x60. d) Sample 24/15 (TS) x200. e) Sample 8/15 (TS) x60. f) Sample 2/14 (TS) x60. g) Sample 3/15 (TS) x200. h) Sample 22/15 (TS) x60. i) Sample 6/15 (TS) x60. j) Sample 7/15 (TS) x60. k) Sample 5/14 (TS) x60. Sediment with fossils and calcareous rock.

samples analysed. This leads to the hypothesis that these ceramics could have been manufactured locally or in a calcareous setting similar to the site. The presence of palygorskite and sanidine was detected in the XRD analysis (Fig. 4.7: f, g, h).

- Group four: Calcareous. This is the most numerous group, corresponding to the calcareous degreasers, with twelve samples. In five cases, micritic limestone was detected; in others, fossils (shells and sea urchin spines) and occasionally, opaque minerals such as pyrite and limonite (M7/14), aragonite (M23/15), and minerals that form part of igneous rocks. Like the third group, this group is coherent with the geology of the surroundings. It could have been manufactured on the site or with similar geological characteristics. The presence of diopside was detected through XRD (Fig. 4.7: i, j, k).

To conclude, in terms of the mineralogical composition, all the clays come from calcareous environments, but the degreasers are of two different origins: calcareous and volcanic. This confirms the macroscopic subdivision in two distinct fabric groups, already visible at a macroscopic level. The most common fabric group appeared to be clearly local (groups three and four), and two different processes were followed with the calcareous degreasers. One uses calcareous grains, sometimes accompanied by shell fossils; in the other, shell fossils are separated from the calcareous sediment and used mainly as a degreaser. In the second fabric group, two samples with a dark reddish, rounded degreaser (iron oxides, possibly hematite) were detected.

[EC, JDR]

Qualitative, Quantitative, and Spatial Analysis of the Pottery Types

As described in the previous sections, the study of pottery was based mainly on macroscopic observation of the fabric, manufacturing process, and morphological seriation of the diagnostic sherds, and only a small sample was analysed by archaeometric analysis. In this section, the first endeavour is to recognize the relationship between pottery types and families, manufacturing traces, and the fabric groups. The combination of these three aspects pointed to the identification of two distinct pottery productions. The most common production group (Production Group 1 or PG1) is an orange-buff ware, low fired, with a high frequency of small and medium grits. This fabric shows a high variability between fine to coarse and can be attributed to serving, storage, and cooking activities. The second production group (Production Group 2, or PG2) is dark orange to red in colour, and a hard-compact texture characterizes it with a high frequency of black volcanic grits, probably basalt or hematite.

Production Group 1 (PG1)

Production Group 1 (PG1) is the most represented of the two groups. It represents the locally produced simple ware at the site, as demonstrated by comparing the fine mass of the pottery samples and the soil samples selected for the archaeometric analysis (groups three and four, see below). The macroscopic and mesoscopic analysis of the fabrics highlights a high variability of the PG1, subdivided between fine — PG1.1 — medium/coarse — PG1.2 — and coarse — PG1.3 — (Fig. 4.1). This can be interpreted as the result of the different functional implication of this group. Related to PG1 are the great majority of shapes and types, as shown in Graph 4.3. Here, PG1.1 and PG1.2 are considered together because of the actual difficulty in the distinction between the two for the non-diagnostic sherds, indicating that their distinction could be subjective, especially for the small and medium-sized closed vessels (Fig. 4.8). The repertoire is comprised of small cups, bowls, and necked jugs/bottles, usually produced in a fine or medium fine fabric (PG1.1, Fig. 4.1: left). A group of medium-sized jars of different families and types is produced in a coarser fabric, hard-compact with a high quantity of angular, medium to large mineral inclusions. It can be related to storage practices (PG1.2, Fig. 4.1:central). A cylindrical or out-flaring neck characterizes medium-large storage jars. Holemouth jars are represented in a wide variety of rims. Both necked and holemouth jars are attested in a very coarse fabric, dark brown to purple, with a high frequency of large calcareous grits, interpreted as cooking ware (PG1.3, Fig. 4.1: right; Fig. 4.9).

Almost all the sherds are handmade and coarsely finished, with little care for the appearance of the final products. These characteristics point to the domestic production of the pottery assemblage. The degree of variability of the profiles indicates the repetitiveness of gestures in the vessel manufacture. The high morphological variability, also expressed by the number of types associated with some specific families, points to a non-specialized production of the pottery assemblage.

4. THE POTTERY: FUNCTION AND TYPOLOGIES

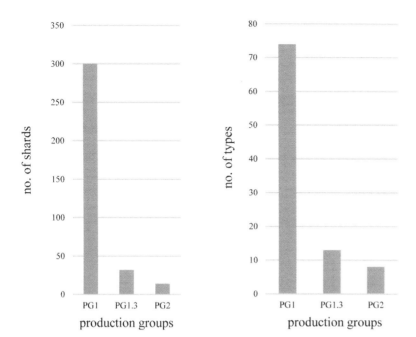

Graph 4.3: Quantitative analysis of production groups.

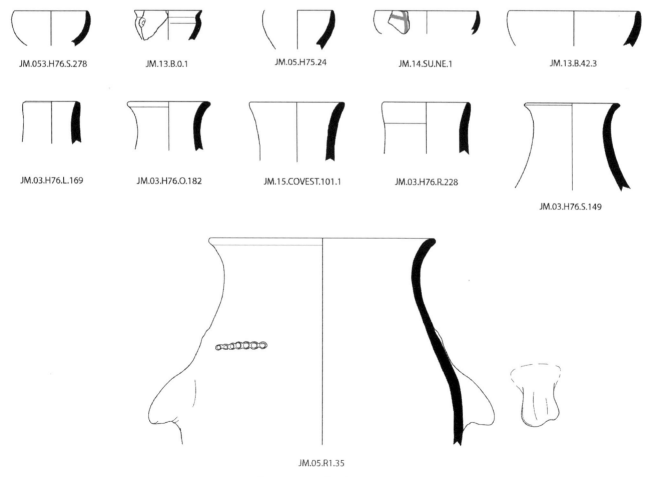

Figure 4.8: Production Group 1.

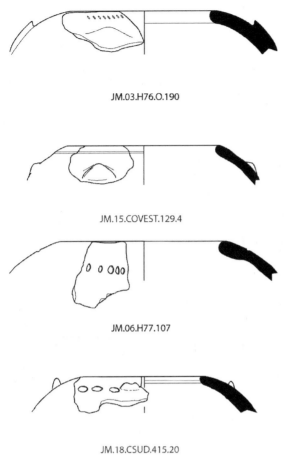

Figure 4.9: Production Group 1 (continued).

In conclusion, PG1 represents the simple local ware used to produce consuming, storage, and cooking ware, indicating a household mode of production due to the lack of specialized production techniques and the high variability of the morphological features across shapes and genres.

Production Group 2 (PG2)

The second macro-group is firmly restricted to the funerary contexts of Area C, with some — rare — exceptions (Fig. 4.10). The presence of black mineral inclusions, possibly hematite (group two, see below), makes this group easily recognizable. Volcanic rock outcrops are visible at c. 1 km from the base of Jebel al-Mutawwaq, and they could constitute the point of supply for the raw materials. The types associated with it are represented by small hemispherical bowls (B.A.6-b), also with disc base, inturned rim platters (D.A.1), small jugs and jars (JB.A.3, JB.B.4, JB.C.2–3, LSJ.A.1, LSJ.B.2), with traces of slow-wheel production and double-mode of production used for the closed shapes. Almost all the PG2 sherds have traces of red burnished slip, sometimes polished. Among the nine types attested, five are exclusive to the funerary contexts of Area C (D.A.1, JB.B.4, JB.C.3, LSJ.A.1, and the disc bases). The small hemispherical bowls B.A.6-b and the everted-rim bottles/jugs JB.A and

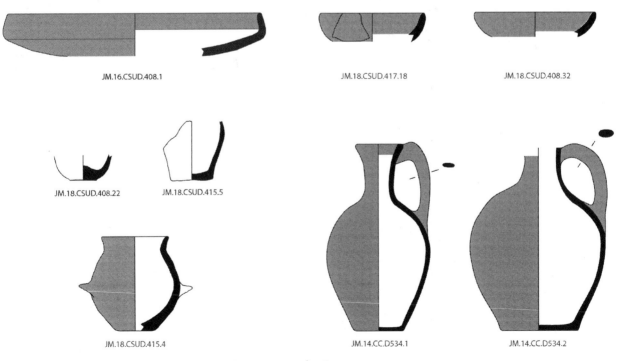

Figure 4.10: Production Group 2.

4. THE POTTERY: FUNCTION AND TYPOLOGIES

JB.C.2 are also attested in PG1, but all the PG2 sherds are from the closing layer 415 of the funerary cave in Area C South. One single sherd of PG2 (JM.05.R4.32, Pl. 11:10, type LSJ.B.2) comes from a different context, Room 4 of the temple area. Some rare non-diagnostic sherds have been found scattered on the surface close to Area C.

Distribution of Pottery Productions, Genres, and Types: Interpreting the Site through Pottery

In the present section, distribution analysis of production groups, shapes, families, and types will give some insights into the general organization of the site.

Analysing the distribution of the shapes among the different contexts could help the functional reconstruction of the different areas at Jebel al-Mutawwaq.

The distribution of PG1 shapes per area is represented in Graph 4.4, where the number given is the percentage of the total number of diagnostic sherds per area (e.g. of the total number of diagnostic sherds from that specific area, x number are cups, x number are bowls, etc.). Looking at the distribution of the shapes, we can see that cups are very well attested inside the temple area, the main attested shapes in the rooms and House 75. In general, it seems that the proportion between cups and bowls is inverted in the East Sector and the temple area, while in the Central Sector (Area C), the propor-

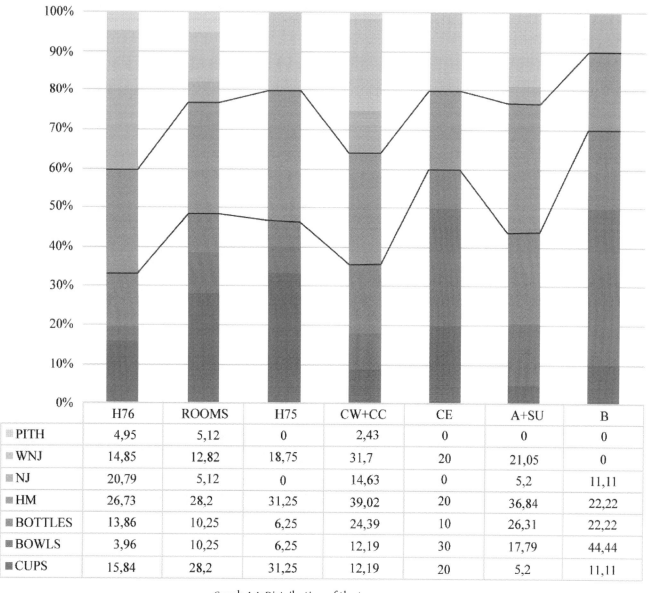

	H76	ROOMS	H75	CW+CC	CE	A+SU	B
PITH	4,95	5,12	0	2,43	0	0	0
WNJ	14,85	12,82	18,75	31,7	20	21,05	0
NJ	20,79	5,12	0	14,63	0	5,2	11,11
HM	26,73	28,2	31,25	39,02	20	36,84	22,22
BOTTLES	13,86	10,25	6,25	24,39	10	26,31	22,22
BOWLS	3,96	10,25	6,25	12,19	30	17,79	44,44
CUPS	15,84	28,2	31,25	12,19	20	5,2	11,11

Graph 4.4: Distribution of the types per area.

tion between the two is *c.* 1:1. This diversification may point to a functional peculiarity of the temple area, with cups that played different specific functions not employed in the other areas of the site. Bottles and jugs are particularly frequent in the public/production compound, Area CW and CC and in the domestic sector of Area A. The holemouth jars are frequent in almost all the contexts analysed, with a particular concentration in the Areas A and CW+CC. The necked jars are a shape typical of the temple area, and in particular of House 76; here are the best-represented closed shapes. They are also frequent in Area B, and no other medium or large necked jars are attested here. The large jars (WNJ and LSJ.C.3 and LSJ.D) are very well represented in the two domestic compounds, while they are absent in funerary contexts.

This analysis of the distribution of the shapes highlights a clear functional distinction among the different contexts at Mutawwaq. The two compounds, Area CW+CC, and Area A, show similar functional repertoire, with the same proportion of open vessels, bottles/jugs, holemouth, and large-sized vessels. Also, the two funerary contexts are similar in the general functional distribution, with the predominance of small instead of large closed vessels. The main room of the temple area, House 76, represents a particular situation in which two shapes, the cups, and the necked jars, seem to be characteristic of this room, possibly indicating some specific functions not carried out in other parts of the settlement. The general assemblage of shapes from Building C in the Central Sector (H.81 and the adjacent court, Areas CW+CC) is similar to that of the temple area (see the black lines in Graph 4.4). Looking at the distribution of types between the two contexts, the same proportion of exclusive types emerges. On a total of eighty-two types identified, forty-four types are exclusive to one single context. Considering the total number of types per area, the temple area has 4.6 per cent exclusive types, while the complex of Area C has 4.1 per cent. This means that the functional character of the two areas, as expressed by the pottery shapes, is marked as similar, but the morphological characterization expressed by types differs. This could be the consequence of a chronological gap between the two contexts and a general diversification in the production organization. Considering the two different areas occupied by two groups of individuals, the morphological diversification of the assemblages can reflect two different production places.

A completely different situation is visible for the repertoire from the two dolmens of Area C, D.534 and D.535.

Here, PG2 is predominant. The range of parallels of the pottery types exclusive to the PG2 indicated a later date in the final phase of the EB I, or EB IB (see below). The evident relation between PG2 and the funerary contexts of the Central Sector testifies to a new need for diversification of the funerary goods, marking a clear break in the tradition with the funerary good repertoire of the dolmens of the eastern necropolis (Area B).

[EC]

Parallels and Chronology

In this section, a preliminary analysis of the Mutawwaq ceramic horizon is intended to fix the geographical and chronological limits of the repertoire. That said, while the C14 dates shed light on the chronology of the different areas of the site, the local simple ware PG1 does not seem to reflect any marked difference in the repertoire from the Great Circle area and the rest of the settlement.

Unfortunately, a clear periodization of the ceramic horizon of the EB I in the southern Levant, including the transitional phases between Late Chalcolithic and EB II, is still undefined, and few contexts help to subdivide the repertoire. Nevertheless, two subphases can be distinguished: early EB I (or EB IA) and late EB I (EB IB). The first one is characterized by the presence of the Grey Burnished Ware and Impressed Slash Ware (Stager 1992). The latter is characterized by the band slip and grain wash's presence and the so-called Umm Hammad Ware. The most extended stratigraphic sequences of the period are attested at Tell Umm Hammad, Jebel Abu Tawwab, Tell Shuna, Bab edh 'Dhra, and Jericho. Megiddo could offer a good parallel, even if the very early phase of the EB I is not attested. The funerary contexts at Tell el-Far'ah N constitute a good repertoire for the later phase of the EB I. Unfortunately, a strong regionalism attested for the very beginning of the EB I impacted the construction of a ceramic periodization for the entire southern Levant, and Jebel al-Mutawwaq suffers the absence of some of the most diagnostic features attested in other regions west of the Jordan River.

The first aim of the present section is the identification of borders of the ceramic 'province' in which Mutawwaq is inserted. A good amount of Jawa 'style' decoration is attested on the holemouth jars. The typical EB IA Grey Burnished Ware attested neither at Jawa nor in the closer site of Jebel Abu Tawwab, and in the small assemblage of the Umayri Dolmen 7, could suggest

4. THE POTTERY: FUNCTION AND TYPOLOGIES

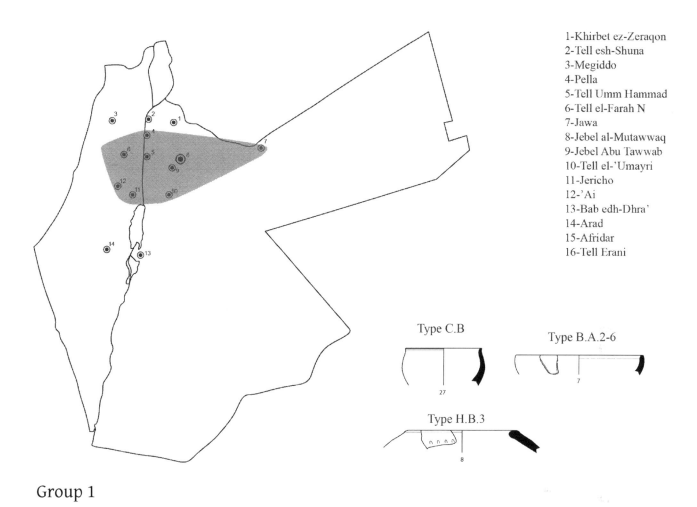

Figure 4.11: Distribution of the parallels of types C.b, B.A.2–6, H.B.3.

a clear border of this ware east of the Jordan Valley. The same conclusion is valid for the Umm Hammad Ware, a hallmark of the EB IB horizon, as recently demonstrated by Bar (2010, 88, fig. 1).[121] Considering the different chronological ranges of the two productions, their absence at Mutawwaq may be related to geographic factors instead of chronology.

On the other hand, thanks to the first surveys effectuated during the eighties by Hanbury-Tenison (1985), the pottery assemblage reflects a strong regionalism that links Jebel al-Mutawwaq with the other site spread along the central Wadi Zarqa and the Jerash area. The repertoire found during the survey showed an organic range of shapes and decorations that could indicate the effective presence of a small province connecting the middle portion of the Zarqa Valley and the immediate northern area.[122]

The series of Figures 4.11–4.15 show the diffusion of the most diagnostic types attested at Mutawwaq. A high number of types is only attested in the site's immediate vicinity, including the area along the Wadi Far'ah, as far as Tell el-Far'ah N (Fig. 4.15). Several types indicate parallels in the east–west direction are quite consistent, from Tell el-Far'ah N to Jawa (Figs 4.11–4.13). Only types in group 4 seem to spread as far south as Bab edh-Dhra (Fig. 4.14).

In the tentatively dated repertoire from Jebel al-Mutawwaq, it is worth noting that, until now, no spe-

---

121 Even though a good number of sherds from Mutawwaq present plastic decorations, they are too poorly preserved to be clearly related to such Ware.

122 Already Hanbury-Tenison (1985, 136) indicate 'a different group of people' than those at Jawa and Umm Hammad, living in the Jerash region. Here, we prefer the idea of 'ceramic tradition' more than a group of people.

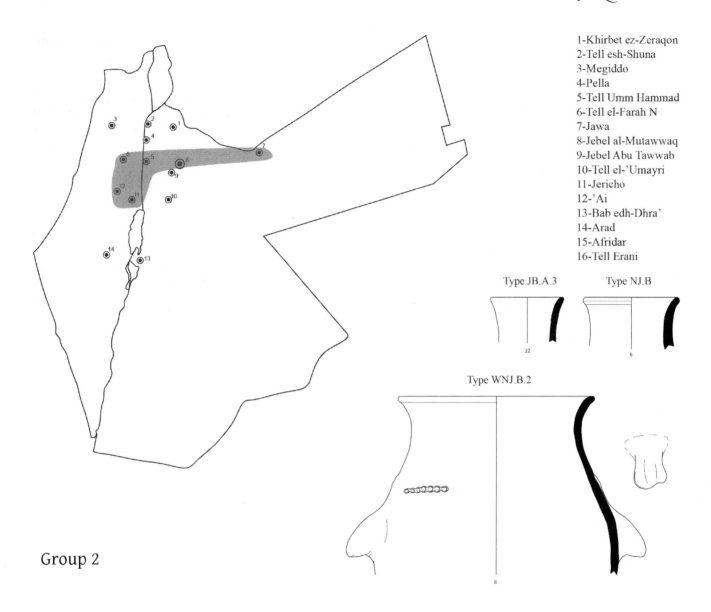

Figure 4.12: Distribution of the parallels JB.A.3, NJ.B, WNJ.B.2.

cialized production or 'Ware' has been found.[123] On the other hand, the presence of PG2 could have a solid chronological connotation.

In general, the morphological assemblage points to a clear EB I dated, as shown by the high frequency of hemispherical cups, the vertical necked jugs and juglets, the necked jars with short necks, and simple everted rims.[124]

Looking at the regional context, the whole pottery repertoire from Jebel al-Mutawwaq seems strongly related to the EB I phase at Jebel Abu Tawwab (Kafafi 2001, figs 33–42), not far south of Mutawwaq. Except for the necked jars, the two assemblages are almost identical: at Tawwab, the excavator identified two phases, marking the second one for the higher amount of simple painted ware. This kind of decoration is attested only for a few red-painted small cups and one amphoriskos handle; for this reason, the Mutawwaq repertoire seems closer to the earlier instead of the later phase of Tawwab. On the other hand, the presence of some 'net-painted' style could point to a later, instead of earlier phase of the EB I period. The most interesting feature of this style is a jug (Fig. 4.16), from the Temple of the

---

123 The term Ware as well as style is controversial, and in this occasion, I prefer to use the capital letter to delineate well-defined parameters usually based on purely subjective observations (Braun 2012, 5).

124 See for example the repertoire from 'Ai/Et-Tell, phases I–II (Callaway 1972, 59, fig. 15) and Jericho, Tomb K2, phase I (Kenyon 1960, fig. 4:1–2, 4–6, 11, fig. 8:1–3, 5–11, 22, 23, 25).

4. THE POTTERY: FUNCTION AND TYPOLOGIES

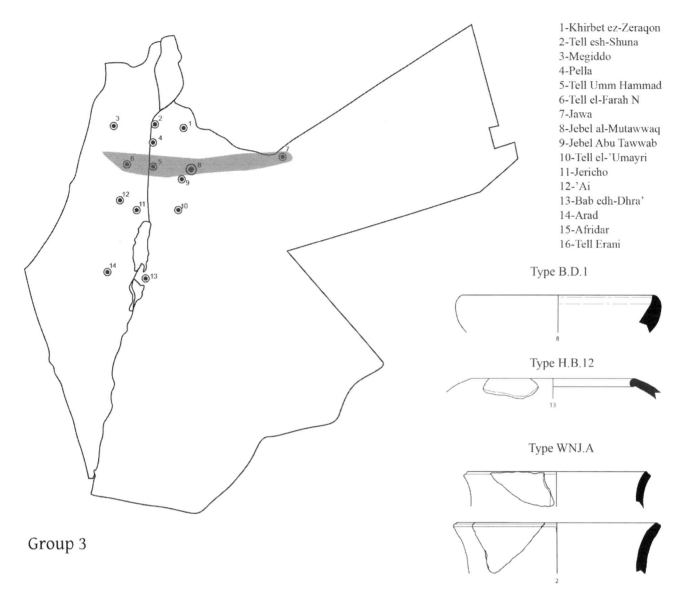

Figure 4.13: Distribution of the parallels of types B.D.1, W.NJ.A, H.B.12.

Serpent, that represents a very peculiar object, with a shape close to the EB IA horizon, but with a clear net-painted decoration, even if it is roughly made. Its character fits well with the transitional period EB IA–EB IB or early EB IB, as attested thanks to the C14 dates.

Close parallels are recognized at the site of Tell Umm Hammad, along the Wadi Zarqa Valley. Here several chronological stages were recognized by the excavator. During stage 2, the holemouth jars with impressed decoration are very popular, and the variant with four knobs on the shoulder might also correlate to the Jawa repertoire.[125]

Looking to the east, at the site of Jawa (Betts & Helms 1991, 71–99), many vessel types are similar to those of Mutawwaq. The Jawa-type cooking holemouth jars, decorated with dot-impressed lines and small triangular knobs, are characteristic of the whole region. Another element of connection is the presence of the 'grapes' impressed decoration (Fernández-Tresguerres Velasco 2005a, 19–20), identical to the 'stamp seal impressions' found at Jawa, Umm Hammad, Tell Mafluq, Tell el-Handaquq N, and Karatet es-Samra (Betts & Helms 1991, 113, fig. 165, fig. 167).

Moving North from Mutawwaq, the excavation at Tell Abu Kharaz constitutes the best parallel for the

---

[125] Repertoires 1–7 are dated to EB I according to parallels in close proximity (Betts 1992, 101–10).

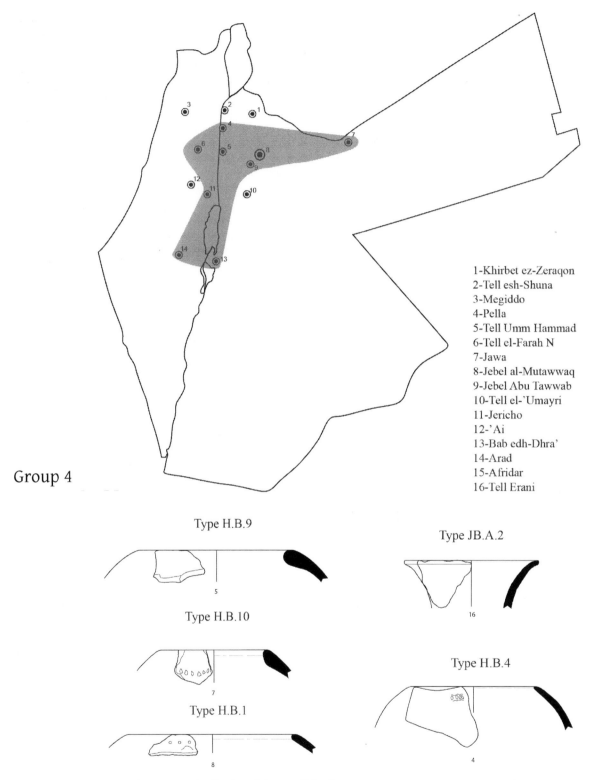

Figure 4.14: Distribution of the parallels of types JB.A.2, H.B.9, H.B.10, H.B.11, H.B.4.

4. THE POTTERY: FUNCTION AND TYPOLOGIES

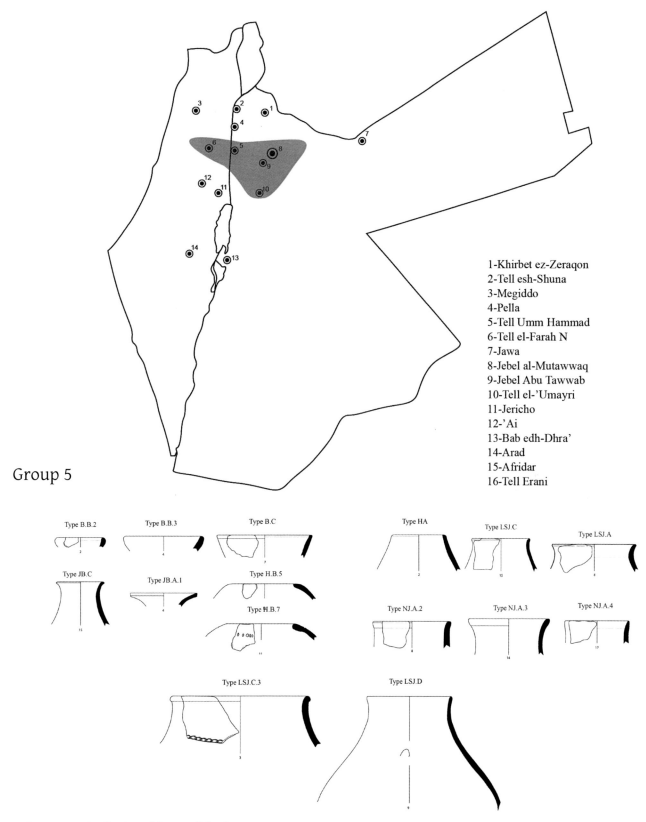

Group 5

1-Khirbet ez-Zeraqon
2-Tell esh-Shuna
3-Megiddo
4-Pella
5-Tell Umm Hammad
6-Tell el-Farah N
7-Jawa
8-Jebel al-Mutawwaq
9-Jebel Abu Tawwab
10-Tell el-'Umayri
11-Jericho
12-'Ai
13-Bab edh-Dhra'
14-Arad
15-Afridar
16-Tell Erani

Figure 4.15: Distribution of the parallels of types B.B.2, B.B.3, B.C, JB.C, JB.A.1, H.B.5, H.B.7, H.A, LSJ.C, LSJ.A, N.A.2, NJ.A.3, NJ.A.4, LSJ.C.3, LSJ.D.

Figure 4.16: Net painted jug from the Temple of the Serpent (Fernández-Tresguerres 2005a, fig. 18).

PG2 assemblage.[126] Rounded, carinated, and S-shaped bowls, and bowls with incurved rims are represented in both subphases IA and IB, and they find close parallels at Mutawwaq.[127] Straight side cups appear during phase IB and can be related to the small cup with string-cut base found in the burial cave of Area C South (Pl. 4.1:9, JM.18.CSUD.W1013/1).[128] Looking at the jugs and juglets, though the rim shapes are very similar, the high manufacturing level is attested in the rim sherds from Mutawwaq only in the PG2 exemplars. Nevertheless, it is impossible to identify such differences as a chronological or regional factor. The necked storage jars are completely different, except for two examples which are probably residual in phase IB.[129] The type with a simple, slightly flaring rim is similar to examples from Kharaz, even if the poor state of preservation of the fragments from Mutawwaq never shows the shape of vessels. Moreover, virtually no grain wash typical of this later phase has been found. Some similarities can be seen again with EB II jars, but they are thought to be attested firstly in the previous period.[130] In Mutawwaq, the great majority of holemouth jars in phase I also present plastic decorations.

Western and north-western areas of the Jordan Valley returned the best sequence of the LC–EB I–EB II period. Unfortunately, the best chronological hallmarks identified in this region are not attested in the Mutawwaq repertoire, once again testifying to the marked regionalism of the end of the fourth and the very beginning of the third millennia BCE. Some parallels can be detected at Tel Teo and in the Hula Valley,[131] Afridar,[132] and Yftah'el.[133] In the Hula Valley, two traditions have been identified: local tradition (derived from Neolithic Jericho IX and Wadi Rabah'/Bet Shean Ware) and Grey Burnished Ware tradition.[134] The local tradition is characterized by coarse, poorly fired, pale-coloured fabric, rich in organic temper, with a thin red slip. The prominent types are hemispherical bowls with roughly scraped bases, deep, sometimes carinated bowls, and jars with splayed or upright rims made separately and inserted into the body of the vessels. The same technique is reproduced in amphoriskoi and miniature jars. Kraters and holemouth, some with rope or slashed decoration, as well as loop-handled cups, round out the group. Greenberg (2002, 44) links this assemblage to Tell el-Far'ah N Tomb 3 (the earliest), Yftah'el II, Meser II, Bet Shean XVI (Braun 1991), Tell Umm Hammad (Chalcolithic–EB I), offering a good overview of the early assemblage of the region during the EB IA. Very few of these types find parallels in the Mutawwaq repertoire, such as the hemispherical bowls and the holemouth jars with rope decorations, confirming the C14 dates at the EB IB for the temple and the settlement.

Trying to broaden the comparisons to other regions, simpler morphological elements can be detected in a broader zone. The small hemispherical cups are a widespread type that is gradually replaced by shallower bowls during the final phase of the EB IB. Known as far north as Byblos, they are recognized in small excavations in the south, such as Umm Saysaban (Linder et al. 2005, figs 17–22), an open site without fortification, but at a strategically defensible site in the Petra region, dated to EB I. Deep cups identical to those found at Jebel al-Mutawwaq were found in the rock-cut tombs A.3 and B.3 at Tell al-Kafrayn,[135] in the central region, among the grave goods of the EB I dolmen at Tell el-Umairy field K,[136] and Wadi Fidan excavation in Area A.[137] Parallels are

---

126 Dated by the excavator to the EB IB, around 3100 BCE, phases I A–B (Fischer 2008, 251).

127 Fischer 2008, fig. 258:1, 3–4, 6, 7, 9–11, 13–17.

128 Fischer 2008, figs 21–22.

129 Fischer 2008, fig. 273:1, 3.

130 Phase II, Fischer 2008, fig. 278:1, 4–7.

131 Greenberg 2002, 25–26.

132 Golani 2004, fig. 27.

133 Braun 1997, figs 9.15–9.18.

134 Greenberg 2002, 42–44.

135 Ji & Lee 2002, fig. 3.

136 Dubis & Dabrowski 2002, figs 3–5.

137 Adams & Genz 1995, figs 3–5.

also attested at al-Basta, along the Wadi Ziqlab.[138] Those parallels should be regarded with caution for their morphological simplicity. They could testify to a sort of connection that involves a broad region, following the main seasonal water courses (Casadei 2018).

To conclude, the ceramic repertoire of Jebel al-Mutawwaq can be considered a good EB I assemblage of the central sector of the Zarqa Valley. Because of the lack of good stratigraphic sequences in the region, it is impossible to fix a relative periodization of the Simple Ware (PG1), and the absence of the LC and EB I hallmarks impacts a more precise dating of the excavated contexts. On the other hand, the continuation with the tradition of the Late Chalcolithic pottery expressed only in the storage vessels could suggest an occupational phase during EB IA.

The funerary context of the Central Sector (Area C) is dated to the EB IB or the very beginning of the EB II, as shown by parallels from domestic and funerary contexts in the region. The presence of miniature vessels in the funerary goods from Cave 1012 confirms the tradition of the EB IB well attested in many other contemporary sites. This fact confirms the possibility of detecting a later phase in other parts of the settlement that could be hidden in the long-lasting types of the PG1.

[EC]

---

138 Banning et al. 2005, fig. 13.

4. THE POTTERY: FUNCTION AND TYPOLOGIES

Plate	Exc. Num.	Type	Description	Parallels
4.1:1	JM.03.H76.O.207	C.A.1	Handmade, low fired, pale brown surfaces and grey core. Rare small limestone grits, chamotte. Simple ware.	Amiran et al. 1978, pl. 7:3; Betts & Helms 1991, fig. 148:528; 1992, fig. 213:18–20; fig. 214:14, 26; fig. 215:13–17; Callaway 1964, pl. IV:855–60, 738–1017; Dubis & Dabrowski 2002, fig. 8.3:4, 8.4:3; Kafafi 2001, fig. 33; pl. XIII: 646–721; Kenyon & Holland 1982, fig. 34:12–13 (type D.I); Schaub & Rast 1989, type 075; de Vaux 1955, fig. 5:3.
4.1:2	JM.03.H76.S.280	C.A.1	Handmade, low fired, grey core, pink surfaces and grey core. Rare small limestone grits. Simple ware.	
4.1:3	JM.03.H76.C.17	C.A.1	Handmade, low fired, pinkish red surfaces, light grey core. Rare small limestone grits. Simple ware.	
4.1:4	JM.15.CC.304.1	C.A.1	Handmade, medium-low fired, pink surfaces and core. Frequent small limestone grits. Simple ware.	
4.1:5	JM.05.R3.1	C.A.1	Handmade, medium-high fired, pink surfaces and core. Frequent small and medium dark rare light grits. Simple ware.	
4.1:6	JM.14.COVEST.110.1	C.A.1	Handmade, medium-high fired, pink surfaces and core. Frequent small and medium dark rare light grits. Simple ware.	
4.1:7	JM.14.SU.SO.5	C.A.1	Handmade, medium fired, pink surfaces and core. Rare small limestone grits. Simple ware.	
4.1:8	JM.03.H76.S.289	C.A.1	Handmade, medium fired, pink surfaces and core. Rare small limestone grits. Simple ware.	
4.1:9	JM.18.CSUD.1013.1	C.A.1	Handmade and wheel-finished, medium-high fired, reddish brown surfaces and core. Frequent small and medium dark rare light grits. Group 2 ware.	
4.1:10	JM.03.H76.O.212	C.A.1	Handmade, medium fired, reddish yellow surfaces, pink core. Rare small limestone and basalt grits. Simple ware.	
4.1:11	JM.05.R2.66	C.A.2	Handmade, medium fired, light red surfaces, reddish yellow core. Rare small dark and light mineral grits. Simple ware.	Amiran et al. 1978, pl. 7:4, 7, 19; Betts 1992, fig. 214:10–11, 13, 21, 25; Callaway 1964, pl. II:1; pl. III:7; pl. IV: 832–1326; pl. XIII: 667–94; Dubis & Dabrowski 2002, fig. 8.3:3, 5; fig. 8.4:6; 8.5:3; Kenyon & Holland 1982, fig. 34, 18 (type D.III).
4.1:12	JM.15.COVEST.131.1	C.A.2	Handmade, medium-high fired, reddish yellow surfaces and core. Very frequent small light and rare dark grits, chamotte. Simple ware.	
4.1:13	JM.053.H76.S.278	C.A.2	Handmade, low fired, light pinkish brown surface and core. Rare small limestone grits. Simple ware.	
4.1:14	JM.05.PS.42	C.A.2	Handmade, medium fired, dark grey inside, light reddish outside, pinkish white core. Medium-frequent small limestone grits, chamotte. Simple ware	
4.1:15	JM.05.R2.25	C.A.2	White wash and traces of red slip inside. Handmade, medium fired, light pinkish red surfaces, light red core. Frequent small light and dark grits. Simple ware.	
4.1:16	JM.03.H76.O.206	C.A.2	Handmade, medium-low fired, reddish yellow surfaces and core. Frequent small and medium limestone grits. Simple ware.	

Plate	Exc. Num.	Type	Description	Parallels
4.1:17	JM.15.COVEST.124.1	C.B.1a	Handmade, medium fired, reddish yellow surfaces and core. Frequent small light and dare dark grits. Simple ware.	Betts & Helms 1991, pl. 145: genre 470; 1992, genre 56; Kenyon & Holland 1982, fig. 36:15–16 (type O.IV, I.IV.b); Kenyon & Holland 1982, fig. 55:26 (type M.I.b).
4.1:18	JM.03.H76.O.195	C.B.1a	Handmade, low fired, light pinkish brown surfaces and core. Rare small limestone grits. Simple ware.	
4.1:19	JM.05.H75.47	C.B.1a	Handmade, medium fired, light reddish yellow surfaces and core. Frequent small light grits, rare dark grits. Simple ware.	
4.1:20	JM.05.H75.94	C.B.1a	Handmade, low fired, reddish yellow surfaces, grey core. Rare small limestone grits. Simple ware.	
4.1:21	JM.03.H76.S.282	C.B.1a	Handmade, low fired, reddish yellow surfaces, grey core. Rare small limestone grits. Simple ware.	
4.1:22	JM.05.R3.25	C.B.1a	Handmade, medium fired, light reddish yellow surfaces and core. Frequent small light grits, rare dark grits. Simple ware.	
4.1:23	JM.14.CEST.L101.3	C.B.1b	Handmade, medium fired, reddish yellow surfaces and core. Frequent small light grits, rare dark grits. Simple ware.	
4.1:24	JM.13.B.0.1	C.B.1b	Handmade, medium fired, reddish yellow surfaces and core. Frequent small light grits, rare dark grits. Simple ware.	
4.1:25	JM.05.R2.2	C.B.1b	Handmade, medium fired, reddish yellow surfaces and core. Frequent small light grits, rare dark grits. Simple ware.	
4.1:26	JM.06.H77.C1.7	C.B.2	Handmade, medium fired, reddish yellow surfaces and core. Frequent small light grits, rare dark grits. Simple ware.	Betts & Helms 1991, fig. 145:476; 1992, fig. 230:3, 5–6 (G 60); Callaway 1964, pl. III:8; Dubis & Dabrowski 2002, fig. 8.3:2; Kenyon & Holland 1982, fig. 34:31 (type F.1).
4.1:27	JM.03.H76.M.153	C.B.2	Traces of red slip (?). Handmade, low fired, pink inside, light red outside, and pink core. Frequent small limestone and basalt grits. Simple ware.	
4.1:28	JM.03.H76.S.283	C.B.2	Handmade, medium-low fired, reddish yellow surface and core. Rare small and medium limestone and rare quartz grits. Simple ware.	
4.1:29	JM.18.CSUD.417.4	C.B.2	Handmade, medium-low fired, reddish yellow surface and core. Rare small and medium limestone and rare quartz grits. Simple ware.	

4. THE POTTERY: FUNCTION AND TYPOLOGIES

Type C.A.1

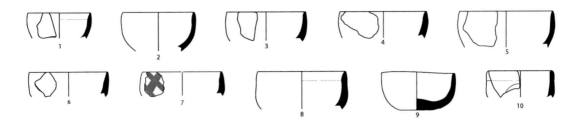

Type C.A.2

Type C.B.1

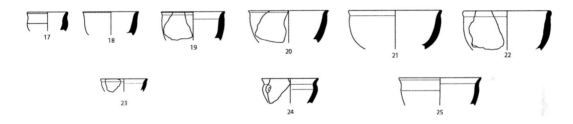

Type C.B.2

Plate 4.1: Types C.A.1, C.A.2, C.B.1a, C.B.1b, C.B.2.

Plate	Exc. Num.	Type	Description	Parallels
4.2:1	JM.05.H75.24	C.C.1	Traces of white wash. Handmade, medium fired, light red surfaces, reddish yellow core. Rare small light and dark grits. Simple ware.	Bets & Helms 1991, fig. 145:481; 1992, fig. 225:6; fig. 226:13, 25; Kenyon & Holland 1983, fig. 13:7; fig. 16:11, 21, 31 (burnished); fig. 17:13 (painted); fig. 18:8; Kenyon & Holland 1982, fig. 34:10 (type C.II); Rast & Schaub 2003, fig. 7.3:6.
4.2:2	JM.05.R2.1	C.C.1	Handmade, medium fired, reddish yellow surface and core. Frequent small limestone grits. Simple ware.	
4.2:3	JM.15.CC.302.7	C.C.1	Handmade, medium-high fired, reddish yellow surfaces and core. Frequent small limestone grits, chamotte. Simple ware.	
4.2:4	JM.05.H75.19	C.C.1	Handmade, medium fired, reddish yellow surface and core. Frequent small limestone grits. Simple ware.	
4.2:5	JM.03.H76.I.239	C.C.1-L	Handmade, low fired, reddish yellow surface and pink core. Rare small limestone grits. Simple ware.	
4.2:6	JM.05.R2.65	C.C.2	Handmade, medium fired, light red surfaces and core. Rare small limestone grits. Simple ware.	Amiran et al. 1978, pl. 7:4; Callaway 1964, pl. III:2; pl. V: 983–1015 (shallower); Kenyon & Holland 1982, fig. 34:19–20 (type D.III), 26–27 (type E.II); Fischer 2008, fig. 258:25; de Vaux 1955, fig. 3:1, 3–5 (with knob handles).
4.2:7	JM.05.R4.8	C.C.2	Handmade, medium fired, reddish yellow surfaces and core. Frequent small light and brown grits. Simple ware.	
4.2:8	JM.05.R5.8	C.C.2	Handmade, medium fired, light red surfaces, reddish yellow core. Rare small light and dark grits. Simple ware.	
4.2:9	JM.05.R2.68	C.C.2	Handmade, medium fired, reddish yellow surfaces and core. Rare limestone grits. Simple ware.	
4.2:10	JM.03.H76.I.251	C.C.3	Handmade, low fired, pink surfaces and core. Rare small limestone grits. Simple ware.	Amiran et al. 1978, pl. 7:21; Betts 1992, fig. 225:5; Kenyon & Holland 1982, fig. 36:10–12 (types O.I, O.II, O.II.b).
4.2:11	JM.05.R2.36	C.C.3	Handmade, medium fired, light red surfaces, reddish yellow core. Rare small light and dark grits. Simple ware.	
4.2:12	JM.14.COVEST.103.2	C.C.3	Handmade, medium fired, light red surfaces, reddish yellow core. Rare small light and dark grits. Simple ware.	
4.2:13	JM.03.H76.I.237	C.C.3	Handmade, low fired, light grey surfaces and core. Rare small and medium limestone grits. Simple ware.	
4.2:14	JM.03.H76.G.245	C.C.3-L	Handmade, low fired, light grey surfaces and core. Rare small and medium limestone grits. Simple ware.	
4.2:15	JM.05.H75.45	C.C.3-L	Handmade, medium fired, reddish yellow surfaces and core. Frequent small and medium limestone grits. Simple ware.	
4.2:16	JM.05.R2.34	C.C.3-L	Traces of red slip (?). Handmade, medium fired, reddish yellow surfaces and core. Frequent small limestone grits.	
4.2:17	JM.03.H76.K.256	C.C.3-L-	Handmade, low fired, light red inside, pink outside and core. Frequent small and medium limestone grits. Simple ware.	
4.2:18	JM.14.CEST.L101.4	C.C.4	Handmade, medium fired, light red surfaces, reddish yellow core. Rare small light and dark grits. Simple ware.	Hanbury-Tenison 1986, fig. 5:29.

4. THE POTTERY: FUNCTION AND TYPOLOGIES

Type C.C.1

Type C.C.2

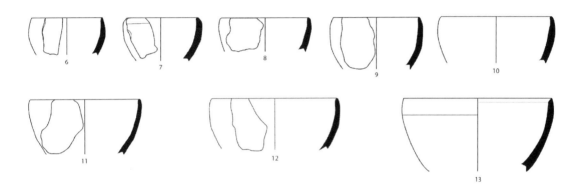

Type C.C.3

Type C.C.4

Plate 4.2: Types C.C.1, C.C.2, C.C.3, C.C.4.

4. THE POTTERY: FUNCTION AND TYPOLOGIES

Plate	Exc. Num.	Type	Description	Parallels
4.3:1	JM.15.CW.123.1	B.A.1	Handmade, medium-high fired, reddish brown surfaces and core. Rare small light and dark grits. Simple ware.	Amiran et al. 1978, pl. 7:6; Betts 1992, fig. 226:22; Callaway 1964, pl. II:2, pl. III:1, pl. IV:913, 951, 773, 906, 917; pl. V:853–990; Kenyon & Holland 1982, fig. 34:14–16 (type D.II); de Vaux 1955, fig. 7:2; fig. 11:2, 8.
4.3:2	JM.14.SU.NE.1	B.A.1	Line red painted. Handmade, medium-low fired, reddish yellow surfaces, light red core. Rare small limestone grits. Simple ware.	
4.3:3	JM.05.R2.3	B.A.1	Knob decoration, traces of red paint (?). Handmade, medium fired, reddish yellow surfaces and core. Rare small limestone and basalt grits. Simple ware.	
4.3:4	JM.14.SU.W12.1	B.A.1	Handmade, medium-high fired, reddish brown surfaces and core. Rare small light and dark grits. Simple ware.	
4.3:5	JM.05.H75.42	B.A.2	Knob decoration. Handmade, medium fired, red surfaces and core. Frequent small limestone grits and rare basalt grits. Simple ware.	Betts & Helms 1991, fig. 148:522, 527; 1992, fig. 255:3, 20–22, 28; Callaway 1964, pl. III:3; pl. V:947, 925, 916; Kenyon & Holland 1982, fig. 34:21–22 (type D.III); de Vaux 1955, fig. 7:1; fig. 11:7 (omphalos bases).
4.3:6	JM.13.B.42.3	B.A.2	Handmade, medium-low fired, reddish yellow surfaces and core. Frequent small limestone and basalt grits. Simple ware.	
4.3:7	JM.15.COVEST.123.12	B.A.2	Handmade, medium-high fired, reddish brown surfaces and core. Rare small light and dark grits. Simple ware.	
4.3:8	JM.05.R4.6	B.A.3	Handmade, low fired, reddish yellow surfaces and core. Rare limestone and basalt grits. Slightly porous simple ware.	Betts & Helms 1991, fig. 146:495–96; Callaway 1964, pl. V:768; Kenyon & Holland 1982, fig. 34:29 (type F.I); Kenyon & Holland 1982, fig. 54:8 (type F.II).
4.3:9	JM.03.H76.D.23	B.A.4	Handmade, low fired, reddish yellow surfaces and core. Rare limestone and basalt grits. Slightly porous simple ware.	Betts & Helms 1991, fig. 146:489; Callaway 1964, pl. III:10; pl. V:857a; Kenyon & Holland 1982, fig. 54:11–16 (type F.II.b).
4.3:10	JM.18.CSUD.417.5	B.A.5	Handmade, low fired, reddish yellow surfaces and core. Rare limestone and basalt grits. Slightly porous simple ware.	Betts 1992, fig. 226:9, 11; Callaway 1964, pl. V:848; Kenyon & Holland 1983, fig. 15:1; de Vaux 1955, fig. 7:9; fig. 11:4.

Plate	Exc. Num.	Type	Description	Parallels
4.3:11	JM.15.CEST.0.2	B.A.6-a	Handmade, medium fired, reddish yellow surfaces and core. Rare small light and dark grits. Simple ware.	Betts & Helms 1991, fig. 148:527; 1992, fig. 225:25; Gustavson-Gaube 1985, fig. 8:2a; Hanbury-Tenison 1986, fig. 10:4 (larger); Kenyon & Holland 1982, fig. 34:2 (type B.I); fig. 51:30 (type D.I.d); fig. 53:25–35 (type F.I.a-b); fig. 55:36–37 (type N.III); de Vaux 1955, fig. 5:2, 5; fig. 14:11.
4.3:12	JM.15.CC.305.1	B.A.6-a	Single red painted circle inside. Handmade, high fired, pink surfaces and core. Frequent small limestone grits. Chamotte. Simple ware.	
4.3:13	JM.05.R5.5	B.A.6-a	Handmade, low fired, reddish yellow surfaces and core. Rare limestone and basalt grits. Slightly porous simple ware.	
4.3:14	JM.06.H77.1	B.A.6-a-L	Handmade, low fired, reddish yellow surfaces and core. Rare limestone and basalt grits. Slightly porous simple ware.	
4.3:15	JM.18.CSUD.417.18	B.A.6-b	Red burnished. Handmade, medium-high fired, reddish brown surfaces and core. Frequent small and medium dark rare light grits. Group 2 ware.	
4.3:16	JM.18.CSUD.408.32	B.A.6-b	Red burnished. Handmade, medium-high fired, reddish brown surfaces and core. Frequent small and medium dark rare light grits. Group 2 ware.	
4.3:17	JM.H76.M.181	B.A.6-	Knob decoration. Handmade, medium-low fired, reddish yellow inside, pink outside and core. Rare small limestone grits. Simple ware.	
4.3:18	JM.18.CSUD.415.21	B.A.6-	Handmade, low fired, reddish yellow surfaces and core. Rare limestone and basalt grits. Slightly porous simple ware.	
4.3:19	JM.03.H76.G.32	B.A.7	Handmade, low fired, pink surfaces and core. Rare small limestone grits. Porous simple ware.	Betts 1992, fig. 225:27; Gustavson-Gaube 1985, fig. 8:8a; Kenyon & Holland 1983, fig. 16:10; Rast & Schaub 2003, fig. 7.3:1.

4. THE POTTERY: FUNCTION AND TYPOLOGIES

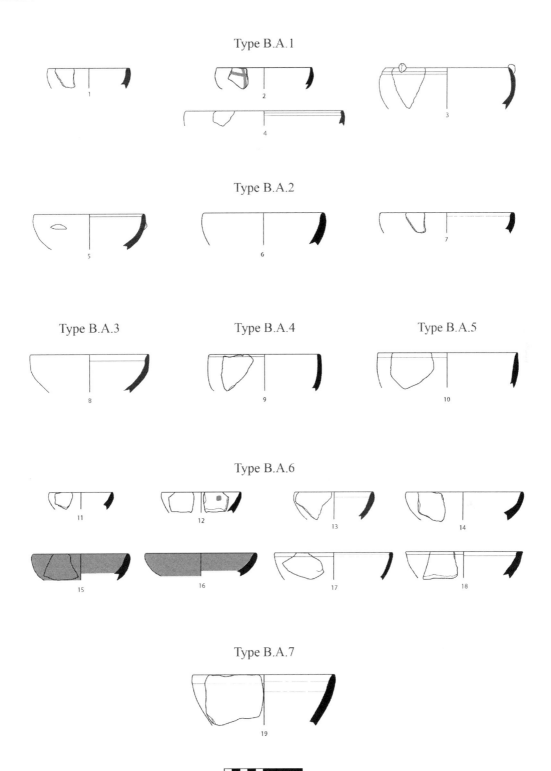

Plate 4.3: Types B.A.1, B.A.2, B.A.3, B.A.4, B.A.5, B.A.6, B.A.7.

Plate	Exc. Num.	Type	Description	Parallels
4.4:1	JM.13.A.5.1	B.B.1	Handmade, medium fired, reddish brown surfaces and core. Frequent small white grits. Coarse simple ware.	
4.4:2	JM.13.B.0.1	B.B.2	Handmade, medium fired, reddish brown surfaces and core. Frequent small white grits. Coarse simple ware.	Kenyon & Holland 1983, fig. 17:20
4.4:3	JM.03.H76.B.109	B.B.3	Handmade, medium fired, whitish surfaces and core. Basalt grits. Coarse white ware.	Betts 1992, fig. 233:6; Gustavson-Gaube 1985, fig. 9:5, 14c, 20; Kenyon & Holland 1983, fig. 18:1; fig. 121:22.
4.4:4	JM.13.B.42.1	B.B.3	Handmade, medium fired, reddish brown surfaces and core. Frequent small white grits. Coarse simple ware.	
4.4:5	JM.15.CEST.0.4	B.C.1	Handmade, medium-high fired, pink surfaces and core. Rare small light and dark grits. Simple ware.	Hanbury-Tenison 1986, fig. 6:2; Kenyon & Holland 1983, fig. 12:2 (only shape).
4.4:6	JM.05.R3.29	B.C.1	Handmade, medium-low fired, yellowish red. Frequent small and medium limestone and basalt grits. Cooking ware.	
4.4:7	JM.14.COVEST.102.1	B.C.2	Handmade, medium fired, grey surfaces and core. Medium frequent small and medium white grits. Cooking (?) ware.	Betts 1992, 231:2; Hanbury-Tenison 1986, fig. 5:45; Kenyon & Holland 1982, fig. 34:16 (type J.I.d).
4.4:8	JM.13.B.41.14	B.D.1	Handmade, medium fired, grey surfaces and core. Medium frequent small and medium white grits. Cooking (?) ware.	Betts & Helms 1991, fig. 147:511, 516; Hanbury-Tenison 1986, fig. 6:27.
4.4:9	JM.16.CSUD.408.1	D.A.1	Red burnished inside and outside. Handmade and wheel-finished, medium fired, light red inside, red outside and core. Very frequent small and medium basalt grits. Group 2 ware.	Amiran et al. 1978, pl. 13:38; Betts 1992, fig. 228:8–13; Fischer 2008, fig. 29:12–13; fig. 48:14–15; fig. 133:16; Kenyon & Holland 1982, fig. 49:27 (type A.II.c); de Vaux 1955, fig. 13:15, 17, 20; fig. 14:16 (larger).

4. THE POTTERY: FUNCTION AND TYPOLOGIES

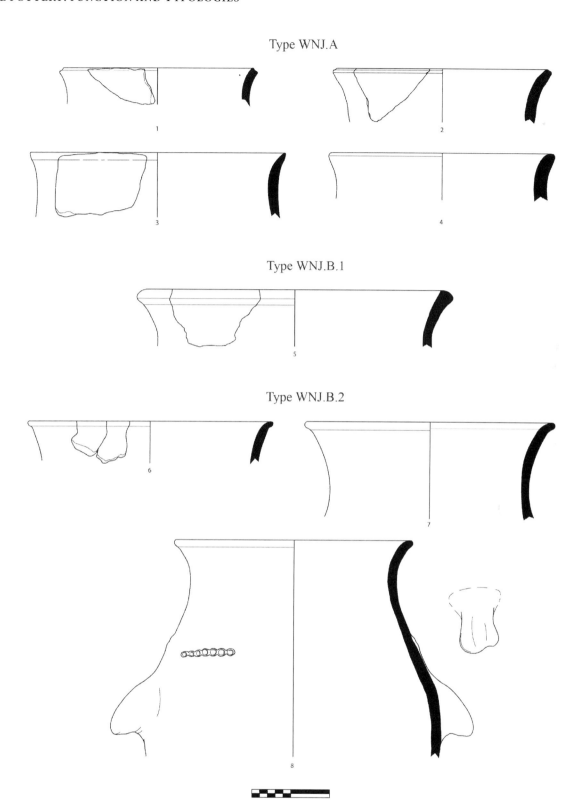

Plate 4.4: Types B.B.1, B.B.2, B.B.3, B.C.1, B.C.2, B.D.1, D.A.1.

4. THE POTTERY: FUNCTION AND TYPOLOGIES

Plate	Exc. Num.	Type	Description	Parallels
4.5:1	JM.14.SU.NO.1	JB.A.1	Handmade, low fired, reddish yellow inside, pink outside and core. Frequent medium limestone grits. Storage ware.	Amiran et al. 1978, pl. 12:4; Hanbury-Tenison 1985, fig. 9:8.
4.5:2	JM.14.COVEST.101.3	JB.A.1	Handmade, low fired, reddish yellow inside, pink outside and core. Frequent medium limestone grits. Storage ware.	
4.5:3	JM.14.SU.W12.3	JB.A.1	Handmade, low fired, reddish yellow inside, pink outside and core. Frequent medium limestone grits. Storage ware.	
4.5:4	JM.03.H76.S.129	JB.A.1	Handmade, low fired, reddish yellow inside, pink outside and core. Frequent medium limestone grits. Storage ware.	
4.5:5	JM.05.PS.27	JB.A.1	Handmade, high fired, pink outside, grey inside and core. Medium frequent small sandy grits. Simple ware.	
4.5:6	JM.03.H76.K.253	JB.A.1	Handmade, medium-low fired, pinkish white inside, pink outside and core. Rare small and medium limestone grits. Simple ware.	
4.5:7	JM.03.H76.O.193	JB.A.1	Handmade, medium-low fired, pink surfaces and core. Rare small limestone grits. Simple ware.	
4.5:8	JM.03.H76.O.192	JB.A.1	Handmade, medium-low fired, pink surfaces and core. Rare small limestone grits. Simple ware.	
4.5:9	JM.03.H76.S.272	JB.A.1	Handmade, medium fired, reddish yellow surfaces and core. Rare small limestone grits. Simple ware.	
4.5:10	JM.14.COVEST.0.10	JB.A.1	Handmade, medium fired, reddish yellow surfaces and core. Rare small limestone grits. Simple ware.	
4.5:11	JM.05.R2.37	JB.A.2-s	Handmade, medium fired, light red inside, reddish yellow outside and core. Frequent small limestone grits, rare brown grits. Simple ware.	Amiran et al. 1978, pl. 12:5 — here pl. 5:12; Betts & Helms 1991, fig. 144:464; 1992, fig. 205:14; Callaway 1972, pl. XIX:44; Gustavson-Gaube 1985, fig. 16:64, with red slip (n. 11); Kenyon & Holland 1982, fig. 58:28 (type D.I.a); fig. 59:8–10 (type E.II); Rast & Schaub 2003, fig. 7.2:8.
4.5:12	JM.14.COVEST.0.9	JB.A.2-L	Handmade, low fired, reddish yellow inside, pink outside and core. Frequent medium limestone grits. Storage ware.	
4.5:13	JM.15.CC.301.1	JB.A.2-s	Handmade, medium-high fired, reddish yellow surfaces and core. Very frequent small light and rare dark grits. Simple ware.	
4.5:14	JM.15.COVEST.131.2	JB.A.2-L	Handmade, medium fired, reddish yellow surface, and core. Frequent small light and rare dark grits. Simple ware.	
4.5:15	JM.05.PS.43	JB.A.2-s	Handmade, medium fired, reddish yellow surface, pink core. Medium frequent small limestone grits, chamotte and porous. Simple ware.	
4.5:16	JM.05.H75.50	JB.A.2-L	Traces of red paint (?). Handmade, medium fired, reddish yellow surfaces, pink core. Frequent small brown grits, rare white grits. Simple ware.	

Plate	Exc. Num.	Type	Description	Parallels
4.5:17	JM.13.B.42.2	JB.A.3	Handmade, low fired, reddish yellow inside, pink outside and core. Frequent medium limestone grits. Storage ware.	Amiran et al. 1978, pl. 10:3; Betts & Helms 1991, fig. 140:393–94; 1992, fig. 205:15–17; Callaway 1964, pl. XII:1451; pl. XIX:39; Fischer 2008, figs 1, 4–5; fig. 269:7–11; fig. 270:2; Gustavson-Gaube 1985, pl. 16:65; Kenyon & Holland 1982, fig. 38:29 (type B.III); de Vaux 1955, fig. 13:23; fig. 1:19, 22; fig. 3:11, 14.
4.5:18	JM.15.COVEST.114.1	JB.A.3	Traces of white wash. Handmade, medium-high fired, reddish yellow surfaces and core. Frequent small light and rare dark grits. Simple ware.	
4.5:19	JM.15.COVEST.111.1	JB.A.3	Handmade, medium-high fired, reddish yellow inside and core, pink outside. Frequent small and medium light and dark grits. Simple ware.	
4.5:20	JM.06.H77.C2.1	JB.A.3	Handmade, low fired, reddish yellow inside, pink outside and core. Frequent medium limestone grits. Storage ware.	
4.5:21	JM.03.H76.E.51	JB.A.3	Handmade, unevenly fired, reddish yellow inside, very pale brown outside and core. Rare small limestone grits. Simple ware.	
4.5:22	JM.15.COVEST.101.1	JB.A.3	Handmade, medium-high fired, yellow inside and core, reddish yellow outside. Frequent small light and dark grits. Simple ware.	
4.5:23	JM.03.H76.S.143	JB.A.3-L	Traces of red slip. Handmade, low fired, reddish yellow outside, pink inside and core. Rare small limestone grits. Simple ware.	

4. THE POTTERY: FUNCTION AND TYPOLOGIES

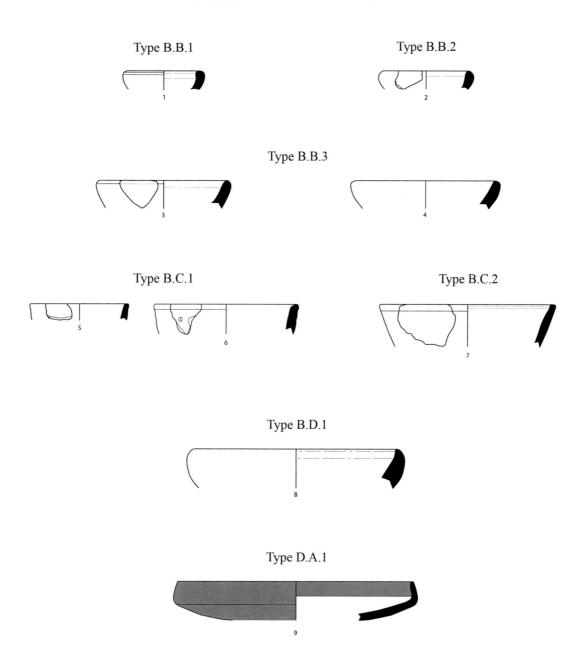

Plate 4.5: Types JB.A.1, JB.A.2, JB.A.3.

Plate	Exc. Num.	Type	Description	Parallels
4.6:1	JM.15.CEST.202.2	JB.B.1	Handmade, medium-high fired, reddish yellow surfaces and core. Very frequent small and medium light grits. Coarse simple ware.	
4.6:2	JM.06.H77.C1.1	JB.B.1	Handmade, medium-low fired, reddish yellow outside, pink inside and core. Frequent small and medium limestone grits. Simple ware.	
4.6:3	JM.14.SU.W12.1	JB.B.2	Handmade, medium-high fired, reddish yellow surfaces and core. Very frequent small and medium light grits. Coarse simple ware.	Callaway 1972, fig. 17:21; Fischer 2008, fig. 269:4, 12; fig. 270:2
4.6:4	JM.03.H76.L.169	JB.B.2	Handmade, medium-low fired, reddish yellow outside, pink inside and core. Frequent small and medium limestone grits. Simple ware.	
4.6:5	JM.03.H76.R.228	JB.B.2	Handmade, low, reddish yellow outside, pink inside and core. Rare small limestone grits. Simple ware.	
4.6:6	JM.03.H76.I.234	JB.B.3	Handmade, low, reddish yellow outside, pink inside and core. Rare small limestone grits. Simple ware.	
4.6:7	JM.18.CSUD.408.4	JB.B.4	Handmade and wheel-finished, medium fired, light red inside, red outside and core. Very frequent small and medium basalt grits. Group 2 ware.	
4.6:8	JM.18.CSUD.417.16	JB.C.3	Handmade and wheel-finished, medium fired, light red inside, red outside and core. Very frequent small and medium basalt grits. Group 2 ware.	Betts 1992, fig. 208:6.
4.6:9	JM.03.H76.I.238	JB.C.1	Handmade, low fired, reddish yellow outside, pink inside and core. Rare small limestone and basalt grits. Simple ware.	Hanbury-Tenison 1986, fig. 6:12; de Vaux 1955, fig. 13:19.
4.6:10	JM.05.R1.28	JB.C.1	Traces of red paint (?). Handmade, medium fired, reddish yellow surfaces and core. Frequent small and medium light and dark grits. Storage ware.	
4.6:11	JM.05.R2.45	JB.C.1-L	Red paint, trickled. Handmade, medium fired, light red surfaces and core. Frequent small and medium light and dark grits. Storage ware.	
4.6:12	JM.13.A.1.6	JB.C.2	Handmade, medium-high fired, reddish yellow surfaces and core. Very frequent small and medium light grits. Coarse simple ware.	Betts 1992, fig. 205:2; Kenyon & Holland 1982, fig. 45:4 (type D.2); de Vaux 1955, fig. 1:20; fig. 14:7, 23.
4.6:13	JM.03.H76.O.182	JB.C.2	Handmade, unevenly medium-low fired, pink surfaces, grey core. Rare small limestone grits. Simple ware.	
4.6:14	JM.03.H76.E.66	JB.C.2	Handmade, low fired, reddish yellow surfaces and core. Medium frequent medium limestone grits and rare basalt grits. Storage ware.	
4.6:15	JM.03.H76.S.149	JB.C.2	Handmade, medium-low fired, reddish yellow outside, very pale brown inside and core. Rare small and medium limestone grits. Simple ware.	
4.6:16	JM.18.CSUD.415.13	JB.C.2	Handmade and wheel-finished, medium fired, light red inside, red outside and core. Very frequent small and medium basalt grits. Group 2 ware.	

4. THE POTTERY: FUNCTION AND TYPOLOGIES

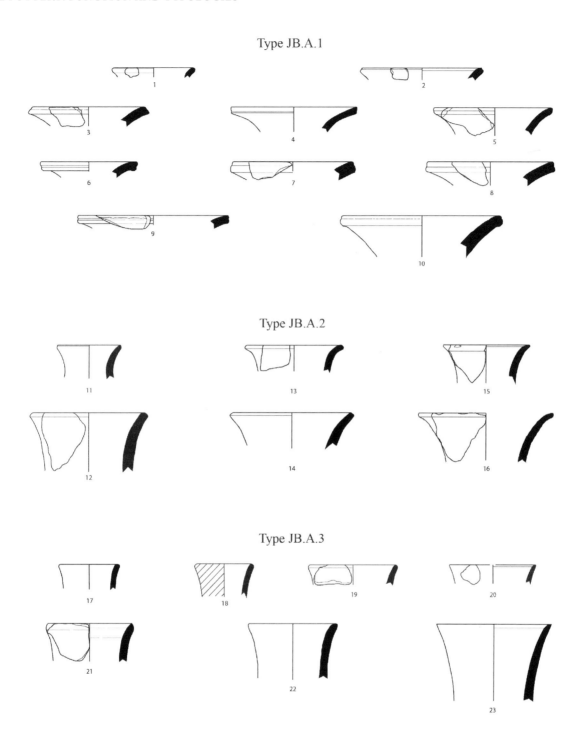

Plate 4.6: Types JB.B.1, JB.B.2, JB.B.3, JB.B.4, JB.C.1, JB.C.2, JB.C.3.

Plate	Exc. Num.	Type	Description	Parallels
4.7:1	JM.03.H76.M.174	NJ.A.1-a	Handmade, unevenly low fired, reddish yellow surfaces, grey core. Rare small limestone and basalt grits. Simple ware.	Callaway 1964, pl. XVIII:56; Dubis & Dabrowski 2002, 8.5:2 (painted); Kenyon & Holland 1982, fig. 59:16–17 (type F.I.a-b); Schaub & Rast 1989, type 0161, 0225, 0234; Rast & Schaub 2003, fig. 7.2:11.
4.7:2	JM.03.H76.D.22	NJ.A.1-a	Handmade, low, reddish yellow surfaces and core. Rare small limestone grits. Simple ware.	
4.7:3	JM.03.H76.O.186	NJ.A.1-a	Handmade, unevenly low fired, pinkish red surfaces, grey core. Rare small limestone grits. Simple ware.	
4.7:4	JM.15.COVEST.125.4	NJ.A.1-L	Handmade, low, reddish yellow surfaces and core. Rare small limestone grits. Simple ware.	
4.7:5	JM.03.H76.E.62	NJ.A.1-b	Handmade, medium fired, very pale brown inside and core, pink outside. Rare small limestone grits. Simple ware.	
4.7:6	JM.03.H76.Q.82	NJ.A.1-b	Handmade, low fired, reddish yellow surfaces and core. Rare small limestone grits. Simple ware.	
4.7:7	JM.14.SU.NE.2	NJ.A.2	Handmade, low, reddish yellow surfaces and core. Rare small limestone grits. Simple ware.	Callaway 1964, pl. XV:681; Dubis & Dabrowski 2002, fig. 8.3:1; Hanbury-Tenison 1986, fig. 10:1; Kenyon & Holland 1982, fig. 59:18 (type F.I.b).
4.7:8	JM.03.H76.M.179	NJ.A.2	Handmade, unevenly medium fired, reddish yellow surfaces, light grey core. Frequent small, medium, and large limestone grits. Storage ware.	
4.7:9	JM.05.R2.54	NJ.A.2	Handmade, low fired, light red surfaces and core. Frequent small white grits. Storage ware.	
4.7:10	JM.03.H76.K.162	NJ.A.2	Handmade, unevenly low fired, reddish yellow outside, pink inside and core. Rare small limestone grits. Storage ware.	
4.7:11	JM.14.COVEST.102.20	NJ.A.2	Traces of trickle red wash from the rim. Handmade, low, reddish yellow surfaces and core. Rare small limestone grits. Simple ware.	
4.7:12	JM.13.B.42.4	NJ.A.3-s	Handmade, low fired, reddish yellow surfaces, pink core. Rare small limestone and basalt grits. Storage ware.	Hanbury-Tenison 1986, fig. 6:6.
4.7:13	JM.03.H76.T.121	NJ.A.3	Handmade, low fired, reddish yellow surfaces, pink core. Rare small limestone and basalt grits. Storage ware.	
4.7:14	JM.03.H76.G.27	NJ.A.3	Handmade, well fired, reddish yellow surfaces, pink core. Medium frequent small and medium limestone and rare basalt grits. Storage ware.	
4.7:15	JM.05.R3.22	NJ.A.4	Handmade, medium fired, light red surfaces, reddish yellow core. Frequent small limestone and rare basalt grits. Simple ware.	Dubis & Dabrowski 2002, fig. 8.4:1; Kenyon & Holland 1982, fig. 59:23.27 (type F.II.b).
4.7:16	JM.03.H76.O.180	NJ.A.4	Handmade, low fired, very pale brown surfaces, light grey core. Rare small limestone grits. Simple ware.	
4.7:17	JM.03.H76.T.102	NJ.A.4	Handmade, low fired, reddish yellow surfaces and core. Rare small limestone and rare basalt grits. Simple ware.	
4.7:8	JM.15.CC.302.3	NJ.A.4-L	Handmade, medium fired, pink surfaces and core. Frequent small and medium limestone grits. Storage ware.	

4. THE POTTERY: FUNCTION AND TYPOLOGIES

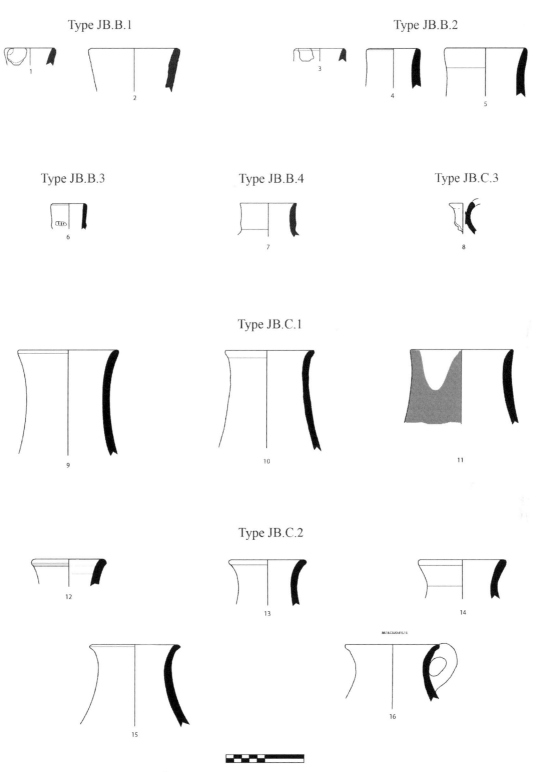

Plate 4.7: Types NJ.A.1, NJ.A.2, NJ.A.3, NJ.A.4.

Plate	Exc. Num.	Type	Description	Parallels
4.8:1	JM.03.H76.K.158	NJ.B.1	Handmade, low fired, reddish yellow outside, pink inside and core. Rare small limestone and basalt grits. Simple ware.	Betts 1992, fig. 210:9; fig. 205:10–13; Kenyon & Holland 1982, fig. 59:1 (type E.I.a); de Vaux 1955, fig. 13:3, 14; fig. 14:21
4.8:2	JM.03.H76.D.25	NJ.B.1	Handmade, unevenly low fired, reddish yellow surfaces and core. Rare small limestone grits, porous. Simple ware.	
4.8:3	JM.03.H76.T.119	NJ.B.1	Handmade, medium fired, pink surfaces and core. Rare small limestone grits. Simple ware.	
4.8:4	JM.05.PS.2	NJ.B.1	Handmade, medium fired, reddish yellow surfaces and core. Frequent small light and dark grits. Simple ware.	
4.8:5	JM.03.H76.S.290	NJ.B.2	Handmade, medium-low fired, reddish yellow surfaces and core. Rare small limestone grits. Simple ware.	Betts & Helms 1991, fig. 126:200–03; 1992, fig. 258:1; Hanbury-Tenison 1986, fig. 6:50; Kenyon & Holland 1982, fig. 59:29 (type F.II.c).
4.8:6	JM.03.H76.O.188	NJ.B.2	Handmade, low fired, reddish surfaces, grey outside. Frequent small and medium limestone grits. Storage ware.	
4.8:7	JM.03.H76.G.247	NJ.B.2	Handmade, unevenly low fired, pinkish red surfaces, grey core. Rare small limestone grits. Simple ware.	
4.8:8	JM.03.H76.S.136	NJ.B.2	Handmade, medium-low fired, reddish yellow surfaces, pink core. Frequent small limestone grits. Simple ware.	
4.8:9	JM.03.H76.S.276	NJ.B.2	Handmade, medium-low fired, reddish yellow surfaces, very pale brown core. Rare small and medium limestone and basalt grits. Storage ware.	
4.8:10	JM.03.H76.M.175	NJ.B.2	Handmade, medium-low fired, reddish yellow inside, pink outside and core. Rare small limestone grits. Simple ware.	
4.8:11	JM.03.H76.S.139	NJ.B.2	Handmade, low fired, reddish yellow inside, pink outside and core. Rare small limestone grits. Simple ware.	
4.8:12	JM.15.COVEST.111.6	NJ.B.3	Handmade, medium-high fired, yellow surfaces and core. Very frequent small light and dark grits. Storage ware.	Betts & Helms 1991, fig. 127:211; Hanbury-Tenison 1986, fig. 7:44.
4.8:13	JM.15.COVEST.125.5	NJ.B.3	Handmade, medium-high fired, reddish yellow surfaces and core. Rare small limestone grits. Storage ware.	
4.8:14	JM.05.R4.34	NJ.B.3	White wash. Handmade, medium fired, light red surfaces, reddish yellow core. Frequent small limestone grits, rare dark grits. Storage ware.	
4.8:15	JM.15.COVEST.127.2	NJ.B.3	Handmade, medium fired, pink surfaces and core. Very frequent limestone grits. Storage ware.	

4. THE POTTERY: FUNCTION AND TYPOLOGIES

Type NJ.B.1

Type NJ.B.2

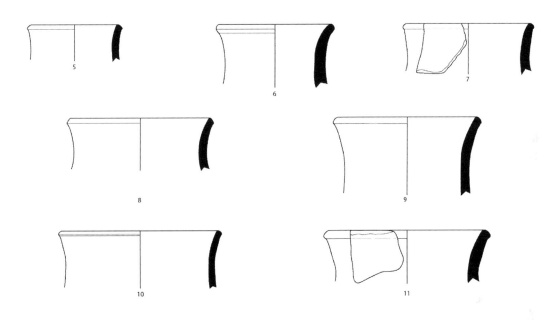

Type NJ.B.3

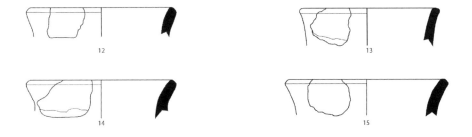

Plate 4.8: Types NJ.B.1, NJ.B.2, NJ.B.3.

Plate	Exc. Num.	Type	Description	Parallels
4.9:1	JM.14.COVEST.103.4	NJ.C.1	Handmade, low, reddish yellow surfaces and core. Rare small limestone grits. Storage ware.	Callaway 1964, pl. XV:380 (only shape); pl. XVIII:103, 35 (?); pl. XIX:97, 1192 (?); Hanbury-Tenison 1986, fig. 6:24 (different orientation); Kenyon & Holland 1983, fig. 16:12; fig. 18:12; 114:1.
4.9:2	JM.15.COVEST.116.1	NJ.C.1	Handmade, medium-high fired, reddish yellow surfaces and core. Very frequent small and medium limestone grits. Storage ware.	
4.9:3	JM.15.COVEST.123.1	NJ.C.2	Handmade, medium-high fired, reddish yellow surfaces and core. Very frequent small and medium limestone grits. Storage ware.	Callaway 1964, pl. XII:741; Hanbury-Tenison 1986, fig. 5:41.
4.9:4	JM.06.H77.101	NJ.C.2	Handmade, medium-high fired, reddish yellow surfaces and core. Very frequent small and medium limestone grits. Storage ware.	
4.9:5	JM.15.COVEST.135.1	NJ.C.3	Handmade, medium-high fired, reddish yellow surfaces and core. Very frequent small and medium limestone grits. Storage ware.	Callaway 1972, fig. 17:16.
4.9:6	JM.03.H76.P.230	NJ.C.4	Handmade, unevenly low fired, reddish yellow surfaces, grey core. Rare small limestone and basalt grits. Storage ware.	Hanbury-Tenison 1986, fig. 7:17; Kenyon & Holland 1982, fig. 37:27 (type C.II.b).
4.9:7	JM.03.H76.C.15	NJ.C.4	Handmade, not well fired, reddish yellow surfaces, light grey core. Medium frequent small and medium limestone grits. Storage ware.	
4.9:8	JM.06.H77.102	NJ.D.1	Handmade, unevenly low fired, reddish yellow surfaces, grey core. Rare small limestone and basalt grits. Storage ware.	Hanbury-Tenison 1986, fig. 6:8; Kenyon & Holland 1983, fig. 121:6, 13–14; 1982, fig. 59:11–12 (type E.II).
4.9:9	JM.14.CEST.L101.0.5	NJ.D.2	Handmade, medium fired, reddish yellow surfaces, pinkish grey core. Frequent small light and dark grits.	
4.9:10	JM.05.R4.35	NJ.D.3	Handmade, medium fired, reddish yellow surfaces, pinkish grey core. Frequent small light and dark grits.	
4.9:11	JM.05.H75.110	NJ.D.4	Handmade, medium fired, reddish yellow surfaces, pinkish grey core. Frequent small light and dark grits.	De Vaux 1955, fig. 4:10.

4. THE POTTERY: FUNCTION AND TYPOLOGIES 149

Type NJ.B.1

Type NJ.B.2

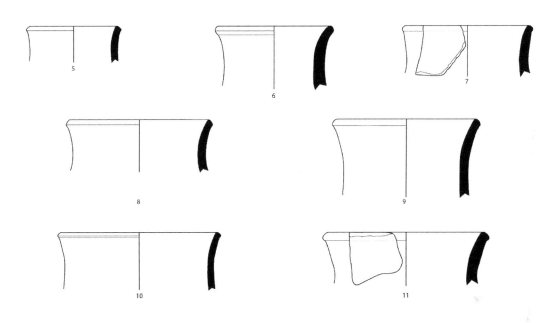

Type NJ.B.3

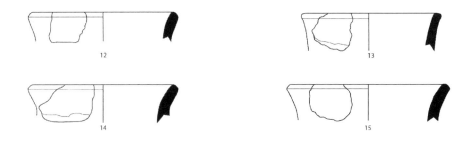

Plate 4.9: Types NJ.C.1, NJ.C.2, NJ.C.3, NJ.C.4, NJ.D.1, NJ.D.2, NJ.D.3, NJ.D.4.

Plate	Exc. Num.	Type	Description	Parallels
4.10:1	JM.03.H76.B.113	WNJ.A.1	Handmade, medium fired, pink outside, reddish yellow inside and core. Rare small limestone grits. Simple ware.	Betts & Helms 1991, fig. 126:193, 195; Douglas & Kafafi 2000, fig. 6.4:1.
4.10:2	JM.06.H77.C2.2	WNJ.A.1	Handmade, medium fired, pink outside, reddish yellow inside and core. Rare small limestone grits. Simple ware.	
4.10:3	JM.03.H76.S.275	WNJ.A.2	Handmade, unevenly medium-low fired, light red inside, reddish yellow outside, grey core. Rare small and medium limestone grits. Storage (?) ware.	Betts & Helms 1991, fig. 126:194; 1992, fig. 196:4, 8.
4.10:4	JM.03.H76.E.47	WNJ.A.3	Handmade, badly fired, reddish yellow surfaces, grey core. Rare small limestone grits. Storage (?) ware.	Betts & Helms 1991, fig. 123:197.
4.10:5	JM.15.COVEST.125.6	WNJ.B.1	Handmade, medium fired, reddish yellow inside, pink outside and core. Frequent small light and dark grits. Storage ware.	Betts & Helms 1991, fig. 127:209; 1992, fig. 185:1.
4.10:6	JM.15.CC.305.2	WNJ.B.2	Handmade, medium-high fired, pink surfaces and core. Very frequent small light and rare dark grits. Storage ware.	Betts & Helms 1991, fig. 124:180–81; fig. 125:182–87; fig. 126:200–03; 1992, fig. 178:4–6; Kenyon & Holland 1983, fig. 19:1; fig. 113:22, 26.
4.10:7	JM.03.H76.K.156	WNJ.B.2	Handmade, low fired, reddish yellow surfaces and core. Rare medium limestone and basalt grits. Storage (?) ware.	
4.10:8	JM.05.R1.35	WNJ.B.2	Applied rope decoration. Handmade, medium fired, light red inside, reddish yellow outside and core. Frequent small and medium light and dark grits. Storage ware	

4. THE POTTERY: FUNCTION AND TYPOLOGIES

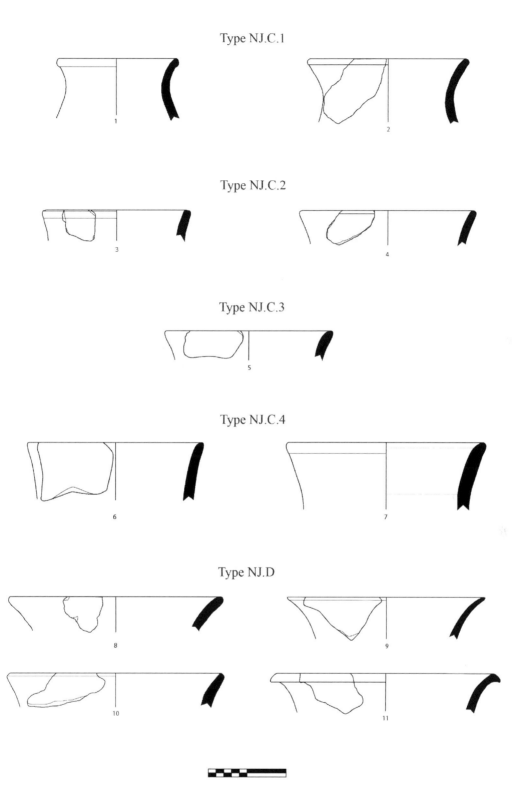

Plate 4.10: Types WNJ.A.1, WNJ.A.2, WNJ.A.3, WNJ.B.1, WNJ.B.2.

Plate	Exc. Num.	Type	Description	Parallels
4.11:1	JM.03.H76.S.287	OJ.A.1	Handmade, low fired, reddish yellow surfaces and core. Rare medium basalt and limestone. Simple ware.	Amiran et al. 1978, pl. 9:7; Betts 1992, fig. 193:16; Callaway 1964, pl. III:16; Hanbury-Tenison 1986, fig. 5:44; Dubis & Dabrowski 2002, fig. 8.4:2; Kenyon & Holland 1982, fig. 37:4 (type A.I.d); de Vaux 1955, fig. 13:5.
4.11:2	JM.03.H76.K.257	OJ.A.1	Handmade, low fired, reddish yellow surfaces and core. Rare small limestone grits. Simple ware.	
4.11:3	JM.05.H75.40	OJ.B.1	Handmade, well fired, red surfaces and core. Frequent small limestone grits. Simple ware.	
4.11:4	JM.15.COVEST.116.4	OJ.C.1	Handmade, medium-high fired, reddish yellow surfaces and core. Frequent small and medium limestone grits. Storage ware.	Amiran et al. 1978, pl. 12:13; de Vaux 1955, fig. 11:22; fig. 1:18.
4.11:5	JM.18.CSUD.415.4	LSJ.A.1	Red burnished inside and outside. Handmade and wheel-finished, medium fired, light red inside, red outside and core. Very frequent small and medium basalt grits. Group 2 ware.	Betts 1992, fig. 201:4; Gustavson-Gaube 1985, type 51d; Douglas & Kafafi 2000, fig. 6.4:4; de Vaux 1955, fig. 6:11; 1:6, 17.
4.11:6	JM.03.H76.T.125	LSJ.A.2	Handmade, low fired, reddish yellow inside, pink outside and core. Rare small limestone grits. Simple ware.	
4.11:7	JM.03.H76.T.120	LSJ.A.2	Handmade, low fired, light red outside, reddish yellow inside and core. Frequent small limestone and basalt grits. Storage ware.	
4.11:8	JM.03.H76.I.240	LSJ.A.3	Handmade, low fired, very pale brown inside, pink outside and core. Rare small limestone grits. Storage ware, porous.	
4.11:9	JM.18.CSUD.415.7	LSJ.B.1	Handmade, unevenly medium-low fired, reddish yellow surface, grey core. Rare small limestone grits. Simple ware.	Amiran 1978, pl. 9:5; 2 Callaway 1972, fig. 27:17
4.11:10	JM.05.R4.32	LSJ.B.2	Handmade and wheel-finished, medium fired, light red inside, red outside and core. Very frequent small and medium basalt grits. Group 2 ware.	
4.11:11	JM.14.CEST.L101.1	LSJ.B.3	Handmade, unevenly medium-low fired, reddish yellow surface, grey core. Rare small limestone grits. Simple ware.	
4.11:12	JM.03.H76.Q.84	LSJ.B.3	Handmade, unevenly medium-low fired, reddish yellow surface, grey core. Rare small limestone grits. Simple ware.	
4.11:13	JM.18.CSUD.415.9	LSJ.B.4	Handmade, unevenly medium-low fired, reddish yellow surface, grey core. Rare small limestone grits. Simple ware.	
4.11:14	JM.03.H76.S.133	LSJ.C.1	Handmade, medium-low fired, pink surfaces and core. Rare small limestone grits. Simple ware.	Gustavson-Gaube 1985, type 48h.
4.11:15	JM.05.R1.38	LSJ.C.1	Handmade, medium fired, reddish yellow surfaces and core. Frequent small and medium light and dark grits. Storage ware.	
4.11:16	JM.03.H76.S.130	LSJ.C.2	Handmade, low fired, pink surfaces and core. Rare small and medium limestone grits. Simple (?) ware.	Betts 1992, fig. 180:5.

4. THE POTTERY: FUNCTION AND TYPOLOGIES

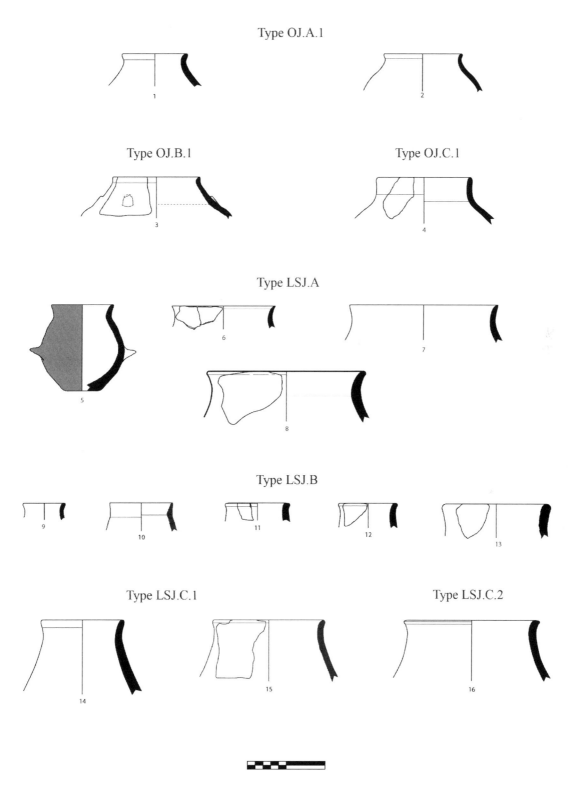

Plate 4.11: Types OJ.A.1, OJ.B.1, OJ.C.1, LSJ.A.1, LSJ.A.2, LSJ.A.3, LSJ.B.1, LSJ.B.2, LSJ.B.3, LSJ.B.4, LSJ.C.1, LSJ.C.2.

Plate	Exc. Num.	Type	Description	Parallels
4.12:1	JM.03.H76.S.144	LSJ.C.3	Handmade, unevenly low fired, reddish yellow surfaces, dark grey core. Frequent small limestone and rare quartz grits. Storage ware.	Hanbury-Tenison 1986, fig. 7:1; Kenyon & Holland 1982, fig. 37:8 (type A.III).
4.12:2	JM.15.COVEST.136.1	LSJ.C.3	Handmade, medium fired, light red surfaces and core. Very frequent small light and dark grits, chamotte. Storage ware.	
4.12:3	JM.03.H76.S.140	LSJ.C.3	Applied rope decoration. Handmade, unevenly low fired, reddish yellow surfaces, grey core. Rare small limestone and basalt grits. Storage (?) ware.	
4.12:4	JM.03.H76.K.254	LSJ.D.1	Handmade, low fired, reddish yellow surfaces and core. Frequent small and medium limestone grits. Storage ware.	Betts 1992, fig. 177:3; Kenyon & Holland 1982, fig. 38:28 (type B.II.b); Hanbury-Tenison 1986, fig. 7:49.
4.12:5	JM.03.H76.S.266	LSJ.D.1	Handmade, low fired, reddish yellow surfaces and core. Rare small limestone grits. Simple (?) ware.	
4.12:6	JM.03.H76.K.249	LSJ.D.1	Knob decoration. Handmade, low fired, pink surfaces and core. Rare small and medium limestone grits. Storage (?) ware.	
4.12:7	JM.03.H76.K.259	LSJ.D.1	Handmade, low fired, reddish yellow surfaces, pinkish grey core. Frequent medium limestone and rare basalt grits. Storage ware.	
4.12:8	JM.03.H76.C.14	LSJ.D.1	Handmade, well fired, very pale brown surfaces, grey core. Rare small and medium limestone and rare basalt grits. Storage (?) ware.	
4.12:9	JM.03.H76.S.74	LSJ.D.1	Knob decoration. Handmade, very low fired, reddish yellow surfaces and core. Rare small limestone, chamotte, and silex (?) grits. Storage (?) ware.	

4. THE POTTERY: FUNCTION AND TYPOLOGIES 155

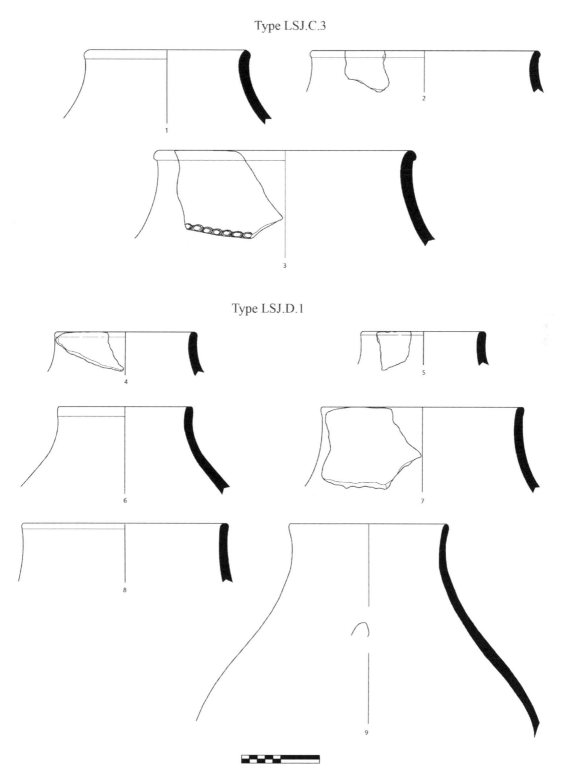

Plate 4.12: Types LSJ.C.3, LSJ.D.1.

Plate	Exc. Num.	Type	Description	Parallels
4.13:1	JM.03.H76.Q.80	LSJ.D.2	Traces of white wash on the rim. Handmade, low fired, pink surfaces and core. Rare small and medium limestone grits. Storage (?) ware.	Hanbury-Tenison 1986, fig. 6:47.
4.13:2	JM.18.CSUD.415.22	LSJ.D.2	Handmade, low fired, reddish yellow surfaces and core. Frequent small and medium limestone grits. Storage ware.	
4.13:3	JM.14.SU.W12.4	LSJ.D.2	Handmade, low fired, reddish yellow surfaces and core. Frequent small and medium limestone grits. Storage ware.	
4.13:4	JM.14.SU.SO.2	LSJ.D.2	Handmade, low fired, reddish yellow surfaces and core. Frequent small and medium limestone grits. Storage ware.	
4.13:5	JM.05.R2.55	LSJ.D.3	Handmade, medium fired, reddish yellow surfaces and core. Frequent small and medium light and dark grits. Storage ware.	Betts 1992, fig. 177:6–7; Gustavson-Gaube 1985, type 56c-d.
4.13:6	JM.14.CEST.201.4	LSJ.D.3	Red painted band from the rim. Handmade, low fired, reddish yellow surfaces and core, frequent small limestone grits. Storage (?) ware.	
4.13:7	JM.14.COVEST.102.11	LSJ.D.3	Red painted band from the rim, applied vertical decoration with small circular impressions. Handmade, low fired, reddish yellow surfaces and core, frequent small limestone grits. Storage (?) ware.	
4.13:8	JM.05.H75.51	H.A.1	Handmade, medium fired, pink inside, pinkish grey outside and core. Frequent small and medium limestone grits, chaff and porous. Storage ware.	Gustavson-Gaube 1985, type 54; Kenyon & Holland 1983, fig. 12:20, fig. 14:12 (larger).
4.13:9	JM.15.CC.302.5	H.A.1	Handmade, low fired, reddish yellow surfaces and core, frequent small limestone grits. Storage (?) ware.	
4.13:10	JM.05.R3.34	H.A.1	Handmade, medium fired, pink inside, pinkish grey outside and core. Frequent small and medium limestone grits, chaff and porous. Storage ware.	
4.13:11	JM.05.H75.36	H.A.1	Knob decoration. Handmade, medium fired, reddish grey outside, reddish yellow outside and core. Frequent small and medium light, rare dark grits. Storage ware.	
4.13:12	JM.15.COVEST.133.2	H.A.1	Handmade, medium-high fired, light red inside, reddish yellow outside and core. Very frequent small and medium light, rare small dark grits. Storage ware.	

4. THE POTTERY: FUNCTION AND TYPOLOGIES

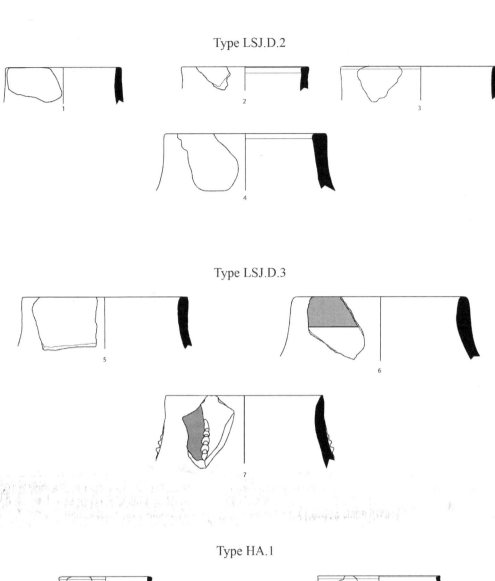

Plate 4.13: Types LSJ.D.2, LSJ.D.3, H.A.1.

Plate	Exc. Num.	Type	Description	Parallels
4.14:1	JM.14.COVEST.102.4	H.A.2	Handmade, low fired, reddish yellow surfaces and core, frequent small limestone grits. Storage (?) ware.	Hanbury-Tenison 1986, fig. 5:43; Kenyon & Holland 1983, fig. 121:30.
4.14:2	JM.03.H76.P.231	H.A.3	Handmade, low fired, reddish yellow surfaces and core, frequent small limestone grits. Storage (?) ware.	Hanbury-Tenison 1986, fig. 5:42.
4.14:3	JM.03.H76.B.110	H.A.3	Handmade, unevenly medium fired, pink inside, reddish yellow outside, grey core. Rare small limestone grits. Storage ware.	
4.14:4	JM.14.COVEST.102.6	H.A.3	Handmade, low fired, reddish yellow surfaces and core, frequent small limestone grits. Storage ware.	
4.14:5	JM.05.R4.18	H.A.4	Handmade, medium fired, red surfaces, light red core. Frequent small and medium light and dark grits. Storage ware.	Gustavson-Gaube 1985, type KH; Kenyon & Holland 1983, fig. 13:30.
4.14:6	JM.14.COVEST.0.2	H.A.5	Handmade, low fired, reddish yellow surfaces and core, frequent small limestone grits. Storage ware.	Betts 1992, fig. 141:1–5; Douglas & Kafafi 2000, fig. 6.2:2; Kenyon & Holland 1983, fig. 121:34.
4.14:7	JM.14.SU.L10.1	H.A.5	Handmade, low fired, reddish yellow surfaces and core, frequent small limestone grits. Storage ware.	
4.14:8	JM.14.SU.L10.4	H.A.5	Handmade, low fired, reddish yellow surfaces and core, frequent small limestone grits. Storage ware.	

4. THE POTTERY: FUNCTION AND TYPOLOGIES

Type HA.2

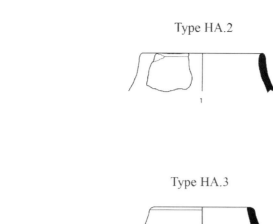

Type HA.3

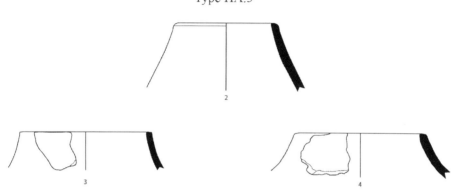

Type HA.4

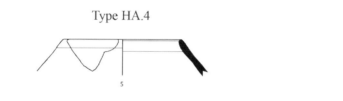

Type HA.5

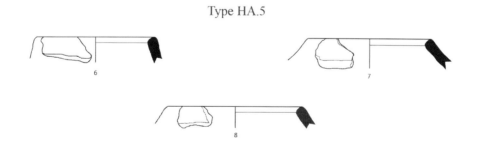

Plate 4.14: Types H.A.2, H.A.3, H.A.4, H.A.5.

Plate	Exc. Num.	Type	Description	Parallels
4.15:1	JM.05.R3.27	H.B.1	Handmade, low fired, yellowish red inside, reddish yellow outside, dark grey core. Very frequent small and medium light and dark grits. Cooking ware.	
4.15:2	JM.14.COVEST.102.3	H.B.1	Handmade, low fired, yellowish red inside, reddish yellow outside, dark grey core. Very frequent small and medium light and dark grits. Cooking ware.	
4.15:3	JM.05.R3.23	H.B.1	Horizontal line of seed-like impressions. Handmade, medium fired, light red surfaces, reddish yellow core. Frequent small light and dark grits. Simple ware.	
4.15:4	JM.03.H76.G.243	H.B.1	Horizontal line of seed-like impressions. Handmade, low fired, reddish brown outside, light red inside and core. Very frequent small and medium limestone grits. Cooking ware.	
4.15:5	JM.03.H76.O.213	H.B.1	Horizontal line of seed-like impressions. Handmade, low fired, grey outside, reddish yellow inside and core. Rare small limestone grits. Cooking (?) ware.	
4.15:6	JM.18.CSUD.417.18	H.B.1	Handmade, low fired, yellowish red inside, reddish yellow outside, dark grey core. Very frequent small and medium light and dark grits. Cooking ware.	
4.15:7	JM.03.H76.G.41	H.B.1	Handmade, very low fired, reddish yellow surfaces, pinkish grey core. Frequent small and medium limestone and quartz grits. Cooking ware.	
4.15:8	JM.03.H76.G.28	H.B.1	Knob decoration and horizontal line of seed-like impressions. Handmade, low fired, reddish brown outside, light red inside and core. Very frequent small and medium limestone grits. Cooking ware.	Amiran et al. 1978, pl. 8:13, 24; Betts & Helms 1991, fig. 116:83–84; 1992, fig. 146:4; Gustavson-Gaube 1985, type 32; Hanbury-Tenison 1986, fig. 6:4, 16; 7:45; Douglas & Kafafi 2000, fig. 6.2:1; fig. 6.3:3, fig. 36:3–4; Kenyon & Holland 1982, fig. 39:1–4 (type A.I); fig. 64:5 (type A.I.b), 17 (type A.II.e), 31 (type C.I.a); Rast & Schaub 2003, fig. 7.1:1.
4.15:9	JM.05.H75.27	H.B.1	Applied decoration with oblique impressions. Handmade, medium fired, reddish yellow surfaces, red core. Frequent small light and rare dark grits. Simple ware.	
4.15:10	JM.14.COVEST.110.2	H.B.1	Knob decoration and horizontal line of seed-like impressions. Handmade, low fired, reddish brown outside, light red inside and core. Very frequent small and medium limestone grits. Cooking ware.	
4.15:11	JM.03.H76.C.1	H.B.1	Handmade, badly low fired, light pinkish grey surfaces and core. Frequent small and medium limestone and basalt grits. Storage ware.	
4.15:12	JM.03.H76.K.164	H.B.1	Handmade, low fired, reddish yellow inside, light reddish brown outside, pink core. Rare small limestone grits. Storage ware.	
4.15:13	JM.15.COVEST.0.4	H.B.1	Handmade, medium fired, reddish yellow surfaces and core. Frequent small light and dark grits. Storage ware.	
4.15:14	JM.13.A.5.4	H.B.1	Handmade, medium fired, reddish yellow surfaces and core. Frequent small light and dark grits. Storage ware.	
4.15:15	JM.03.H76.K.256	H.B.1	Horizontal line of seed-like impressions. Handmade, low fired, light red inside, pink outside and core. Frequent small and medium limestone grits. Storage ware.	
4.15:16	JM.18.CSUD.415.10	H.B.1	Horizontal line of seed-like impressions. Handmade, low fired, reddish brown outside, light red inside and core. Very frequent small and medium limestone grits. Cooking ware.	
4.15:17	JM.18.CSUD.417.17	H.B.1	Handmade, low fired, reddish brown outside, light red inside and core. Very frequent small and medium limestone grits. Cooking ware.	
4.15:18	JM.05.H75.41	H.B.1	Rope-impressed decoration. Handmade, low fired, grey surfaces, reddish yellow core. Very frequent small and medium light and dark grits. Cooking ware.	

4. THE POTTERY: FUNCTION AND TYPOLOGIES

Type H.B.1

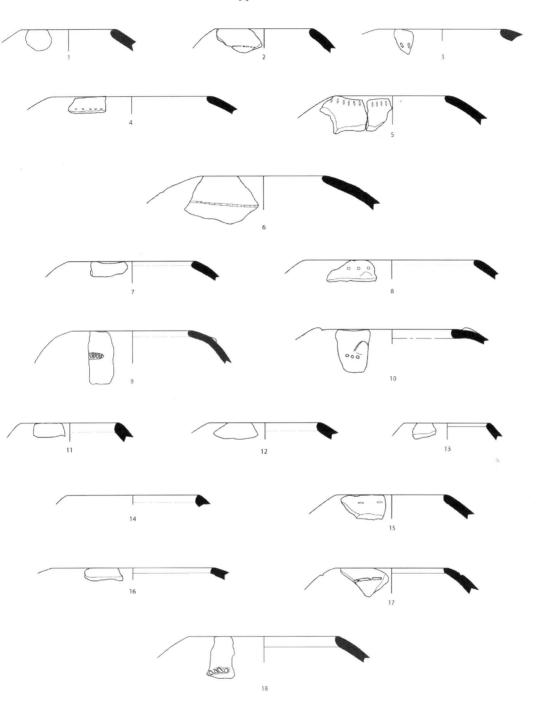

Plate 4.15: Types H.B.1.

Plate	Exc. Num.	Type	Description	Parallels
4.16:1	JM.03.H76.D.13	H.B.2	Handmade, low fired, pink surfaces, grey core. Frequent medium limestone and basalt grits. Cooking pot.	Betts & Helms 1991, fig. 117:88; Kenyon & Holland 1982, fig. 39:5, 8–10 (type A.I.c, A.II).
4.16:2	JM.03.H76.S.99	H.B.2	Knob decoration and horizontal line of circular impressions. Handmade, low fired, reddish yellow surfaces, light reddish brown core. Frequent medium limestone grits. Cooking ware.	
4.16:3	JM.03.H76.O.190?	H.B.2	Knob decoration and horizontal line of circular impressions. Handmade, low fired, dark grey outside, pinkish grey inside and core. Rare small and medium limestone grits. Cooking ware.	
4.16:4	JM.03.H76.D.9	H.B.2	Couple of pointed impressed lines with vertical orientation alternating with single horizontal line of circular impressions. Handmade, low fired, pink surfaces and core. Rare small limestone grits. Simple ware.	
4.16:5	JM.03.H76.D.11	H.B.2	Couple of pointed impressed lines with vertical orientation alternating with single horizontal line of circular impressions. Handmade, low fired, pink surfaces and core. Rare small limestone grits. Simple ware.	
4.16:6	JM.03.H76.D.10	H.B.2	Spouted vessel, horizontal line of circular impression. Handmade, low fired, pink surfaces and core. Rare small limestone grits. Simple ware.	
4.16:7	JM.03.H76.P.224	H.B.3	Horizontal line of seed-like impressions. Handmade, low fired, reddish yellow surfaces, pink core. Rare small limestone grits. Storage ware.	Betts & Helms 1991, fig. 117:92; Gustavson-Gaube 1985, type 36; Hanbury-Tenison 1986, fig. 10:13 (different orientation); Douglas & Kafafi 2000, fig. 6.3:1; Kenyon & Holland 1982, fig. 64:7–8 (type A.I.c); Rast & Schaub 2003, fig. 7.1:5.
4.16:8	JM.05.R3.31	H.B.3	White wash. Handmade, medium-high fired, reddish yellow outside, red inside and core. Frequent small and medium light and rare dark grits. Storage ware.	
4.16:9	JM.05.R3.24	H.B.3	Horizontal line of seed-like impression. Handmade, medium fired, red surfaces, reddish yellow core. Very frequent small and medium light and dark grits. Cooking ware.	
4.16:10	JM.05.R3.28	H.B.3	Applied decoration with oval impressions. Handmade, medium fired, yellowish red outside, reddish yellow inside and core. Very frequent small and medium light and dark grits. Cooking ware.	

4. THE POTTERY: FUNCTION AND TYPOLOGIES

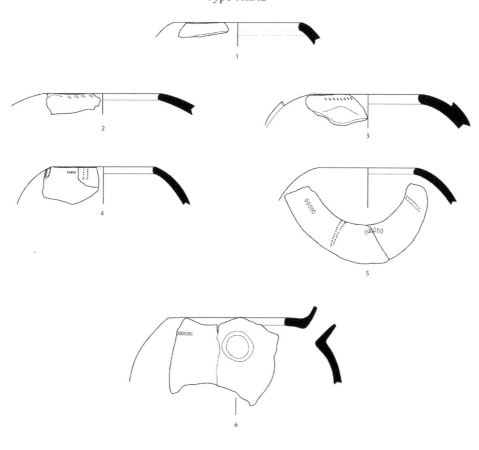

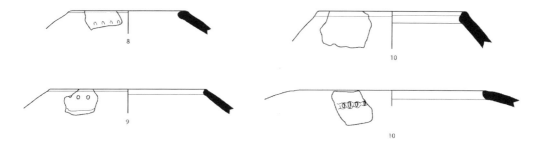

Plate 4.16: Types H.B.2, H.B.3.

Plate	Exc. Num.	Type	Description	Parallels
4.17:1	JM.05.R3.33	H.B.4	Handmade, medium-low fired, reddish yellow surfaces and core. Very frequent small and medium light and dark grits. Storage ware.	Amiran et al. 1978, pl. 8:31; Betts & Helms 1991, fig. 120:132, 135; Gustavson-Gaube 1985, type 32c, 33c; Hanbury-Tenison 1986, fig. 6:17; Kenyon & Holland 1983, fig. 12:13 (decorated); fig. 14:19 (decorated); fig. 16:3; Rast & Schaub 2003, fig. 7.1:12, 14.
4.17:2	JM.14.COVEST.101.1	H.B.4	Handmade, medium-low fired, reddish yellow surfaces and core. Very frequent small and medium light and dark grits. Storage ware.	
4.17:3	JM.03.H76.I.241	H.B.4	Horizontal line of seed-like impressions. Handmade, low fired, reddish yellow surfaces and core. Very frequent small and medium limestone grits. Storage ware.	
4.17:4	JM.03.H76.K.255	H.B.4	Applied decoration with oval impressions. Handmade, low fired, reddish yellow surfaces and core. Frequent small and medium limestone grits. Storage ware.	
4.17:5	JM.03.H76.P.201	H.B.4	Applied decoration with oval impressions. Handmade, low fired, reddish yellow surfaces and core. Frequent small and medium limestone grits. Storage ware.	
4.17:6	JM.05.R3.20	H.B.4	Horizontal line of seed-like impressions. Handmade, medium fired, light red surfaces, reddish yellow core. Rare small light and dark grits. Simple ware.	
4.17:7	JM.03.H76.N.217	H.B.4	Handmade, low fired, pink inside, light brown outside and core. Rare small limestone grits, porous. Cooking ware.	
4.17:8	JM.14.COVEST.103.6	H.B.4	Handmade, medium-low fired, reddish yellow surfaces and core. Very frequent small and medium light and dark grits. Storage ware.	
4.17:9	JM.14.SU.SE.2	H.B.4	Handmade, medium-low fired, reddish yellow surfaces and core. Very frequent small and medium light and dark grits. Storage ware.	
4.17:10	JM.05.R1.37	H.B.5	Traces of red wash (?) outside. Handmade, medium fired, reddish yellow surfaces and core. Frequent small light and dark grits. Storage (?) ware.	Betts 1992, fig. 147:10; Gustavson-Gaube 1985, type 47; Douglas & Kafafi 2000, fig. 6.3:4; Kenyon & Holland 1982, fig. 39:14 (type A.IV); fig. 65:20 (type C.II.c).
4.17:11	JM.03.H76.B.108	H.B.5	Handmade, medium-high fired, light greyish brown surfaces, pale brown core. Rare small limestone grits. Cooking (?) pot.	
4.17:12	JM.13.A.1.3	H.B.5	Handmade, medium-low fired, reddish yellow surfaces and core. Very frequent small and medium light and dark grits. Storage ware.	

4. THE POTTERY: FUNCTION AND TYPOLOGIES

Type H.B.4

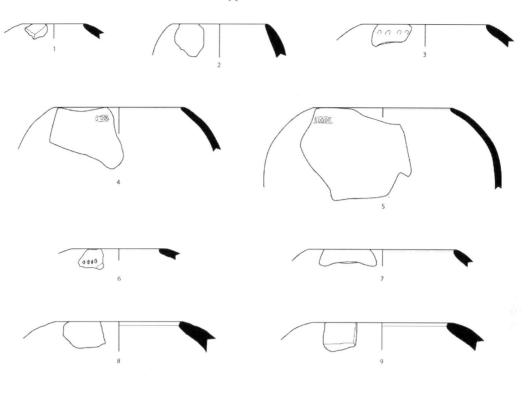

Type H.B.5

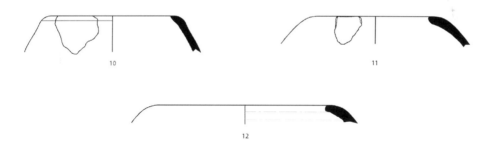

Plate 4.17: Types H.B.4, H.B.5.

Plate	Exc. Num.	Type	Description	Parallels
4.18:1	JM.13.SU.NE.3	H.B.6	Handmade, medium-low fired, reddish yellow surfaces and core. Very frequent small and medium light and dark grits. Storage ware.	Kenyon & Holland 1982, fig. 64:9–10 (type A.II.a).
4.18:2	JM.14.COVEST.103.5	H.B.6	Handmade, medium-low fired, reddish yellow surfaces and core. Very frequent small and medium light and dark grits. Storage ware.	
4.18:3	JM.06.H77.104	H.B.6	Handmade, medium-low fired, reddish yellow surfaces and core. Very frequent small and medium light and dark grits. Storage ware.	
4.18:4	JM.14.SU.W12.5	H.B.6	Handmade, medium-low fired, reddish yellow surfaces and core. Very frequent small and medium light and dark grits. Storage ware.	
4.18:5	JM.14.A.0.11	H.B.6	Handmade, low fired, light brown inside, light red outside and core. Frequent small limestone grits, chaff. Storage ware.	
4.18:6	JM.06.H77.105	H.B.6	Handmade, medium-low fired, reddish yellow surfaces and core. Very frequent small and medium light and dark grits. Storage ware.	
4.18:7	JM.14.CEST.205.1	H.B.6	Horizontal line of seed-like impressions. Handmade, medium-low fired, reddish yellow surfaces and core. Very frequent small and medium light and dark grits. Storage ware.	
4.18:8	JM.06.H77.106	H.B.7	Handmade, low fired, red surfaces, light red core. Very frequent medium and large light and dark grits. Cooking ware.	Callaway 1964, pl. XIX:2269; Kenyon & Holland 1982, fig. 39:19 (type B.I.b); De Vaux 1955, fig. 4:7.
4.18:9	JM.15.COVEST.136.3	H.B.7	Handmade, medium fired, brownish yellow surfaces and core. Very frequent small and large light and dark grits. Cooking ware.	
4.18:10	JM.15.COVEST.111.3	H.B.7	Handmade, low fired, red surfaces, light red core. Very frequent medium and large light and dark grits. Cooking ware.	
4.18:11	JM.06.H77.107	H.B.7	Handmade, medium fired, brownish yellow surfaces and core. Very frequent small and large light and dark grits. Cooking ware.	
4.18:12	JM.15.COVEST.129.4	H.B.7	Knob decoration. Handmade, low fired, pink surfaces, dark red core. Very frequent small, medium, and large light and dark grits. Cooking ware.	
4.18:13	JM.06.H77.108	H.B.7	Handmade, medium fired, brownish yellow surfaces and core. Very frequent small and large light and dark grits. Cooking ware.	
4.18:14	JM.18.CSUD.415.20	H.B.8	Knob decoration, horizontal line of circular impressions. Handmade, light grey surfaces and core. Rare small white and dark grits. Cooking ware.	Kenyon & Holland 1982, fig. 65:28 (type D.I.d).
4.18:15	JM.03.H76.S.101	H.B.8	Handmade, very low fired, reddish yellow surfaces and core. Frequent medium limestone and basalt grits. Storage ware.	
4.18:16	JM.05.R2.6	H.B.8	Applied knob. Handmade, medium fired, red surfaces, reddish yellow core. Very frequent medium light and dark grits. Storage ware.	
4.18:17	JM.14.COVEST.102.22	H.B.8	Horizontal line of seed-like impressions. Handmade, medium-low fired, reddish yellow surfaces and core. Very frequent small and medium light and dark grits. Storage ware.	

4. THE POTTERY: FUNCTION AND TYPOLOGIES

Type H.B.6

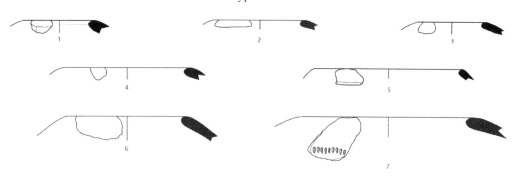

Type H.B.7

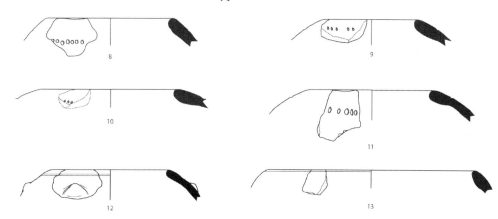

Type H.B.8

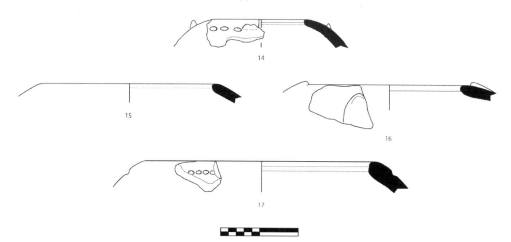

Plate 4.18: Types H.B.6, H.B.7, H.B.8.

Plate	Exc. Num.	Type	Description	Parallels
4.19:1	JM.14.SURF.2	H.B.9	Handmade, low fired, reddish yellow inside and core, light red outside. Rare medium limestone grits. Cooking ware.	Amiran et al. 1978, pl. 18:24; Betts & Helms 1991, fig. 110:7–10; 1992, fig. 151:1–4; Kenyon & Holland 1982, fig. 39:22–24 (type C.II); fig. 40:18 (type F.I.a); fig. 68:14–16 (type G.II.c).
4.19:2	JM.05.R2.29	H.B.9	Handmade, medium fired, reddish yellow surfaces, pink core. Very frequent small and medium light and dark grits. Storage ware.	
4.19:3		H.B.9	Handmade, medium fired, reddish yellow surfaces, pink core. Frequent small and medium light and dark grits. Storage ware.	
4.19:4	JM.03.H76.F.55	H.B.9	Handmade, very low fired, brownish yellow surfaces and core. Frequent medium limestone grits. Cooking ware.	
4.19:5	JM.03.H76.L.170	H.B.9	Handmade, low fired, reddish yellow inside and core, light red outside. Rare medium limestone grits. Cooking ware.	
4.19:6	JM.05.H75.21	H.B.9	Handmade, medium fired, red surfaces and core. Very frequent small and medium light and dark grits. Cooking ware.	
4.19:7	JM.13.B.48.1	H.B.10	Handmade, low fired, reddish yellow inside and core, light red outside. Rare medium limestone grits. Cooking ware.	Amiran et al. 1978, pl. 8:17; Betts & Helms 1991, fig. 121:146; 1992, fig. 144:1; Hanbury-Tenison 1986, fig. 5:30, 34–35; Kenyon & Holland 1982, fig. 39:25 (type D.I).
4.19:8	JM.05.H75.34	H.B.10	Handmade, low fired, red surfaces and core. Frequent small and medium light and rare dark grits. Cooking ware.	
4.19:9	JM.03.H76.T.126	H.B.10	Handmade, low fired, reddish yellow inside, light red outside and core. Frequent medium limestone grits. Cooking ware.	
4.19:10	JM.03.H76.P.227	H.B.11	Handmade, unevenly low fired, reddish yellow surfaces, grey core. Frequent small limestone and rare basalt grits. Cooking ware.	Betts & Helms 1991, fig. 120:137–40.
4.19:11	JM.03.H76.O.198	H.B.11	Horizontal line of seed-like impressions. Handmade, low fired, light reddish brown surfaces and core. Rare small limestone grits. Storage ware.	
4.19:12	JM.15.CC.302.2	H.B.12	Handmade, medium fired, pink surfaces and core. Very frequent small and medium limestone grits. Storage ware.	Betts & Helms 1991, fig. 114:56–58; 1992, fig. 145:9.
4.19:13	JM.15.COVEST.136.2	H.B.12	Handmade, medium fired, light red surfaces and core. Very frequent small and medium light and dark grits. Storage (?) ware.	
4.19:14	JM.15.COVEST.105.2	H.B.12	Handmade, medium fired, light reddish brown surfaces and core. Frequent small white and dark grits. Storage ware.	
4.19:15	JM.15.COVEST.124.10	H.B.12	Applied decoration with small oval impressions. Handmade, medium fired, light reddish brown surfaces and core. Frequent small white and dark grits. Storage ware.	

4. THE POTTERY: FUNCTION AND TYPOLOGIES

Type H.B.9

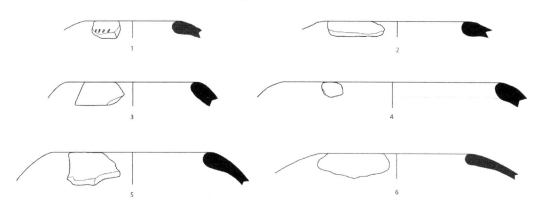

Type H.B.10

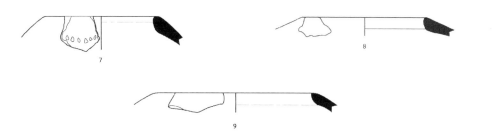

Type H.B.11

Type H.B.12

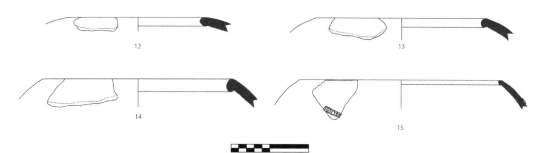

Plate 4.19: Types H.B.9, H.B.10, H.B.11, H.B.12.

Plate	Exc. Num.	Type	Description	Parallels
4.20:1	JM.05.H75.20		Red painted on white slip. Handmade, medium-high fired, reddish yellow surfaces and core. Frequent small light and rare dark grits. Simple ware.	
4.20:2	JM.05.R1.43		Handmade, medium fired, light reddish brown surfaces and core. Frequent small dark (basalt?) grits, rare light grits. Simple ware.	
4.20:3	JM.18.CSUD.408.22		Handmade and wheel-finished, medium-high fired, reddish brown surfaces and core. Frequent small and medium dark rare light grits. Group 2 ware.	
4.20:4	JM.16.CSUD.408.30		Handmade and wheel-finished, medium-high fired, reddish brown surfaces and core. Frequent small and medium dark rare light grits. Group 2 ware.	
4.20:5	JM.18.CSUD.415.5		Handmade and wheel-finished, medium-high fired, reddish brown surfaces and core. Frequent small and medium dark rare light grits. Group 2 ware.	
4.20:6	JM.15.COVEST.101.3		Handmade, medium fired, reddish yellow surfaces and core. Frequent small light and dark grits. Simple ware.	
4.20:7	JM.15.CC.302.12		Handmade, high fired, pinkish white surfaces and core. Frequent small white and dark grits. Simple ware.	
4.20:8	JM.14.SU.NO.2		Handmade, medium fired, light red inside, pink outside, reddish yellow core. Medium frequent small limestone grits, chamotte. Storage ware.	
4.20:9	JM.05.H75.56		Handmade, medium fired, light red inside, pink outside, reddish yellow core. Medium frequent small limestone grits, chamotte. Storage ware.	
4.20:10	JM.15.CEST.0.7		Handmade, medium fired, light red surfaces, weak red core. Frequent small white and dark grits. Coarse simple ware.	
4.20:11	JM.05.R4.25		Handmade, medium-high fired, reddish yellow surfaces, dark grey core. Frequent small light and rare dark grits. Simple ware.	
4.20:12	JM.14.COVEST.107.6		Traces of red painted bands. Handmade, medium fired, reddish yellow surfaces and core. Frequent small white and rare dark grits. Storage ware.	
4.20:13	JM.14.CEST.L101.8		Handmade, medium fired, reddish yellow surfaces and core. Frequent small light and rare medium and small dark grits. Storage ware.	Amiran et al. 1978, pl. 11: 17 (with red slip and burnished); Callaway 1972, fig. 15:11.
4.20:14	JM.14.COVEST.102.7		Handmade, medium fired, reddish yellow surfaces and core. Frequent small light and rare medium and small dark grits. Storage ware.	
4.20:15	JM.15.COVEST.111.5		Handmade, medium-low fired, yellow surfaces and core. Very frequent small and medium white and dark grits. Storage ware.	
4.20:16	JM.14.SU.H3.2		Traces of red painted bands. Handmade, medium fired, reddish yellow surfaces and core. Frequent small white and rare dark grits. Storage ware.	Amiran et al. 1978, pl. 11:12–16; Hanbury-Tenison 1986, fig. 7:59; Kenyon & Holland 1983, fig. 14:7–8.
4.20:17	JM.05.R1.27		Light red painted band. Handmade, medium fired, reddish yellow surfaces and core. Frequent small light and dark grits. Chamotte. Storage ware.	
4.20:18	JM.05.R4.22		Handmade, medium fired, reddish yellow surfaces and core. Frequent small light and rare medium and small dark grits. Storage ware.	

4. THE POTTERY: FUNCTION AND TYPOLOGIES

Plate	Exc. Num.	Type	Description	Parallels
4.20:19	JM.05.H75.2		Handmade, medium fired, reddish yellow surfaces and core. Frequent small light and rare medium and small dark grits. Storage ware.	Hanbury-Tenison 1986, fig. 10:17.

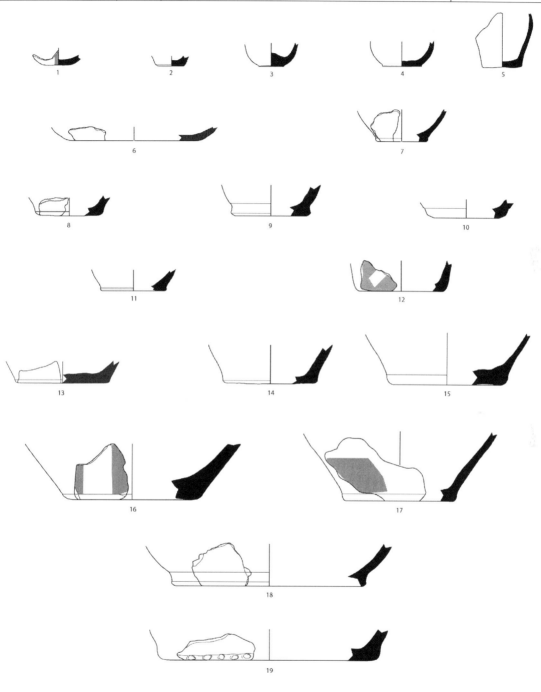

Plate 4.20: Bases.

Plate	Exc. Num.	Type	Description	Parallels
4.21:1	JM.03.H76.S.95		Red slip painted decoration that shows a couple of wavy lines. Handmade, medium fired, pink inside and core, reddish yellow outside. Rare small limestone grits. Simple ware.	
4.21:2	JM.05.H75.22		Line of red paint on white slip outside, red dots painted inside. Handmade, medium fired, red inside, light red outside, reddish yellow core. Frequent small light and rare dark grits. Simple ware.	Kenyon & Holland 1982, fig. 93:5 (crude dots); Schaub & Rast 1989, fig. 75:3.
4.21:3	JM.05.R4.24		Red painted crossing bands on white wash. Handmade, medium fired, light pink surfaces, light grey core. Frequent small dark, rare small light grits. Simple ware.	Kafafi 2001, fig. 34:2329; Kenyon & Holland 1982, fig. 59:23; fig. 87:26; fig. 91:3–4.
4.21:4	JM.15.COVEST.111.7		Traces of crossing red painted bands. Handmade, low fired, brown inside and core, yellow outside. Very frequent small and medium white and dark grits. Cooking (?) ware.	
4.21:5	JM.05.R2.4		Two parallel incised lines vertically oriented on a wavy incised line. Under that there are two wavy crossed incised lines. Handmade, medium-high fired, reddish yellow surfaces and core. Frequent small and medium light and dark grits. Storage ware.	Amiran et al. 1978, pl. 17:4, pl. 105:5 (incised lines).
4.21:6	JM.03.H76.F.59		Applied body snake. Handmade, unevenly medium-low fired, pink inside, reddish yellow outside, light grey core. Frequent small limestone and basalt grits, chamotte. Storage ware.	
4.21:7	JM.03.H76.S.68		Applied body snake. Handmade, low fired, pink surfaces, very pale brown core. Rare small limestone grits. Simple ware.	
4.21:8	JM.05.H75.39		Applied decoration impressed by a line of parallel impressions. Handmade, medium-high fired, reddish yellow. Frequent small light, rare dark grits. Simple ware.	
4.21:9	JM.05.PS.26		Rope decoration. Handmade, medium-high fired, pink surfaces, light red core. Rare small and medium light and dark grits. Simple ware.	
4.21:10	JM.05.R4.12		Applied decoration impressed by a line of parallel circular impressions. Handmade, medium fired, reddish yellow surfaces and core. Frequent small light and dark grits. Chamotte. Storage ware.	
4.21:11	JM.05.R2.57		Snakes applique, white wash. Handmade, medium fired, pink outside, reddish yellow inside and core. Frequent small dark and rare small light grits. Chamotte (?). Storage ware.	

4. THE POTTERY: FUNCTION AND TYPOLOGIES

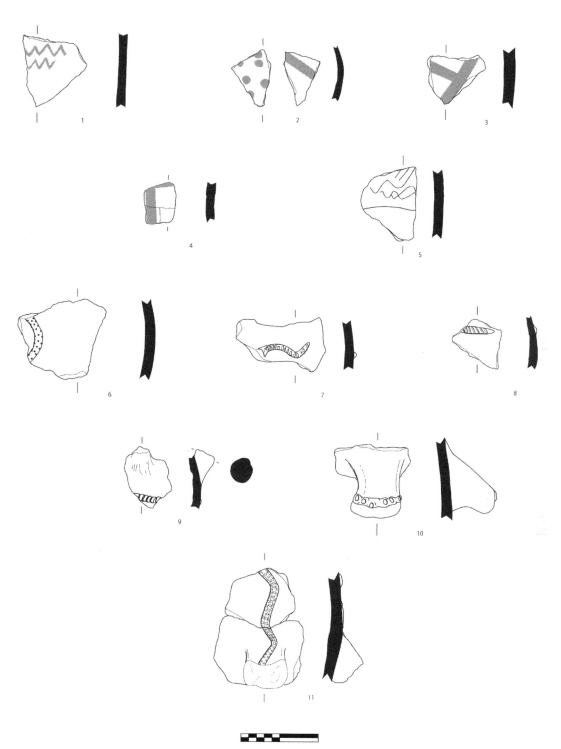

Plate 4.21: Decorations.

Plate	Exc. Num.	Type	Description	Parallels
4.22:1	JM.03.H76.P.205		Three small knobs. Handmade, unevenly low fired, reddish yellow surfaces, grey core. Frequent small and medium limestone, basalt, and flint grits. Storage (?) ware.	
4.22:2	JM.05.R2.56		Applied decoration impressed by a line of parallel circular impressions. Handmade, medium fired, reddish yellow surface, dark grey core. Frequent small and medium light and dark grits. Storage ware.	
4.22:3	JM.05.R2.18		Applied decoration impressed by two parallel lines of parallel impressions. Handmade, medium fired, reddish yellow surfaces and core. Frequent small light and rare dark grits. Storage ware.	
4.22:4	JM.03.H76.G.38		Thin rope decoration. Handmade, low fired, pink surfaces and core. Frequent small limestone and basalt grits. Simple ware.	Hanbury-Tenison 1986, fig. 5:50.
4.22:5	JM.03.H76.C.6		Handmade, low fired, light grey outside, pink inside and core. Medium frequent small limestone and basalt grits. Simple ware.	Hanbury-Tenison 1986, fig. 5:16 (similar).
4.22:6	JM.03.H76.O.78		Applied decoration with small vertical impressions. Handmade, unevenly low fired, pink surfaces, grey core. Rare small limestone grits. Simple ware.	
4.22:7	JM.03.H76.P.229		Applied decoration with circular impressions. Handmade, unevenly low fired, pink surfaces, grey core. Rare small limestone grits. Simple ware.	
4.22:8	JM.05.PS.34		Groups of small circular impressions. Handmade, medium-high fired, reddish yellow surfaces, pink core. Small and medium limestone grits, porous. Storage ware.	
4.22:9	JM.05.R2.27		Two parallel lines of small circular incisions. Handmade, medium fired, reddish yellow surfaces and core. Frequent small light and dark grits. Storage ware.	
4.22:10	JM.14.COVEST.106.1		Knob decoration and double horizontal circular impressed lines, loop handle. Handmade, mat impression on the base, reddish yellow surfaces and grey core. Small and medium limestone grits, porous. Storage ware.	Hanbury-Tenison 1986, fig. 6:36.

4. THE POTTERY: FUNCTION AND TYPOLOGIES

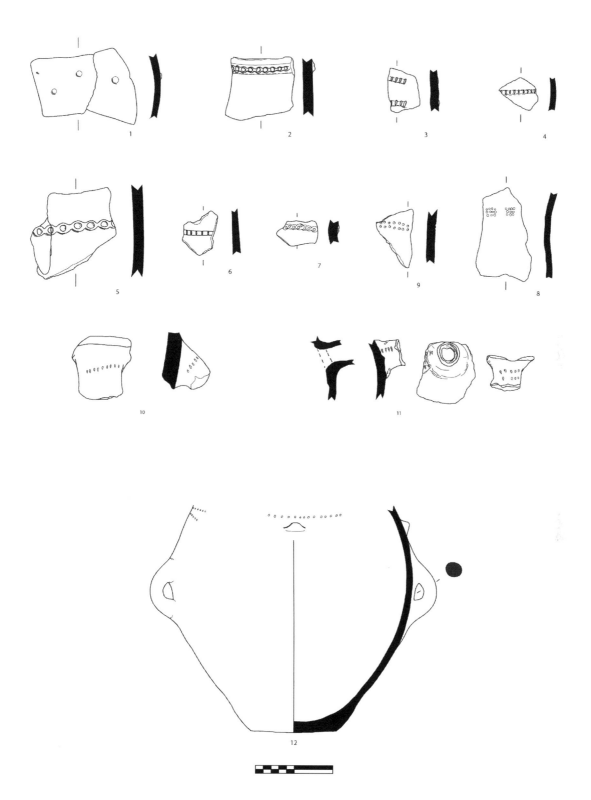

Plate 4.22: Decorations (continued).

Plate	Exc. Num.	Type	Description	Parallels
4.23:1	JM.18.CSUD.417.1		Handmade, low fired, yellowish brown surfaces and core. Frequent small and medium light and rare medium and small dark grits. Miniaturistic.	
4.23:2	JM.18.CSUD.415.1		Handmade, low fired, yellowish brown surfaces and core. Frequent small and medium light and rare medium and small dark grits. Miniaturistic.	
4.23:3	JM.18.CSUD.417.2		Handmade, low fired, yellowish brown surfaces and core. Frequent small and medium light and rare medium and small dark grits. Miniaturistic.	
4.23:4	JM.18.CSUD.417.3		Handmade, low fired, yellowish brown surfaces and core. Frequent small and medium light and rare medium and small dark grits. Miniaturistic.	
4.23:5	JM.18.CSUD.415.27		Handmade, low fired, yellowish brown surfaces and core. Frequent small and medium light and rare medium and small dark grits. Miniaturistic.	
4.23:6	JM.18.CSUD.415.3		Handmade, low fired, yellowish brown surfaces and core. Frequent small and medium light and rare medium and small dark grits. Miniaturistic.	Hanbury-Tenison 1986, fig. 6:1.
4.23:7	JM.16.411.2		Handmade, low fired, buff pinkish surfaces and core. Frequent small and medium light and rare medium and small dark grits. Miniaturistic.	Kenyon & Holland 1982, fig. 44:2-31 (similar shapes); Rast & Schaub 2003, fig. 7.2:16.
4.23:8	JM.18.CSUD.415.2		Handmade, low fired, yellowish brown surfaces and core. Frequent small and medium light and rare medium and small dark grits. Miniaturistic.	Amiran et al. 1978, pl. 10:1-3; Kenyon & Holland 1982, fig. 87:33-37, 39 (globular body)
4.23:9	JM.18.CSUD.417.15		Handmade, low fired, yellowish brown surfaces and core. Frequent small and medium light and rare medium and small dark grits. Miniaturistic.	
4.23:10	JM.18.CSUD.417.9		Handmade, low fired, yellowish brown surfaces and core. Frequent small and medium light and rare medium and small dark grits. Miniaturistic.	
4.23:11	JM.18.CSUD.417.25		Handmade, low fired, yellowish brown surfaces and core. Frequent small and medium light and rare medium and small dark grits. Miniaturistic.	Kenyon & Holland 1982, fig. 93:4 (body shape); fig. 47:4-6, 8-10; 1983, fig. 119:13; Rotem 2012, pl. 30:5.
4.23:12	JM.18.CSUD.417.26		Handmade, low fired, yellowish brown surfaces and core. Frequent small and medium light and rare medium and small dark grits. Miniaturistic.	
4.23:13	JM.14.CC.D534.1		Red burnished. Coil made, medium fired, red surfaces and core. Frequent small and medium basalt grits. Group 2 ware.	Amiran et al. 1978, pl. 14:21-31; Callaway 1980, fig. 62:11-12, 18-19; Kenyon & Holland 1982, fig. 85:3; fig. 87:1 (only to 4.23:13); Fischer 2008, fig. 30:8; fig. 48:5-6; fig. 1091-95; Kenyon & Holland 1983, fig. 119:10-11; Rotem 2012, pl. 13:9-10.
4.23:14	JM.14.CC.D534.2		Red burnished. Coil made, medium fired, red surfaces and core. Frequent small and medium basalt grits. Group 2 ware.	

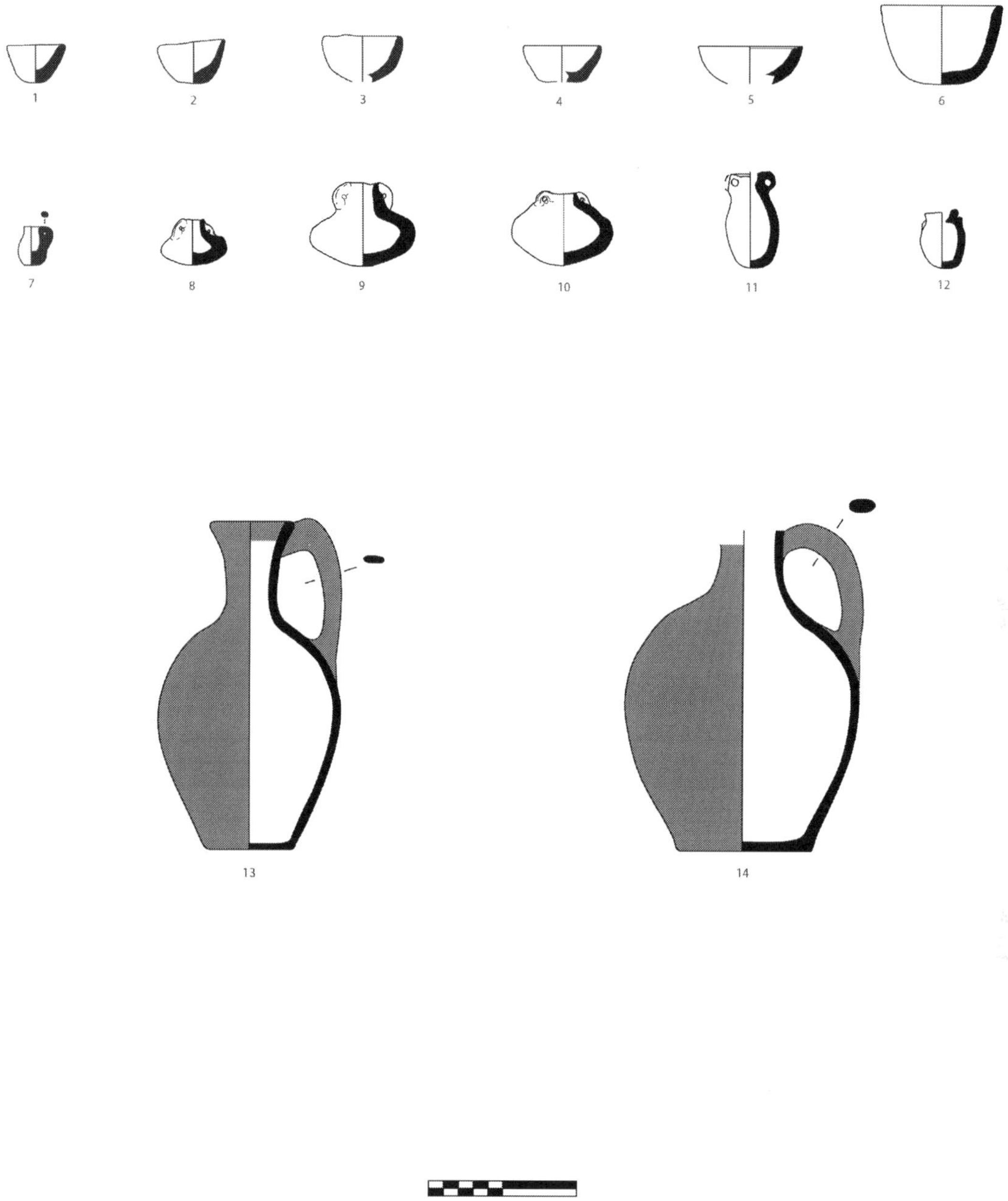

4. THE POTTERY: FUNCTION AND TYPOLOGIES

Plate 4.23: Miniature and Production Group 2 jugs.

5. The Lithics: Function and Typologies

Alessandra Caselli

General Description and Provenance of the Lithic Assemblages

In this chapter the analysis focuses on the lithic repertoire comprised of both chipped and ground stone tools.

The chapter includes the analysis of the lithic objects unearthed during the 2012 to 2018 Spanish-Italian excavations carried out at the site, that is, in the Central and Eastern Sectors, which includes Area B, Area A, the 2014 one-day survey, and Area C. Finally, the data coming from the study of the materials found in the Temple of the Serpents, which have been re-analysed since 2014, are included in this analysis.

During the 2012 to 2018 excavations, all the objects were gathered together and photographed. The selected objects were described in a database and detailed drawings and pictures were taken. The percentages regarding the distribution of the objects described in this chapter only concern the selected objects, and not the unselected objects comprised of cores and flakes. All the typologies are represented in the plates, but not all the objects studied for this analysis are presented.

The assemblage of lithic objects is mainly comprised of flint tools and ground stones. Many flint flakes and cores have been found at the site, and this information suggests that the flint objects were realized at the site itself. The main typologies of the flint objects are represented by: blades, bladelets, and retouched blades, scrapers, tabular scrapers, burins and borers, points.

Amongst the blades, there are several Canaanean blades; these blades used to be viewed as a type of tool particular to the southern Levant during the Early Bronze Age I (EB I) period. However, recent studies and excavations have revealed that this kind of object was already present in the Late Chalcolithic period, especially in Cisjordan (Milevski et al. 2011). Blades and bladelets are the most numerous objects found at the site, together with scrapers and *ad hoc* tools.

With regard to hard stone, the analysis in this chapter includes ground stones, that is, mortars, lower grinding slabs and handstones (comprising mainly of polishing tools and pestles), textile production tools, mace-heads, and stone vessels. Basalt was mainly used to realize this kind of object, although some of them were made of limestone.

Typologies of the Chipped Stone Tools

Chipped stone tools form the larger part of the lithic repertoire from Jebel al-Mutawwaq. In fact, the total number of artefacts in this category is 329 (Table 5.1). This category has been divided into five functional categories. They are as follows:

(1) Non-Canaanean blades, bladelets, and sickles (101 in total);

(2) Canaanean blades (twenty-one in total);

(3) Scrapers and *ad hoc* tools (152 in total);

(4) Tabular scrapers (twenty-eight in total);

(5) Borers and points (fifty-two in total).

Alessandra Caselli (alessandra.caselli@unipg.it) is a Research Fellow in Near Eastern Archaeology at Perugia University (Italy).

Table 5.1: Distribution of the typologies of the chipped stone tools.

Typology	Non-Canaanean blades	Canaanean blades	Scrapers and *ad hoc* tools	Tabular scrapers	Borers and points
Total	101	21	152	27	52
Surface	6	0	10	0	1
Area A	6	0	15	0	4
Area B	21	1	31	6	22
Area C East	34	6	23	0	12
Area C Centre (Building 131)	5	4	16	5	0
Area C West	10	5	23	0	4
Area C South	13	0	16	0	2
Dolmen 534	1	1	3	0	3
House 75 (Temple Area)	0	0	5	6	2
House 76 (Temple Area)	1	4	7	7	0
House 77 (Temple Area)	0	0	0	0	0
Rooms (Temple Area)	0	0	0	1	0
Courtyard (Temple Area)	4	0	3	2	2

The artefacts are presented, taking into consideration their use and their distribution throughout the site, with the aim of better understanding the purpose of the areas where they were collected and, consequently, to frame the activities performed at the site in the domestic and in the public and/or ritual spheres. For this reason, the technological aspect of the productive process of the chipped stone tools is not discussed. Moreover, it was not possible to perform any wear and tear analysis on the objects, and it has not been easy to define the exact function of some typologies, such as the scrapers and the *ad hoc* tools.

Non-Canaanean Blades (Plates 5.1–5.2)

This category includes sickle blades, bladelets, and retouched blades. Non-Canaanean sickle blades can be backed truncated segments or unbacked truncated segments (Rosen 1997, 50). The backed segments are typical of the Late Chalcolithic and Early Bronze Age I periods. Cores are not large, usually *c.* 8 cm in length and wadi cobbles, geologically from Transjordan, are a common raw material (Rosen 1997, 44). The blades are short and the section varies; it can be trapezoidal, triangular, or irregular. Considering the use of this typology, in some cases the artefacts could be used as knives or as sickle fragments.

At Jebel al-Mutawwaq 101 fragments of blades/sickles were collected. This typology, because of its use in the daily life of the community and because of the variability of their function, is widespread throughout the entire site. Concerning the distribution, it is interesting to notice that the larger number of non-Canaanean blades and sickles has been collected in Area C East, inside the Great Enclosure, where several Canaanean blades were also collected.

5. THE LITHICS: FUNCTION AND TYPOLOGIES

Similar blades were found at Tell Abu Kharaz (Fischer 2008, fig. 121.2), at Jebel Abu Thawwab (Kafafi 2001, fig. 2.7), and at Tell Umm Hammad (Betts (ed.) 1992, fig. 182.3).

Canaanean Blades (Plate 5.1)

Canaanean blades are specialized prismatic blades, with a trapezoidal section; they can be either sickle segments or reaping knives, with a complete blade without the truncation. Blades are long and wide, usually up to 15 cm in length and 2 cm in width (Rosen 1997, 48). Backing is virtually absent. The Canaanean blade technology and the system that saw its spread have been the focus of several specialist studies in recent years.[1] At the beginning of the research about this typology, archaeologists focused their studies on the shape and the morphological aspects of Canaanean blades, but gradually scholars started to consider the Canaanean technology as the most peculiar aspect of this tool.[2]

The blades were produced by specialists using high-quality flint and then distributed regionally (Rosen 2011, 250). The primary function of this type of tool was reaping, but it could also be used as a knife. In some cases, the Canaanean blades have a glossy surface that has been interpreted as being due to the constant contact with and rubbing of the blades against vegetal elements, thereby causing their surfaces to shine. For this reason, the presence of a glossy surface was frequently used to identify the blade as being a sickle blade.[3]

At Jebel al-Mutawwaq twenty-one Canaanean blades have been collected between 2012 and 2018. It is interesting to note that the Canaanean blades are concentrated mainly in Area C and in the Temple area. In fact, sixteen of them were found in Area C (six in Area C West, four inside Building 131, and five in Area C East), while four of them come from House 76, the main building of the Temple area.

Canaanean blades could be used as sickles or as knives, and the presence of the glossy surface on some examples confirms the relation between this typology and the agricultural activities, as will be stressed in the

Figure 5.1: An example of a Canaanean blade with glossy surface found in the Temple area (JM.17.O.113).

conclusions of this Chapter (Fig. 5.1). The specialized technology needed to realize these blades determines that Canaanean blades were not produced and used in domestic contexts and their finding contexts at Jebel al-Mutawwaq confirm this aspect. In fact, Area C is a communal food production area and these sickle blades, used for reaping, come from the same context where several ground stone tools, used to process the cereal harvest, were found. This information confirms that both the typologies of objects were used in association with each other to perform activities linked to the agricultural exploitation of the surroundings of the site.

Furthermore, the presence of four Canaanean blades inside House 76 in the Temple area is significant. In fact, while only the 4.95 per cent of non-Canaanean blades were recovered in the Temple area, the 19 per cent of the twenty-one Canaanean blades come from the Temple area. This information, associated with the percentages of the other typologies of objects found at Jebel al-Mutawwaq, confirms that the Canaanean blades are a peculiar class used for communal activities and not in the daily life of the inhabitants.

Similar Canaanean blades were found at Tell Abu Kharaz (Fischer 2008, fig. 34.6, fig. 50.4), at Jawa (Betts & Helms (eds) 1991, fig. 276.2) and at Tell Umm Hammad (Betts (ed.) 1992, fig. 182.4).

---

1 The first researcher who identified the Canaanean typology was Macalister (1912). See also Shimelmitz et al. 2000; Hartenberger et al. 2000.

2 See Rosen 1989; 1997; Coqueugniot 2006.

3 Rosen 1997, 57. For a discussion about the interpretation of the glossy surface and, consequently, of the use of Canaanean blades see Anderson et al. 2004.

Scrapers and *ad hoc* Tools (Plate 5.3)

The technology used to realize scrapers varies and is used on an *ad hoc* basis. For this reason, scrapers have different dimensions and shapes and as such are non-standardized. Because of their variability, it is difficult to distinguish the function of the various scraper shapes. They were produced for a specific use and then discarded. Thus, scrapers and other *ad hoc* tools are widespread throughout the southern Levant.

The production of these objects was not specialized but rather it was carried out in a domestic context and connected to daily life. This feature determines the large number of scrapers found during the excavations, but the *ad hoc* nature of production also made it difficult to use this category for the definition of the chronological time span of the archaeological context.

Across the millennia, it is possible to recognize the variation in the distribution of some typologies in comparison with others, but it is not possible to recognize a specific class produced and used only during Early Bronze Age I (Rosen 1997, 87). The typologies are defined by the shape of the object and by the way the scraper was used based on the retouching on the sides. The main typologies are endscrapers, side scrapers, and steep scrapers.

Scrapers and *ad hoc* artefacts are the most numerous chipped stone tools at Jebel al-Mutawwaq. The total number is 152 and it is the typology most widespread on the site because of their domestic and multifunctional use. Considering the distribution of the tools, it is quite homogeneous throughout the site, concentrations of scrapers and *ad hoc* tools are not attested. It is interesting to notice that few tools were collected in the temple area, consistent with the domestic use of these typologies.

Similar tools were found at Bab edh-Dhra (Rast & Schaub 2003, fig. 16.3) and at Jericho (Kenyon & Holland 1983, fig. 344.2).

Tabular Scrapers (Plates 5.4–5.5)

Tabular scrapers are large, retouched flakes indicating intentional retention of the cortex on the dorsal surface. The presence of this kind of tool is attested in archaeological sites from the southern Sinai and Lower Egypt in the south to south-eastern Turkey in the north; they are attested in the Late Neolithic period, but they become common during the Chalcolithic and Early Bronze Age periods (4500 to 2500 BCE).[4]

---

4 Barket & Bell 2011, 56; Rosen 1997, 75.

As for the Canaanean blades, also for this typology one of the most interesting aspects is linked to the specialist production process. Large mines where noticeable quantities of tabular scrapers were realized have been found in south-eastern Jordan and in the North-Eastern Badia (Muller-Neuhof 2013). The presence of few mines could imply that the communities should move through the regions to obtain these objects. The fact that one of the mines was in the Eastern Badia, where Jawa was settled in EB I, confirms direct contact between the two settlements, as suggested already by some similarities in the pottery assemblage.

The typologies of these tools are based on their shape. The most common and regular shapes are the fan scrapers, the oval, the elongated, or the rounded, but several other more irregular shapes are present.

The function of this kind of object is still under debate, but it was probably used for shearing and butchering animals, or to scrape fresh reeds. The debate about tabular scrapers mainly concerns the use of these objects in ritual activities; this is because in some sites, such as Bab edh-Dhra,[5] this kind of tool was recovered in the sacred areas. Furthermore, in some cases, Early Bronze Age tabular scrapers show some incisions on the cortex which have been interpreted as signs connected to ritual activities.[6]

Several experimental studies have been performed to understand the function of these tools, but the differing results suggest that tabular scrapers could be used to cut 'soft substances' easily (Barket & Bell 2011, 59). Of course, it was noted that while the tool can be used for different activities, the traces on the edges of the scraper differ depending on the type of use.[7] Unfortunately the Spanish-Italian expedition to Jebel

---

5 For Bab edh-Dhra see McConaughy 1980.

6 Elliott 1977, McConaughy 1980 p. 53. McConaughy conducted a use-wear examination of several tabular scrapers from the Early Bronze site of Bab edh-Dhra, Jordan, and concluded that they may have been used as butchering knives and, because they were found in the sacred area, he suggested that they could have been used as sacrificial knives.

7 The results of the experimental studies are described by Barket & Bell 2011. Here, the author reported how, in 1991, Rowan and Levy examined ten tabular scrapers collected at Shiqmim and, observing the wear traces, observed that some tools were used for cutting, some for scraping, and some of them show traces of both the activities. During 1995, Henry was the first to conduct experimental procedures to test the hypothesis of a sheep-shearing function. Several other experimental tests have been conducted since then, but the results do indicate that the tools could be used for different activities.

al-Mutawwaq has not yet had the opportunity to analyse the traces on the tabular scrapers found in the site. The fact that in the last seven campaigns the tabular scrapers were mainly found in funerary and cultic contexts could suggest that these tools were related to an activity that was performed in the productive area of the Temple of the Serpents.

Twenty-seven tabular scrapers have been found at Jebel al-Mutawwaq, that is, sixteen in the Temple of the Serpents, six in the megalithic necropolis, and five in Building 131 (Table 5.2).

Tabular scrapers found in Dolmen 317 constitute the grave goods of the intact burial B. 25, unearthed during the 2013 campaign (Polcaro & Muñiz 2014). Grave goods included a fan scraper (JM.13.O.70) and an elongated tabular scraper (JM.13.O.69), and their presence as grave goods could indicate the activities performed by the deceased women during their lives, as well as suggesting that they were important activities for the community of Jebel al-Mutawwaq (Fig. 5.2).[8]

In the portion of the megalithic necropolis investigated, known as Area B, in addition to the tabular scrapers found inside Dolmen 317, four other artefacts were discovered, that is, one inside Dolmen 228, one inside Dolmen 316, and two inside Dolmen 318. While artefacts JM.13.O.70 and JM.13.O.69 were the grave goods of the burial B. 25 and were found in a sealed context, the funerary chambers of the other dolmens were found to have been violated. Furthermore, the objects were not intact but only partially preserved. Consequently, it has not been possible to affirm if the objects were originally inside the dolmens.

In 2015 an elongated tabular scraper (JM.15.O.54) was found inside Building 131. Building 131 was not just a domestic unit, but was a structure where productive activities were performed, as testified by the presence of two large circular installations, as well as being suggested by its proximity to the Great Enclosure (Polcaro & Muñiz 2019); probably a huge communal place used by the inhabitants to gather their livestock and to perform ritual activities. This elongated tabular scraper is very

---

[8] It is interesting to notice that the same couple of objects was found in the EB IB burial Cave F-55 of Nesher-Ramla Quarry in Cisjordan (Avrutis 2012, 215, fig. 7.3:C; 214, fig. 7.2: B), as already reported by Andrea Polcaro in Chapter 3. This aspect can be related to the use of those two different types of tabular scrapers to perform distinct activities in the same context. As already stressed, it is not possible to delineate a univocal function of tabular scrapers and the various shapes of these tools can suggest that the shape was linked to the activity.

Figure 5.2: The tabular scrapers found as grave goods of the burial B. 25 inside Dolmen 317. JM.13.O.70 on the right, JM.13.O.69 on the left.

similar to example JM.13.O.69 even though it is slightly bigger. Inside Building 131, three other tabular scrapers were found. While in keeping with the function of the building, they are fragmentary, but it is possible to understand the shape of these three artefacts: two of them have a trapezoidal shape, while one is elongated in shape.

The larger number of tabular scrapers come from the sacred area, the Temple of the Serpents, where sixteen tabular scrapers were found, they are mainly fanned, elongated, or oval but there are also some rounded examples.

With regard to the distribution of tabular scrapers in the sacred area, seven of them were found in the main building, House 76, the cultic centre of the complex, amongst them, four were found grouped together close to the entrance door (Fernández-Tresguerres 2008a, 32); six of them were found in the eastern sector of House 75; while one of them was found in the rooms and the other two were found in the courtyard. The high concentration of this kind of tool in the eastern sector of House 75 suggests that the activities performed with such tools were carried out in that area, and indicates that the activities were linked to ritual. The importance of these activities is also testified by the presence of the tabular scrapers in the cultic building, perhaps an offering to the gods.

Hopefully, further analysis of the traces of use on these tools will clarify the communal function of the tabular scrapers found at the site of Jebel al-Mutaw-

Table 5.2: Details about the tabular scrapers found at Jebel al-Mutawwaq.

ID	Archaeological context	Shape	Preservation	Length	Width	Thickness
JM.17.O.1	House 75	Fan scraper	Fragmentary	3.9 cm	6.1 cm	0.3–0.5 cm
JM.17.O.104	House 76	Fan scraper	Fragmentary	4.9 cm	6.5 cm	0.6 cm
JM.17.O.110	House 76	Fan scraper	Fragmentary	5.4 cm	7.2 cm	0.4 cm
JM.17.O.107	House 76	Elongated	Fragmentary	7 cm	7.1 cm	0.9 cm
JM.17.O.108	House 76	Rounded	Intact	6.1 cm	5.4 cm	0.5–0.8 cm
JM.17.O.109	House 76	Elongated	Intact	11.6 cm	3–5.5 cm	0.3–0.8 cm
JM.17.O.111	House 76	Fan scraper	Fragmentary	4.5 cm	5.4 cm	0.5 cm
JM.17.O.117	Room 1	Fan scraper	Intact	14.8 cm	8.8 cm	0.3 cm
JM.17.O.123	Building 131	Rounded	Fragmentary	4.5 cm	5.1 cm	0.7 cm
JM.17.O.134	Building 131	Fan scraper	Fragmentary	7.8 cm	7.3 cm	0.5 cm
JM.17.O.138	Building 131	Fan scraper	Fragmentary	6.7 cm	6.2 cm	0.5 cm
JM.17.O.2	House 75	Fan scraper	Intact	11.4 cm	6.5 cm	0.2 cm
JM.17.O.3	House 75	Elongated	Intact	9.7 cm	4.4 cm	0.3 cm
JM.17.O.35	Area B	Fan scraper	Fragmentary	5.6 cm	6.7 cm	0.5 cm
JM.17.O.4	Building 131	Fan scraper	Intact	11.3 cm	10.2 cm	0.4 cm
JM.17.O.48	Area B	Fan scraper	Fragmentary	3.4 cm	5.9 cm	0.4 cm
JM.17.O.5	House 75	Fan scraper	Intact	13.9 cm	9.7 cm	0.5 cm
JM.17.O.53	Area B	Fan scraper	Fragmentary	5.1 cm	4.5 cm	0.5 cm
JM.17.O.6	House 75	Fan scraper	Intact	11.7 cm	8.1 cm	0.2 cm
JM.17.O.7	House 75	Fan scraper	Intact	14.5 cm	6.8 cm	0.2 cm
JM.17.O.70	Temple area	Rounded	Intact	7.4 cm	6.4 cm	1.1 cm
JM.17.O.73	House 76	Elongated	Fragmentary	2.9 cm	3.1 cm	0.2 cm
JM.17.O.92	Temple area	Fan scraper	Fragmentary	3.8 cm	3.6 cm	0.8 cm
JM.17.O.77	Area B	Fan scraper	Fragmentary	3.1 cm	4.5 cm	0.4 cm
JM.15.CC.O.54	House 131	Elongated	Intact	15.3 cm	6 cm	0.9 cm
JM.13.O.69	Area B (Dolmen 317)	Elongated	Intact	12 cm	5.2 cm	0.8 cm
JM.13.O.70	Area B (Dolmen 317)	Fan scraper	Intact	14 cm	9.5 cm	0.6 cm

waq, both in the sacred area and in the productive area (Area C, Building 131). The communal use of Building 131 is confirmed by the presence of tools as the tabular scraper as in the sacred area.

Similar tabular scrapers were found at Tell Umm Hammad (Betts (ed.) 1992, fig. 279), Bab edh-Dhra (Rast & Schaub 2003, fig. 16.5), Tell Abu Kharaz (Fischer 2008, fig. 142.1) and Jebel Abu Thawwab (Kafafi 2001, fig. 14.4).

Points and Borers (Plates 5.6–5.7)

Borers are usually realized by retouching blades. The technology used to realize them is frequently *ad hoc* and so non-standardized. These kinds of objects were probably used for engraving activities (Rosen 1997, 68). Concerning the points, the technology seems to have been similar to that used for the borers and they were manufactured from bladelets and elongated flakes.

At Jebel al-Mutawwaq fifty-two tools interpreted as points or borers have been collected. Concerning the distribution of these artefacts, they have been found in every investigated context, even though it is possible to observe a concentration of those typologies in Area B (22) and in Area C East (12). Area B is constituted by

5. THE LITHICS: FUNCTION AND TYPOLOGIES

Figure 5.3: The flint tools found gathered in L. 51, Area C West.

the funerary monuments of the first phase of occupation of the site. In this area an intact burial (B. 25) was identified inside Dolmen 317 and, even if the C14 analysis did not give an exact absolute chronology because of the bad state of preservation of the collagen in the bones, the architectural characteristics of the funerary structure and the material culture dated the area to Early Bronze Age I.[9] Area C East correspond to the Great Enclosure, an open area surrounded by a massive semicircular wall around 60 m in diameter. Concerning this area, the C14 analysis performed in 2020 on samples collected in 2019 and constituted by olive seeds proved that the structure pertains to Early Bronze Age IA, the first phase of occupation of the site.[10]

It is not possible to identify the exact function of these tools in the contexts where they were collected but it is interesting to observe that these typologies were preferred in the first phase in comparison with the second phase, it is not clear if the slow reduction of these tools depended on the evolution of the technology and in the choice of the tools for specific activities or on the change in activities performed by the community.

---

9 The details about Area B and Dolmen 317 are reported in Chapter 3.

10 The results are: 5470–5316 cal BP = 3521–3367 cal BCE — Beta Analytic 576901.

Figure 5.4: The Neolithic point found in L. 51, Area C West (JM.14.0.57).

An interesting archaeological discovery occurred during the 2014 excavation campaign. The team was investigating Area C, and specifically the Courtyard L. 51 located between Building C and Building 131. The courtyard had a storage function, as confirmed by the presence, in the northern portion of the area on a raised levelled bedrock, of two installations (I. 66 and I. 65) carved into the limestone in which two almost complete storage jars were found (Polcaro & Muñiz 2019). In the courtyard, a group of eight flint tools was collected, made up of four blades and four scrapers (Fig. 5.3). In addition to these tools, a Neolithic point was also found. Morphologically, it is a Haparsa point and it can be dated to the Pre-Pottery Neolithic B period (Fig. 5.4). It is an interesting find as it seems to be the only intrusion of a Neolithic object in the site. Along the valley of the Wadi Zarqa, at the base of the mountain where Jebel al-Mutawwaq is settled, a Neolithic site, Kheraysin, was discovered and is now under investigation by a Spanish team directed by J. Ibañez.[11] This piece of data could suggest that inhabitants from Jebel al-Mutawwaq found the object close to the river and decided to keep it and use it together with their daily tools.

Similar chipped stone tools were found at Jawa (Betts & Helms (eds) 1991, fig. 278.2), Tell Umm Hammad (Betts (ed.) 1992, fig. 179.11), Bab edh-Dhra (Rast & Schaub 2003, fig. 16.15).

Concerning the Neolithic Haparsa point, a similar example was found at Jebel Abu Thawwab (Kafafi 2001, fig. 1.3).

Typologies of the Worked Stones

Ground stone artefacts found in Jebel al-Mutawwaq have been divided, following Wright's Classification System into four categories, as follows (Wright 1992):

(1) Grinding implements (querns, grinding slabs, handstones and pestles, mortars);

(2) Textile production tools;

(3) Stone vessels;

During the 2012–2018 excavation campaigns at Jebel al-Mutawwaq, a total of fifty-four worked stone objects were collected in the various investigated areas. As for the other groups of objects, in addition to the finds from the excavations, the objects collected by the Spanish expedition in the temple area between 2003 and 2005 are included in the analysis. This is because the Spanish-Italian team had the opportunity to study the material culture of the temple area in recent years. Consequently, the worked stone artefacts now total sixty-one (Table 5.3). The distinct groups of objects are described in the following sections. The majority of worked stone objects comprise grinding implements which are 70.49 per cent of the total. Concerning the distribution of the artefacts, this matter is discussed later in this chapter. While it is possible to affirm that the distribution appears to be quite homogeneous, the fact that there are only a small number of artefacts imposes caution on the interpretative hypothesis of the functions of the areas under investigation.

In addition to the ground stone tools, this section will present the textile production tools made up of stone, the mace-heads, and the stone vessels. Each category comprises few examples from the site of Jebel al-Mutawwaq but they can provide essential information about the site and its inhabitants. In fact, the textile tools can provide a better understanding of the textile production technology and of the organization of the

---

11 For Kheraisyn see Ibañez et al. 2016.

Table 5.3: Distribution of the worked stone tools throughout the site of Jebel al-Mutawwaq.

Typology	Grinding implements	Textile production tools	Mace-heads	Stone vessels
Total	45	5	8	5
Surface	4	0	0	0
Area A	3	0	0	0
Area B	3	0	0	0
Area C East	6	0	2	0
Area C Centre (Building 131)	9	1	0	1
Area C West	1	0	0	3
Area C South	8	3	1	0
Dolmen 534	0	0	1	0
Building 151	0	1	3	0
House 75 (Temple Area)	6	0	0	0
House 76 (Temple Area)	0	0	1	0
House 77 (Temple Area)	2	0	0	0
Rooms (Temple Area)	0	0	0	0
Courtyard (Temple Area)	3	0	0	1

working process inside the community. Conversely, mace-heads and stone vessels are useful to delineate the evolution of their classes through the fourth millennium BCE as a consequence of the socio-economic transformations that occurred between the Late Chalcolithic and Early Bronze Age I.[12]

Ground Stone Tools

Grinding Slabs (Plates 5.8–5.9)

A grinding slab is the lower of two stones used to grind; it is generally immobile. Thus, the second, smaller stone is rubbed against the grinding slab (Rowan 2003, 185). Twenty-three grinding slabs were collected between 2012 and 2018 at Jebel al-Mutawwaq; the majority of them are fragmentary and are made of basalt, apart from one limestone slab found in the Great Enclosure, Area C East.

The grinding slabs collected during the excavations are fragmentary, the degree of preservation of every slab can be deduced by the dimensions of the fragments reported in the table (Table 5.4). It is possible to observe that most of the slabs have a plano-convex cross-section and that there is not a large variety of shapes. The artefacts mainly have a decidedly rectangular or an elongated shape, and were used unifacially: in fact, the slabs were worked by way of pecking and flaking solely on the ventral and lateral sides, but not on the dorsal side. Some of these slabs present a smooth surface due to the use of the object. The majority of the better-preserved grinding slabs are slightly concave on the ventral side and convex on the dorsal side, but some of them are flat, such as example JM.15.0.72, found inside Building 131 in Area C.

The better-preserved grinding slab is JM.17.0.140. It was found inside Building 131, an interesting archaeological context due to its function as a food production area. The grinding slab was finely worked and smoothed; some traces of pecking are still visible on its lateral sides.

The only grinding slab made of limestone is JM.18.0.37, which was found in Area C East, inside the

---

12 For a description of the fourth-millennium phases in the southern Levant see Philip 2008; van den Brink 2011; Braun 2019.

Figure 5.5: Limestone grinding slab JM.18.O.37.

Table 5.4: Details of the grinding slabs found at Jebel al-Mutawwaq.

ID	Archaeological context	Material	Preservation	Width	Length	Thickness
JM.16.CSUD.0/A	C South	Basalt	Fragmentary	6.2 cm	10.2 cm	5.6 cm
JM.18.O.55	C South	Basalt	Fragmentary	6.8 cm	10.4 cm	11.9 cm
JM.17.O.101	Temple area (House 75)	Basalt	Fragmentary	8.8 cm	8.8 cm	4.7 cm
JM.17.O.129	House 131	Basalt	Fragmentary	6.1 cm	11 cm	5.3 cm
JM.17.O.133	House 131	Basalt	Fragmentary	6.4 cm	19 cm	6 cm
JM.17.O.140	House 131	Basalt	Almost intact	11.2 cm	30.5 cm	5.2 cm
JM.15.O.37	House 131	Basalt	Fragmentary	2.5 cm	9.9 cm	2.9 cm
JM.15.O.55	House 131	Basalt	Fragmentary	9.5 cm	12.1 cm	5 cm
JM.15.O.58	House 131	Basalt	Fragmentary	5.2 cm	6.4 cm	5.8 cm
JM.15.O.71	House 131	Basalt	Fragmentary	4.3 cm	6.7 cm	3.4 cm
JM.15.O.72	House 131	Basalt	Fragmentary	5.5 cm	16.2 cm	3 cm
JM.18.O.35	C East	Basalt	Fragmentary	7.1 cm	10.5 cm	5.6 cm
JM.18.O.37	C East	Limestone	Fragmentary	7 cm	13 cm	5 cm
JM.14.O.45	C East	Basalt	Fragmentary	9.9 cm	6.1 cm	4.9 cm
JM.14.O.46	C East	Basalt	Fragmentary	9.6 cm	7 cm	3.1 cm
JM.14.O.79	C East	Basalt	Fragmentary	9.3 cm	12.1 cm	6.6 cm
JM.14.O.5	Area A	Basalt	Fragmentary	4.6 cm	7.6 cm	3.9 cm
JM.14.O.6	Area A	Basalt	Fragmentary	5.1 cm	7.8 cm	3.3 cm
JM.14.O.22	Surface	Basalt	Almost intact	6.3 cm	4.1 cm	1.6 cm
JM.14.O.25	Surface	Basalt	Fragmentary	10.6 cm	8.4 cm	4.8 cm
JM.14.O.39	Surface	Basalt	Fragmentary	7.8 cm	8.1 cm	6 cm
JM.14.O.75	Surface	Basalt	Fragmentary	4.7 cm	5.4 cm	2.6 cm
JM.14.O.62	C West	Basalt	Fragmentary	8 cm	7.3 cm	3.5 cm
JM.13.A.02	Area A	Basalt	Fragmentary	4.2 cm	7.3 cm	4.4 cm
JM.13.B.65	Area B	Basalt	Fragmentary	13 cm	9.2 cm	5.2 cm

5. THE LITHICS: FUNCTION AND TYPOLOGIES

Table 5.5: Details of the handstones and pestles found at Jebel al-Mutawwaq.

ID	Archaeological context	Artefact	Material	Preservation	Length	Width	Thickness
JM.18.0.1	C South	Polishing tool	Limestone	Intact	4.9 cm	6.8 cm	4.3 cm
JM.18.0.18	C South	Pestle	Limestone	Half preserved	5.5 cm	3.9 cm	3.4 cm
JM.18.0.20	C South	Polishing tool	Limestone	Intact	6.4 cm	6.4 cm	5.6 cm
JM.18.0.27	C South	Polishing tool	Limestone	Almost intact	6.9 cm	5.4 cm	5.1 cm
JM.18.0.28	C South	Polishing tool	Basalt	Fragmentary	6.2 cm	4.8 cm	5.1 cm
JM.18.0.33	C East	Pestle	Basalt	Intact	7.9 cm	3.1 cm	2.7 cm
JM.17.0.81	House 77	Polishing tool	Limestone	Intact	9.1 cm	6 cm	4 cm
JM.17.0.82	House 77	Pestle	Limestone	Intact	9.6 cm	8 cm	6.9 cm
JM.17.0.84	House 75	Polishing tool	Limestone	Intact	7.2 cm	4.5 cm	4 cm
JM.17.0.85	House 75	Polishing tool	Limestone	Intact	5.9 cm	4.1 cm	3 cm
JM.17.0.97	House 75	Polishing tool	Limestone	Intact	9.1 cm	7 cm	4.2 cm
JM.17.0.98	House 75	Polishing tool	Limestone	Intact	7.5 cm	4.5 cm	4.4 cm
JM.17.0.36	Dolmen 232	Polishing tool	Basalt	Fragmentary	13.3 cm	7 cm	9.1 cm
JM.13.B.18	Dolmen 228	Pestle	Basalt	Fragmentary	6 cm	3.4 cm	ND
JM.17.0.122	House 131	Pestle	Basalt	Fragmentary	3.2 cm	4.9 cm	ND

Great Enclosure (Fig. 5.5). The object presents several traces of pecking on its sides and the surface is not finely smoothed. The peculiar aspect of the slab is the fact that, on its ventral surface, the area dedicated to grinding activity is clearly visible thanks to several traces of polishing on the surface. The slab is 30 cm in length while the portion dedicated to the activity is 16.5 cm in length. The fact that it is made of limestone and that the short sides are fragmentary could suggest that the slab was originally part of the bedrock and that it was broken intentionally or broke naturally after the end of its use. As the slab was found in a collapsed layer, its archaeological context was not sealed; that is consistent with the possibility that it was originally part of the bedrock.

Regarding the distribution of the grinding slabs throughout the site, despite their small number, it is noticeable that out of a total of twenty-three artefacts, eight were collected inside Building 131. The structure has been interpreted as a food production area, as discussed in Chapter 3, and the concentration of ground stone artefacts in this context is perfectly consistent with the function of the building.

Similar objects are attested at Qyriat Ata (Rowan 2003, fig. 6.1), at Arad (Amiran 1978, pl. 79.3), at Tell Umm Hammad (Betts (ed.) 1992, fig. 194.696), and at Jebel Abu Thawwab (Kafafi 2001, fig. 5).

Handstones/Polishing Tools and Pestles (Plates 5.10–5.11)

This category includes different objects used in the grinding and pounding of food. They can be divided into pestles and grinders. Handstones are the upper mobile ground stone artefacts used in association with the grinding slabs, while pestles are mobile tools used for the pounding activity in association with mortars. The distinction between handstones and pestles is mainly based on the wear and tear traces on the objects.

In total, fifteen tools were found between 2012 and 2018, there are five pestles and ten polishing tools. The polishing tools are characterized by the presence of traces of wear on the sides; usually one of the sides appears smoother than the others. Conversely, pestles are characterized by traces of use on one of the short sides where the object appears smoother. Despite the small number of artefacts, a predominance of handstones can be observed; this may be due to the fact that, as opposed to the handstones, the community may have chosen to use a different perishable material for pounding, such as wood.

Concerning the material used, 80 per cent of the polishing tools are made of limestone and 20 per cent of basalt, while 40 per cent of pestles are made of limestone and 60 per cent of basalt (Table 5.5).

Concerning the distribution of the artefacts throughout the site, it is quite homogeneous in the different areas. It is of note that just one polishing tool was found inside Building 131, although eight grinding slabs were collected there. Another point of interest is the presence of four polishing tools in the Temple area, inside House 75, where food production activities were performed.

Similar objects were found at Jawa (Betts & Helms (eds) 1991, fig. 193.692), at Jebel Abu Thawwab (Kafafi 2001, fig. 8), and at Beth Shean (Mazar 2012, fig. 9.15).

Mortars (Plate 5.12)

The main characteristic of this category is that the surface use is sub-circular in plan and variable in section, from shallow and concave to U-shaped. Usually, they are not shaped on the external surface.

At Jebel al-Mutawwaq five fragmentary mortars were found. Four of them were found in the Temple area (Table 5.6). They are as follows:

(1) JM.17.0.40 is a shallow, limestone mortar with a diameter of *c.* 10 cm; it was found in the courtyard of the sacred area;

(2) JM.17.0.41 is a U-shaped, basalt mortar with a diameter of 14 cm; it was found close to the northeastern gate of Building 76;

(3) JM.17.0.74 is a shallow, basalt mortar with a diameter of 20 cm; it was found in the courtyard;

(4) JM.17.0.80 is a shallow, limestone mortar with a diameter of 16 cm found in Building 75.

The fifth basalt mortar, JM.16.403.A, was found in Area C South. It is quite squared in shape with a very sharply defined base. The diameter of the artefact is 13.2 cm. This mortar was found in a surface layer; thus, it does not relate to any sealed archaeological context.

The mortars pertaining to a reliable archaeological context were found in the Temple area; two of them were found in the courtyard, while one of them was found close to the main building, House 76, and one inside House 75, where the presence of several ground stone artefacts suggests that the function of the structure was connected to food production activities for the community.

The small number of this typology found throughout the site, especially in the areas where several other ground stone artefacts had been found, could be explained when considering that some of the identified cup marks dug directly into the bedrock were probably used as mortars, given their shape and internal traces.[13] In some cases, it is possible to observe a concentration of ground stone artefacts associated with the presence of a mortar or of a cup mark, for example, this occurs in the Temple area, inside House 75, and in Area C, inside Building 131.[14] These data suggest that both typologies of tools were used for the same activities.

If it were to be assumed that the ground stone artefacts were used to grind cereals, it could be hypothesized that the mortars were useful for another function, that is, initially the spikes of hard cereals needed to be beaten to break the protective film on the caryopsis, and so to isolate the seeds from the pericarp. Only after this initial phase was it possible to proceed with the grinding activities using ground stones and handstones.

Similar mortars were found at Tell Umm Hammad (Betts (ed.) 1992, fig. 189), at Tell Abu Kharaz (Fischer 2008, fig. 200.6), and at Al-Khawarij (Lovell et al. 2007, fig. 15).

Textile Production Tools (Plate 5.11)

Five stone objects were identified as loom weights or spindle whorls during the 2012–2018 excavation campaigns (Fig. 5.6). three of them were found in Area C South; one of them was in Building 131. Concerning the tools found in Area C South, they are mainly made of limestone, except for JM.18.0.56 which is made of basalt. None of these specimens are intact, but it is possible to reconstruct the dimensions of the objects and the diameter of their central holes. All the objects present

---

13 During a survey conducted in 2019 at Jebel al-Mutawwaq with the aim of identifying all the visible cup marks on the site, it was possible to recognize the distinct typologies and shapes of them. Some of them could be interpreted as postholes because they are characterized by a noticeable depth, a small diameter, and a sharp regular rim; conversely, others present a shallow depth, a larger diameter, and a raised rim. Those characteristics together with the location of this kind of cup mark, also inside the Building 131, suggest that these features were used as mortars. For Building 131 this hypothesis is consistent with the proposed function of the structure, interpreted as a community productive area (see Caselli 2023).

14 In addition to the contexts described in this volume, the excavations performed in Area EE in 2019 and in 2021 have to be considered. In fact, in 2019, during the investigations of the surroundings of Dolmen 11, several ground stone artefacts together with a cup mark were found, suggesting that food production activities were performed there, close to the funerary structure, perhaps in association with the funerary rituals (see Polcaro & Muñiz 2023). Moreover, in 2021 a structure was identified and partially excavated. Inside the structure, Building 1214, two slabs were found together with two querns and a cup mark engraved in a mobile limestone block.

5. THE LITHICS: FUNCTION AND TYPOLOGIES

Table 5.6: Details of the mortars found at Jebel al-Mutawwaq.

ID	Archaeological context	Preservation	Material	Diameter	Thickness
JM.17.O.40	Temple area	Fragmentary	Limestone	16 cm	4 cm
JM.17.O.41	Temple area	Fragmentary	Basalt	14 cm	4 cm
JM.17.O.74	Temple area	Fragmentary	Basalt	19 cm	7 cm
JM.17.O.80	Temple area	Fragmentary	Limestone	26 cm	5.5 cm
JM.16.403.A	Area C South	Fragmentary	Basalt	ND	8 cm

Figure 5.6: The intact limestone loom weight/spindle whorl found in Building 151 (JM.17.O.34).

a smooth surface. The object collected in Building 131 is similar to the other loom weights as regards material and dimensions (Table 5.7), but it has an irregular surface, as well as an irregular central hole. This object is half preserved.

During the various campaigns, it was also possible to analyse some of the finds collected by the Spanish team between 1989 and 2011. During this activity, it was possible to identify an intact limestone loom weight found in Building 151. This object presents a very smooth and regular surface, a regular circular central hole, and a somewhat circular cross-section. Due to their small number and their state of preservation, it is difficult to identify an internal division of these objects into groups. However, it is possible to observe that the majority of them had a rather circular cross-section, while at least one of them has an ovoid cross-section. The dimensions are quite homogeneous; the objects present an inner diameter of between 1 cm and 1.8 cm, while the outer diameter measures between 3 cm and 6 cm. It was not possible to analyse the exact weight of the objects because of their state of preservation, in particular the more irregular ones.

Concerning the material, it is possible to observe a predominance in the use of limestone, probably because of the high availability of this material at the site. In fact, the stone loom weights, not described in this publication as they come from the 2019 and 2021 excavation campaigns, are also mainly made of limestone.[15]

As already stressed, the typology of these objects is usually interpreted as pertaining to spindle whorls or to loom weights. In this case, the majority of the objects probably relate to loom weights as the irregularity of the central holes and of the outer surfaces suggests that it would have been difficult to attach them to wooden sticks without being wobbly and unstable.[16] Despite that, the regularity of the hole and of the entire shape and surface of the intact example (JM.17.O.34) suggest that this object could be interpreted also as a spindle whorl.

Concerning the archaeological contexts where these objects were found, they come from Building 131, investigated in 2015, from Building 151, investigated by the Spanish expedition in 2009, and from Area C South, which was investigated between 2016 and 2018. Building 131, located in Area C and already described in Chapter 3, is an interesting structure because it is connected to Dolmen 534, and because it seems to have been used as a productive structure for the entire community.

In addition, in Area C, two cup marks used as mortars and two large circular platforms have been identified, further testifying to the fact that food production activities were performed there. The presence of a loom weight may suggest that distinct activities were performed there, including textile production, even though only a single loom weight was found. In fact, the presence of four tabular scrapers in the same context of

---

15 The stone loom weights found during the later excavation campaigns are described in Polcaro et al. *in press*, in Polcaro & Muñiz 2023.

16 As suggested by Fischer 2008, 354. He divided the objects into two groups and identified the use of each of them, in particular thanks to the finding of some spindle whorls still connected to a wooden stick.

Table 5.7: Details of the textile production tools found at Jebel al-Mutawwaq.

ID	Archaeological context	Preservation	Material	Height	Inner diameter	Outer diameter
JM.16.CSUD.406/b	Area C South	Half preserved	Limestone	2.6 cm	1.5 cm	5 cm
JM.18.O.24	Area C South	Half preserved	Limestone	3.5 cm	1.1 cm	3 cm
JM.18.O.56	Area C South	Half preserved	Basalt	2.6 cm	1 cm	3 cm
JM.17.O.126	Building 131	Half preserved	Limestone	5.2 cm	1.8 cm	6 cm
JM.17.O.34	Building 151	Intact	Limestone	3.6 cm	1.2 cm	4 cm

loom weights can be related to the wool cycle, including distinct processes conducted using different tools.[17]

Building 151 is a structure located in the northeastern area of the site. It is of interest because it is part of a complex made up of several structures that, due to the dimensions of the structures and the finds found there, probably had a public function (Fernández-Tresguerres 2011c). The smooth surface of the loom weight found there and its preservation confirm that the object did not pertain to a domestic context.

Most of the loom weights collected between 2012 and 2018 come from Area C South where, as described in Chapter 3, during the excavation of Dolmen 535 and its entrance, a funerary cave connected to the dolmen was identified and investigated. During the excavations, it was possible to identify two different phases of use of the cave: the first phase relates to the domestic use of the cave (Early Bronze Age IA), while the second phase relates to its funerary use (Early Bronze Age IB). The loom weights collected in this area probably relate to the domestic use of the area.

Similar tools were found at Jebel Abu Thawwab (Kafafi 2001, fig. 10.2–11), at Tell Abu Kharaz (Fischer 2008, fig. 34.3–4), and at Bab edh-Dhra (Rast & Schaub 2003, fig. 21.1.10).

Mace-Heads (Plate 5.13)

Mace-heads are pierced spherical objects. They could be used as actual weapons, using a stick as a handle, or as a status symbol (Bourke 2001, 142).

Chalcolithic mace-heads present a high degree of variability in terms of material, having been found in granite, basalt, hematite, limestone. The most common materials used appear to have been limestone and hematite.[18] Conversely, the Early Bronze Age I examples are mainly made of limestone, and it is possible to observe the disappearance of some materials (such as granite) in preference to such hard white stone as calcite and limestone. Another change regarding mace-heads is their shape. In fact, during the Early Bronze Age I period, the variability slowly decreased and the most attested shapes are the piriform, globular, and barrel shapes. Furthermore, it is interesting to note that, in EB I contexts, the finding of unfinished mace-heads is much more frequent than in Chalcolithic contexts.

The low variability of the shapes, the propensity to choose locally available material, and the presence of unfinished items suggest that the mace-heads were produced in loco and that, after the end of Late Chalcolithic period, they lost their value as goods to be exchanged.[19]

Eight mace-heads were found and studied during the 2012–2018 campaigns at Jebel al-Mutawwaq (Table 5.8). Two of them come from the Great Enclosure, one from Area C South, one from the Temple of the Serpents (Fernández-Tresguerres 2005a), one from Dolmen 534, and three from the Northern Sector of the site, where House 151 was investigated by the Spanish team.

The Temple of the Serpents' find (JM.17.O.119) is comprised of half a mace-head. This almost hemispherical object shows traces of working on its two short sides, similar to the start of the perforating process, probably to create the hole in the mace-head. This is only

---

17 In this regard, during the 2019 campaign at Jebel al-Mutawwaq, Area EE was investigated on the southern slope of the mountain. During the excavations, Cave 1210 was investigated and, in front of its entrance, several tabular scrapers and loom weights/spindle whorls were found, suggesting that the tools were associated because used in the same processes linked to the wool cycle. Further investigations will give more data about the archaeological context and the material culture.

18 As discussed by Rowan & Levy 2011, the percentage of the chosen materials changes if the Nahal Mishmar hoard is included in the count because of the large amount of copper artefacts in that context (see Bar-Adon 1980).

19 For a discussion about the role of Pre-Dynastic and Proto-Dynastic Egypt and its influence on this phenomenon, see Rowan & Levy 2011.

5. THE LITHICS: FUNCTION AND TYPOLOGIES

the start of the working process, that is, solely the first polishing of the surface and the starting of the perforating process. It is likely that the object broke during this process. The object has a slightly elongated spherical shape, perhaps slightly piriform in shape. The object was found in the pit close to the altar inside Building 76.

The mace-head found in Area C South (JM.18.O.19), similar to the one found in the Temple, is unfinished and the central hole does not pierce the entire object; this is probably because the mace-head broke before the end of the process. The object has a globular shape, is made out of limestone, and its surface is not polished. The mace-head was found in SU 412, a layer located under floor L. 1007 which is in front of the entrance to Dolmen 535.[20] Layer SU 412 was part of the sealing layers of Cave C. 1012. For this reason, this is probably not its primary context.

A fragment of a mace-head was found in Area C during the excavation of Dolmen 534 in 2014. The fragment was in one of the surface layers, which was not its primary context. Almost one half of the fragment is preserved. It is unfinished, probably because it broke during the manufacturing process. The holes on both sides are not deep. Several traces of working and polishing (radial lines starting from the centre of the preserved portion to the edges of the object) are visible. The polished surface shows some breaks but the object probably broke before it was used. The object is white in colour. It appears to be different to the other stone tools from the site in that it appears that the limestone is chalky and softer that the common limestone used, suggesting the object had no practical use.

The mace-heads found in the Great Enclosure in 2014 have a quite regular globular shape and are made of a different material in comparison to the other examples. One of them (JM.14.O.74) is black in colour, and the analysis performed by the University of Cagliari[21] has revealed that it is not made of basalt. The mace-head is half preserved; the hole has an irregular shape and the surface is very smooth, with no traces of use being identified. The other example (JM.14.O.73) has a reddish colour with yellowish and black spots. It is probable that the object is made of a specific type of limestone rich in iron oxide. The two mace-heads found in the Great Enclosure are better worked, having smooth surfaces, and do not seem to have been used as mace-heads. It is not clear why the community of Jebel al-Mutawwaq chose to use these particular materials solely for these two objects, and the context in which they were found is not sealed. In fact, they were found within a collapse layer of the Great Enclosure wall, and the scarcity of material from the Great Enclosure does not enable any interpretations.

All the mace-heads described here were not intact at the moment of their discovery. Between 2007 and 2009, the Spanish expedition, directed by J. A. Fernández-Tresguerres, investigated the northern portion of the site, where they identified a complex comprising of at least three buildings with a central courtyard.[22] During the excavations, four intact mace-heads were recovered.

Mace-head JM.17.O.31 is an intact piriform-shaped mace-head with a smooth, polished surface. On the smaller side the object there is a circular hole that does not reach the other side of the mace-head. Internally, the hole shows several concentric circular lines of working. The hole is 2.7 cm in depth, 1.8 cm wide at the top, and 0.9 cm wide at the bottom.

Mace-head JM.17.O.32 is an intact, almost spherical (slightly flattened) mace-head with a smooth, polished surface. On the upper side of the object there is a circular hole that does not reach the other side of the mace-head. Internally, the hole presents several concentric circular lines of working. The object is an unfinished mace-head; in fact, the hole is only 0.9 cm in depth, 1.3 cm wide at the top, and 0.9 cm wide at the bottom. Traces of use are visible on one of its sides.

Mace-head JM.17.O.33 is intact and has a circular hole that goes through its entire centre. The mace-head has a bi-conical rhomboidal shape. The surface of the object is not smooth and polished, but indicates many instances of irregular retouching. The irregular surface of the object has not been attested at the site, and it was not possible to identify any similar mace-heads in the region during Early Bronze Age I.

It is interesting to note that the intact mace-heads found in House 151 have some peculiar characteristics: examples JM.17.O.31 and JM.17.O.32 appear to be unfinished as they are not completely 'through-holed'. Despite this fact, the objects are very well smoothed in comparison to the unfinished objects from the Temple of the Serpents and Area C South. This would appear to suggest that the objects could have a different function, or that the choice to not realize a through-hole

---

20 Polcaro, Chapter 3 in the current volume.

21 The Raman analysis was performed by Prof. Carlo Ricci and Dr Daniele Chiriu from the University of Cagliari.

22 Fernández-Tresguerres 2007; 2008b; 2009.

Table 5.8: Details of the mace-heads found at Jebel al-Mutawwaq.

ID	Archaeological context	Preservation	Material	Height	Inner diameter	Width
JM.17.0.119	Temple area	Half preserved	Limestone	6.5 cm	-	6.4 cm
JM.17.0.31	Building 151	Intact	Limestone	5.4 cm	0.9–1.8 cm	4.9 cm
JM.17.0.32	Building 151	Intact	Limestone	5 cm	0.9–1.3 cm	5.8 cm
JM.17.0.33	Building 151	Intact	Limestone	6.5 cm	1.4 cm	5 cm
JM.17.0.63	Dolmen 534	Half preserved	Limestone?	3.9 cm	0.3–0.9 cm	5.9 cm
JM.14.0.73	Area C East	Half preserved	Limestone?	5.4 cm	0.9 cm	6.4 cm
JM.14.0.74	Area C East	Half preserved	?	5 cm	1 cm	5.2 cm
JM.18.0.19	Area C South	Half preserved	Limestone	4.8 cm	1 cm	5 cm

Figure 5.7: Some examples of mace-heads from Jebel al-Mutawwaq: 1 (JM.14.0.74) and 2 (JM.14.0.73) were found in Area C East; 3 (JM.17.0.31) and 4 (JM.17.0.32) were found inside Building 151.

was intentional. In addition, example JM.17.0.33 has a rather unique shape; it has not been possible to find any comparisons at the site or in the surrounding regions.

A fourth mace-head was found in this excavation area. Unfortunately, it has not been possible to study it, and so for this reason it has not been included in this analysis. The object, unlike the other mace-heads from the excavation area, presents a shape that is consistent with the Early Bronze Age I repertoire from the southern Levant. The mace-head is in fact piriform in shape, with a very smoothed surface and a through-hole. Concerning the material, it appears to be basalt, but the absence of specific analysis does not permit any confirmation and so doubts remain. Even if the piriform shape is peculiar to Early Bronze Age I, this object is the only one with this shape found at the site of Jebel al-Mutawwaq. Furthermore, the archaeological context in which it was found is the same context as where the two unfinished mace-heads and JM.17.0.33 were found.

Unfortunately, it has not been possible to perform any other archaeological investigations in the area as a portion of the site is located on private land. For this reason, it is not possible to understand if the peculiar findings in the area depend upon a different chronological subphase of occupation of that area or are due to a different reason, such as import from another region.

Concerning the shape of the mace-heads from Jebel al-Mutawwaq, all of them are globular and not piriform in shape, as are most of the Early Bronze Age mace-heads (Fig. 5.7). The dimensions of the mace-heads are between 5 and 6 cm in height and width, and the holes have a diameter of between 0.8 and 1.4 cm.

Of interest is the use of different materials to realize mace-heads. They were principally made of limestone, as suggested by the Raman analysis, but different types of limestone. However, some of them, such as the chalky example JM.17.0.63, or the reddish one, JM.14.0.73, have only been attested to now amongst the stone object repertoire of the site. It could be suggested that the choice of the material was not functional, that is, the material was not chosen taking into consideration the practical use of the object, as suggested by the different degrees of hardness of the stones. It more probably depends on the fact that mace-heads primarily had a representative function, and for this reason the community chose not to use the same stone as they used for the tools utilized in daily life.

Similar mace-heads were found at Bab edh-Dhra (Rast & Schaub 1989, fig. 167.1–3) and at Tell Umm Hammad (Betts (ed.) 1992, figs 194–95).

Stone Disc

During the 2018 excavations in Area C South, Cave 1012 was found and investigated. At the end of the campaign, it was possible to recognize two different phases of use of the cave.[23] In fact, before its use as a funerary chamber, the cave was used for a different function; the hearth and the artefacts collected inside it suggest that the structure could have a domestic purpose or that the remains were functional to the creation of the funerary chamber. Inside the cave, directly on the bedrock, a peculiar object was found (Fig. 5.8).

It is a limestone disc-shaped object which measures 10 cm in width and 2.9 cm in thickness. and it is the only one pertaining to this typology throughout the site. The retouches on the edges suggest that the object was used as a chopper or a percussor, but the chosen material is not common, because usually those tools were made out of flint. It is not clear if the tool originally had a different function, as, for example a stopper for storage jars (consistent with its presence in the same context as several examples of ledge handles), and that its function changed over time and it was retouched and used as a chopper. The possibility that the tool originally had a different function is suggested also by the fact that the object presents a very well polished and refined upper side, while the other side has a roughly worked surface. This aspect could indicate that one side was more important than the other and a different degree of refinement on the two sides is not understandable for a percursor. Moreover, some traces of burning on a portion of the edges of the object suggest that it was exposed to heat but not uniformly.

An interesting parallel can be detected at the Late Chalcolithic sanctuary of Gilat, where two limestone scrapers were collected (see Levy (ed.) 2006, 571, fig. 11.37:2; 559, fig. 11.25:7). Moreover, also a limestone chopper was identified (Levy (ed.) 2006, 571, fig. 11.37:4).

Stone Vessels (Plate 5.14)

Stone vessels, especially basalt vessels, form a high percentage of the ground stone tool assemblages of many

Figure 5.8: The stone disc (JM.18.O.36) found in Area C South.

Late Chalcolithic settlements in the southern Levant.[24] They are usually characterized by a wide V-shaped profile and flat or fenestrated pedestal bases, and they are highly polished inside.

They were often decorated with a band of hatched triangles located on the inner edge of the rim, whilst the outer rim was sometimes decorated with parallel incised bands (Rutter 2003, 136). They are usually found in both domestic and public contexts, but Chalcolithic basalt vessels are considered to be prestige items (Chasan & Rosenberg 2019, 54). The production of basalt vessels decreased in number with the decline of craft specialization after the collapse of the Late Chalcolithic. However, despite this, these objects are well attested in Early Bronze Age I sites. Braun has identified three main typologies of Early Bronze Age I basalt vessels, the most common of them having flaring walls and a flat base, for example, such as the Late Chalcolithic bowls. The items have been found in both occupation and funerary contexts, and slowly decreased in number at the beginning of Early Bronze Age II (Braun 1990, 87). Fenestrated bowls are not attested in Early Bronze Age I sites; this is probably due to their peculiar manufacturing technology disappearing, together with the end of craft specialization at the end of the Chalcolithic.

Few basalt vessels have been found at Jebel al-Mutawwaq (Table 5.9). This assemblage is made up of six fragmentary basalt bowls.

One example of this assemblage (JM.15.O.34), found in Area C West, is an hemispherical bowl; it presents a

---

23 See Chapter 3 for the detailed description of the archaeological context.

24 See Rowan et al. 2006; Ilan et al. 2015; Rosenberg et al. 2016.

Table 5.9: Details of the stone vessels found at Jebel al-Mutawwaq.

ID	Archaeological context	Preservation	Material	Diameter	Thickness
JM.15.0.34	Area C West	Fragmentary	Basalt	10 cm	2.8 cm
JM.15.0.31	Area C West	Fragmentary	Limestone	11 cm	2.2 cm
JM.17.0.118	Temple area	Fragmentary	Limestone	17 cm	1.5 cm
JM.14.0.81	Area C East	Fragmentary	Basalt	16 cm	1.5 cm
JM.17.0.125	Building 131	Fragmentary	Basalt	19 cm	1.7 cm
JM.15.0.69	Building 131	Fragmentary	Basalt	ND	2.6 cm

thick rounded rim with a maximum diameter of 12 cm. Another stone vessel from Area C West (JM.15.0.31) has the same shape, but a thinner, pointed rim, the maximum diameter measures 14 cm.

The hemispherical stone vessel found in the Temple area (JM.17.0.118) presents a thin pointed rim, the base is preserved and its maximum diameter measures 17 cm. The artefact was found inside Room 2, one of the rooms of the multicellular structure inside the *temenos*.

It is interesting to note the presence of two V-shaped basalt vessels characterized by the presence of knobs on the external surface. This vessel typology of vessel is typical of the Late Chalcolithic period (Braun 2011b, 172). These vessels come from Area C East (JM.14.0.81) and from Building 131 (JM.17.0.125). Their maximum diameter measures 20 cm and 19 cm, respectively. Inside Building 131, another fragment of a basalt bowl was found (JM.15.0.69) but its fragmentary state does not permit the reconstruction of its maximum diameter or the precise shape of the vessel.

Despite the paucity of this kind of artefact, it is worth noting that the stone vessels were collected in archaeological contexts interpreted as communal productive and storage areas. In fact, Area C West comprising a large courtyard between Building C and Building 131, has already been interpreted as a productive centre. In the courtyard, L. 51, several storage installations were carved into the bedrock in order to place storage jars, consistent with the presence of stone vessels.[25] This information explains the presence of four of the six vessels in Area C West and inside Building 131.

With regard to the Temple area, a stone vessel was found inside Room 2, which is part of the multicellular structure inside the *temenos*.[26] Thus, the structure was interpreted as a storage area because of the concentration of storage jars inside it. This fact, together with the proximity of House 75, which has been interpreted as a productive area due to the presence of several ground stone artefacts together with a working slab and a fireplace, suggests that the objects were used for storage purposes.

It is worth noting that only one of the stone vessels collected during the excavations has a knob decoration on its outer surface and that it was found in Area C East. In fact, the knob decoration was frequently used in the Late Chalcolithic period and in the first phase of Early Bronze Age (Rosenberg & Golani 2012, 38). As already explained by Andrea Polcaro in Chapter 3 of the present volume, the C14 analysis performed in 2020 confirmed the hypothesis, already proposed by the directors of the expedition, of two main phases of occupation of the site: the first during EB IA and the second during EB IB.[27] The first phase of occupation has been attested in Area C East, the Great Enclosure, with the presence of a fragmentary stone vessel with a knob decoration on the surface possibly being related to the slow transition from the Late Chalcolithic material culture to the Early Bronze Age I tradition.

Similar stone vessels were found at Jebel Abu Thawwab (Kafafi 2001, fig. 9.2) and at Tell Umm Hammad (Betts (ed.) 1992, fig. 192:689).

---

25 See Chapter 3 for the description of the archaeological context and Chapter 4 for the description of the storage jars found in L. 51, in Area C West.

26 See Chapter 3.

27 The first phase of occupation of the site is dated to EB IA by the C14 analysis performed on some samples collected in the 2019 campaign in the Great Enclosure (5470-5316 cal BP = 3521-3367 cal BCE — Beta Analytic 576901); the EB IB phase is attested in the necropolis, in the Temple of the Serpents, and in the domestic contexts (from Cave C. 1012: 5190-5053 cal BP = 3241-3104 cal BCE — Beta Analytic 561343; from Dolmen 11: 4980-4856 cal BP = 3031-2907 cal BCE — Beta Analytic 576899; from the Temple of the Serpents: 5290-5040 cal BP = 3340-3090 cal BCE — Beta Analytic 194526; from House 400: 5064-4870 cal BP = 3115-2921 cal BCE — Beta Analytic 576900). See Polcaro & Muñiz 2023.

5. THE LITHICS: FUNCTION AND TYPOLOGIES

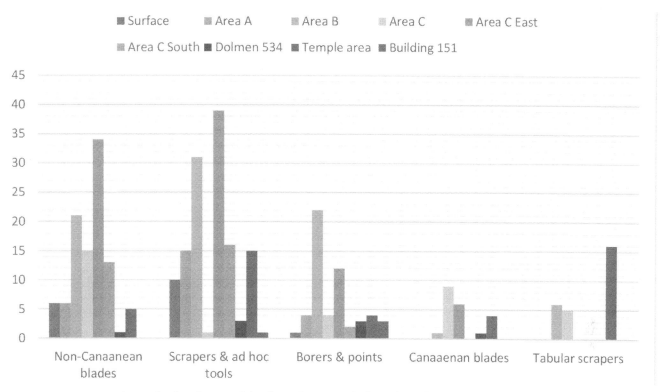

Graph 5.1: The distribution of the chipped stone tools throughout the site of Jebel al-Mutawwaq.

Spatial Analysis of the Lithic Assemblage

The main aim of this analysis was to delineate the function of the various excavated contexts by way of the study of the material culture.

Concerning the chipped stone tools, it is essential to divide the artefacts into two groups, the tools used in a domestic context in daily life by the inhabitants of Jebel al-Mutawwaq and the tools mainly found in peculiar contexts linked to communal activities. Non-Canaanean blades, scrapers, *ad hoc* tools, borers, and points pertain to the first group. These classes of materials are homogeneously distributed throughout the site, except for the Temple area where a scarcity of these typologies can be observed (Graph 5.1).

Conversely, the opposite situation can be noted if the distribution of Canaanean blades and tabular scrapers is under analysis. Regarding the Canaanean blades, the majority of them were found in the Temple area, in Area C East and in Area C, that is two sacred areas and the communal productive area. Concerning the tabular scrapers, the majority of them were found in the Temple area, in Area C and in the necropolis. This aspect confirms that these two classes of material had a specific function and a symbolic value, especially for the tabular scrapers that were linked to the spirituality of the community. In the case of Canaanean blades, their specialized technology determined its presence solely in public contexts.

Regarding the worked stone tools assemblage, the total number of the artefacts (sixty-one) is smaller than the total number of chipped stone tools (329). However, some observations can be made taking into account the distribution of the findings throughout the site (Graph 5.2).

The grinding implements comprise 70.49 per cent of the worked stone objects found at Jebel al-Mutawwaq. The objects present a quite homogeneous distribution throughout the site, except for Area C, where nine grinding tools were found inside Building 131, confirming the productive function of the structure.

Moreover, eleven grinding implements were collected in the Temple area where a distribution analysis of the objects is essential to understand the internal organization of the sacred area and the activities performed in the distinct structures located inside the *temenos*. Four Canaanean blades and seven tabular scrapers were found inside House 76, the main building of the complex, indicating maybe an offering to the gods. Conversely, no grinding implements were found in House 76, suggesting the mere functional use of these typologies without any symbolic or peculiar value. At

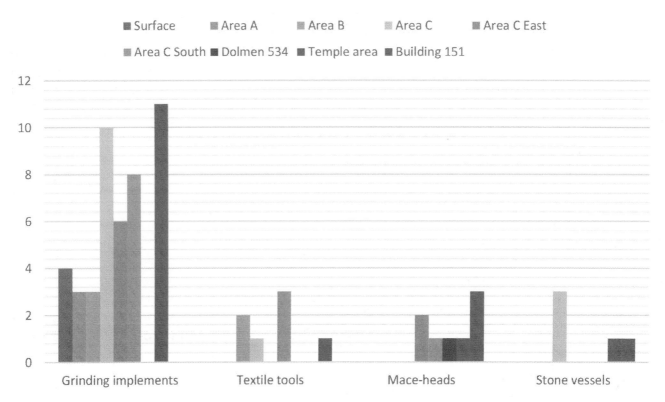

Graph 5.2: The distribution of the worked stone tools throughout the site of Jebel al-Mutawwaq.

the same time, two ground stone tools were collected inside House 77 and six inside House 75. These two structures had a productive and storage function. House 75 was internally divided into two rooms and a working table was identified inside one of them. The grinding implements were found in the eastern sector of the building and the tools collected here comprise 54.45 per cent of the total number of grinding implements collected in the temple area, confirming that the food production activities performed in association with the rituals of the inhabitants of Jebel al-Mutawwaq were conducted in this structure.

Regarding the other classes of worked stone materials described in this Chapter, that is the textile production tools, the stone vessels, and the mace-heads, the small number of examples pertaining to these typologies does not permit proposing any interpretation of the distribution analysis.

It is possible to observe that, regarding the mace-heads, none were found in domestic contexts, consistent with the interpretation of these objects as status symbols. In fact, the eight mace-heads presented in this Chapter were found in the Temple area, in Area C East (which was an open sacred area in the first phase of occupation of the site), in the necropolis, and inside House 151 that is part of a complex that surely had a specific function and value for the inhabitants of Jebel al-Mutawwaq (Fernández-Tresguerres 2011c).

In conclusion, the spatial analysis of the distribution of chipped and worked stone tools confirms that the society at Jebel al-Mutawwaq during Early Bronze Age I had an economy based on agro-pastoral activities. The presence of several tabular scrapers in specific archaeological contexts indicates the importance of pastoralism for the community. At the same time, the presence of areas and buildings dedicated to the grinding activity proves the importance of activities deriving from the agricultural exploitation of the surrounding landscape. The increase in agriculture attested throughout the southern Levant at the end of the fourth millennium BCE appears to have had an impact also on the community living at Jebel al-Mutawwaq, as confirmed by the presence of several olive seeds in distinct archaeological contexts, including domestic and public ones.[28]

Parallels and Chronology

The lithic repertoire from the site of Jebel al-Mutawwaq is quite homogeneous and reflects the traditions of the

---

[28] For the detail about the presence of olive seeds on the site and of the exploitation of olive trees see Chapter 7.

5. THE LITHICS: FUNCTION AND TYPOLOGIES

material culture of the southern Levant during the Early Bronze Age I period. In fact, with regard to the chipped stone tools, few typo-technological classes were widespread in the region during the fourth and third millennia BCE and, regarding the functional aspects, only two classes indicate continuity over these millennia: sickle segments and the multifunctional *ad hoc* tools (Manclossi & Rosen 2022, 304). This continuity depends on the use of these classes in domestic contexts and daily activities that were not directly subject to the effects of socio-economic changes and the transition between the Late Chalcolithic and Early Bronze Ages, which were to lead to the urbanization process. The changes in the lithic repertoire could have depended upon the evolution of technology; for instance, the axes slowly disappeared because of the increasing spread of metal objects. The changes in rituality may have had an influence on the material culture too, as happened with the disappearance of the Chalcolithic star tool (Manclossi & Rosen 2022, 308).

The long duration of some typologies throughout the fourth and third millennia BCE determines the difficulty in using the lithic repertoire, both chipped and ground stone, to better understand the chronology of an archaeological context. It is possible to use some classes, such as the tabular scrapers or the Canaanean blades, to fix a chronological *terminus ante quem* or *post quem* but there is no class that only spreads during the Early Bronze Age I period. For this reason, the main resource in order to frame a lithic repertoire are the comparisons with other sites located in the same region.

The lithic repertoire of the site is consistent with the repertoire of the Early Bronze Age I repertoire in the southern Levant, as shown by the assemblages of EB I sites in the southern Levant, such as Jawa, Tell Umm Hammad, and Tell Abu Kharaz.[29] The majority of the chipped and worked stone is comprised of tools with a domestic use, such as sickle fragments, scrapers, and *ad hoc* tools, as well as peculiar Early Bronze Age tools, such as the tabular scrapers that do not present incisions on the surface. The incisions on the tabular scrapers seem to appear during Early Bronze Age I, when the rituality of the Late Chalcolithic had already collapsed (Rosen 1997, 75). This aspect, linked to a peculiar typology used in community activities suggests that the incisions could have had a spiritual meaning.[30] The evolution of rituality in a community is a complex phenomenon that can have a distinct development in the different regions, especially at the beginning of the process in a society that is still at the proto-urban stage of development.

---

29 See Betts & Helms (eds) 1991; Betts (ed.) 1992; Fischer 2008.

30 The incisions were usually geometric but during a survey in the Sinai a tabular scraper with incisions representing an orant was collected (see Rosen & Gopher 2003, fig. 5.46:5).

Plate	Exc. No.	Area	Description	Parallels
5.1:1	JM.17.O.105	Building 76	Canaanean blade	Betts 1991, fig. 276.2; 1992, fig. 182.4; Mazar 2012, fig. 11.10.1; Kenyon & Holland 1983, fig. 345.5; Fischer 2008, fig. 34.6, fig. 50.4; Amiran 1978, pl. 83.1
5.1:2	JM.14.O.54	C West	Canaanean blade	
5.1:3	M.14.O.49	C West	Knife	Levy 2006, fig. 11.13.1; Kafafi 2001, fig. 3.1; Rast & Schaub 2003, fig. 16.1.a
5.1:4	JM.17.O.42		Knife	
5.1:5	JM.17.O.112	Building 76	Denticulated sickle	Betts 1991, fig. 277.2; Kafafi 2001, fig. 2.7; Levy 2006, fig. 11.12.5, fig. 11.13.1; Betts 1992, fig. 182.3; Mazar 2012, fig. 11.2; Fischer 2008, fig. 121.2
5.1:6	JM.17.O.113	Building 76	Denticulated sickle	
5.1:7	JM.17.O.130	Building 131	Denticulated sickle	
5.1:8	JM.16.CEST.708/A	C East	Denticulated sickle	Betts 1991, fig. 277.2; Kafafi 2001, fig. 2.7; Levy 2006, fig. 11.12.5, fig. 11.13.1; Betts 1992, fig. 182.3
5.1:9	JM.16.CEST.0/A	C East	Denticulated sickle	
5.1:10	JM.16.CEST.0/I	C East	Denticulated sickle	Betts 1991, fig. 277.2; Kafafi 2001, fig. 2.7; Levy 2006, fig. 11.12.5, fig. 11.13.1; Betts 1992, fig. 182.3; Fischer 2008, fig. 50.6
5.1:11	JM.14.O.44	C East	Denticulated sickle	
5.1:12	JM.16.CEST.0/A	C East	Denticulated sickle	Betts 1991, fig. 277.2; Kafafi 2001, fig. 2.7; Levy 2006, fig. 11.12.5, fig. 11.13.1; Betts 1992, fig. 182.3
5.1:13	JM.17.O.132	Building 131	Denticulated sickle	
5.1:14	JM.17.O.106	Building 76	Denticulated sickle	Betts 1991, fig. 277.2; Kafafi 2001, fig. 2.7; Levy 2006, fig. 11.12.5, fig. 11.13.1; Betts 1992, fig. 182.3; Getzov 2006, fig. 7.1.1–2; Amiran 1978, pl. 85.1
5.1:15	JM.17.O.124	Building 131	Denticulated sickle	
5.1:16	JM.14.O.72	C East	Denticulated sickle	
5.1:17	JM.14.O.63	C West	Denticulated sickle	
5.1:18	JM.14.O.43	C East	Denticulated sickle	Kafafi 2001, fig. 2.8; Betts 1992, fig. 182.3
5.1:19	JM.14.O.41	C East	Denticulated sickle	
5.1:20	JM.16.CEST.0/X	C East	Denticulated sickle	
5.1:21	JM.14.O.50	C West	Denticulated sickle	
5.1:22	JM.14.O.63	C West	Denticulated sickle	Kafafi 2001, fig. 2.8; Betts 1992, fig. 182.3
5.1:23	JM.14.O.60	C West	Denticulated sickle	
5.1:24	JM.14.O.56	C West	Denticulated sickle	Kafafi 2001, fig. 2.8; Betts 1992, fig. 182.3
5.1:25	JM.16.CSUD.0/D	C South	Denticulated sickle	
5.1:26	JM.18.O.34	C East	Canaanean blade	
5.1:27	JM.16.CEST.0/R	C East	Canaanean blade	Lovell et al. 2005, fig. 14.5
5.1:28	JM.13.O.27	Area B	Canaanean blade	

5. THE LITHICS: FUNCTION AND TYPOLOGIES

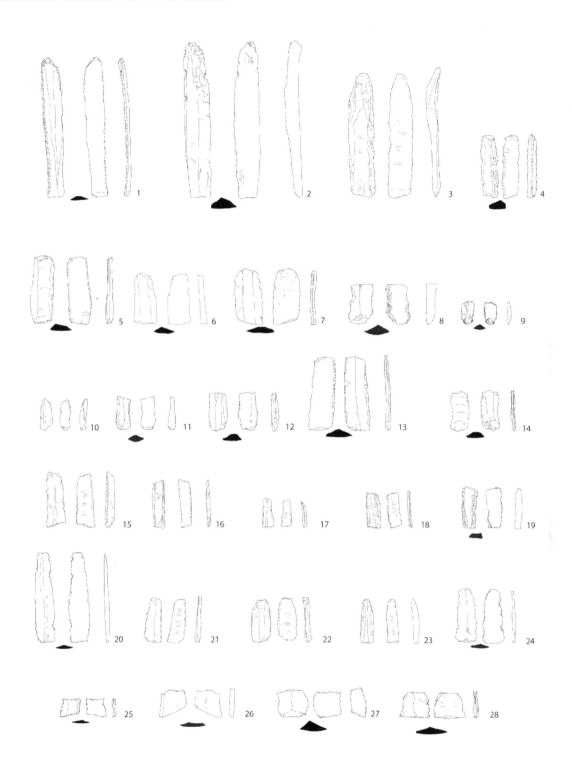

Plate 5.1: Canaanean and non-Canaanean blades.

Plate	Exc. No.	Area	Description	Parallels
5.2:1	JM.14.O.52	C West	Knife	Kafafi 2001, fig. 3.8; Rast & Schaub 2003, fig. 16.11.b; Fischer 2008, fig. 78.6; Amiran 1978, pl. 88.7
5.2:2	JM.13.A.0.3	Area A	Knife	
5.2:3	JM.17.O.103	Building 76	Sickle blade	Kafafi 2001, fig. 2.2; Rast & Schaub 2003, fig. 16.9.e
5.2:4	JM.13.O.23	Area B	Sickle blade	
5.2:5	JM.17.O.102	Building 76	Sickle blade	
5.2:6	JM.13.O.48	Area B	Sickle blade	Levy 2006, fig. 11.12.1
5.2:7	JM.13.A.0.5	Area A	Sickle blade	
5.2:8	JM.13.A.10.1	Area A	Sickle blade	Levy 2006, fig. 11.12.1; Rast & Schaub 2003, 16.2.g
5.2:9	JM.18.O.11	C East	Sickle blade	
5.2:10	JM.13.O.21	Area B	Sickle blade	Levy 2006, fig. 11.12.1
5.2:11	JM.13.O.22	Area B	Sickle blade	
5.2:12	JM.13.A.1.4	Area A	Blade	Levy 2006, fig. 11.12.5; fig. 11.13.1
5.2:13	JM.14.O.23	Survey	Blade	
5.2:14	JM.13.A.2.1	Area A	Blade	Levy 2006, fig. 11.12.5; fig. 11.13.1; Rast & Schaub 2003, fig. 16.9.f
5.2:15	JM.14.O.4	Area A	Blade	
5.2:16	JM.16.CSUD.0/B	C South	Blade	Levy 2006, fig. 11.12.5; fig. 11.13.1
5.2:17	JM.18.O.30	C South	Blade	

5. THE LITHICS: FUNCTION AND TYPOLOGIES

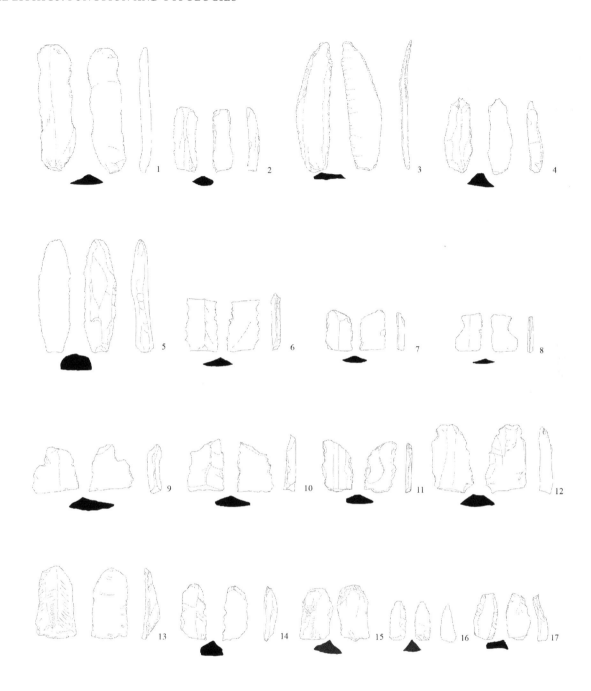

Plate 5.2: Non-Canaanean blades.

Plate	Exc. No.	Area	Description	Parallels
5.3:1	JM.18.O.32	C South	Flint chopper	Seaton 2008, pl. 100.a
5.3:2	JM.14.O.53	C East	Scraper	Levy 2006, fig. 11.25.5
5.3:3	JM.17.O.83	Building 75	Scraper	Levy 2006, fig. 11.25.7
5.3:4	JM.17.O.120	Courtyard of the Temple of the Serpents	Scraper	
5.3:5	JM.16.CEST.O/T	C East	Endscraper	Levy 2006, fig. 11.24.4
5.3:6	JM.14.O.58	C East	Endscraper	
5.3:7	JM.14.O.1	Area A	Endscraper	
5.3:8	JM.13.A.1.3	Area A	Scraper	Seaton 2008, pl. 101.i; Rast & Schaub 2003, 16.3.d
5.3:9	JM.14.O.51	C West	Scraper	Levy 2006, fig. 11.24.4
5.3:10	JM.14.O.47	C West	Scraper	
5.3:11	JM.14.O.13	Area A	Scraper	Seaton 2008, pl. 101.i
5.3:12	JM.13.AIV.1D	Area A	Scraper	
5.3:13	JM.14.O.55	C East	Axe?	Seaton 2008, pl. 102.6; Levy 2006, fig. 11.26.2; Kenyon & Holland 1983, fig. 344.2

5. THE LITHICS: FUNCTION AND TYPOLOGIES

Plate 5.3: Scrapers.

Plate	Exc. No.	Area	Description	Parallels
5.4:1	JM.13.O.70	B (Dolmen 317)	Fan scraper	Avrutis 2012, pl. 7.2.3
5.4:2	JM.13.O.69	B (Dolmen 317)	Elongated tabular scraper	Betts 1991, fig. 178.1
5.4:3	JM.17.O.5	Building 75	Fan scraper	Betts 1991, fig. 174
5.4:4	JM.15.O.54	Area CC (Building 131)	Elongated tabular scraper	Betts 1991, fig. 178.2; Rast & Schaub 2003, fig. 16.8.a; Fischer 2008, fig. 34.8
5.4:5	JM.17.O.117	Room 1	Fan scraper	Avrutis 2012, pl. 7.2.3
5.4:6	JM.17.O.3	Building 75	Elongated tabular scraper	Betts 1991, fig. 178.1; Kenyon & Holland 1983, 347.2

5. THE LITHICS: FUNCTION AND TYPOLOGIES

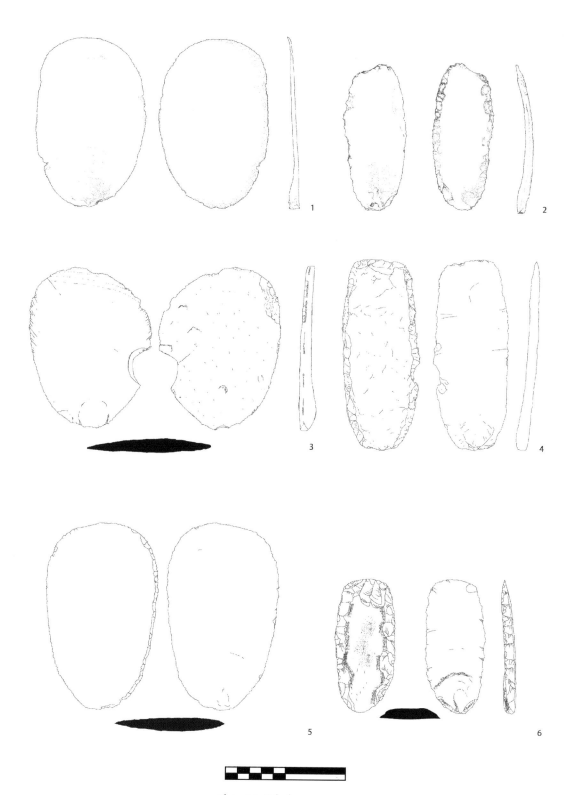

Plate 5.4: Tabular scrapers.

Plate	Exc. No.	Area	Description	Parallels
5.5:1	JM.17.O.7	Building 75	Fan scraper	Levy & Alon 1985, fig. 3.4
5.5:2	JM.17.O.134	Courtyard Temple of the Serpents	Fan scraper (fragment)	Levy 2006, fig. 11.20.2
5.5:3	JM.17.O.2	Building 75	Oval tabular scraper	Levy & Alon 1985, fig. 3.4; Amiran 1978, pl. 87.4
5.5:4	JM.17.O.108	Building 76	Rounded tabular scraper	Levy 2006, fig. 11.22.4; Rast & Schaub 2003, fig. 16.5.a
5.5:5	JM.17.O.109	Building 76	Elongated tabular scraper	Betts 1992, fig. 277.4; Mazar 2012, fig. 11.5.1
5.5:6	JM.17.O.70	Courtyard of the Temple of the Serpents	Rounded tabular scraper	Kafafi 2001, fig. 14.4; Fischer 2008, fig. 142.1; Amiran 1978, pl. 90.7
5.5:7	JM.17.O.138	Courtyard of the Temple of the Serpents	Irregular tabular scraper	Betts 1992, fig. 279
5.5:8	JM.17.O.107	Building 76	Oval tabular scraper (fragment)	Muller-Neuhof 2006, fig. 9d

5. THE LITHICS: FUNCTION AND TYPOLOGIES

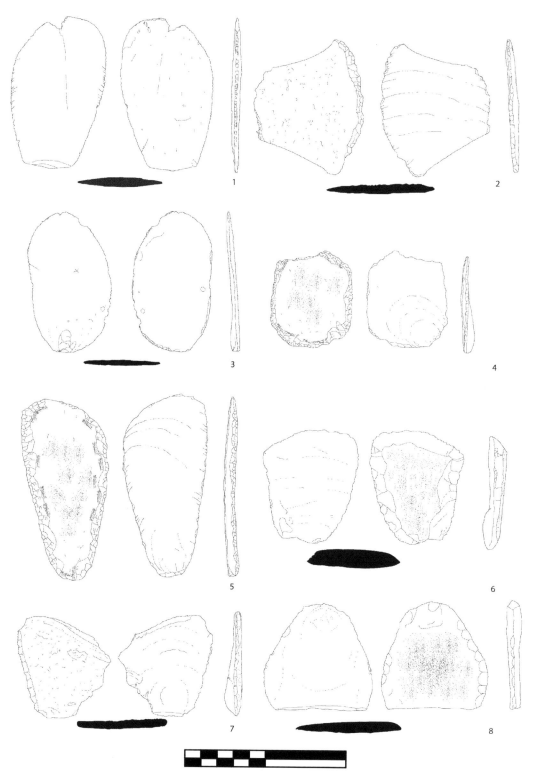

Plate 5.5: Tabular scrapers.

Plate	Exc. No.	Area	Description	Parallels
5.6:1	JM.17.0.115	Building 76	Perforator	
5.6:2	JM.13.0.24	Area B	Perforator	Betts 1991, fig. 278.2
5.6:3	JM.13.0.50	Area B	Perforator	
5.6:4	JM.17.0.131	Building 131	Perforator/Point	Betts 1992, fig. 180.1; Seaton 2008, pl. 102.f
5.6:5	JM.13.A.0/6	Area A	Point	Betts 1992, fig. 180.1; Mazar 2012, fig. 11.9.1
5.6:6	JM.14.0.59	C West	Perforator/Point	Lovell 2007, fig. 14.14; Betts 1992, fig. 180.2
5.6:7	JM.16.CEST.0/P	C East	Perforator/Point	Lovell 2007, fig. 14.18; Betts 1992, fig. 180.4; Golani 2008, fig. 13.6
5.6:8	JM.CEST.0/M	C East	Perforator	Lovell 2007, fig. 14.18; Betts 1991, fig. 278.2
5.6:9	JM.14.0.28	Survey	Borer	Levy 2006, fig. 11.17.15; Rast & Schaub 2003, fig. 16.13.d
5.6:10	JM.13.0.35	Area B	Borer	Levy 2006, fig. 11.17.15; Golani 2008, fig. 13.7
5.6:11	JM.13.0.53	Area B	Borer	Levy 2006, fig. 11.17.15
5.6:12	JM.13.0.36	Area A	Borer	Levy 2006, fig. 11.17.14–15
5.6:13	JM.13.0.58	Area B	Perforator	Betts 1992, fig. 180.1; Seaton 2008, pl. 102.f; Amiran 1978, pl. 81.4
5.6:14	JM.13.0.20	Area B	Borer	Levy 2006, fig. 11.18.2
5.6:15	JM.13.0.51	Area B	Burin	Seaton 2008, pl. 103.c
5.6:16	JM.13.0.43	Area B	Borer	Levy 2006, fig. 11.18.5
5.6:17	JM.16.CEST.0/H	C East	Borer	Seaton 2008, pl. 103.6; Levy 2006, fig. 11.17.15
5.6:18	JM.CEST.0/N	C East	Borer	Seaton 2008, pl. 103.6; Levy 2006, fig. 11.17.15; Rast & Schaub 2003, fig. 16.13.e
5.6:19	JM.14.0.66	C East	Borer	Seaton 2008, pl. 103.6; Levy 2006, fig. 11.17.15
5.6:20	JM.14.0.24	Survey	Borer	Levy 2006, fig. 11.17.1; Mazar 2012, fig. 11.8.5; Rast & Schaub 2003, 16.3.c; Barzilai et al. 2013, fig. 23.3
5.6:21	JM.14.0.36	Survey	Borer	Levy 2006, fig. 11.17.14–15
5.6:22	JM.14.0.11	Area A	Borer	Levy 2006, fig. 11.17.14–15; Rast & Schaub 2003, 16.3.j
5.6:23	JM.14.0.14	Area A	Borer	Levy 2006, fig. 11.17.14–15; Rast & Schaub 2003, fig. 16.3.g

5. THE LITHICS: FUNCTION AND TYPOLOGIES

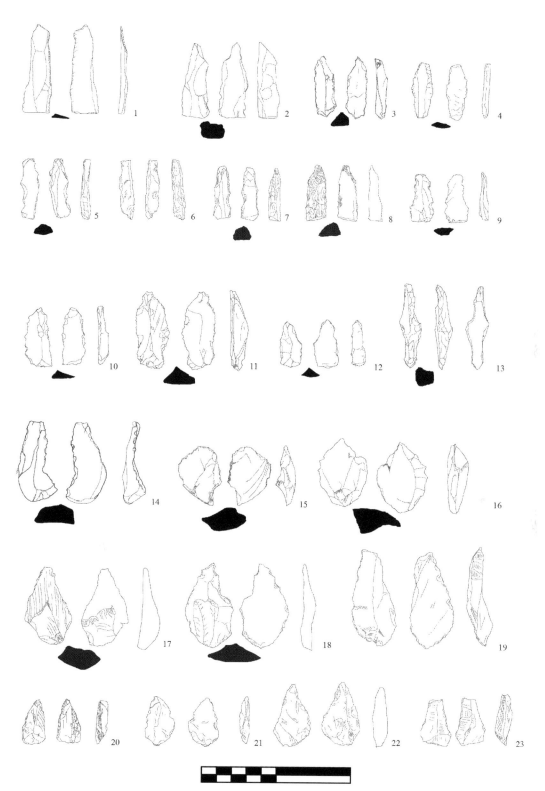

Plate 5.6: Borers.

Plate	Exc. No.	Area	Description	Parallels
5.7:1	JM.14.O.57	C West	Neolithic point (Haparsa type)	Kafafi 2001, fig. 1.3 (p. 127); Kenyon & Holland 1983, fig. 308.4
5.7:2	JM.13.O.54	Area B	Point	Levy 2006, fig. 11.17.4; Seaton 2008, pl. 101.4
5.7:3	JM.13.O.26	Area B	Point	Betts 1992, fig. 179.11; Rast & Schaub 2003, 16.3.h
5.7:4	JM.17.O.43	Area B	Point	
5.7:5	JM.16.CSUD.406/A	C South	Point	Levy 2006, fig. 11.17.4
5.7:6	JM.16.CEST.709/B	C East	Point	Levy 2006, fig. 11.17.4; Rast & Schaub 2003, 16.15.b
5.7:7	JM.16.CEST.709/A	C East	Point	
5.7:8	JM.16.CEST.709/C	C East	Point	Levy 2006, fig. 11.17.4
5.7:9	JM.17.O.128	Building 131	Point	Seaton 2008, pl. 103.6
5.7:10	JM.17.O.51	Area B	Point	Levy 2006, fig. 11.17.14

5. THE LITHICS: FUNCTION AND TYPOLOGIES

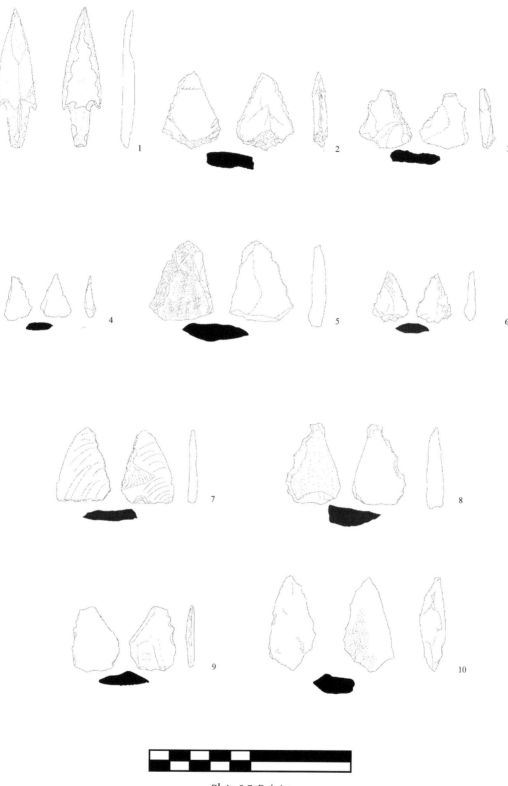

Plate 5.7: Points.

Plate	Exc. No.	Area	Description	Parallels
5.8:1	JM.17.O.140	Building 131	Saddle quern (basalt)	Betts 1992, fig. 194.696; Kafafi 2001, fig. 5; Amiran 1978, pl. 79.3; Callaway 1980, fig. 67.1

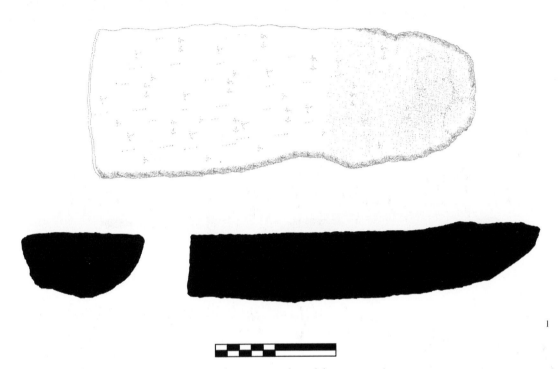

Plate 5.8: Grinding slab.

5. THE LITHICS: FUNCTION AND TYPOLOGIES

Plate	Exc. No.	Area	Description	Parallels
5.9:1	JM.17.O.36	Dolmen 232	Saddle quern (basalt)	Betts 1992, fig. 194.696; Kafafi 2001, fig. 5; Amiran 1978, pl. 79.1
5.9:2	JM.17.O.101	Building 75	Saddle quern (basalt)	Betts 1992, fig. 194.696; Kafafi 2001, fig. 5; Amiran 1978, pl. 79.7; Mazar 2012, fig. 9.13.4
5.9:3	JM.18.O.35	C East	Saddle quern (basalt)	Betts 1992, fig. 194.696; Kafafi 2001, fig. 5; Amiran 1978, pl. 79.6

Plate 5.9: Grinding slabs.

Plate	Exc. No.	Area	Description	Parallels
5.10:1	JM.17.O.84	Building 75	Handstone	
5.10:2	JM.17.O.85	Building 75	Handstone	
5.10:3	JM.17.O.98	Building 75	Handstone	Kafafi 2001, fig. 8; Betts 1991, fig. 193.692; Mazar 2012, 9.15
5.10:4	JM.17.O.100	Building 75	Handstone	
5.10:5	JM.18.O.1	C South	Handstone	Kafafi 2001, fig. 3.1–2; Mazar 2012, fig. 9.11.8–10
5.10:6	JM.18.O.20	C South	Handstone	Kafafi 2001, fig. 3.1–2

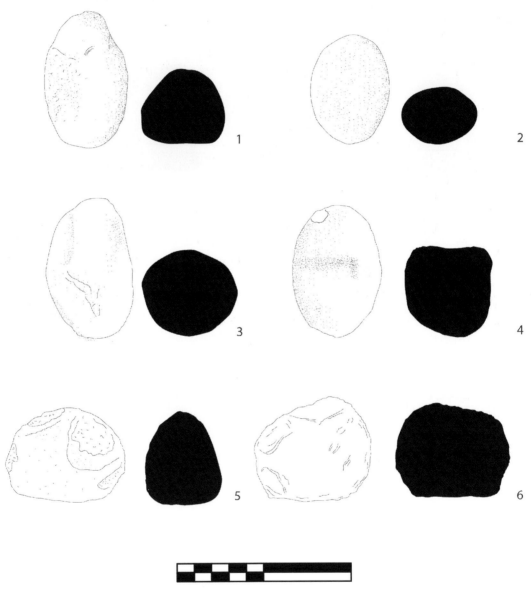

Plate 5.10: Handstones.

5. THE LITHICS: FUNCTION AND TYPOLOGIES

Plate	Exc. No.	Area	Description	Parallels
5.11:1	JM.18.O.33	C East	Pestle (basalt)	Betts 1991, fig. 283.15–26; Kafafi 2001, fig. 2; Seaton 2008, pl. 91; Amiran 1978, pl. 80.13; Mazar 2012, fig. 9.11.11
5.11:2	JM.18.O.18	C South	Pestle (limestone)	Betts 1991, fig. 283.15–26; Kafafi 2001, fig. 2; Seaton 2008, pl. 91; Amiran 1978, pl. 80.16
5.11:3	JM.18.O.56	C South	Loom weight (basalt)	Kafafi 2001, fig. 10.2–11; Amiran 1978, pl. 76; Rast & Schaub 2003, fig. 21.1.10; Mazar 2012, fig. 9.9
5.11:4	JM.18.O.24	C South	Loom weight (limestone)	Kafafi 2001, fig. 10.2–11; Amiran 1978, pl. 76.7; Rast & Schaub 2003, fig. 21.1.10
5.11:5	JM.16.406/B	C South	Loom weight (limestone)	Kafafi 2001, fig. 10.2–11; Lovell 2007, fig. 15.12; Amiran 1978, pl. 76.7; Rast & Schaub 2003; Mazar 2012, fig. 21.1.10; Rosenberg & Golani 2012, fig. 7.5
5.11:6	JM.13.O.19	Area B	Loom weight (basalt)	Kafafi 2001, fig. 10.2–11; Amiran 1978, pl. 76.8; Rast & Schaub 2003, fig. 21.1.10; Getzov 2006, fig. 2.18.11; Fischer 2008, fig. 34.3–4

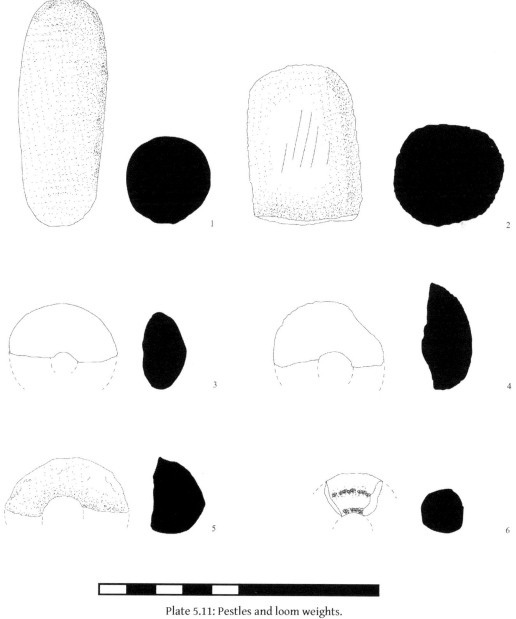

Plate 5.11: Pestles and loom weights.

Plate	Exc. No.	Area	Description	Parallels
5.12:1	JM.17.O.74	Courtyard of the Temple of the Serpents	Shallow mortar (basalt)	Betts 1992, fig. 189; Lovell 2007, fig. 15.13; Amiran 1978, pl. 78.22
5.12:2	JM.17.O.40	Courtyard of the Temple of the Serpents	Shallow mortar (limestone)	Betts 1992, fig. 189; Lovell 2007, fig. 15.13; Amiran 1978, pl. 78.8–9
5.12:3	JM.17.O.80	Building 75	Shallow mortar (limestone)	Betts 1992, fig. 189; Lovell 2007, fig. 15.13; Amiran 1978, pl. 78.9; Fischer 2008, fig. 142.3
5.12:4	JM.17.O.41	Building 76	U-shaped mortar (basalt)	
5.12:5	JM.16.O.403/a	C South	U-shaped mortar (Basalt)	Betts 1992, figs 190, 191; Fischer 2008, fig. 200.6; Rosenberg & Golani 2012, fig. 5.1

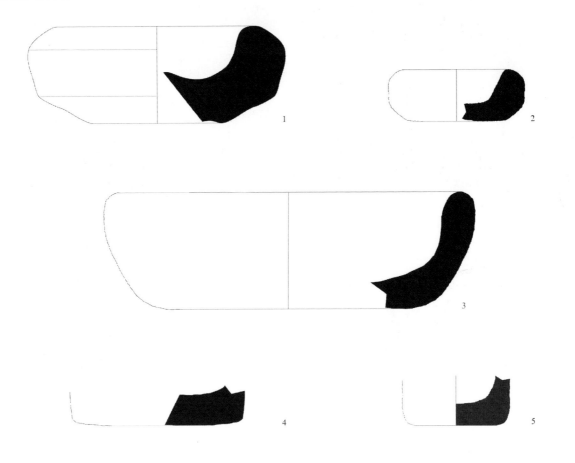

Plate 5.12: Mortars.

5. THE LITHICS: FUNCTION AND TYPOLOGIES

Plate	Exc. No.	Area	Description	Parallels
5.13:1	JM.18.O.19	C South	Mace-head	
5.13:2	JM.17.O.119	Building 76	Mace-head	Betts 1992, figs 194–95; Seaton 2008, pl. 87.a; Elliott 1977, fig. 5.7; Avrutis 2012, fig. 5.18; Amiran 1978, pl. 76.3; Rast & Schaub 1989, fig. 167.1–3; Mazar 2012, fig. 9.8.2; Kenyon & Holland 1983, fig. 365.6
5.13:3	JM.14.O.73	C East	Mace-head	
5.13:4	JM.14.O.74	C East	Mace-head	

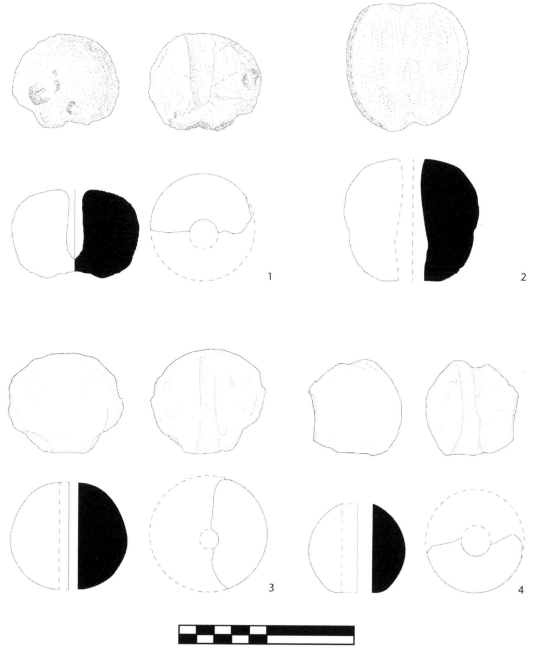

Plate 5.13: Mace-heads.

Plate	Exc. No.	Area	Description	Parallels
5.14:1	JM.15.O.34	C East	Stone vessel	Kafafi 2001, fig. 9.2
5.14:2	JM.15.O.31	C East	Stone vessel	Kafafi 2001, fig. 9.2; Amiran 1978, pl. 77.4
5.14:3	JM.17.O.118	Building 76	Stone vessel	Seaton 2008, pl. 94.d
5.14:4	JM.14.O.76	Surface	Stone vessel	
5.14:6	JM.17.O.125	Building 131	Stone vessel	
5.14:5	JM.14.O.81	C East	Stone vessel	Betts 1992, fig. 192:689

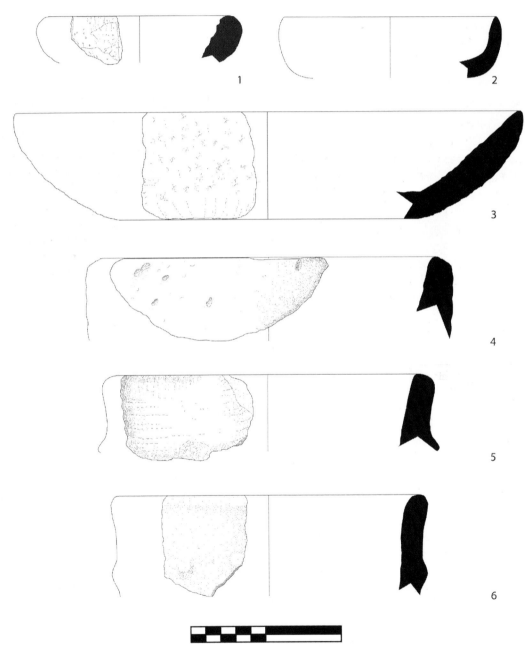

Plate 5.14: Stone vessels.

6. Biomolecular Archaeology: Preliminary DNA Analysis of Skeletal Remains from Jebel al-Mutawwaq

Chiara Panicucci, Sara Silvestrini, Giorgio Gruppioni, Donata Luiselli, Elisabetta Cilli & Patrizia Serventi

Overview

Today the study of archaeological contexts requires the synergy of many research areas in order to be able to conduct and interpret in a comprehensive way an archaeological excavation and the consequent reconstruction of past events. Of great importance in recent years is certainly the field of biology applied to the preservation and knowledge of archaeological heritage. Specifically, this study is focused on the study of ancient DNA of human remains from Jebel al-Mutawwaq, an Early Bronze Age site located in Jordan. The aim of this project was a preliminary genetic survey through ancient DNA analyses of the remains collected in this peculiar site, starting from the analysis of the mitochondrial DNA (specifically the HVS-I region). The first step is necessary to determine the state of preservation of the DNA in such ancient remains from an area that, until now, had been poorly investigated from a genetic point of view. This preliminary analysis, carried out on five individuals retrieved in different burials (from Dolmen 317 and Dolmen 534), investigated the presence, quality, and amount of DNA, the sex of individuals, and any maternal relationship among them. Thanks to the preliminary data obtained here, in the future steps of the project it would be possible to obtain more information by using recently developed techniques, such as the capture of complete mitochondrial genomes or some nuclear regions, coupled with high-throughput DNA sequencing (HTS) technologies.

Chiara Panicucci (panicuccichiara@gmail.com) MA in Archaeogenetics at Bologna University Alma Mater Studiorum, was collaborator of the Spanish-Italian Archaeological Expedition to Jebel al-Mutawwaq (Italy).

Sara Silvestrini (sara.silvestrini6@unibo.it) is a Research Fellow in Paleoproteomics and Archaeozoology at the University of Bologna Alma Mater Studiorum (Italy).

Giorgio Gruppioni (giorgio.gruppioni@unibo.it) is a Full Professor in Anthropology at the University of Bologna Alma Mater Studiorum (Italy).

Donata Luiselli (donata.luiselli@unibo.it) is a Full Professor in Archaeogenetics at the University of Bologna Alma Mater Studiorum (Italy).

Elisabetta Cilli (elisabetta.cilli@unibo.it) is an Adjunct Professor in Archaeogenetics at the University of Bologna Alma Mater Studiorum (Italy).

Patrizia Serventi (p.serventi87@gmail.com) is a Research Fellow in Paleogenomics at University of Rome Tor Vergata (Italy).

Ancient DNA Molecules: A Brief Review of the State of Art

History of Ancient DNA Study

The first ancient DNA (aDNA) study was published thirty-five years ago, when Russell Higuchi and co-workers reported in the journal *Nature* the molecular cloning of short mitochondrial DNA (mtDNA) sequence fragments from a piece of dry tissue of a 140-year-old quagga museum specimen, an equid species that became extinct in the nineteenth century. The quagga research captured international attention, demonstrating how preserved old tissues can retain amplifiable DNA sequences. This finding was shortly followed by

---

Jebel al-Mutawwaq: A Fourth Millennium BCE Village and Dolmen Field at the Beginning of the Bronze Age: Six Years of Spanish-Italian Excavations by Pontificia Facultad San Esteban and Perugia University (2012–2018), ed. by Andrea Polcaro, Juan Ramon Muñiz, and Alessandra Caselli, LEMA, 3 (Turnhout, 2024), pp. 221–231.
DOI 10.1484/M.LEMA-EB.5.136128

a report of the first detection of human nuclear DNA (nuDNA) in an extract of muscle from an infant boy of a pre-Dynastic Egyptian mummy. These first approach that yielded aDNA sequences by the cloning of end-repaired DNA molecules into *in vivo* vectors, showed that the genetic material surviving in ancient specimens was often principally microbial or fungal, and that endogenous DNA was generally limited to very low concentrations of short, damaged fragments of multi-copy loci, such as mtDNA. In fact, after an organism dies, genetic material is damaged under the effect of cellular nucleases, microbial enzymes, and physical factors. As a result, aDNA sequences contain chemical modifications, including strand breaks, DNA crosslinks, and modified bases, that make their recovery challenging (Pääbo 1989).

A few years later, the development of the polymerase chain reaction (PCR) technique (Mullis et al. 1986), made it possible to amplify minute amounts of specific genomic targets up to a level compatible with downstream sequencing (Pääbo 1989; Pääbo & Wilson 1988; Pääbo et al. 2004). Certainly, without the invention of PCR, it is unlikely that ancient DNA research would ever have resulted in more than a few reports of short DNA fragments with little biological significance. Nevertheless, the combination of the high sensitivity of the PCR reaction and the damaged nature of aDNA made modern contamination a key issue for these studies. In fact, due to the post-mortem DNA degradation processes, there is a high chance that an error is introduced in the early cycles of the PCR reaction, thus increasing the risk for preferential amplification of exogenous contaminant sequences (Rizzi et al. 2012). Thus, researchers have outlined a series of guidelines to ensure the quality of aDNA data and the reliability of consequent conclusions. Afterwards, these guidelines have gradually evolved into a more detailed and extensive list of requirements, resulting in a rigorous set of criteria for aDNA field (Knapp et al. 2015; Llamas et al. 2017; Cilli 2023).

Although the retrieval of multi-copy DNA sequences was often possible, the study of single-copy nuclear DNA from diploid organisms was particularly tough due to high rates of nucleotide damage, short DNA fragment lengths, low endogenous DNA content, and the possibility of modern contamination. Within the last decade, with the advent of high-throughput DNA sequencing (HTS) technologies, many of the issues with endogenous aDNA retrieval have been at least partially overcome. Whereas PCR method makes it possible to amplify a limited number of specific DNA targets at a time, the HTS combines amplification and sequencing of up to several billions of individual DNA library templates at a time (Llamas et al. 2017), thus reducing the sequencing costs. In HTS method, the extracts are used to yield DNA libraries that can then be sequenced or used to isolate DNA fragments of interest by hybridization capture (Burbano et al. 2010). One of the most relevant advantages coming from HST is that short molecules (<50 base pairs, bp) can be studied. As described above, there is the possibility to enrich the endogenous DNA fraction from highly contaminated aDNA extracts. Nowadays, one of the most popular enrichment approaches is the selective capture of particular regions of interest by hybridization of the ancient molecules with pre-designed oligonucleotide probes (Burbano et al. 2010). The targets of such selective capture assays can be complete mitochondrial genomes (Llamas et al. 2016; Posth et al. 2016), genome-wide SNPs analysis (Lazaridis et al. 2016; Uterländer et al. 2017; Mathieson et al. 2017; O'Sullivan et al. 2018), exomes capture (Castellano et al. 2014; Lindo et al. 2016), chromosomes, or complete genomes. These advances allow aDNA researchers to generate a huge amount of data that were inconceivable using previous techniques (Marciniak & Perry 2017).

Refinements of the techniques that allow short DNA sequences to be extracted efficiently (Rohland & Hofreiter 2007), as well as the finding that DNA is particularly likely to survive in the petrous part of the temporal bones of humans and animals (Gamba et al. 2014; Pinhasi et al. 2015), and also teeth (Higgins et al., 2013; Gamba et al. 2014, Damgaard et al. 2015; Hansen et al. 2017), have made it possible to retrieve genome-wide DNA data from large numbers of remains.

The aDNA Challenges: Degradation and Contamination

An understanding of the degradation of ancient molecules is an essential complement to the use of these molecules to address archaeological issues. Most recoverable fragments of aDNA are shorter than 150 bp and contain miscoding lesions that can result in erroneous sequences (Prüfer et al. 2010; Sawyer et al. 2012). A wide range of degradation patterns result in the fragmentation and chemical modification of DNA templates causing the nucleic acids' post-mortem instability.

After the death of an organism, cellular DNA repair mechanisms are blocked and without them, the DNA naturally and gradually degrades into short fragments.

Initially, endogenous nucleases start the process of DNA degradation, after that a combination of exogenous nucleases (released by microorganisms and environmental invertebrates) and environmental processes, such as exposure to oxygen and water, carry on the damage process.

Compared to the previously described enzymatic degradation processes, non-enzymatic reactions are slower but persistent. The depurination, which is a hydrolytic damage and the principal mechanism of DNA degradation, falls into this category. It consists of the hydrolysis of an N-glycosidic bond base-sugar resulting in a base loss. In correspondence of this abasic site, the strand breaks more easily. In detail, purines are liberated from DNA at similar rates with guanine being released slightly more rapidly, whereas pyrimidines are lost at 5 per cent of the rate of the purines. At a site of base loss, the DNA chain is weakened and undergoes strand cleavage by β-elimination.

The best characterized degradation reaction is the deamination, another hydrolytic damage, that also induces miscoding lesions that cause base misincorporations. The most common deamination reaction is from cytosine to uracil, thus resulting in a C to T transition. Deamination of purines, even if it occurs, is a minor reaction.

Hydroxyl radicals cause oxidative lesions that generate modifications in sugars and in bases, resulting in base misincorporations and/or block of DNA replication. In detail, the more common mutagenic lesions are the formation of an 8-hydroxyguanine, which basepairs with adenine rather than cytosine, and of a ring-saturated derivative of a pyrimidine, which occurs in several forms and results in noncoding bases. Moreover, abasic sites may proceed to DNA crosslinks between DNA and proteins or between the ring-opened sugar of the abasic sugar and an amino group located on the opposite strand and may prevent the amplification of endogenous DNA. A variety of lesions including oxidative damages, single and double-strand breaks, base modifications, destruction of sugars, intra and interstrand crosslinks, and formation of dimers could be caused by radiation. All these decay processes are responsible for the characteristics of aDNA recovered from the samples and they begin almost immediately after the organism dies.

Researchers have assumed that DNA survival correlates negatively with the age of the material. Nevertheless, several studies suggest that more than age, it is the sedimentary environment that influences the rate of decay of a sample (Pääbo et al. 1989; Poinar et al. 1996). Constant low temperatures, rapid desiccation, the absence of microorganisms, high salt concentrations, absence of oxygen, and neutral or slightly alkaline environments have the possibility to enhance the preservation of ancient DNA. In addition, few environmental situations can properly exclude the microbial activity, for example, if DNA binds to mineral surfaces and even fermentation activities of anaerobic bacteria and the presence of humic acids. Bollongino et al. (2008) also suggested that fresh excavated samples show a better preservation state (evaluated as PCR successful rate) than samples stored in the museum. As a result, extracted aDNA is always a mixture of endogenous and exogenous DNA, including that from bacteria, fungi, and other organisms that colonize the sample during burial, and any contamination occurring during excavations and processing from people who handle the specimens (Shapiro & Hofreiter 2014).

Given the conditions described above, the endogenous DNA is often contaminated with some level of exogenous DNA, as a result of post-mortem juxtaposition of organisms, or modern human DNA from the researchers themselves (Morozova et al. 2016). PCR-based studies had shown the extent of human contamination introduced during handling of bone and tooth samples when stringent aDNA precautions are not applied (Pilli et al. 2013). For example, laboratory instruments and reagents could be contaminated by modern human DNA during their production, before arriving at an aDNA laboratory (Deguilloux et al. 2011).

In order to avoid contamination, the experiment must be properly managed, including special requirements for sample collection, sterilization of the working area, DNA authentication, and independent reproducibility (Knapp et al. 2015; Llamas et al. 2017). These protocols are constantly being refined and improved. For example, there are several guidelines for sampling (Pilli et al. 2013; Llamas et al. 2017; Cilli 2023), which are equally relevant for archaeologists working in the field, physical anthropologists, and museum curators who handle the remains once unearthed. Regarding the protocols used for working in the aDNA laboratory (Poinar 2003; Pääbo et al. 2004; Champlot et al. 2010), in addition to mechanical removal of the outer layer and UV and/or sodium hypochlorite treatment of the sample, a brief pre-digestion step was recently suggested, consisting of short-term sample incubation (fifteen–thirty minutes) in an extraction buffer and its subsequent removal (Korlević et al. 2015; Damgaard et al. 2015). According to the authors, this step alone increases the fraction of endogenous DNA several fold (Damgaard et al. 2015). Irrespective of which decontamination method is used, aDNA researchers have to balance the removal of contaminating DNA with preserving the remaining endogenous DNA (Llamas et al. 2017).

Mitochondrial DNA (mtDNA)

Mitochondria are organelles present in multiple copies in almost all eukaryotic cells and mitochondrial DNA occurs in hundreds to thousands of copies in each cell. These double membrane-bound rod-shaped organelles are responsible for the energy supply of the cell, as they are the sites where the Krebs cycle and the oxidative phosphorylation take place. Mitochondrial DNA is a circular, double-stranded, 16,569 base pairs (bp) long molecule. Its high copy number, small genome size, maternal inheritance, and the presence of a fast-evolving region made mtDNA the chosen molecule for many genetic applications, ranging from forensic analyses, genealogical purposes, and population genetic studies. MtDNA contains thirty-seven genes coding for thirteen proteins involved in the energy metabolism, twenty-two transfer RNAs (tRNAs), and two ribosomal RNAs (rRNAs). The control region, also called D-loop, is about 1100 bp long and has an important regulatory function. This region consists of three hypervariable segments (namely HVSI, HVSII, and HVSIII) with a higher mutation rate than the coding region of the genome and a decreasing mutation rate between themselves. These distinct mutation rates in separate regions allow for different levels of analysis within the same molecule (Jobling et al. 2014). The mutation sites of the D-loop with respect to the revised Cambridge Reference Sequence (rCRS) (Andrews et al. 1999) define the haplotype of each individual while the sharing of defined mutations for biallelic markers (SNPs) in the coding region determines the affinity with a haplogroup. The study of the distribution of haplogroups along maternal lineages led to the construction of a mtDNA mutational tree that allows following the accumulation of genetic variants throughout human dispersal events, starting from 'Out of Africa'. Mitochondrial DNA, due to its maternal inheritance, absence of recombination, high mutation rate, and population-level variability, is a useful tool for reconstructing the past demographic events. In fact, it was successfully used in several projects to identify the demographic changes that shaped past and modern genetic variation of populations (Ghirotto et al. 2013; Serventi et al. 2018).

The Peopling of the Middle East

Since prehistoric times the Middle East has constituted a key area in the dispersal and admixture of modern humans, in fact its history was deeply marked by considerable movements of different populations through time, along with their goods and genes. From this area several fossils, for their morphological characteristics, archaeological contexts, and antiquity, have been the subject of numerous investigations and reconstructions of the evolutionary and population dynamics of modern humans (Caramelli 2009; Jobling et al. 2014).

The discovery of important fossils, such as those retrieved in the Qafzeh, Es Skhul, and Kebara Caves in Israel constitutes the earliest and most important proof of the first contact between the anatomically modern humans, who migrated about ± 125,000 years ago out of Africa, and Neanderthals, who lived in these territories hundreds of thousands of years before (Jobling et al. 2014). Those fossils have made it possible to clarify important steps in the reconstruction of the relationship between these two species, by studying the morphological features and by dating them with electron paramagnetic resonance and thermoluminescence techniques. Data showed that Neanderthals occupied the sites both before and after the anatomically modern humans (Caramelli 2009).

Moreover, during the tenth millennium and early ninth millennium calibrated BCE, this area was the epicentre of the Neolithic expansion through the origin and spread of agriculture, characterized by the domestication of plants and animals (Asouti & Fuller 2013). The same phenomenon independently arose also in Mesoamerica and the Yangtze region of south-east Asia.

The spread of farming from the Fertile Crescent was driven westward and northward over five millennia, but it has been a long-standing debate whether agricultural practices were diffused via migration of people (demic diffusion) or ideas (cultural diffusion) (Cavalli-Sforza et al. 1994).

Until recently, to discern patterns of human migration and admixture from human populations, data from archaeology, combined with anthropology, linguistics, the study of ancient texts, and also the analysis of modern DNA, constituted the only tools available. However, their resolution was often not sufficient and produced more unanswered questions.

Analysis of ancient DNA allows us to come back to the past and to follow the evolution and the population dynamics in real time. Sequencing of ancient genomes has addressed key questions about migration patterns, evolutionary pathways, kinship or personal identification, physiological or morphological features. Some paleogenetic studies have highlighted the important role of migrations in the Neolithization process (Skoglund et al. 2014) and in Bronze Age period migrations.

However, for a long time, owing to the poor preservation of DNA in warm climates, it has been impossible to study the population structure and genetic history of some peculiar populations, such as the first farmers of the Fertile Crescent, and to trace their contribution to later populations (Lazaridis et al. 2016). Recent improvements made it possible to partially overcome the obstacle of poor DNA preservation, such as the discovery of the optimal preservation of genetic material in the inner ear region of the petrous bone (Gamba et al. 2014; Pinhasi et al. 2015) and the continuous development of protocols (Carøe et al. 2018; Xavier et al. 2021). Thanks to these methodological ameliorations it was also possible to analyse DNA from some individuals retrieved in warm climates (Lazaridis et al. 2016; Harney et al. 2018), but conspicuous uncertainties remain about the whole process and the relative roles of migration, cultural diffusion, and proportion of admixture with local hunter-gatherers in the early Neolithization of Europe and in subsequent millennia with the different waves of migration (Hofmanová et al. 2016).

Materials and Methods

Samples for Genetic Analysis

The human skeletal remains of five individuals from the Early Bonze Age site of Jebel al-Mutawwaq were selected based on the archaeological information and on the state of preservation of the samples. In general, the specimen selection should be based on good preservation and minimal diagenetic alteration. The sampling of teeth and petrous bones was carried out throughout the archaeological campaigns between 2013 and 2016 field seasons with all the necessary precautions described in Fortea et al. (2008) to minimize the occurrence of contamination from modern human DNA. Briefly, samples were collected using disposable lab coats, sterile gloves, facemasks, and over-shoes and all the instruments used were decontaminated with 3 per cent sodium hypochlorite and ethanol before and after each sampling. All the specimens were delivered to the laboratory, stored in a cold and dry place in specific plastic bags, and annotated with sample description, location, number of

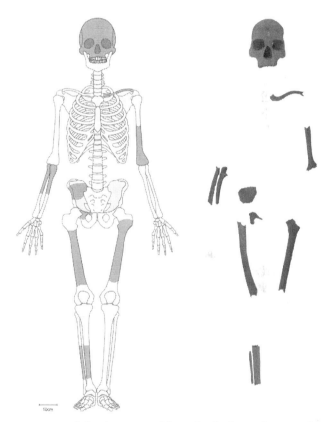

Figure 6.1: Skeletal remains of the individual B. 25 discovered in archaeological campaign of 2013.

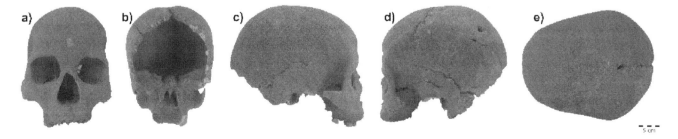

Figure 6.2: Skull detail of the individual B. 25.

burial, and stratigraphic unit. Moreover, buccal swab samples from all the archaeologists and anthropologists were taken to monitor potential sources of contamination.

In detail, from Dolmen 317 the skeletal remains of the individual B. 25 were discovered in the 2013 archaeological campaign (Fig. 6.1). In particular, the petrous bones coming from the skull of B. 25 were collected for the aDNA analysis (Fig. 6.2). Moreover, from this grave two more well-preserved petrous bones — belonging to two different individuals — were selected among a group of several bones situated in the same dolmen (B. 26). Moreover, from Dolmen 534 excavated in 2016 a jaw of an infant individual was recovered from which the teeth were collected.

Ancient DNA Procedures

DNA extractions and PCR setup were performed in physically isolated work areas dedicated to ancient DNA analysis at the Ancient DNA Laboratory, Department of Cultural Heritage (DBC), University of Bologna, according to rigorous aDNA standards to avoid contamination (Knapp et al. 2015). Suitable disposable clothing (coverall suit, face mask, plastic face shield, double pair of gloves, and over-shoes) were worn during the handling and extraction of materials. Chemical cleaning procedures with ≥3 per cent commercial sodium hypochlorite and DNA degrading detergent such as DNA-AWAY™ solution (Thermo Scientific™) were regularly performed of all the laboratory worktop and instruments after each experiment (Champlot et al. 2010). In addition, the ancient DNA laboratory was exposed to ultraviolet radiation (λ = 245 nm) overnight for approximately four hours, in order to degrade the DNA on laboratory surfaces and equipment. Sterile materials and dedicated pipettes with aerosol-resistant tips were used at each step of work. All the reagents were screened for modern DNA and stored in small-volume aliquots before use. Specimens, DNA extracts, and reagents were stored in separate fridges and freezer. Multiple blank extractions were processed in parallel and negative controls were included in all reactions. Post-PCR laboratory procedures (amplification and sequencing) were carried out in a separate facility at the Laboratory of Molecular Anthropology and at the Centre for Genome Biology, Department of Biological, Geological, and Environmental Sciences (BiGeA), University of Bologna. In addition, the HVS-I sequences of the personnel involved in this study (archaeologists, anthropologists, and laboratory researchers) were compared with the genetic profiles obtained from the ancient specimens to make sure of the absence of modern contamination.

Samples Preparation

Sample treatment prior to DNA isolation is required to remove pre-laboratory surface contamination. After the photographic documentation step, the samples were decontaminated by removing the external layer with a Dremel® drill and then irradiated with UV light (λ = 254 nm) for fifteen minutes on each side. The teeth extracted from the jaw discovered in Dolmen no. 534 were cut at the cementum-enamel junction with a diamond cut-disc and the cementum in the outer layer of the root was targeted by removing as much dentine as possible according to Damgaard et al. (2015). Instead, the petrous bones coming from Dolmen no. 317 were sampled by cutting off the apex part until the otic capsule was reached, since this denser part provides higher endogenous DNA yields (Gamba et al. 2014; Pinhasi et al. 2015). All the samples were then cut into small pieces (not pulverized) and stored in a 5 mL tube at 4°C until use.

aDNA Extraction and Quantification

DNA isolation was performed by means of a silica-based method with a few modifications. This method of extraction exploits the presence of a siliceous resin inside the test tubes that can absorb nucleic acids on its surface. This happens by adding a chaotropic salt that destroys hydrogen bonds and denatures proteins (Fig. 6.3). All the samples were 'pre-digested' in 1 mL of extraction buffer (0.45M EDTA pH 8.0, 0.25 mg/mL Proteinase K) for fifteen–thirty minutes at 37°C under constant rotation. After centrifugation for two minutes at 16,000 rpm, the supernatant was discarded. An identical fresh extraction buffer was transferred again to the pre-digested and sedimented pellet, then the sample was vortexed and incubated overnight at 37°C. This treatment facilitates the removal of surface contaminants and hence results in a higher proportion of endogenous DNA in the final extract (Damgaard et al. 2015).

After that, samples were centrifuged at maximum speed and the supernatant was removed and transferred in a new 15-mL falcon tube with 10 mL of binding buffer (5M Guanidine Hydrochloride, 90 mM Sodium Acetate, 40 per cent Isopropanol, 0.05 per cent Tween-20 and nuclease-free water). A binding apparatus was constructed by

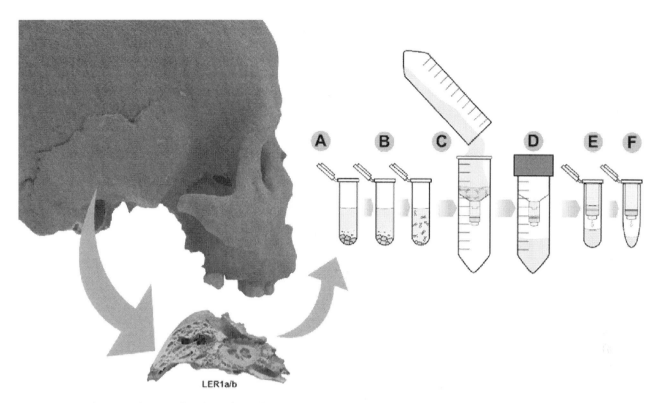

Figure 6.3: The several steps of analysis, from the petrous bone collection, to DNA extraction (A–F). In particular, this procedure consists of different phases: digestion (A–B), binding to the silica matrix (C–D), washing (E), and final elution (F).

forcefully fitting an extension reservoir removed from a Zymo-Spin™ V column (Zymo Research — Irvine, CA, USA) into a MinElute silica spin column (Qiagen GmbH, Hilden, Germany) and then placed into a 50-mL falcon tube. To avoid contamination, the Zymo-Spin™ V extension reservoir was previously submerged in a 3 per cent commercial sodium hypochlorite bath for twenty minutes, washed with nuclease-free water, and UV irradiated for fifteen minutes before use. Moreover, the binding apparatus was tested in the centrifuge for four minutes at 1500 rpm before the use. The solution containing the binding buffer and the supernatant was then poured into the extension reservoir apparatus, which was centrifuged (1500 rpm for four minutes), rotated at 90°, and centrifuged again at 1500 rpm for two minutes.

Afterwards, the silica membrane was centrifuged and washed twice with 750 µl of PE buffer (Qiagen GmbH, Hilden, Germany) at 6000 rpm for thirty seconds and, after putting the column in a new 1.5 ml tube, the DNA was eluted by adding 35 µl of TET buffer (10 mM Tris-HCL, 1 mM EDTA, 0.05 per cent Tween-20, and nuclease-free water) directly on the silica membrane. The column was incubated at room temperature for five minutes and finally centrifuged at 8000 rpm for one minute and then at 10,000 rpm for two minutes.

At the end, 1 µl of eluted DNA was used for DNA quantification with Qubit® dsDNA HS Assay Kit (Invitrogen™ Life Technologies — Carlsbad, CA, USA), following the manufacturer's instructions (Wales et al. 2014). Given that the Qubit® fluorometer quantifies all the double-stranded DNA inside the extract, then also bacterial or fungal DNA which is often present in aDNA, it was decided to proceed to a more precise analysis by PCR Real Time.

The quantification of the collected samples was carried out with the Quantifiler® Trio DNA Quantification Kit (Thermo Fisher Scientific, Oyster Pint, CA) according to manufacturer's protocol. The Quantifiler® Trio Kit detects three different human multi-copy autosomal targets producing a small amplicon (SA — small autosomal target), a larger amplicon (LA — large autosomal target), and Y-Chromosome target. The SA target is the primary quantification target for total human genomic DNA. Its smaller amplicon size (80 bp) is aligned with the sizes of typical 'mini' STR loci and makes it better able to detect degraded DNA samples. The LA target is used mainly as an indicator of DNA degradation (DI), by comparing the ratio of its quantification result with that of the SA target. The Y target allows the quantification of a sample's human male genomic DNA component and is particularly useful in assessing mixture samples of male and female genomic DNAs. Moreover, an internal PCR control (IPC) makes it possible to check the presence of inhibitors in the reaction mix.

The standard curve was generated with tenfold serial dilutions obtaining five standard concentrations from 50 ng/µL to 0.005 ng/µL, and duplicate reactions of each standard curve sample were run per plate. Each Real-Time PCR amplification reaction contained 8 µL of Quantifiler® Trio Primer Mix and 10 µL of Quantifiler® Trio PCR Reaction Mix and 2 µL of sample DNA. Quantitative PCR was performed using the 7500 Real-Time PCR System (Thermo Fisher Scientific, Oyster Point, CA) with 96-well Optical MicroAMP plates following the manufacturer's instruction. The data were analysed using the HID Real-Time PCR Analysis Software v1.2 with the default setting provided with the Quantifiler® templates.

mtDNA Amplification and Sanger Sequencing

Three sets of PCR primers pairs (L15995-H16132: 179 bp, L16107-H16261: 197 bp, L16247-H16402: 156 bp) were used to amplify overlapping DNA fragments of the first hypervariable segment (HVS-I) of the mtDNA control region, to obtain 360 bp, spanning from nucleotide position (np) 16024 to np 16383.

The amplification of each fragment was carried out in independent PCR reactions. For each ancient sample at least two extractions were undertaken at different time points, moreover two amplifications for each extraction were made and both strands of the DNA were sequenced, to verify the repeatability of the mtDNA data and to confirm the authenticity of the results (Hervella et al. 2015; Lorkiewicz et al. 2015).

Briefly, PCR reaction was performed in a final volume of 25 µl of reaction mix (DNA template, 1X AmpliTaq Gold-Buffer (Applied BioSystems, Foster City, USA), AmpliTaq Gold DNA Polymerase (2.5 U) (Applied BioSystems, Foster City, USA), 0.25 mM dNTP mix, 0.2 mM of primers, 2 mM of $MgCl_2$, 0.8 mg/mL of BSA and nuclease-free water). The temperature profile of the thermal cycler program was as follows: initial denaturation at 94°C for ten minutes, forty cycles of forty-five seconds at 94°C, one minute at 53°C and one minute at 72°C, followed by a final extension for ten minutes at 72°C.

Furthermore, all DNA extracts were screened to test their appropriate molecular behaviour with L15996-H16401 primers pairs (Vigilant et al. 1989), which amplify a larger fragment (~400 bp), to detect possible contaminations, given that ancient DNA molecules are often fragmented to very short pieces encompassed between 60 and 150 bp (Prüfer et al. 2010; Sawyer et al. 2012). The temperature profile of the thermal cycler program was as follows: initial denaturation step at 95°C for ten minutes, thirty-five cycles consisting of forty-five seconds at 94°C, one minute at 60°C, one minute at 72°C, followed by a final extension for ten minutes at 72°C. Afterwards, PCR products were checked on 1.5 per cent agarose gel and subsequently purified using a QIAquick® PCR Purification Kit (Qiagen GmbH, Hilden, Germany) following manufacturer's recommendation. Sanger sequencing experiment was performed on a 3730 DNA Analyzer (Applied BioSystems, Foster City, USA) at the 'Unità Operativa di Genetica Medica dell'Azienda Ospedaliera di Bologna'. In detail, the purified PCR product was added to the sequencing reaction mixture (Big Dye Terminator, 5X Buffer, 1 µM of primer and nuclease-free water), with a volume ranging from 0.5 to 1.5 µl, determined based on the intensity of the bands on the electrophoresis gel. For the sequencing reaction the thermal cycler profile was set as follows: thirty cycles consisting of two minutes and ten seconds at 96°C, fifteen seconds at 50°C, and four minutes at 60°C.

Then, the reaction products were purified by means of a precipitation mixture (ethanol, sodium acetate, and nuclease-free water) that, combined with a long centrifugation at 3000 rpm at 4°C for thirty minutes, let the DNA precipitate at the bottom of the well plates. The supernatant was discarded by quickly inverting the plate over the sink and another washing step, with 70 µl of ethanol 70 per cent, was carried out. Several centrifugations followed, even with the plate upside down on an absorbent pad, to remove the supernatant and guarantee no presence of residual ethanol. Before loading the plate into the sequencer, 20 µl of injection solution was added to each well to resuspend the sample and a silicone septa mat was used to cover the plate.

DNA Analysis of the Researchers

Mitochondrial DNA genotypes of the researchers who handled the ancient specimens were determined. The epithelial cells were collected from the mucosa on both sides of the oral cavity using buccal swabs. DNA extraction, as well as PCR and sequencing reaction setup involving modern samples, was carried out in at the laboratory of Molecular Anthropology (University of Bologna) that was physically separated from the

6. BIOMOLECULAR ARCHAEOLOGY: PRELIMINARY DNA ANALYSIS OF SKELETAL REMAINS

Table 6.1: HVS-I motifs of the researchers who had been in contact with the ancient samples during the archaeological excavation and the laboratory work. * Overall quality: 1–0.9 the haplogroup assignment is quite reliable.

Researcher	HVS-I range	HVSI Haplotype based on rCRS	Haplogroup based on HaploGrep	Overall quality *
R1	15997–16400	16223T 16325C 16362C	G1a1	1.000
R2	15997–16400	16126C 16189C 16294T 16296T	T2+16189C	1.000
R3	15997–16400	16168T 16192T 16256T 16270T 16304C	U5a2b3	0.903
R4	15997–16400	rCRS	H2a2a1	1.000

laboratory where the ancient samples were analysed. DNA was extracted using QIAmp DNA Mini Kit (Qiagen GmbH, Hilden, Germany) which enzymatically lyses the cells and, again, uses spin columns with a silica gel membrane that selectively binds nucleic acids and allows their purification from cellular residuals. The entire mtDNA HVS-I region was amplified using a single pair of primer (L15996-H16401) reported in Vigilant et al. (1989). The amplification products were purified with the MinElute PCR purification Kit (Qiagen GmbH, Hilden, Germany), and then sequenced directly with the same amplification primers (forward and reverse) following the BigDye Terminator v1.1 Cycle Sequencing Kit supplier's instructions. Sanger sequencing experiment was performed on a 3730 DNA Analyzer instrument (Applied BioSystems, Foster City, USA).

Haplogroup Assignment

The data obtained — three HVS-I sequences (forward and reverse) for each extracted ancient sample — were aligned and compared to the revised Cambridge Reference Sequence (rCRS, GenBank Accession Number NC 012920) using BioEdit v7.2.5 (Andrews et al. 1999) and MEGA7 software (Kumar et al. 2016), to define the HVS-I mutational motif. The types and frequency of nucleotide variations among the sequences were checked by hand, such as C->T transitions, which represent the prevalent signal of post-mortem miscoding lesions in authentic aDNA (Stiller et al. 2009; Bollongino et al. 2013). Haplogroups assignment was determined using Haplogrep2 software with a further check based on the PhyloTree mtDNA phylogeny, build 17 (<www.phylotree.org>).

Results and Discussion
Authentication Criteria

Contamination from modern human DNA cannot yet be totally ruled out, and a strong logical chain of evidence is required to authenticate aDNA results. Indeed, sporadic contamination can still be observed, especially when amplifying human mtDNA with high PCR cycle numbers. In this study, it is possible to exclude contamination with a high level of confidence and to attest the authenticity of mtDNA results on the following grounds *(i)* samples were collected during the archaeological excavations in a virtually modern human 'DNA-free' conditions, a circumstance that has been suggested to facilitate the discrimination between endogenous and contaminant DNA (Llamas et al. 2017); *(ii)* the analyses were undertaken in a dedicated aDNA laboratory, under strictly controlled conditions; *(iii)* no systematic contamination was ever observed in either the extraction or the amplification negative controls; *(iv)* aDNA data was considered as genuine whenever a clear sequence was reproduced in all the overlapping fragments portion of each adjacent fragment; *(v)* when possible, replicas of DNA extraction were undertaken on different skeletal elements of the same individual, or during the preparation step, all the specimens were divided and stored in two different aliquots and then analysed in different experimental batches at different times; *(vi)* all HVS-I sequences obtained from Jebel al-Mutawwaq samples showed different haplotypes from those of operators involved in this study (Table 6.1); *(viii)* all the ancient samples tested with the L15996-H16401 primer pair, yielded no long amplification products, indicating the absence of undamaged modern exogenous DNA.

DNA Quantification and Haplogroup Assignment

Ancient DNA was successfully extracted from three of five individuals and the quantification performed by Qubit® fluorometer highlighted good amounts of DNA. All samples were thus analysed with the amplification of the three fragments of the first hypervariable region (HVS-I) of the mitochondrial DNA and then tested on agarose gel. The three fragments were successfully amplified from the samples LER1, MU3, and MUR4

Table 6.2: Qubit® quantification and PCR amplification results.

Burial	Skeletal elements	ID	Powder (g)	Qubit® (ng/µl)	PCR amplification		
					Fr.1	Fr.2	Fr.3
Dolmen 317 (B. 25)	Petrous bone	LER 1	0.3	7.04	ok	ok	ok
Dolmen 317 (B. 26)	Petrous bone	MUR 1	0.3	22.4	/	/	/
Dolmen 317 (B. 26)	Petrous bone	MUR 2	0.3	9.74	/	/	/
Dolmen 534	Molar tooth	MU3	0.012	41	ok	ok	ok
Dolmen 49/b	Petrous bone	MUR4	0.3	8.54	ok	ok	ok

and as pointed out by agarose gel (Table 6.2). Both the extraction controls and negative PCR controls did not produce a positive amplification, therefore contamination by exogenous DNA introduced during the molecular analyses could be ruled out.

With the aim to test nuclear DNA content in the samples analysed, in order to try an amplification of nuclear loci, a quantification of DNA Real-Time PCR coupled with Quantifiler® Trio Kit (Thermo Scientific) was performed. This analysis, currently performed on the LER1 sample only, allows us to identify the sex of the individuals and also to calculate the DNA degradation index. These early steps show good preservation of both mitochondrial and nuclear DNA, and the Quantifiler® Trio Kit attests that the individual of the B. 25 tomb is female (Table 6.3), which is very important since the only anthropological study of the skeleton had not successfully determined this, given the intermediate position of the measures and morphology observed in this individual.

The data highlighted the lack of amplification of large autosomal target in almost all the specimens analysed, thus it was not possible to obtain the values of the degradation index included in the Quantifiler® Trio Kit (Thermo Scientific), as it is calculated as large autosomal/small autosomal data. This situation is compatible with an intense degradation of the nuclear genetic material. For these reasons we decided to analyse only the mitochondrial DNA.

After that, the three HVS-I short overlapping fragments of the ancient samples were sequenced and edited by software to reconstruct the whole HVS-I region and the consensus sequences were obtained in three out of the five ancient specimens (Table 6.4). The remaining two samples were excluded from subsequent analyses because they yielded no amplification products (MUR1 and MUR2).

As shown in the table above, LER1 belongs to haplogroup H (hg H), while the MUR4 belongs to haplogroup V (hg V). In the mitochondrial phylogeny these lineages can be reconducted to the major clade HV, which comprises at least eighteen recognized subclades, constituted by the haplogroup H and seventeen subclades numerically labelled from HV0 to HV17 (the label HV3 is not used). Furthermore, haplogroup V is a nested sub-haplogroup within the HV0 clade. The hg H is today the most prevalent mitochondrial haplogroup gene pool of Europeans (~40–45 per cent on average) (Roostalu et al. 2007), and was investigated in human genetic diversity studies for more than a decade (Achilli et al. 2004; Roostalu et al. 2007; Alvarez-Iglesias et al. 2009; Behar et al. 2012). Phylogeographic studies suggest that hg H arrived in Europe from the Near East prior to the Last Glacial Maximum (~21,000 years ago), and survived in glacial refugia in south-west Europe before undergoing a postglacial re-expansion. Hg H lineages also spread outside of Europe and a pertinent example is found in North Africa.

Indeed, the sample MUR4 is ascribed to the haplogroup V9a1, that is a subclade of haplogroup V (hg V). The mutations defining the subclade HV0 are thought to have taken place around the Last Glacial Maximum (~ 19,000–26,000 years ago), while hg V, which is a sub-haplogroup derived from HV0, would have arisen in the Late Glacial Period, sometime between 16,000 and 12,000 years ago. Their places of origin remain highly controversial and could be anywhere in Europe, North Africa, or the Near East. The extremely high prevalence of hg V among the Sami, who have very little Neolithic farmer admixture, and maintained a hunter-gather lifestyle throughout the ages, is the best evidence that hg V did not originate in the Near East but in Mesolithic Europe (Tambets et al. 2004). Another argument is that hg HV0 and V are much rarer in the Near East than in Europe, and practically absent in the Arabian Peninsula,

Table 6.3: DNA quantification analysis of LER samples using Quantifiler® trio kit. This sample was extracted twice (LER1a and LER 1b) and each extraction was amplified in two replicas.

Sample	T.Large Autosomal (ng/µl)	T.Small Autosomal (ng/µl)	(Y ng/µl)	Index of degradation
LER1a	N/A	0.0006	N/A	N/A
LER1 (replicate)	N/A	0.001	N/A	N/A
LER1b	0.0002	N/A	N/A	N/A
LER1 (replicate)	N/A	0.0005	N/A	N/A

Table 6.4: mtDNA results of samples from Jebel al-Mutawwaq site. [1] sample MU3 shows ambiguous results for haplogroup assignments based only this portion of mtDNA. * Overall Quality: 1–0.9 the haplogroup assignment is quite reliable.

Sample ID	HVS-I range	HVS-I Haplotype based on rCRS	Haplogroup based on HaploGrep	Overall quality*
LER1	15996–16401	16213A	H7h	1.000
MU3	15996–16401	16311C	[1]	-
MUR4	15996–16401	16192T 16219G 16311C	V9a1	0.941

Mesopotamia, and Georgia, three of the regions with the highest ancestry derived from the Neolithic Fertile Crescent — because they were less affected by later Indo-European migrations, Persian, Greek, and Roman conquests, or the settlements of European crusaders in the Middle Ages (Pereira et al. 2010).

Instead, based on the only mutation retrieved (16311C) in the sample MU3, it was not possible to identify the haplogroup to it belongs, but future analyses of the polymorphisms in the mtDNA coding region will help to resolve its assignment.

Conclusions

In conclusion, the analyses carried out on Jebel al-Mutawwaq site involved the mitochondrial DNA, and in particular the hypervariable region, a marker that in humans is transmitted only by maternal line. Moreover, on the LER1 sample, analyses aimed to determine the sex were performed. This preliminary study focuses mainly on the description of the approaches of a biological study aimed at understanding an archaeological context and testing the DNA preservation of samples recovered from this particular area. In fact, samples preserved at this latitude and in this particular area, usually showed poor DNA content and little genetic data from this region has been published so far. These results are in fact preliminary and of circumstantial value on the genetics of the populations who settled in this area. It will therefore be necessary to implement this research with a wider number of samples and deepen the study with the sequencing of the entire genome. Moreover, in the future, to better understand the microevolutionary and population dynamics of this area, it would be very interesting to sample the current inhabitants of the same geographic area of the necropolis, and neighbouring areas.

7. The Development of Olive Growing at the Jebel al-Mutawwaq Site: Preliminary Data

Alessia D'Auria & Gaetano Di Pasquale

The olive tree (*Olea europaea*) is considered one of the most important and iconic fruit trees of the Mediterranean basin, especially in the Levant, whose origins are tied to the appearance of some of the first civilizations about six millennia ago.[1] This tree is one of the most sustainable crops in low fertility soils and it belongs to the first group of domesticated trees.[2]

Indeed, the history of olive domestication is characterized by vegetative propagation of the most valuable genotypes[3] selected for the ability of the plant to grow in anthropogenic environment, for the facility of their propagation though cutting, and for their agronomic value such as larger fruits and higher oil content.[4] Two taxonomic varieties are currently recognized: *Olea europaea* var. *sylvestris*, the wild tree and *Olea europaea* var. *europaea*, the cultivated olive. The wild form is the ancestor of the modern varieties of cultivated olive, and it is a long-lived evergreen sclerophyllous tree that usually grows in the thermo Mediterranean belt and in typical Mediterranean climates with hot summers and low winter temperatures; it can survive under 200 mm of annual rainfall.[5] By contrast, an olive orchard requires instead at least 400–500 mm of annual precipitation to be profitable, the fruit production starting five to six years after the planting and if well managed a long-lived tree can produce fruits for hundreds of years.[6] *O. europaea* var. *sylvestris* is an element of maquis and garrigue formation and it is distributed over large areas around the Mediterranean basin.[7] In the southern Levant the olive grows especially in its original natural habitat in the hilly Mediterranean forest zones.

The first archaeobotanical data recovered in the archaeological site of Jebel al-Mutawwaq suggests the presence of olive trees as an important element of the landscape probably especially for its commercial value. The site was settled during the Early Bronze Age I, a crucial period for southern Levant civilizations, when the semi-nomadic communities started to establish permanent villages and consequently to increase the complexity of the society. For this reason, the Early Bronze Age I is considered a proto-urban phase. According to the map of potential vegetation of the east Mediterranean region[8] the site of Jebel al-Mutawwaq falls in the region characterized by two types of vegetation: a) a presteppic open forest vegetation with *Quercus calliprinos* and *Juniperus excelsa* and b) a presteppic maquis formation with *Pistacia atlantica* and *Amigdalus*. Here the wild olive was widely

---

1 Zohary & Hopf 2000, 145; Loumou & Giourga 2003; Kaniewski et al. 2012; Zohary et al. 2012.

2 Zohary & Hopf 2000.

3 Zohary et al. 2012.

4 Besnard & de Casas 2016.

Alessia D'Auria (alessia.dauria@unina.it) is a Research Fellow in Archaeobotany at University of Naples Federico II (Italy).

Gaetano Di Pasquale (gaetano.dipasquale@unina.it) is an Associate Professor in Archaeobotany at University of Naples Federico II (Italy).

5 Ozenda 1975; Zohary & Hopf 2000, 145; Langgut et al. 2016.

6 Zohary et al. 2012, 116.

7 Zohary & Spiegel-Roy 1975.

8 Quézel & Barbero 1985.

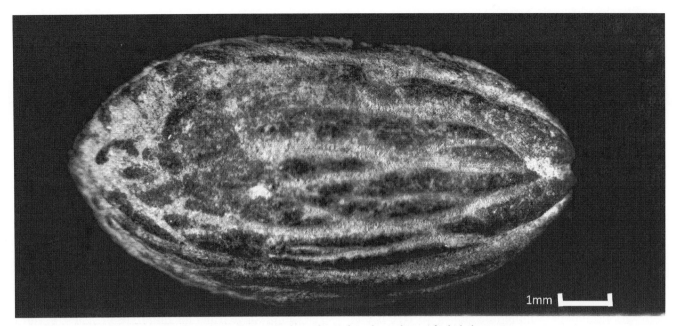

Figure 7.1: Whole olive stone from the archaeological site of Jebel al Mutawwaq.

present.[9] The first archaeobotanical analysis coming from this site returned twenty-eight charred fragments and only one whole olive stone (Fig. 7.1) dated to the Early Bronze Age I (Table 7.1). Our hypothesis is to verify if the above-mentioned socio-economic change was caused by the richness linked to olive oil production or if olive cultivation was a consequence of sedentarization.

This preliminary data is very interesting because it fits into the great debate on the origin of olive growing. Based on archaeobotanical evidence the classical theory assumes that olive cultivation began ~6000 BP in the Near East.[10]

Instead, more recent genetic studies propose a multiple origin of cultivars across the Mediterranean area, indicating that olive domestication occurred at different moments and olive exploitation and management were also present in the central and western Mediterranean in particular during the Early Bronze Age (4500–4000 BP).[11] Recent archaeological and archaeobotanical records indeed confirm the existence of a primary domestication area in the eastern Mediterranean basin.[12]

Multidisciplinary data (palynological records and molecular evidence about olive oil production) dated to the Early Chalcolithic period and to the Late Neolithic[13] suggest that the southern Levant was probably the region where olive trees were first domesticated during the above-cited period (Late Neolithic-Early Chalcolithic).[14] On the other hand, the palynological diagrams indicate that the wild olive was a minor component in the natural Levantine environments during the Late Pleistocene.[15] Domestication is probably also linked to the active participation of the major cultures that lived in the settlement of this historical period, at the start of the olive/oil culture.[16] For example, data shows early olive cultivation in Palestine during the Middle and Late Chalcolithic where the *O. europaea* var. *sylvestris* is present since the Early Palaeolithic (at Negev, about 43000 BCE; Table 7.1)[17] and in Syria, in the same time; in these periods, the olive was probably collected in the wild.[18] In the southern Levant significant olive exploitation appeared during the Early Bronze Age (EBA), in particular during the EBA IB (3100–2900 BCE),[19]

---

9 Quézel & Barbero 1985.

10 van Zeist 1980, 129–45; Liphschitz et al. 1991; Zohary & Hopf 2000; Brun 2003.

11 Terral & Arnold-Simard 1996, Terral 2000; Terral et al. 2004; Margaritis 2013; D'Auria et al. 2017.

12 Besnard et al. 2018; Julca 2020.

13 See van Zeist et al. 2009, 29–64; Neumann et al. 2007; Litt et al. 2012; Schiebel 2013 for palynological data and see Galili et al. 1997; Galili et al. 2007; Namdar et al. 2015 for evidence of oil production and molecular evidence for actual olive oil.

14 Langgut et al. 2011.

15 Horowitz 1979; Weinstein-Evron 1983; Langgut et al. 2011.

16 Liphschitz et al. 1991; Galili et al. 1997; Kanjewski et al. 2012; Zohary et al. 2012; Newton et al. 2014.

17 Liphschitz et al. 1991, 448.

18 van Zeist & Bakker-Heeres 1984.

19 Riehl 2009.

Table 7.1: Archaeobotanical data of *Olea europaea* referred to the Levantine area (Neolithic–Early Bronze Age).

Archaeological site	Region	Coordinates (Lat/Long)	Chronology	Archaeobotanical data	References
Pella	Jordan	32°26'15"N 35°36'20"E	Neolithic to Iron Age	Charcoal and endocarp	Dighton et al. 2016
Kfar Samir	Israel	32°49'04"N 34°57'13"E	Late Neolithic	Crushed stones with pulp	Galili et al. 2007
Tel Masos	Israel	31°12'44"N 34°58'05"E	Chalcolithic	Charred wood	Liphschitz et al. 1991
Tell Esh Shuna North	Israel	32°36'36"N 35°36'29"E	Chalcolithic	Wood and stone	Bottema et al. 1989
Abu Hamid	Syria	33°17'08"N 33°39'55"E	Chalcolithic	Wood and stones	Bottema et al. 1989
Teleilat Ghassul	Jordan	31°51'35"N 35°38'30"E	Chalcolithic	Wood and stones	Bottema et al. 1989
Jebel el-Mutawwaq	Jordan	32°12'44" N 35°59'38" N	Early Bronze Age I	Stones	In this chapter
Tell Mastuma	Syria	35°52'06"N 36°38'16"E	Early Bronze Age II–III	Seeds	Yasuda 1997
Tell Fadous	Lebanon	34°13'44"N 35°39'20"E	Early Bronze Age II–III	Charred seeds (and olive pits?)	Genz et al. 2009; Höflmayer et al. 2014
Zeraqun	Jordan	31°42'07"N 34°57'04"E	Early Bronze Age II–III	Wood and stones	Bottema et al. 1989

in Syria (Tell Mastuma,[20] Table 7.1) and in northern Lebanon (Tell Fadous;[21] Table 7.1) during the EBA II–III, while in the northern Levant it was recorded only about 2900 BCE, indicated by the pollen record from Tell Sukas on the Syrian coast.[22] The evidence of expansive olive cultivation during the Early Bronze Age in the southern Levant is confirmed by Riehl (2009), who has recovered archaeobotanical data from 138 Levantine archaeological sites with a chronology spanning the period of 5500–2600 cal BP.

In the specific case of Jordan, archaeobotanical research confirms the presence of large amounts of wood and stone fragments of olive in the Jordan Valley during the Chalcolithic period; this proves that the olive tree played an important role in these communities. In particular, olive remains were found at Abu Hamid and Tell esh Shuna North where the inhabitants had probably gathered the olives from wild trees (Table 7.1).[23]

The hypothesis is that these olives were first cultivated for their oil content and not food as such because fresh olives have an obnoxiously bitter taste.[24]

Olive cultivation was attested in the Chalcolithic site of Teleilat Ghassul (southern Jordan Valley) where the presence of olive stones probably could not have come from local trees considering that the site is outside or marginal to the natural distribution range of olive (Table 7.1).[25] Moreover olive branches were recovered at this site, which could indicate the pruning of trees. Another proof is the presence of beams of olive wood at Teleilat Ghassul and Abu Hamid that show the use of olive wood for construction. Always in the Jordan Valley, in the archaeological site of Pella, the presence of olive remains from the Early Pottery Neolithic (about 6200 cal BCE; Table 7.1) suggests some of the earliest evidence for olive exploitation in the southern Levant, and the presence of jift with evidence of olive fruit pressing makes it possible to hypothesize oil production from at least about 5200 BCE.[26]

---

20 Yasuda 1997, fig. 8, 258.
21 Genz et al. 2009; Höflmayer et al. 2014.
22 Sorrel & Mathis 2016.
23 Bottema et al. 1990.

24 Bottema et al. 1990.
25 Bottema et al. 1990; Meadows 2005, 241; Weiss 2015, 76.
26 Dighton et al. 2017.

All this evidence supports Zohary and Spiegel-Roy's (1975) theory of olive cultivation beginning in the Chalcolithic period.

Moreover, in Jordan the olive tree is considered a minor constituent of forest dominated by deciduous oak (*Quercus ithaburensis*) while is present at lower altitudes in association with evergreen-oak forest.[27] A first proof of olive culture in the deciduous oak forest was attested in the city-state of Zeraqun, where olive tree cultivation seems to have been important[28] (Table 7.1) during the Early Bronze Age.

All these data suggest a gradually intensifying exploitation of olive trees in the northern Jordan Valley at the beginning of the Early Pottery Neolithic while in the southern Jordan Valley olive domestication was introduced relatively late with management practice during the Late Chalcolithic period.[29] Olive exploitation probably decreases during the final phases of the Early Bronze Age, as demonstrated by the Galilee pollen diagram that shows a drop in the olive curve during the Middle and Late Bronze Age, connected to the decline of the city-states at the end of the Early Bronze Age.[30]

Therefore, it is possible that the expansion of olive orchards is linked with the spread of human civilization probably due to the multiple uses of wild and cultivated olive trees such as olive food, wood, and cattle fodder.[31] It is possible that the cultivated olive has been primarily used as a source of oil but the first use of this oil is still a matter of debate; the first descriptions indicate the use of olive oil as a combustible to produce light and also as body ointment with a ritual significance.[32]

The first traces of olive oil were dated to the Late Pottery Neolithic where organic residue, interpreted as olive oil, has been found in pottery vessels from an archaeological site in northern Syria, at En Zippori.[33] Olive oil production on a large scale can be demonstrated as early as EB I when olive oil was widely produced and become an important trading commodity with Egypt;[34] Egyptian records mention olive oil among the products imported from Palestine.[35] By contrast, the culinary use of olive oil seem to be successive and not widely reported until the ancient Roman epoch[36] and the consumption of pickled olives was probably introduced only in the Hellenistic or Roman period.[37]

---

27 Bottema et al. 1990.
28 Bottema et al. 1990.
29 Dighton et al. 2017.
30 Baruch 1986.
31 Besnard et al. 2018.
32 Besnard & de Casas 2016.
33 Namdar et al. 2015.
34 Langgut et al. 2011.
35 Stager 1985, 172–88.
36 Tardi 2014, 321–37.
37 Borowski 1979.

8. Conclusions: The Importance of the Jebel al-Mutawwaq Settlement at the Beginning of the First Urbanization in the Southern Levant

Andrea Polcaro

After seven years of archaeological excavations by the Spanish-Italian Archaeological Expedition, it is now possible to identify at least three main phases of development at the Jebel al-Mutawwaq settlement and necropolis. The first phase coincides with the Early Bronze Age IA, between 3500 and 3300 BCE. The only structure of the settlement clearly dated to this phase in the settlement is the Great Enclosure, a large open-air structure with a standing stone in the centre used to perform periodical rituals, perhaps connected with activities related to herd exploitation. In this period, it is impossible to reconstruct how large the inhabited area on the mountain was, but it is quite probable that some of the dwellings between the Western and the Central Sectors were already built. All the data coming from the excavations point to a massive change in the urban planning and settlement organization between 3300 and 3100 BCE, during the passage between the EB IA and EB IB. In this second phase, the settlement changes its main cultic place, moving it from the Central to the Western Sector, where the Temple of the Serpent was built. Possibly slightly later the village was enclosed by a wall, and the Western and Southern Gates were built. It is possible to see this as a period of expansion of the urbanized landscape, as the village grows by attracting people from the countryside, as is well attested during urbanization processes in the Near East.[1] The increase in the number of inhabitants also explains the huge megalithic necropolis, which probably grows in the same period, particularly in the area of the eastern necropolis. The village of Jebel al-Mutawwaq in this second phase surely included the Western and Central Sector as far as the Hanbury-Tenison Door, its possible eastern gateway, and it was already well organized with internal pathways crossing the settlement. At present, it is not easy to say when the Eastern Sector was added to the village, but it could have occurred at the end of this phase, as further suggested by the connection between the eastern edge of the sector (Area A) and the nearby funerary area (Area B). The third and final phase is dated between 3100 and 2900 BCE, corresponding to the Early Bronze Age IB. In this phase the southern necropolis was built close to the settlement wall, clearly with a homogenous new funerary ideological programme. It could also be possible that the small area of extramural dwellings in the same zone should be dated to this last phase of expansion of the settlement.[2] This neighbourhood *extra muros*, built close to the Southern

---

Andrea Polcaro (andrea.polcaro@unipg.it) is an Associate Professor in Near Eastern Archaeology at Perugia University (Italy).

1 Concerning the phenomenon of the growth of the communities undergoing urbanization in Transjordan, followed by the partial depopulation of the surrounding areas see also Kafafi 2022, 116–17.

2 Even if the ongoing excavations of one building in the outer neighbourhood Area EE gave a C14 calibrated date of 3243–3102 cal BCE (Beta Analytic — 624947); thus, close to the end of the second phase of settlement expansion. However, further data from the ongoing excavations are needed to securely date the maximum expansion of these extramural neighbourhoods of the EB I settlement.

Gate, extended along a rock terrace which represented the beginning of the road descending downstream. If the double-apsidal buildings in this area could be functionally connected to the southern necropolis they might also not be seen as private dwellings, but only the continuing excavations begun in this area in 2021 can answer that question. It is also possible that, during this last phase of occupation, some further work was done on the settlement wall's Western Sector, involving the construction of the two western towers, giving it the aspect of a more solid fortification system.

Even if public buildings clearly associated with a centralized economy organized by a main institution have not so far been recognized by the excavations at the site, it is clear from the existing data that the settlement of Jebel al-Mutawwaq experienced a rapid development in an urban direction during the last centuries of the fourth millennium BCE. At least three hundred years before this moment, it is likely that a few semi-nomadic tribes, living from sheep-herding and possible seasonal agriculture along the valley of the Zarqa River, began to forge blood ties and to identify the mountain of Mutawwaq as a sacred place where they could gather to hold periodic rituals. The Great Enclosure is the symbol of this first community; its shape reflects the heterarchical society of the EB IA, as the communities were starting to reorganize their social and political relationships within a new landscape that was itself changing[3] due to natural climate variations. Compared to its predecessor of the Late Chalcolithic period, the landscape of the EB IA must have been less fertile for centuries, with less biodiversity and spontaneous food resources, before starting to improve at the end of the millennium. The Great Enclosure is a wide place, where more people can gather not only to perform periodic rituals, but also, eventually, to take decisions. The settling of numerous people on the site at the end of the EB IA, with the shift of the main sacred area to the Temple of the Serpents reflects a further change to the society. The Temple of the Serpent is a closely circumscribed area, surrounded by a *temenos* wall, where specific production could also be organized by the people who looked after the cult. This suggests a restricted number of people involved in decision-making and power. The inception of a settlement wall, even if only with the purpose of defining the urban space, is a strong indication of the definition of a new boundary separating the Jebel al-Mutawwaq community from the countryside. At the same time, it offers an instrument of defence for the people, especially if the fortification aspect of the wall is confirmed by future research at the site. All this points to a further reorganization of the urban space and countryside, with a new political relation system for the region. The implementation of oliviculture in these centuries had surely played a role in this change to landscape organization. Oliviculture is a good response as an agricultural strategy in the face of a changing environment. As already quoted, it needs a very well-planned, organized landscape to be productive. The olive grower must constantly be careful to protect and care for his plants, all year round, with a greater need not only to stay on the territory but also to organize water resources. The data from the Jebel al-Mutawwaq excavations attests to a growth in olive exploitation from the first to the third phase of the settlement's development. Some of the data could also suggest that one of the purposes of oliviculture was the production of olive oil, a product that, as already noted at the beginning of the volume, had a great relevance in the southern Levant in EB IB, in part due to the growth in export demand from Egypt. This important productive sector of the village economy could easily be centralized under the control of one or more extended families within the settlement, who were perhaps also involved in cult organization. At the same time, the necessity of defence of the agricultural landscape, spread over the slopes of the hills along the valley, grows. The territory is changed, as are the power relationships between the communities, which are rapidly transforming themselves. It is easy to imagine also periodic contrasts between smaller regional pastoral communities, which continued to undertake transhumance along the river, and new, more fixed olive growers defending their crop. In this context, it is possible that another group of the Jebel al-Mutawwaq community started to cover and centralize in their hands the role of protection of the urban space and of the new agricultural landscape. This is well represented by the warrior burial discovered in Dolmen 534, built close to the settlement wall and in connection with a large area possibly dedicated to the veneration of the ancestors of a specific element of the society.

In this picture, the southern necropolis represents the maximum evolution toward urbanization of the Jebel al-Mutawwaq society before its fall and the sub-

---

[3] Possibly it is not the case that the landscape around Jebel al-Mutawwaq, along the whole Middle Wadi az-Zarqa Valley, is characterized, as it seems, during the EB IA only by the presence of smaller settlements and dolmen fields; furthermore, it may be that not all of them are permanent villages: some could also be temporary camps by pasture or for the performance of seasonal agricultural activities.

8. Conclusions: The Importance of the Jebel al-Mutawwaq Settlement

Figure 8.1: Dolmen 534 in the southern necropolis, with its external 'stone box' shape well preserved.

sequent abandonment of the site. In fact, in this area dolmens are not casually spread along the mountain slopes, as in the eastern necropolis, but they are carefully organized along the rocky terrace that follows one of the main roads entering the settlement. The dolmens are particularly monumental, the largest examples of megalithic tombs within the whole necropolis of the site, and their shape, thanks to their regular tumuli made of large regularly cut stone blocks, recall a huge box of rock. This shape transforms the older circular tumulus into a larger and more visible and regular structure.

Their image therefore is bound up with the need to identify and mark one of the main entrances to the walled village.[4] Thus, from one side, these monuments shape the new urban landscape, identifying the settlement itself with specific clans or families owning these megalithic tombs, reflecting the representative needs of the new elites of the EB IB. From the other, thanks to their location, they have an easier access to the centre of the village, through a street starting from the Central Sector, not far from the Temple of the Serpent. This means direct access to the urban space, in the case of religious processions and festivities dedicated to the memories of the ancestors of the specific families which owned the dolmens in the southern necropolis. The food production areas connected to these megalithic monuments strongly point to this picture. In this case, the ancestors of these specific clans were no longer venerated exclusively by their relatives but by the whole community, which recognized them as their 'founding heroes'. If the aforementioned social and political organization of the Jebel al-Mutawwaq settlement at the end of its life is accepted as plausible, it is noteworthy that in the same final phase of the settlement some clusters of buildings were built in different extramural areas close to the walled site. This is another typical sign of the urbanization process, when the city creates a sort of 'buffer zone' around the urban centre. This area represents a middle space between the countryside and the city, settled by people coming and going for commer-

---

4 Concerning the role of dolmens in shaping the landscape, both ritual and socio-economical, see also Kerner 2022.

cial or religious purposes, connected to the main centre of the new power. It defines an outer space, inhabited or frequented by those who probably cannot not live 'inside the wall', but can participate in urban life and in particular in specific economic or production activities.

Around 2900 BCE the settlement of Jebel al-Mutawwaq was abandoned. No sign of a devastating fire or destruction layer has ever been identified at the site, either in the private areas or in the public buildings. The dwellings were sealed at the end of their use, sometimes with all the furniture left inside. Often the funerary monuments were emptied and sealed with stones, a practice identified at least in the excavations of the eastern necropolis. These leave us with several possible causes for the abandonment of the site. The first plausible hypothesis involves a single devastating natural event, like a large earthquake. An earthquake can be preceded by other smaller seismic events, warning the population to move outside of the buildings before the stronger wave strikes. This could explain why the people left most of their possessions inside the dwellings, but could recover them after the serious collapse of the stone structures. It must be considered in this case that the dry-stone architecture of Jebel al-Mutawwaq could be very sensitive to a seismic event. The peculiar typology of the foundations of several building of the settlement, constructed along the slope, such as the lateral wall of the Great Enclosure or the eastern and western north–south segments of the settlement wall, with small stones and rubble filling the gaps in the bedrock and sustaining the weight of tons of huge stone blocks, makes most of the structures in the site very sensitive to seismic activity. If there were a strong ground shake, the devastation in the settlement must have been catastrophic. A detail which could support this theory might be the deep crack in the rock identified by Fernández-Tresguerres in House 77, even if it is not in itself enough. However, other Early Bronze Age settlements suffered from strong earthquakes in the region, close as it is to the rift valley of the River Jordan and the attendant high seismic risk. In particular, at Tell Abu Kharaz on the Jordan Valley, a strong earthquake possibly ended the EB IB–EB II phase.[5]

The second possible hypothesis again sees the abandonment as having a natural origin, but strictly connected with the huge gathering of people clearly present in the site, with a constant growth of population till the end of its use. In the agro-pastoral society of Jebel al-Mutawaq, more than one thousand people lived in less than twenty hectares, crowded together inside the urban space with a lot of animals, such as sheep, goats, and pigs, to which a large number of poultry must probably be added. Such a number of humans and animals living together can be a paradise for the spread of infections, bacteria, and any number of viruses, which often pass from animals to man. In this hypothesis, the settlement of Jebel al-Mutawwaq paid a high cost for its quick development toward a large urban community; and as is well known, even a deadly pandemic usually leaves no trace on human bone.[6] Moreover, there was a change in the alimentation of the Jebel al-Mutawwaq population during EB IB with the transformation of the landscape, the implementation of oliviculture, and a new sedentary life. This change seems to be confirmed by the data from the human bones of Cave 1012, especially compared to those coming from the older inhumations in Dolmen 317. The quick shift toward a diet based mostly on cereals and vegetables can lead to a reduced immune defence in the population, favouring the spread of specific viruses, especially in the absence of favourable hygienic conditions. The natural response of the human being to the spread of infection through overcrowding is dispersion over the territory. It is suggestive that the following EB II fortified settlements, much smaller than Mutawwaq, built slightly after its abandonment, could also reflect the need to avoid an excess of site populations. However, at the moment, there are no further data to support this theory.

The last hypothesis which can be advanced is of an anthropogenic nature. However, in the absence of any traces of destruction layers, it is hard to imagine that a growth of internal social division, or external pressure, led to a sort of pacific abandonment of the site by all the population. Moreover, no clear sign of wounds has been identified on the human bones recovered in the tombs of the necropolis, apart from burial B. 25 in Dolmen 317. However, the typology of the wound identified on the skull of B. 25 suggests an execution more than a killing within the context of fighting; due to the precision of the wound-cut it is possible that the victim was immobile when slaughtered. These considerations point to a ritual event, that, unfortunately, can no longer be reconstructed in the absence of further data.

---

5 See Fischer 2008, 71, 97, 383.

6 See on this topic for a recent re-analysis about the ancient sedentarization and urbanization processes and its cost for the human communities Scott 2017. See in particular concerning the typologies of the spread of infections in the case of crowding of people and animals Scott 2017, 96–113.

8. CONCLUSIONS: THE IMPORTANCE OF THE JEBEL AL-MUTAWWAQ SETTLEMENT

Finally, Jebel al-Mutawwaq is a precious site to study the dynamics behind the urbanization process of the Transjordan communities. In particular, the most important feature is the possibility of investigating both a megalithic necropolis and its contemporary settlement, which is still largely preserved, even if it is suffering continual destruction. The three phases identified in the site, sedentarization, settlement expansion, and first urban development, correspond well to the historical framework of the end of Early Bronze Age I, the moment when the older societies of the fourth millennium BCE start to develop the new fully urbanized settlements of the third millennium BCE.

Works Cited

Achilli, Alessandro; Rengo, Chiara; Magrini, Chiara; Battaglia, Vincenza; Olivieri, Anna; Scozzari, Rosaria; Cruciani, Fulvio; Zeviani, Massimo; Briem, Egill; Carelli, Valerio; Moral, Pedro; Dugoujon, Jean M.; Roostalu, Urmas; Loogväli, Eva L.; Kivisild, Toomas; Bandelt, Hans J.; Richards, Martin; Villems, Richard; Santachiara, Silvana; Semino, Ornella & Torroni, Antonio
2004 'The Molecular Dissection of mtDNA Haplogroup H Confirms that the Franco-Cantabrian Glacial Refuge Was a Major Source for the European Gene Pool', *American Journal of Human Genetics* 75/5: 910–18.

Adams, Russel & Genz, Herman
1995 'Excavation at Wadi Fidan 4: A Chalcolithic Village Complex in the Copper Ore District of Feinan, Southern Levant', *Palestine Exploration Quarterly* 127: 8–20.

Ajlouny, Fardous; Khrisat, Bilal; Al-Masri, Eyad; Ahmad, Hassan; Alyassin, Hassan; Mayyas, Abdulraouf & Kraishan, Dima
2022 'Early Bronze Snake Motifs on Pottery Vessels and their Symbolism in Southern Levant', *Mediterranean Archaeology and Archaeometry* 22/2: 67–96.

Alvarez, Valentin; Muñiz, Juan R. & Polcaro, Andrea
2013 'Preliminary Results of the First Spanish-Italian Excavation Campaign to the Jabal al-Mutawwaq Dolmen Field, August-September 2012', *Annual of the Department of Antiquities of Jordan* 57: 409–24.

Álvarez-Iglesias, Vanesa; Mosquera-Miguel, Ana; Cerezo, Maria; Quintáns, Beatriz; Zarrabeitia, Maria T.; Cuscó, Ivon; Lareu, Maria V.; García, Óscar; Pérez-Jurado, Luis; Carracedo, Ángel & Salas, Antonio
2009 'New Population and Phylogenetic Features of the Internal Variation within Mitochondrial DNA Macrohaplogroup R0', *PLoS One* 5/4: e5112.

Amiran, Ruth K.
1969 *Ancient Pottery of the Holy Land*. Massada, Jerusalem.

Amiran, Ruth K. & Gophna, Ram
1992 'The Correlation between Lower Egypt and Southern Canaan during the EB I Period', in Edwin C. M. van den Brink (ed.), *The Nile Delta in Transition: 4th-3rd Millennium BC*. Israel Exploration Society, Tel Aviv: 357–60.

Amiran, Ruth K. & Ilan, Aaron
1996 *Early Arad, II: The Chalcolithic and Early Bronze Ib Settlements and the Early Bronze II City: Architecture and Town Planning Sixth-Eighteenth Seasons of Excavations, 1971 1978, 1980 1984 Arad Excavation Reports*. Israel Exploration Society, Jerusalem.

Amiran, Ruth K.; Paran, Uzzi; Shiloh, Yigal; Brown, Rafi; Tsafir, Yoran & Ben-Tor, Ammon (eds)
1978 *Chalcolithic Settlement and the Early Bronze Age City, I: First-Fifth Seasons of Excavation 1962-1966*. Israel Exploration Society, Jerusalem.

Anderson, Patricia; Chabot, Jacques & Van Gijn, Annelou
2004 'The Functional Riddle of "Glossy" Canaanean Blades and the Near Eastern Threshing Sledge', *Journal of Mediterranean Archaeology* 17/1: 87–130.

Andrews, Richard M.; Kubacka, Iwona; Chinnery, Patrick F.; Lightowelers, Robert N.; Turnbull, Douglass M. & Howell, Neil
1999 'Reanalysis and Revision of the Cambridge Reference for Human Mitochondrial DNA', *Nature Genetics* 23: 147.

Asouti, Eleni & Fuller, Dorian Q.
2013 'A Contextual Approach to the Emergence of Agriculture in Southwest Asia: Reconstructing Early Neolithic Plant-Food Production', *Current Anthropology* 54/3: 299–345.

Avrutis, Vladimir W.
2010 'Excavation of Burial Cave F-55 and Burial F-257', in Shlomo Kol-Ya'akov (ed.), *Salvage Excavations at Nesher-Ramla Quarry*, I. Ostracon, Haifa: 20–46.
2012 *Late Chalcolithic and Early Bronze Age I Remains at Nesher-Ramla Quarry*. Zinman Institute of Archaeology, Jerusalem.

Banning, Edward B.; Gibbs, Kevin & Kadowaski, Seiji
2005 'Excavations at Late Neolithic al-Bastin, in Wadi Ziqlab, Northern Jordan', *Annual of the Department of Antiquities of Jordan* 49: 217–28.

Bar-Adon, Pessah
1980 *The Cave of the Treasure: The Finds from the Caves in Nahal Mishmar*. Israel Exploration Society, Jerusalem.

Barket, Theresa M. & Bell, Colleen A.
2011 'Tabular Scrapers: Function Revisited', *Near Eastern Archaeology* 74/1: 56–59.

Baruch, Uri
1986 'The Late Holocene Vegetational History of Lake Kinneret (Sea of Galilee), Israel', *Paléorient* 12: 37–48.

Barzilai, Omri; Vardi, Jacob; Liran, Roy; Yegorov, Dmitry; Covello-Paran, Karen; Brink, Edwin C. M. van den; Yaroshevich, Alla & Berger, Uri
2013 'The Nahal Zippori, the Eshkol Reservoir–Somekh Reservoir Pipeline', *Excavations and Survey in Israel* 125 <https://www.jstor.org/stable/26602851> [accessed 1 November 2023].

Behar, Doron M.; Oven, Mannis; Rosset, Saharon; Metspalu, Mait; Loogväli, Eva L.; Silva, Nuno M.; Kivisild, Toomas; Torroni, Antonio & Villems, Richard
2012 'A "Copernican" Reassessment of the Human Mitochondrial DNA Tree from its Root', *The American Journal of Human Genetics* 90/5: 675–84.

Besnard, Guillaume & Casas, Rafael Rubio de
2016 'Single vs Multiple Independent Olive Domestications: The Jury Is (Still) Out', *New Phytologist* 209: 466–70.

Besnard, Guillaume; Terral, Jean Frédéric & Cornille, Amandine
2018 'On the Origins and Domestication of the Olive: A Review and Perspectives', *Annals of Botany* 121/3: 385–403.

Betts, Alison V. G. (ed.)
1992 *Excavations at Tell Um Hammad: The Early Assemblages (EB I-II)*. Edinburgh University Press, Edinburgh.

Betts, Alison V. G. & Helms, Svend W. (eds)
1991 *Excavations at Jawa 1972-1986: Stratigraphy, Pottery and Other Finds*. Edinburgh University Press, Edinburgh.

Bollongino, Ruth; Nehlich, Olaf; Richards, Michael P.; Orschiedt, Jörg; Thomas, Mark G.; Sell, Christian; Fajkošová, Zuzana; Powell, Adam & Burger, Joachim

2013   '2000 Years of Parallel Societies in Stone Age Central Europe', *Science* 342: 479–81.

Bollongino, Ruth; Tresset, Anne & Vigne, Jean D.

2008   'Environment and Excavation: Pre-lab Impacts on Ancient DNA Analyses', *Comptes rendus palevol* 7: 91–98.

Borowski, Oded

1979   'Agriculture in Iron Age Israel' (unpublished doctoral thesis, University of Michigan).

Bottema, Sytze; Entjes-Nieborg, Gertie; Zeist, Willem van (eds)

1990   *Man's Role in the Shaping of the Eastern Mediterranean Landscape: Proceedings of the Symposium on the Impact of Ancient Man on the Landscape of the Eastern Mediterranean Region and the Near East, Groningen, Netherlands, 6–9 March 1989.* CRC Press, Groningen.

Bourke, Stephen J.

2001   'The Chalcolithic Period', in Burton MacDonald, Russell Adams & Piotr Bienkowski (eds), *The Archaeology of Jordan*. Eisenbrauns, Sheffield: 107–62.

Bourke, Stephen J. & Lovell, Jamie

2004   'Ghassul, Chronology and Cultural Sequencing', *Paleorient* 30/1: 179–82.

Bradbury, Jennie; Braemer, Frank & Sala, Maura

2014   'Fitting Upland, Steppe, and Desert into a "Big Picture" Perspective: A Case Study from Northern Jordan', *Levant* 46/2: 206–29.

Brandl, Baruch

1992   'Evidence for Egyptian Colonization in the Southern Costal Plain and Lowlands of Canaan during the EB I Period', in Edwin C. M. van den Brink (ed.), *The Nile Delta in Transition: 4th-3rd Millennium BC*. Israel Exploration Society, Tel Aviv: 441–77.

Braun, Eliot

1990   'Basalt Bowls of the EB I Horizon in the Southern Levant', *Paléorient* 16: 87–96.

1997   *Yiftah'el: Salvage and Rescue Excavations at a Prehistoric Village in Lower Galilee, Israel* (Israel Antiquities Authority Reports 2). Israel Antiquities Authority, Jerusalem.

2009   'South Levantine Early Bronze Age Chronological Correlations with Egypt in Light of the Narmer Serekhs from Tel Erani and Arad: New Interpretations', *British Museum Studies in Ancient Egypt and Sudan* 13: 25–48.

2011a 'Early Interactions between Peoples of the Nile Valley and the Southern Levant', in Emily Teeter (ed.), *Before the Pyramids: The Origin of Egyptian Civilization* (Oriental Institute Publications 33). Oriental Institute, Chicago: 105–22.

2011b 'The Transition from Chalcolithic to Early Bronze Age I in the Southern Levant: A "Lost Horizon" Slowly Revealed', in Jaimie L. Lovell & Yorke M. Rowan (eds), *Culture, Chronology and the Chalcolithic: Theory and Transition*. Oxbow, Oxford: 161–77.

2012   'On Some South Levantine Early Bronze Age Ceramic "Wares" and "Styles"', *Palestine Exploration Quarterly* 144/1: 4–31.

2013   *Early Megiddo on the East Slope (The 'Megiddo Stages'): A Report on the Early Occupation of the East Slope of Megiddo; Results of the Oriental Institute's Excavations, 1925-1933* (Oriental Institute Publications 139). Oriental Institute, Chicago.

2019   'Forging a Link: Evidence for a "Lost Horizon" – The Late Chalcolithic to EB 1 Transition in the Southern Levant in Studies', in Haim Goldfus, Mayer I. Gruber, Shamir Yona & Peter Fabian (eds), *Studies in Archaeology and Ancient Cultures in Honor of Isaac Gilead*. Archaeopress, Oxford: 66–95.

2020 'Reflections on South Levantine Early Bronze Age I Vernacular Architecture', online open access at: <https://www.academia.edu/42805562/Braun_EB_1_Vernacular_Architecture> [accessed 1 November 2023].

Braun, Eliot & Roux, Valentine
2013 'The Late Chalcolithic to the Early Bronze Age I Transition in the Southern Levant: Determining Continuity and Discontinuity or "Mind the Gap"', *Paléorient* 39/1: 15–22.

Brink, Edwin C. M. van den
2011 'Continuity and Change – Cultural Transmission in the Late Chalcolithic – Early Bronze Age I: A View from Early Modi'in, a Late Prehistoric Site in Central Israel', in Jaimie L. Lovell & Yorke M. Rowan (eds), *Culture, Chronology and the Chalcolithic: Theory and Transition*. Oxbow, Oxford: 61–70.

Brun, Jean Pierre
2003 *Archéologie du vin et de l'huile: de la Préhistoire à l'époque Hellénistique*. Errance, Paris.

Burbano, Hernán A; Hodges, Emily; Green, Richard E.; Briggs, Adrian W.; Krause, Johannes; Meyer, Matthias; Good, Jeffrey M.; Maricic, Tomislav; Johnson, Philip L. F.; Xuan, Zhenyu; Rooks, Michelle; Bhattacharjee, Arindam; Brizuela, Leonardo; Albert, Frank W.; De la Rasilla, Marco; Fortea, Javier; Rosas, Antonio; Lachmann, Michael; Hannon, Gregory J. & Pääbo, Svante
2010 'Targeted Investigation of the Neandertal Genome by Array-Based Sequence Capture', *Science* 328: 723–25.

Buxeda i Garrigós, Jaume
1999 'Alteration and Contamination of Archaeological Ceramics: The Perturbation Problem', *Journal of Archaeometrical Science* 26: 295–313.

Cabellos, Teresa; Garralda, Maria Dolores & Fernández-Tresguerres, Juan A.
2002 'Las gentes del Bronce antiguo de Jebel Mutawwaq (Jordania, 3500–2000 a.C.); studio antropologico', *Revista Espanola de Antropologia Biologica* 23: 93–114.

Callaway, Joseph A.
1964 *Pottery from the Tombs at 'Ai (Et-Tell)*; B. Quaritch, London.
1972 *The Early Bronze Age Sanctuary at 'Ai (et-Tell): A Report of the Joint Archaeological Expedition to 'Ai /et-Tell)*, I. American School of Oriental Research, Cambridge, MA.
1980 *The Early Bronze Age Citadel and Lower City at Ai (Et-Tell): A Report of the Joint Archaeological Expedition to Ai (Et-Tell); No. 2*. American School of Oriental Research, Cambridge, MA.

Cameron, Dorothy O.
1981 *The Ghassulian Wall Paintings*. Kenyon-Dean, London.

Caramelli, David
2009 *Antropologia molecolare: manuale base*. University of Florence, Florence.

Carøe, Christian; Gopalakrishnan, Shyam; Vinner, Lasse; Mak, Sarah S. T.; Sinding, Mikkel H. S.; Samaniego, José A.; Wales, Nathan; Sicheritz-Pontén, Thomas & Gilbert, Thomas M.
2018 'Single-Tube Library Preparation for Degraded DNA Methods', *Ecology and Evolution* 9/2: 410–19.

Casadei, Eloisa
2018 'Linking the River and the Desert: The Early Bronze Age I Pottery Assemblage of the Wadi Zarqa Region', in Barbara Horejs, Christoph Schwall, Vera Müller, Marta Luciani, Markus Ritter, Mattia Guidetti, Roderick B. Salisbury, Felix Höflmayer & Teresa Bürge (eds), *Proceedings of the 10th International Congress on the Archaeology of the Ancient Near East, 25-29 June 2016, Vienna*. Harrassowitz, Wiesbaden: 287–301.

Casado, Ángel Martínez; Muñiz, Juan R.; Polcaro, Andrea; Martinez, Valentin; Casadei, Eloisa; Garcia del Rio, Joaquin; Perri, Gianluca; Gonzalez, Sergio R.; Piedra, Gerardo S.; Zambruno, Pablo & Corrada, Marta

2016 'Qareisan Spring: Jebel Mutawwaq Dolmen Field and Bronze Age Site. Trabajos de excavación arqueológica en Jebel Mutawwaq, Jordania. Campaña de 2015', *Informes y trabajos* 14: 276–89.

Caselli, Alessandra

2023 'Jebel al-Mutawwaq and the Middle Wadi az-Zarqa Region during the IV Millennium BC: Results of a Comprehensive Research Based on the Reanalysis of the Hanbury-Tenison's Survey', in Nicolò Marchetti, Francesca Cavaliere, Enrico Cirelli, Claudia D'Orazio, Gabriele Giocosa, Mattia Guidetti & Eleonora Mariani (eds), *Proceedings of the 12th International Congress on the Archaeology of the Ancient Near East, Bologna, 6-9 April 2021*, II: *Field Reports: Islamic Archaeology*. Harrassowitz, Wiesbaden: 115–28.

Castellano, Sergi; Parra, Genís; Sánchez-Quinto, Federico A; Racimo, Fernando; Kuhlwilm, Martin; Kircher, Martin; Sawyer, Susanna; Fu, Qiaomei; Heinze, Anja; Nickel, Birgit; Dabney, Jesse; Siebauer, Michael; White, Louise; Burbano, Hernán A; Renaud, Gabriel; Stenzel, Udo; Lalueza-Fox, Carles; De la Rasilla, Marco; Rosas, Antonio; Rudan, Pavao; Brajković, Dejana; Kucan, Željko; Gušic, Ivan; Shunkov, Michael V.; Derevianko, Anatoli P; Viola, Bence; Meyer, Matthias; Kelso, Janet; Andrés, Aida M. & Pääbo, Svante

2014 'Patterns of Coding Variation in the Complete Exomes of Three Neandertals', *Proceedings of the National Academy of Science of the USA* 111/18: 6666–71.

Cavalli-Sforza, Luigi L.; Menozzi, Paolo & Piazza, Alberto

1994 *The History and Geography of Human Genes*. Princeton University Press, Princeton.

Champlot, Sophie; Berthelot, Camille; Pruvost, Mélanie; Bennett, Andrew E.; Grange, Thierry & Geigl, Eva M.

2010 'An Efficient Multistrategy DNA Decontamination Procedure of PCR Reagents for Hypersensitive PCR Applications', *PLoS One* 5: e13042.

Chasan, Rivka & Rosenberg, Danny

2019 'Getting into Shape: The Characteristics and Significance of Late Chalcolithic Basalt Vessel Decoration in the Southern Levant', *Paleorient* 45/1: 53–68.

Chesson, Meredith S.

2001 'Embodied Memories of Place and People: Death and Society in an Early Urban Community', in Meredith S. Chesson (ed.), *Social Memory, Identity and Death: Ethnographic and Archaeological Perspectives on Mortuary Rituals* (American Anthropological Association Series 10). American Anthropological Association, Arlington: 100–13.

2007 'Remembering and Forgetting in the Early Bronze Age Mortuary Practices', in Nicola Laneri (ed.), *Performing Death: Social Analyses of Funerary Traditions in the Ancient Near East and Mediterranean* (Oriental Institute Seminars 3). Oriental Institute, Chicago: 109–39.

Cilli, Elisabetta

2023 'Archaeogenetics', *Reference Module in Social Sciences*, Elsevier <https://doi.org/10.1016/B978-0-323-90799-6.00017-3>.

Clarke, Joanne; Brooks, Nick; Banning, Edward B.; Bar-Matthews, Miryam; Campbell, Stuart; Clare, Lee; Cremaschi, Mauro; di Lernia, Savino; Drake, Nick; Gallinaro, Marina; Manning, Sturt; Nicoll, Kathleen;

Philip, Graham; Rosen, Steve; Schoop, Ulf-Dietrich; Tafuri, Mary Anne; Weninger, Berhard & Zerboni, Andrea
2015 'Climatic Changes and Social Transformations in the Near East and North Africa during the "Long" 4th Millennium BC: A Comparative Study of Environmental and Archaeological Evidence', *Quaternary Science Reviews* 136: 96–121.

Cocchi-Genick, Daniela
2012 *Le potenzialità informative delle ceramiche nell'analisi storica: le forme vascolari dell'età del rame dell'Italia settentrionale*. QuiEdit, Verona.

Conder, Claude R.
1989 *The Survey of Eastern Palestine*, I. Palestine Exploration Fund, London.

Coqueugniot, Eric
2006 'Outillages en pierre taillée et la question des lames "cananéennes": étude préliminaire', in Jean-Paul Thalmann (ed.), *Tell Arqa*, I: *Les niveaux de l'Âge du Bronze* (Bibliothèque archéologique et historique 177). Institut français du Proche-Orient, Beirut: 195–202.

Cordoba, Joaquin M. & Perez Die, Carmen (eds)
2011 *The Spanish Near Eastern Adventure (1166-1926): Travellers, Museums and Scholars in the History of the Rediscovering of Ancient Near East*. Ministerio de Cultura, Madrid.

D'Andrea, Marta
2014 *The Southern Levant in Early Bronze Age*, IV: *Issues and Perspectives in the Pottery Evidence* (Contributi e materiali di archeologia orientale 17). Sapienza Università di Roma, Rome.

D'Auria, Alessia; Buonincontri, Mauro Paolo; Allevato, Emilia; Saracino, Antonio; Jung, Reinhard; Pacciarelli, Marco & Di Pasquale, Gaetano
2017 'Evidence of a Short-Lived Episode of Olive (*Olea europaea* L.) Cultivation during the Early Bronze Age in Western Mediterranean (Southern Italy)', *The Holocene* 27: 605–12.

Damgaard, Peter B.; Margaryan, Ashot; Schroeder, Hannes; Orlando, Ludovic; Willerslev, Eske & Allentoft, Morten E.
2015 'Improving Access to Endogenous DNA in Ancient Bones and Teeth', *Scientific Report* 5: 11184.

Deguilloux, Marie F.; Ricaud, Séverine; Leahy, Rachael & Pemonge, Marie H.
2011 'Analysis of Ancient Human DNA and Primer Contamination: One Step Backward One Step Forward', *Forensic Science International* 210: 102–09.

Dighton, Anne; Fairbairn, Andrew; Bourke, Stephen; Faith, J. Tyler & Habgood, Philip
2017 'Bronze Age Olive Domestication in the North Jordan Valley: New Morphological Evidence for Regional Complexity in Early Arboricultural Practice from Pella in Jordan', *Vegetation History and Archaeobotany* 26: 403–13.

Douglas, Khaled & Kafafi, Zeidan
2000 'The Main Aspects of the Early Bronze Age I Pottery from Jebel Abu Thawwab, North Jordan', in Graham Philip & Douglas Baird (eds), *Ceramics and Change in the Early Bronze Age of the Southern Levant* (Levantine Archaeology 2). Sheffield Academic Press, Sheffield: 101–12.

Dubis, Elzbieta & Dabrowski, Bogdan
2002 'Field K: The Dolmen and Other Features on the South Slopes of Tall al-'Umayri', in Larry G. Herr, Douglas R. Clark, Lawrence T. Geraty, Øystein S. LaBianca & Randall W. Younker (eds), *Madaba Plains Project: The 1994*

Season at Tall al-'Umayri and Subsequent Studies (Madaba Plains Project Series 5). Andrews University Press, Berrien Springs: 171–77.

Elliott, Carolyn
1977 'The Religious Beliefs of the Ghassulians, c. 4000–3100 BC', *Palestine Exploration Quarterly* 109: 3–25.

Epstein, Claire
1985 'Dolmen Excavated in the Golan', *'Atiqot* 17: 20–58.

Esse, Douglas
1989 'Secondary State Formation and Collapse in Early Bronze Age Palestine', in Pierre de Miroschedji (ed.), *L'urbanisation de la Palestine a l'age du Bronze Ancien* (British Archaeological Reports, International Series 527). Archaeopress, Oxford: 81–96.

Fernández-Tresguerres, Juan A.
1987 'Arpones decorados en el Aziliense Asturiano: Cueva de Los Azules, Cangas de Onis', *Revista de arquelogia* 78: 20–24.

1992 'Jebel Mutawwaq: los inicios de la edad del bronce en la zona de Wadi Zarqa (Jordania)', *Treballs d'arquelogia* 2: 127–43.

1999 'Jebel Mutawwaq, un poblado de Bronce Antiguo IA en la estepa jordana', in Joaquìn Gonzalez Echegaray & Mario Menendez (eds), *De Oriente a Occidente: homenaje al Dr Emilio Olavarri*. Pontificia Facultad de Salamanca, Salamanca: 213–36.

2001 'The Northern Jordanian Plateau at the End of the Fourth Millennium', in Juan Luis Montero Fenollòs & Felip Masò Ferrer (eds), *De la estepa al mediterràneo: actas del 1er Congreso de Arqueologia e Historia Antigua del Oriente Pròximo, Barcelona, 3-5 de Abril de 2000* (Monografies Eridu 1). Eridu, Barcelona: 319–32.

2004a 'Jebel al-Mutawwaq (Jordania)', *Bienes culturales: Revista de Instituto del Patrimonio Historico Espanol* 3: 63–74.

2004b 'La casa 81 y enterramientos de niños en jarras en el Bronce Antiguo I de Jebel Mutawwaq (Jordania)', in Antonino González Blanco, Juan Pablo Vita & José Angel Zamora López (eds), *De la tablilla a la inteligencia artificial: homenaje al Prof. Jesús-Luís Cunchillos en su 65 aniversario*. Instituto de Estudios Islámicos y del Oriente Próximo, Zaragoza: 263–78.

2005a 'El "Templo de Las Serpientes". Un santuario del Bronce Antiguo I en el poblado del Jebel al-Mutawwaq (Jordania)', *ISIMU* 8: 9–34.

2005b 'Jabal Muṭawwaq', *Annual of the Department of Antiquities of Jordan* 49: 365–732.

2006 'Jebel al-Mutawwaq', in Maria Perez Die & Joaquìn Cordoba Zoilo (eds), *La aventura espanola en Oriente (1166-2006)*. Ministerio de Cultura, Subdireccion General de Publicaciones, Informacion y Documentacion, Madrid: 63–67.

2007 'La casa 77 dentro del conjunto del "Tempio de las Serpientes" de Jebel al-Mutawwaq (Jordania)', in Josué J. Juster Vicente, Barbara E. Solans, Juan P. Vita & Josè A. Zamora (eds), *Las aguas primigenias: el Proximo Oriente Antiguo como fuente de civilizacion*. Instituto de Estudios Islamicos y del Oriente Proximo, Zaragoza: 421–38.

2008a 'The Temple of the Serpents, a Sanctuary of the Early Bronze Age I in the Village of Jabal al Muṭawwaq (Jordan)', *Annual of the Department of Antiquities of Jordan* 52: 23–34.

2008b 'Jebel al-Mutawwaq (Jordania)', in Valentin Alvarez Martinez, David Gonzalez Alvarez & Jesus I. Jimenez Chaparro (eds), *Actas de las I Jornadas de Arqueologia de Asturias (abril-mayo de 2005)*. Compana Espanola de Reprografia y Servicios: Madrid: 39–50.

2010 'Biblia y arqueologia', in Maria del Mar Larraza (ed.), *Historia de Israel y del pueblo judio: guerra y paz en al Tierra Prometida*. Ediciones Universidad de Navarra, Navarra: 67–110.

2011a 'Pierres dressées dans la région de Mutawwaq, al-Hawettan and Hmeid (Jordanie) region', in Tara Steimer-Herbet (ed.), *Pierres dressées et statues anthropomorphes* (British Archaeological Reports, International Series 2317). BAR, Oxford.

2011b 'Los dolmenes en Jebel Mutawwaq (1990–1992)', in Fernando Junceda Quintana (ed.), *IV Simposio Biblico Espanol (I Ibero-Americano): biblia y culturas*. Universitad de Granada, Granada: 35–40.

2011c 'Jebel al-Mutawwaq 2009. Excavación de la casa 151. Trabajos en las zonas dolménicas de Mutawwaq y de wadi Hmeid', *Informes y trabajos* 5: 212–21.

Fernández-Tresguerres, Juan A. & Junceda, Quintana F.

1991 'Jebel Mutawwaq (Jordania). Campanas 1989–1991', *Estudios Biblicos* 49: 523–42.

Finkelstein, Israel & Gophna, Raphael

1993 'Settlement, Demographic, and Economic Patterns in the Highlands of Palestine in the Chalcolithic and Early Bronze Periods and the Beginning of Urbanism', *Bulletin of the American Schools of Oriental Research* 289: 1–22.

Fischer, Peter M.

2000 'The Early Bronze Age at Tell Abu al-Kharaz, Jordan Valley: A Study of Pottery Typology and Provenance, Radiocarbon Dates, and Synchronism of Palestine and Egypt during Dynasty 0–2', in Graham Philip & Douglas Baird (eds), *Ceramics and Change in the Early Bronze Age of the Southern Levant* (Levantine Archaeology 2). Sheffield Academic Press, Sheffield: 201–32.

2008 *Tell Abu Kharaz in the Jordan Valley, I: The Early Bronze Age* (Contributions to the Chronology of the Eastern Mediterranean 16). Österreichische Akademie der Wissenschaften, Vienna.

Fortea, Javier; De la Rasilla, Marco; García-Tabernero, Antonio; Gigli, Elena; Rosas, Antonio & Lalueza-Fox, Carles

2008 'Excavation Protocol of Bone Remains for Neandertal DNA Analysis in El Sidrón Cave (Asturias, Spain)', *Journal of Human Evolution* 55: 353–57.

Fraser, Jamie

2018 *Dolmens in the Levant* (Palestine Exploration Fund Annual 14). Routledge, New York.

Fraser, Jamie; Cartwright, Caroline R.; Zoubi, Nasr; Carr, Adam; Handziuk, Natalia; Spry, Beau; Vassiliades, Anthoulla; Wesselingh, Kate & Winter, Holly

2021 'The First Preliminary Report of the Khirbat Umm al-Ghuzlan Excavation Project: Investigating an EB IV Olive Processing Site in North Jordan', *Annual of the Department of Antiquities of Jordan* 60: 487–500.

Galili, Ehud; Rosen, Baruch & Boaretto, Elisabetta

2007 'Haifa, Kafr Samir. Hadashot Arkheologiyot', *Excavations and Surveys in Israel* 119: 1–4.

Galili, Ehud; Stanley, Daniel Jean; Sharvit, Jacob & Weinstein-Evron, Mina

1997 'Evidence for Earliest Olive-Oil Production in Submerged Settlements off the Carmel Coast, Israel', *Journal of Archaeological Science* 24/12: 1141–50.

Gamba, Cristina; Jones, Eppie R.; Teasdale, Matthew D.; McLaughlin, Russell L.; Gonzalez-Fortes, Gloria; Mattiangelli, Valeria; Domboròczki, Làszlò; Kõvàri, Ivett; Pap, Ildikò; Anders, Alexandra; Whittle, Alasdair; Dani, Jànos; Raczky, Pàl; Higham, Thomas F. G.; Hofreiter, Michael; Bradley, Daniel G. & Pinhasi, Ron

2014 'Genome Flux and Stasis in a Five Millennium Transect of European Prehistory', *Nature Communications* 5: 5257.

Genz, Hermann; Çakirlar, Canan; Damick, Alison; Jastrzebska, Emilia; Riehl, Simone; Deckers, Katleen & Donkin, Ann

2009 'Excavations at Tell Fadous-Kfarabida: Preliminary Report on the 2009 Season of Excavations', *Bulletin d'archéologie et d'architecture libanaises* 13: 71–123.

Getzov, Nimrod
2006 *The Tel Beth Yerah Excavations 1994-1995* (Israel Antiquities Authority 28). Israel Antiquities Authority, Jerusalem.

Ghirotto, Silvia; Tassi, Francesca; Fumagalli, Erica; Colonna, Vincenza; Sandionigi, Anna; Lari, Martina; Vai, Stefania; Petiti, Emanuele; Corti, Giorgio; Rizzi, Ermanno; De Bellis, Gianluca; Caramelli, David & Barbujani, Guido
2013 'Origins and Evolution of the Etruscans mtDNA', *PLoS One* 8: e55519.

Gilead, David
1968 'Burial Customs and the Dolmen Problem', *Palestine Exploration Quarterly* 100: 16–26.

Glueck, Nelson
1951 *The Survey of Eastern Palestine*, IV (Annual of the American Schools of Oriental Research 25-28). American Schools of Oriental Research, New Haven.

Golani, Amir
2004 'Salvage Excavations at the Early Bronze Age Site of Ashqelon, Afridar – Area E', *'Atiqot* 45: 9–62.
2008 'The Early Bronze Age Site of Ashqelon, Afridar – Area M', *'Atiqot* 60: 19–51.

Gonzalez Echegaray, Joaquin
1970 'Sondeos y prospecciones en Mogaret-Dalal (Jordania)', *Ampurias: revista de arquelogia, prehistoria y etnologia* 31–32: 233–40.

Gonzales Morales, Manuel R.; Dupré Olivier, Michèle; Corchon Rodriguez, Maria Soledad; Gomez, M. Hovos; Laville, Henri; Fortea Pérez, Francisco Javier; Rodriguez Asensio, Jose Adolfo & Fernández-Tresguerres, Juan A.
1989 'Neue Untersuchungen in den Flusstalern des Nalon und des Sella (Asturien)', *Madrider Mitteilungen* 30: 1–30.

Gophna, Raphael
2002 'Elusive Anchorage Points along the Israel Littoral and the Egyptian-Canaanite Maritime Route during the Early Bronze Age I', in Edwin C. M. van der Brink & Thomas E. Levy (eds), *Egypt and the Levant: Interrelations from the 4th through the Early 3rd Millennium B.C.E.* Leicester University Press, London: 418–21.

Greenberg, Raphael
2001 'Early Bronze Age II–III Palestinian Cylinder Seal Impressions and the North Canaanite Metallic Ware Jar', in Samuel R. Wolff (ed.), *Studies in the Archaeology of Israel and Neighboring Lands in Memory of Douglas L. Esse.* Oriental Institute of the University of Chicago, Chicago: 189–98.
2002 *Early Urbanization in the Levant: A Regional Narrative.* Leicester University Press, London.

Gustavson-Gaube, Carrie
1985 'Tell Esh-Shuna (North): 1984, a Preliminary Report', *Annual of the Department of Antiquities of Jordan* 29: 43–87.

Guy, Philip L. O.
1938 *Megiddo Tombs* (Oriental Institute Publication 33). Oriental Institute, Chicago.

Hanbury-Tenison, Jack W.
1986 *The Late Chalcolithic to Early Bronze Age I Transition in Palestine and Transjordan* (British Archaeological Reports, International Series 311). Archaeopress, Oxford.
1989 'Jebel al-Mutawwaq 1986', *Annual of the Department of Antiquities of Jordan* 33: 137–44.

Hansen, Henrik. B.; Damgaard, Peter B.; Margaryan, Ashot; Stenderup, Jesper; Lynnerup, Niels; Willerslev, Eske & Allentoft, Morten E.
2017   'Comparing Ancient DNA Preservation in Petrous Bone and Tooth Cementum', *PLoS One* 12: e0170940.

Harney, Eadaoin; May, H.; Shalem, Dina; Rohlad, Nadin; Mallick, Swapan; Lazaridis, Iosif; Sarig, Rachel; Stewardson, Kristin; Nordenfelt, Susanne; Patterson, Nick; Hershkovitz, Israel & Reich, David
2018   'Ancient DNA from Chalcolithic Israel Reveals the Role of Population Mixture in Cultural Transformation', *Nature Communications* 9: 3336.

Hartenberger, Britt; Rosen, Steven A. & Matney, Timothy
2000   'The Early Bronze Age Blade Workshop at Titris Hoyuk: Lithic Specialization in an Urban Context', *Near Eastern Archaeology* 63: 51–58.

Helms, Svend W.
1984   'Excavations at Tell Umm Hammad esh-Sharqiya in the Jordan Valley, 1982', *Levant* 16: 35–54.

Hennessy, John B.
1977   *Teleilat Ghassul: An Interim Report*. University of Sydney, Sydney.

Henry, Donald O.
1995   *Prehistoric Cultural Ecology and Evolution: Insights from Southern Jordan* (Interdisciplinary Contributions to Archaeology; Language of Science). Plenum, New York.

Hervella, Montserrant; Rotea, Mihai; Izagirre, Neskuts; Costantinescu, Mihai; Alonso, Santos; Ioana, Mihai; Lazăr, Cătălin; Ridiche, Florin; Soficaru, Andrei D.; Natea, Mihai G. & De la Rua, Concepcion
2015   'Ancient DNA from South-East Europe Reveals Different Events during Early and Middle Neolithic Influencing the European Genetic Heritage', *PLoS One* 10: e0128810.

Higgins, Denice & Austin, Jeremy J.
2013   'Teeth as a Source of DNA for Forensic Identification of Human Remains: A Review', *Science & Justice: Journal of the Forensic Science Society* 53/4: 433–41.

Höflmayer, Felix; Dee, Michael W.; Genz, Hermann & Riehl, Simone
2014   'Radiocarbon Evidence for the Early Bronze Age Levant: The Site of Tell Fadous-Kfarabida (Lebanon) and the End of the Early Bronze III Period', *Radiocarbon* 56: 529–42.

Hofmanová, Zuzana; Kreutzer, Susanne; Hellenthal, Garrett; Sell, Christian; Diekmann, Yoan; Díez-del-Molino, David; Dorp, Lucy van; López, Saioa; Kousathanas, Athanasios; Link, Vivian; Kirsanow, Karola; Cassidy, Laura M.; Martiniano, Rui; Strobel, Melanie; Scheu, Amelie; Kotsakis, Kostas; Halstead, Paul; Triantaphyllou, Sevi; Kyparissi-Apostolika, Nina; Urem-Kotsou, Dushka; Ziota, Christina; Adaktylou, Fotini; Gopalan, Shyamalika; Bobo, Dean M.; Winkelbach, Laura; Blöcher, Jens; Unterländer, Martina; Leuenberger, Cristoph; Çilingiroğlu, Ciler; Horejs, Barbara; Gerritsen, Fokke; Shennan, Stephen J.; Bradley, Daniel G.; Currat, Mathias; Veeramah, Krishna R.; Wegmann, Daniel; Thomas, Mark G.; Papageorgopoulou, Christina & Burger, Joachim
2016   'Early Farmers from across Europe Directly Descended from Neolithic Aegeans', *Proceedings of the National Academy of Sciences* 113/25: 6886–91.

Horowitz, Aharon
1979   *The Quaternary of Israel*. Academic Press, New York.

Humbert, Jean-Baptiste & Desreumaux, Alain
1989   'Khirbet es-Samra', in Jean Marcillet & Jean Starcky (eds), *Contribution française à l'archéologie jordanienne*. Institut français du Proche-Orient, Damascus: 113–21.

Ibañez, Juan J.; Muñiz, Juan R.; Iriarte, Eneko; Monik, Martin; Santana, Jonathan; Teira, Luis; Corrada, Marta; Lagüera, Manuel A.; Lendakova, Zuzana; Regalado, Encarnacion & Rosillo, Rafael

2016 'Kharaysin: A PPNA and PPNB Site by the Zarqa River. 2014 and 2015 Field Seasons', *Neo-Lithics: The Newsletter of Southwest Asian Neolithic Research* 2/15: 11–19.

Ilan, David

2002 'Mortuary Practices in Early Bronze Age Canaan', *Near Eastern Archaeology* 65/2: 92–104.

Ilan, David; Ben-Ari, Nathan & Levitte, Dov

2015 'The Ground Stone Assemblage', *NGSBA Archaeology* 3: 84–93.

Ilan, David & Rowan, Yorke M.

2012 'Deconstructing and Recomposing the Narrative of Spiritual Life in the Chalcolithic of the Southern Levant (4500–3600 B.C.E.)', *Archeological Papers of the American Anthropological Association* 21/1: 89–113.

Ji, Chang-Ho C. & Lee, Keun

2002 'The Survey in the Regions of 'Iraq al-Amir and Wadi al-Kafrayn, 2000', *Annual of the Department of Antiquities of Jordan* 46: 179–95.

Jobling, Mark; Hurles, Matthew & Tyler-Smith, Chris

2014 'Human Evolutionary Genetics: Origins, Peoples and Disease', *American Journal of Human Genetics* 76/6: 1087–88.

Joffe, Alexander H.

2018 'Notes on Early Bronze Age Commensality', in Itzick Shai, Jeffrey R. Chadwick, Louise Hitchcock, Amit Dagan, Chris McKinny & Joe Uziel (eds), *Tell It in Gath: Studies in the History and Archaeology of Israel; Essays in Honor of A. M. Maeir on the Occasion of his Sixtieth Birthday*. Zaphon, Munster: 41–70.

2022 'New Models for the End of the Chalcolithic in the Southern Levant', in Matthew J. Adams & Valentine Roux (eds), *Transitions during the Early Bronze Age in the Levant: Methodological Problems and Interpretative Perspectives* (Ägypten und Altes Testament 101). Zaphon, Münster: 81–115.

Julca, Irene; Marcet-Houben, Marina; Cruz, Fernando; Gòmez-Garrido, Jèssica; Gaut, Brandon S.; Dìez, Concepciòn M.; Gut, Ivo G.; Alioto, Tyler S.; Vargas, Pablo & Gabaldòn, Toni

2020 'Genomic Evidence for Recurrent Genetic Admixture during the Domestication of Mediterranean Olive Trees (*Olea europaea* L.)', *BMC Biology* 18/1: 1–25.

Kafafi, Zeidan A.

2001 *Jebel Abu Thawwab (Er-Rumman) Central Jordan: The Late Neolithic and Early Bronze Age I Occupation* (Monograph of the Institute of Archaeology and Anthropology 3). Ex oriente, Berlin.

2022 'The Lower Jordan Valley, Southern Ghors and Wadi Arabah: A Case for Urban Life in Jordan in the Third Millennium BC', in Jesse C. Long, Jr & William G. Dever (eds), *Transitions, Urbanism, and Collapse in the Bronze Age: Essays in Honor of Suzanne Richard*. Equinox, Sheffield: 111–25.

Kaniewski, David; Van Campo, Elise; Boiy, Tom; Terral, Jean-Frédéric; Khadari, Bouchaïb & Besnard, Guillaume

2012 'Primary Domestication and Early Uses of the Emblematic Olive Tree: Palaeobotanical, Historical and Molecular Evidence from the Middle East', *Biological Reviews* 8: 885–99.

Kenyon, Kathleen M.

1960 *Excavations at Jericho*, I: *The Tombs Excavated in 1952-1954*. British School of Archaeology, London.

Kenyon, Kathleen M. & Holland, Thomas A.

1982 *Excavation at Jericho*, IV: *The Pottery Type Series and Other Finds*. British School of Archaeology in Jerusalem, London.

1983 *Excavation at Jericho*, V: *The Pottery Phase of the Tell*. British School of Archaeology in Jerusalem, London.

Kerner, Susanne

2019 'New Research into the Early and Middle Bronze Age in Central Jordan: The Site of Murayghat', *Journal of Eastern Mediterranean Archaeology and Heritage Studies* 7/2: 165–87.

2022 '"Show Me How to Bury your People": Dolmens, Burials, and Social Development in the Early Bronze Age', in Jesse C. Long, Jr & William G. Dever (eds), *Transitions, Urbanism, and Collapse in the Bronze Age: Essays in Honor of Suzanne Richard*. Equinox, Sheffield: 127–40.

Knapp, Michael; Lalueza-Fox, Carles & Hofreiter, Michael

2015 'Re-inventing Ancient Human DNA', *Investigative Genetics* 6: 4.

Korlević, Petra; Gerber, Tobias; Gansauge, Marie T.; Hajdinjak, Mateja; Nagel, Sarah; Aximu-Petri, Ayinuer & Meyer, Matthias

2015 'Reducing Microbial and Human Contamination in DNA Extractions from Ancient Bones and Teeth', *Biotechniques* 59/2: 87–93.

Kumar, Sudhir; Stecher, Glen & Tamura, Koichiro

2016 'MEGA7: Molecular Evolutionary Genetics Analysis Version 7.0 for Bigger Datasets', *Molecular Biology and Evolution* 33: 1870–74.

Langgut, Dafna; Adams, Matthew J. & Finkelstein, Israel

2016 'Climate, Settlement Patterns and Olive Horticulture in the Southern Levant during the Early Bronze and Intermediate Bronze Ages (ca. 3600–1950 BCE)', *Levant* 48: 117–34.

Langgut, Dafna; Almogi-Labin, Ahuva; Bar-Matthews, Myriam & Weinstein-Evron, Mina

2011 'Vegetation and Climate Changes in the South Eastern Mediterranean during the Last Glacial-Interglacial Cycle (86 ka): New Marine Pollen Record', *Quaternary Science Reviews* 30: 3960–72.

Lazaridis, Iosif; Nadel, Dani; Rollefson, Gary; Merrett, Deborah C.; Rohland, Nadin; Mallick, Swapan; Fernandes, Daniel; Novak, Mario; Gamarra, Beatriz; Sirak, Kendra; Connell, Sarah; Stewardson, Kristin; Harney, Eadoin; Fu, Qiaomei; Gonzalez-Fortes, Gloria; Jones, Eppie R.; Roodenberg, Songul A.; Lengyel, György; Bocquentin, Fanny; Gasparian, Boris; Monge, Janet M.; Gregg, Michael; Eshed, Vered; Mizrahi, Ahuva-Sivan; Meiklejohn, Christopher; Gerritsen, Fokke; Bejenaru, Luminita; Blüher, Matthias; Campbell, Archie; Cavalleri, Gianpiero; Comas, David; Froguel, Philippe; Gilbert, Edmund; Kerr, Shona M.; Kovacs, Peter; Krause, Johannes; McGettigan, Darren; Merrigan, Michael; Merriwether, Andrew D.; O'Reilly, Seamus; Richards, Martin B.; Semino, Ornella; Shamoon-Pour, Michael; Stefanescu, Gheorghe; Stumvoll, Michael; Tönjes, Anke; Torroni, Antonio; Wilson, James F.; Yengo, Loic; Hovhannisyan, Nelli A.; Patterson, Nick; Pinhasi, Ron & Reich, David

2016 'Genomic Insights into the Origin of Farming in the Ancient Near East', *Nature* 536: 419–24.

Levy, Thomas E. (ed.)

2006 *Archaeology, Anthropology and Cult: The Sanctuary at Gilat, Israel*. Routledge, London.

Levy, Thomas E. & Alon, David

1985 'Shiqmim: A Chalcolithic Village and Mortuary Centre in the Northern Negev', *Paleorient* 11/1: 71–83.

Levy, Thomas E. & Brink, Edwin C. M. van den

2002 'Interactions Models, Egypt and the Levantine Periphery', in Edwin C. M. van der Brink & Thomas E. Levy (eds), *Egypt and the Levant: Interrelations from the 4th through the Early 3rd Millennium B.C.E.* Leicester University Press, London: 3-38.

Linder, Manfred; Schreyer, Elisabeth & Gunsam, Elisabeth

2005 'Early Bronze Age Umm Saysaban Excavation Continued in 2001: Insights and Conjectures', *Annual of the Department of Antiquities of Jordan* 49: 217-28.

Lindo, John; Achilli, Alessandro; Perego, Ugo A.; Archer, David; Valdiosera, Cristina; Petzlt, Barbara; Mitchell, Joycelynn; Worl, Rosita; Dixon, James E.; Fifield, Terence E.; Rasmussen, Morten; Willerslev, Eske; Cybulski, Jerome S.; Kemp, Braian M.; DeGiorgio, Michael & Malhi, Ripan S.

2016 'Ancient Individuals from the North American Northwest Coast Reveal 10,000 Years of Regional Genetic Continuity', *Proceedings of the National Academy of Science of the USA* 14/16: 4093-98.

Liphschitz, Nili; Gophna, Ram; Harman, Moshe & Biger, Gideon

1991 'The Beginning of Olive (*Olea europaea*) Cultivation in the Old World: A Reassessment', *Journal of Archaeological Science* 18: 441-53.

Litt, Thomas; Ohlwein, Christian; Neumann, Frank H.; Hence, Andreas & Stein, Mordechai

2012 'Holocene Climate Variability in the Levant from the Dead Sea Pollen Record', *Quaternary Science Reviews* 49: 95-105.

Llamas, Bastien; Valverde, Guido; Fehren-Schmitz, Lars; Weyrich, Laura S.; Cooper, Alan & Haak, Wolfgang

2017 'From the Field to the Laboratory: Controlling DNA Contamination in Human Ancient DNA Research in the High-Throughput Sequencing Era', *Science & Technology of Archaeological Research* 3: 1-14.

Llamas, Bastien; Willerslev, Eske & Orlando, Ludovico

2016 'Human Evolution: A Tale from Ancient Genomes', *Philosophical Transactions of the Royal Society B: Biological Sciences* 372/1713: 20150484.

Lorkiewicz, Wieslaw; Płoszaj, Tomasz; Jędrychowska-Dańska, Kristina; Żądzińska, Elżbieta; Strapagiel, Dominik; Haduch, Elżbieta; Szczepanek, Anita; Grygiel, Ryszard & Witas, Henryk W.

2015 'Between the Baltic and Danubian Worlds: The Genetic Affinities of a Middle Neolithic Population from Central Poland', *PLoS One* 10: e0118316.

Loumou, Angeliki & Giourga, Christina

2003 'Olive Groves: "The Life and Identity of the Mediterranean"', *Agriculture and Human Values* 20: 87-95.

Lovell, Jamie L.

2002 'Shifting Subsistence Patterns: Some Ideas about the End of the Chalcolithic in the Southern Levant', *Paléorient* 28/1: 89-102.

2010 'Community Is Cult, Cult Is Community: Weaving the Web of Meanings for the Chalcolithic', *Paléorient* 36/1: 103-22.

Lovell, Jamie; Richter, Tobias; McLaren, Bruce; McRae, I. Katherine & Abu Shmeis, Adeib

2005 'The First Preliminary Report of the Wadi ar-Rayyan Archaeological Project: The Survey of Al-Khawarij', *Annual of the Department of Antiquities of Jordan* 49: 189-200.

Lovell, Jamie; Thomas, David; Miller, Henry; Wesselingh, Karyn; Kurzawska, Aldona; McRae, I. Katherine; Elias, Christine; Obeidat, E. & Abu Shmais, Adeib

2007 'The Third Preliminary Report of the Wadi ar-Rayyan Archaeological Project: The Second Season of Excavations at Al-Khawarij', *Annual of the Department of Antiquities of Jordan* 51: 103–40.

Mabry, Jonathan

1989 'Investigations at Tell el-Handaquq, Jordan (1978–88)', *Annual of the Department of Antiquities of Jordan* 33: 59–95.

1995 'Early Town Development and Water Management in the Jordan Valley: Investigations at Tell el-Handaquq North', in William G. Dever (ed.), *Preliminary Excavation Reports: Sardis, Idalion, and Tell el-Handaquq North* (Annual of the American Schools of Oriental Research 53). American Schools of Oriental Research Publications, Boston: 115–54.

Macalister, Robert M. A.

1912 *The Excavation of Gezer*, II. Murray, London.

Mallon, Alexis; Koeppel, Robert & Neuville, René

1934 *Teleilat Ghassul*, I. Pontifical Biblical Institute, Rome.

1940 *Teleilat Ghassul*, II. Pontifical Biblical Institute, Rome.

Manclossi, Francesca & Rosen, Steven A.

2022 'Transitions, Truncations, Correlations, and Disassociations in Early Bronze Age Lithic Systems of the Southern Levant: Issues of Process', in Matthew J. Adams & Valentine Roux (eds), *Transitions during the Early Bronze Age in the Levant: Methodological Problems and Interpretative Perspectives*. Zaphon, Munster: 301–18.

Marciniak, Stephanie & Perry, George H.

2017 'Harnessing Ancient Genomes to Study the History of Human Adaptation', *Nature Reviews Genetics* 11: 659–74.

Margaritis, Evi

2013 'Distinguishing Exploitation, Domestication, Cultivation and Production: The Olive in the Third Millennium Aegean', *Antiquity* 87: 746–57.

Mathieson, Iain; Roodenberg, Songül A.; Posth, Cosimo; Szécsényi-Nagy, Anna; Rohland, Nadin; Mallick, Swapan; Olalde, Inigo; Broomandkhoshbacht, Nasreen; Candilio, Francesca; Cheronet, Olivia; Fernandes, Daniel; Ferry, Matthew; Gamarra, Beatriz; González Fortes, Gloria; Haak, Wolfgang; Harney, Eadaoin; Jones, Eppie; Keating, Denise; Krause-Kyora, Ben; Kucukkalipci, Isil; Michel, Megan; Mittnik, Alissa; Nägele, Kathrin; Novak, Mario; Oppenheimer, Jonas; Patterson, Nick; Pfrengle, Saskia; Sirak, Kendra; Stewardson, Kristin; Vai, Stefania; Alexandrov, Stefan; Alt, Kurt W.; Andreescu, Radian; Antonović, Dragana; Ash, Abigail; Atanassova, Nadezhda; Bacvarov, Krum; Balázs Gusztáv, Mende; Bocherens, Hervé; Bolus, Michael; Boroneanţ, Adina; Boyadzhiev, Yavor; Budnik, Alicja; Burmaz, Josip; Chohadzhiev, Stefan; Conard, Nicholas J.; Cottiaux, Richard; Čuka, Maja; Cupillard, Christophe; Drucker, Dorothée G.; Elenski, Nedko; Francken, Michael; Galabova, Borislava; Ganetsovski, Georgi; Gély, Bernard; Hajdu, Tamás; Handzhyiska, Veneta; Harvati, Katerina; Higham, Thomas; Iliev, Stanislav; Janković, Ivor; Karavanić, Ivor; Kennett, Douglas J.; Komšo, Darko; Kozak, Alexandra; Labuda, Damian; Lari, Martina; Lazar, Catalin; Leppek, Maleen; Leshtakov, Krassimir; Lo Vetro, Domenico; Los, Dzeni; Lozanov, Ivaylo; Malina, Maria; Martini, Fabio; McSweeney, Kath; Meller, Harald; Menđušić, Marko; Mirea, Pavel; Moiseyev, Vyacheslav; Petrova, Vanya; Price, T. Douglas; Simalcsik, Angela; Sineo, Luca; Šlaus, Mario; Slavchev, Vladimir; Stanev, Petar; Starović, Andrej; Szeniczey, Tamás; Talamo, Sahra; Teschler-Nicola, Maria; Thevenet, Corinne; Valchev, Ivan; Valentin, Frederique; Vasilyev, Sergey; Veljanovska, Fanica; Venelinova, Svetlana; Veselovskaya, Elizaveta; Viola, Bence; Virag, Cristian; Zaninović, Joško; Zäuner, Steve; Stockhammer, Philipp W.; Catalano,

Giulio; Krauß, Raiko; Caramelli, David; Zariņa, Gunita; Gaydarska, Bisserka; Lillie, Malcolm; Nikitin, Alexey G.; Potekhina, Inna; Papathanasiou, Anastasia; Borić, Dušan; Bonsall, Clive; Krause, Johannes; Pinhasi, Ron & Reich, David

2017 'The Genomic History of Southeastern Europe', *Nature* 555: 197–203.

Mazar, Amihai (ed.)

2012 *Excavations at Tel Beth-Shean 1989-1996*, IV: *The Fourth and Third Millennia* BCE *Jerusalem*. Israel Exploration Society, Jerusalem.

Mazar, Amihai; Miroschedji, Pierre de & Porat, Naomi

1996 'Hartuv, an Aspect of the Early Bronze I Culture of Southern Israel', *Bulletin of the American Schools of Oriental Research* 302: 1–40.

McConaughy, Mark A.

1980 'Chipped Stone Tools', in Walter E. Rast & Thomas R. Schaub, 'Preliminary Report of the 1979 Expedition to the Dead Sea Plain', *Bulletin of the American Schools of Oriental Research* 240: 53–61.

Meadows, John

2005 'The Younger Dryas Episode and the Radiocarbon Chronologies of the Lake Huleh and Ghab Valley Pollen Diagrams, Israel and Syria', *The Holocene* 15: 631–36.

Milevski, Ianir; Fabian, Peter & Marder, Ofer

2011 'Canaanean Blades in Chalcolithic Contexts of the Southern Levant?', in Jaimie L. Lovell & Yorke M. Rowan (eds), *Culture, Chronology and the Chalcolithic: Theory and Transition*. Oxbow, Oxford: 149–59.

Miroschedji, Pierre de

1989 'Le processus d'urbanisation en Palestine au Bronze Ancien: chronologie et rythmes', in Pierre de Miroschedji (ed.), *L'Urbanisation de la Palestine à l'Âge du Bronze Ancien* (British Archaeological Reports, International Series 527). Archaeopress, Oxford: 63–80.

Montanari, Daria

2020 *Le armi in metallo nel Levante Meridionale nel Bronzo Antico* (Rome 'La Sapienza' Studies on the Archaeology of Palestine and Transjordan 14), Sapienza Università di Roma, Rome.

Morozova, Irina; Flegontov, Pavel; Mikheyev, Alexander S.; Bruskin, Sergey; Asgharian, Hosseinali; Ponomarenko, Petr; Klyuchnikov, Vladimir; ArunKumar, GaneshPrasad; Prokhortchouk, Egor; Gankin, Yuriy; Rogaev, Evgeny; Nikolsky, Yuri; Baranova, Ancha; Elhaik, Eran & Tatarinova, Tatiana V.

2016 'Toward High-Resolution Population Genomics Using Archaeological Samples', *DNA Research* 23: 295–310.

Müller-Neuhof, Bernard

2006 'Tabular Scraper Quarry Site in the Wadi Ruwayshid Region (N/E Jordan)', *Annual of the Department of Antiquities of Jordan* 50: 373–83.

2013 'Southwest Asian Late Chalcolithic/Early Bronze Age Demand for "Big-Tools": Specialized Flint Exploitation beyond the Fringes of Settled Regions', *Lithic Technology* 38/3: 220–36.

2015 'Evidences for an Early Bronze Age (EBA) Colonization of the Jawa Hinterland: Preliminary Results of the 2015 Field-Work Season in Tulul al-Ghusayn', *Bulletin of the Council of British Research in the Levant* 10: 74–77.

2017 'The Chalcolithic/Early Bronze Age Hillfort Phenomenon in the Northern Badia', *Near Eastern Archaeology* 80/2: 124–31.

2020 'Defending the "Land of the Devil": Prehistoric Hillforts in the Jawa Hinterland', in Peter M. M. G. Akkermans (ed.), *Landscapes of Survival: The Archaeology and Epigraphy of Jordan's North Eastern Desert and Beyond*. Sidestone, Leiden: 145–63.

2021 'The Smoking Gun? An Uruk Deposit from the Black Desert in Jordan', in Claudia Bührig, Margarete van Ess, Iris Gerlach, Arnulf Hausleiter & Bernd Müller-Neuhof (eds), *Klänge der Archäologie: Festschrift für Ricardo Eichmann*. Harrassowitz, Wiesbaden: 299–308.

Müller-Neuhof, Bernd; Abu-Azizeh, Lorraine; Abu-Azizeh, Wael & Meister, Julia

2013 'East of Jawa: Chalcolithic/Early Bronze Age Settling Activities in the al-Harra (NE-Jordan)', *Annual of the Department of Antiquities of Jordan* 57: 125–39.

Muñiz, Juan R. & Polcaro, Andrea

2016 'Jebel al-Mutawwaq', *Arqueología Bíblica* 91: 39–47.

Muñiz, Juan, R.; Polcaro, Andrea & Alvarez, Valentin

2013 'La evolución del estudio de un yacimiento de la edad del bronce Antiguo I en la estepa jordana', *ISIMU (Revista sobre Oriente Próximo y Egipto en la antigüedad)* 16: 79–95.

2016 'New Spanish – Italian Excavations to the Dolmen Field of Jabal al-Mutawwaq in Middle Wadi az-Zarqa. Preliminary Results of 2012 Campaign', *Studies in the History and Archaeology of Jordan* 12: 477–88.

Namdar, Dvory; Amrani, Alon; Getzov, Nimrod & Milevski, Ianir

2015 'Olive Oil Storage during the Fifth and Sixth Millennia BC at Ein Zippori, Northern Israel', *Israel Journal of Plant Sciences* 62: 65–74.

Neumann, Frank; Schölzel, Christian; Litt, Thomas; Hense, Andreas & Stein, Mordechai

2007 'Holocene Vegetation and Climate History of the Northern Golan Heights (Near East)', *Vegetation History and Archaeobotany* 16: 329–46.

Newton, Claire; Lorre, Christine; Sauvage, Caroline; Ivorra, Sarah & Terral, Jean-Frédéric

2014 'On the Origins and Spread of *Olea europaea* L. (Olive) Domestication: Evidence for Shape Variation of Olive Stones at Ugarit, Late Bronze Age, Syria: A Window on the Mediterranean Basin and on the Westward Diffusion of Olive Varieties', *Vegetation History and Archaeobotany* 23: 567–75.

Nicolle, Christophe

2012 'The Mid-4th Millennium Gathering Site of Mutawwaq in Northern Jordan', in Juan Ramon Muñiz (ed.), *Ad Orientem: Del final del paleolitico en el norte de Espana a las primeras civilizaciones del Oriente Proximo*. Ménsula Ediciones, Oviedo: 431–46.

Nicolle, Christophe & Braemer, Frank

2012 'Settlement Networks in the Southern Levant in the Mid 4th Millennium BC: Sites with Double-Apsed Houses in the Leja Area of Southern Syria during the EBA IA', *Levant* 44: 1–16.

Nigro, Lorenzo (ed.)

2006 *Tell es-Sultan / Gerico alle soglie della prima urbanizzazione: il villaggio e la necropoli del Bronzo Antico I (3300-3000 a.C.)* (Rome 'La Sapienza' Studies on the Archaeology of Palestine and Transjordan 1). Sapienza Università di Roma, Rome.

Nigro, Lorenzo

2013 'Khirbet al-Batrawy. An Early Bronze Age City at the Fringes of the Desert', *Syria* 90: 189–209.

2016 'Khirbat al-Batrawy 2010-2013: The City Defences and the Palace of Copper Axes', *Studies in the History and Archaeology of Jordan* 12: 135–54.

2019 'Archaeological Periodization VS Absolute Chronology: What Does Not Work with High and Low Early Bronze Age in Southern Levant', in Elisabetta Gallo (ed.), *Conceptualizing Urban Experiences: Tell es-Sultan and Tall al-Ḥammām Early Bronze Cities across the Jordan; Proceedings of a Workshop Held in Palermo, G. Whitaker Foundation, Villa Malfitano June, 19th 2017* (Rome 'La Sapienza' Studies on the Archaeology of Palestine and Transjordan 13). Sapienza Università di Roma, Rome: 1–46.

Nigro, Lorenzo; Calcagnile, Lucio; Yasin, Jehad; Gallo, Elisabetta & Quarta, Gianluca
2019 'Jericho and the Chronology of Palestine in the Early Bronze Age: A Radiometric Reassessment', *Radiocarbon* 61/1: 211–41.

Nur el-Din, Hamid
2000 'The Development of the Broadroom House during the Early Bronze Age and its Chieftain Architectural Concept in Palestine', in Paolo Matthiae, Alessandra Enea, Luca Peyronel & Frances Pinnock (eds), *Proceedings of the First International Congress on the Archaeology of the Ancient Near East, Rome, May 18th-23rd 1998*. Sapienza Università di Roma, Rome: 1225–33.

O'Sullivan, Niall; Posth, Cosimo; Coia, Valentina; Schuenemann, Verena J.; Prince, Douglas T.; Wahl, Joachim; Pinhasi, Ron; Zink, Albert; Krause, Johannes & Maixner, Frank
2018 'Ancient Genome-Wide Analyses Infer Kinship Structure in an Early Medieval Alemannic Graveyard', *Science Advances* 4/9: 11262.

Ozenda, Paul
1975 'Sur les étages de végétation dans les montagnes du bassin méditerranéen', *Documents de cartographie écologique* 16: 1–32.

Pääbo, Svante
1989 'Ancient DNA: Extraction, Characterization, Molecular Cloning, and Enzymatic Amplification', *Proceedings of the National Academy of Science of the USA* 86: 1939–43.

Pääbo, Svante; Poinar, Hendrik; Serre, David; Jaenicke-Déprés, Viviane; Hebler, Juliane; Rohland, Nadine; Kuch, Melanie; Krause, Johannes; Vigilant, Linda & Hofreiter, Michael
2004 'Genetic Analyses from Ancient DNA', *Annual Review of Genetics* 38: 645–79.

Pääbo, Svante & Wilson, Allan C.
1988 'Polymerase Chain Reaction Reveals Cloning Artefacts', *Nature* 334/6181: 387–88.

Pereira, Luìsa; Černý, Viktor; Cerezo, Maria; Hájek, Martin; Vašíková, Alžběta; Kujanová, Martina; Brdička, Radim & Salas, Antonio
2010 'Linking the Sub-Saharan and West Eurasian Gene Pools: Maternal and Paternal Heritage of the Tuareg Nomads from the African Sahel', *European Journal of Human Genetic* 18: 915–23.

Peroni, Roberto
1998 'Classificazione tipologica, seriazione cronologica, distribuzione geografica', *Aquileia Nostra* 69: 9–28.

Philip, Graham
1989 *Metal Weapons of the Early and Middle Bronze Ages in Syria-Palestine* (British Archaeological Reports, International Series 526). Archaeopress, Oxford.
2003 'The Early Bronze Age of the Southern Levant: A Landscape Approach', *Journal of Mediterranean Archaeology* 16/1: 103–32.
2008 'The Early Bronze Age I–III', in Russell B. Adams (ed.), *Jordan: An Archaeological Reading*. Equinox, London: 161–226.
2011 'The Later Prehistory of the Southern Levant: Issues of Practice and Context', in Jamie L. Lovell & Yorke M. Rowan (eds), *Culture Chronology and the Chalcolithic: Theory and Transition* (Levant Supplementary Series 9). Oxbow, Oxford: 192–209.

Philip, Graham & Baird, Douglas (eds)
2000 *Ceramics and Change in the Early Bronze Age Southern Levant* (Levantine Archaeology 2). Sheffield Academic Press, Sheffield.

Pilli, Elena; Modi, Alessandra; Serpico, Ciro; Achilli, Alessandro; Lancioni, Hovirag; Lippi, Barbara; Bertoldi, Francesca; Gelichi, Sauro; Lari, Martina & Caramelli, David
2013 'Monitoring DNA Contamination in Handled vs. Directly Excavated Ancient Human Skeletal Remains', *PLoS One* 8: e52524.

Pinhasi, Ron; Fernandes, Daniel; Sirak, Kendra; Novak, Mario; Connell, Sarah; Alpaslan-Roodenberg, Songül; Gerritsen, Fokke; Moiseyev, Vyacheslav; Gromov, Andrey; Raczky, Pál; Anders, Alexandra; Pietrusewsky, Michael; Rollefson, Gary; Jovanovic, Marija; Trinhhoang, Hiep; Guy, Bar-Oz; Oxenham, Marc; Matsumura, Hirofumi & Hofreiter, Michael
2015 'Optimal Ancient DNA Yields from the Inner Ear Part of the Human Petrous Bone', *PLoS One* 10/6, e0129102.

Poinar, Hendrik; Höss, Matthias; Bada, Jeffrey L. & Pääbo, Svante
1996 'Amino Acid Racemization and the Preservation of Ancient DNA', *Science* 272: 864–66.

Poinar, Hendrik; Kuch, Melanie; McDonald, Gregory; Martin, Paul & Pääbo, Svante
2003 'Nuclear Gene Sequences from a Late Pleistocene Sloth Coprolite', *Current Biology* 13/13: 1150–52.

Polcaro, Andrea
2006 *Necropoli e costumi funerari in Palestina dal Bronzo Antico I al Bronzo Antico III* (Contributi e materiali di archeologia orientale 11). Sapienza Università di Roma, Rome.

2008 'The Ideology of Ancestors in the EB I Palestine and Transjordan: The Cult of Dead as Social Structure and Factor of Territorial Unification of Early Urban Development', in Hartmut Kühne, Rainer M. Czichon & Florian J. Kreppner (eds), *Proceedings of the 4th International Congress of the Archaeology of the Ancient Near East, 29 March – 3 April 2004, Freie Universität Berlin*. Harrassowitz, Wiesbaden: 521–36.

2013 'The Stone and the Landscape: The Phenomenon of Megalithic Constructions in Jordan in the Main Historical Context of Southern Levant at the Beginning of the 3rd Millennium BC', in Luca Bombardieri, Anacleto D'Agostino, Guido Guarducci, Valentina Orsi & Stefano Valentini (eds), *Identity and Connectivity: Proceeding of the 16th Symposium on Mediterranean Archaeology, 1st-3rd March 2012 Florence, Italy* (British Archaeological Reports, International Series 2581). Archaeopress, Oxford: 127–36.

2018 'Esplorazioni e primi contatti commerciali egizi con il Levante Meridionale nel IV millennio a.C.', in Agnese Vacca, Sara Pizzimenti & Maria Gabriella Micale (eds), *A Oriente del Delta: scritti sull'Egitto ed il Vicino Oriente antico in onore di Gabriella Scandone Matthiae* (Contributi e materiali di archeologia orientale 18). Sapienza Università di Roma, Rome: 539–66.

2019a 'The Jordan Valley and its Eastern Tributaries at the Beginning of the Bronze Age: Dolmen Fields and Settlements in the 4th Millennium BC', in Elisabetta Gallo (ed.), *Conceptualizing Urban Experiences, Tell es-Sultan and Tall al-Ḥammām Early Bronze Cities across the Jordan: Proceedings of a Workshop Held in Palermo, G. Whitaker Foundation, Villa Malfitano June, 19th 2017* (Rome 'La Sapienza' Studies on the Archaeology of Palestine and Transjordan 13). Sapienza Università di Roma, Rome: 47–60.

2019b 'On Pots and Serpents: An Iconographic and Contextual Analysis of the Cultic Vessels with Serpent Figurines in the 4th-3rd Millennium BC Transjordan', in Marta D'Andrea, Maria Gabriella Micale, Davide Nadali, Sara Pizzimenti & Agnese Vacca (eds), *Pearls of the Past* (MARRU 8). Zaphon, Münster: 775–94.

2021 'EBI and Early Urbanism in Jordan: New Lights on a Formative Period from Jebel Mutawwaq', in Jesse C. Long & William G. Dever (eds), *Transitions, Urbanism, and Collapse in the Bronze Age: Essays in Honor of Suzanne Richard*. Equinox, Sheffield: 95–109.

Polcaro, Andrea & Muñiz, Juan R.
2017 'Jebel al Mutawwaq, the Mountain Surrounded by Water. The Importance of Water Resources during the 4th Millennium BC in the Transjordanian Highlands', in Lorenzo Nigro, Michele Nucciotti & Elisabetta Gallo (eds), *Precious Water: Paths of Jordanian Civilizations as Seen in the Italian Archaeological Excavations; Proceedings of the International Conference Held in Amman, October 18th 2016* (Rome 'La Sapienza' Studies on the Archaeology of Palestine and Transjordan 12). Sapienza Università di Roma, Rome: 15–27.

2018 'Dolmen 534: A Megalithic Tomb of the Early Bronze Age II in Jebel al-Mutawwaq, Jordan. Preliminary Results of the 2014 Spanish-Italian Expedition in Area Cc South', in Barbara Horejs, Christoph Schwall, Vera Müller, Marta Luciani, Markus Ritter, Mattia Guidetti, Roderick B. Salisbury, Felix Höflmayer & Teresa Bürge (eds), *Proceedings of the 10th International Congress on the Archaeology of the Ancient Near East, 25-29 June 2016, Vienna*. Harrassowitz, Wiesbaden: 589–600.

2019 'Preliminary Results of the 2014–2015 Excavations Campaigns at the Early Bronze Age I Settlement of Jebel al-Mutawwaq, Middle Wadi az-Zarqa, Area C', in *Proceedings of the International Congress on the History and Archaeology of Jordan, Amman Princess Sumaya University 22-26 May 2016* (Studies on History and Archaeology of Jordan 13). Department of Antiquities of Jordan, Amman: 85–96.

2021 'Preliminary Report of the Seventh Season (2018) of Spanish-Italian Excavations to Jebel al-Mutawwaq, Wadi az-Zarqa, Jordan', *Annual of the Department of Antiquities of Jordan* 60: 301–09.

2023 'The 2018–2019 Spanish-Italian Archaeological Campaigns at Jebel al-Mutawwaq: The Early Bronze Age I Site and the Megalithic Necropolis', in Nicolò Marchetti, Francesca Cavaliere, Enrico Cirelli, Claudia D'Orazio, Gabriele Giocosa, Mattia Guidetti & Eleonora Mariani (eds), *Proceedings of the 15th International Congress on the Archaeology of the Ancient Near East, Alma Mater Studiorum, University di Bologna 6-9 April 2021, Bologna*. Harrassowitz, Wiesbaden: 499–510.

Polcaro, Andrea; Muñiz, Juan R.; Alvarez, Valentin; Mogliazza, Silvia

2014 'Dolmen 317 and its Hidden Burial: An Early Bronze Age I Megalithic Tomb from Jebel al-Mutawwaq (Jordan)', *Bulletin of American Schools of Oriental Research* 372: 1–17.

Polcaro, Andrea; Muñiz, Juan R. & Caselli, Alessandra

In press _ 'Preliminary Report of the Eighth Spanish-Italian Archeological Expedition to Jebel al-Mutawwaq, Middle Wadi az-Zarqa, September 2019', *Annual of the Department of Antiquities in Jordan* 61.

Posth, Cosimo; Renaud, Gabriel; Mittnik, Alissa; Drucker, Dorothée G.; Rougier, Hélène; Cupillard, Christophe; Valentin, Frédérique; Thevenet, Corinne; Furtwängler, Anja; Wißing, Christoph; Francken, Michael; Malina, Maria; Bolus, Michael; Lari, Martina; Gigli, Elena; Capecchi, Giulia; Crevecoeur, Isabelle; Beauval, Cédric; Flas, Damien; Germonpré, Mietje; Plicht, Johanne van der; Cottiaux, Richard; Gély, Bernard; Ronchitelli, Annamaria; Wehrberger, Kurt; Grigorescu, Dan; Svoboda, Jiří; Semal, Patrick; Caramelli, David; Bocherens, Hervé; Harvati, Katerina; Conard, Nicholas J.; Haak, Wolfgang; Powell, Adam & Krause, Johannes

2016 'Pleistocene Mitochondrial Genomes Suggest a Single Major Dispersal of Non-Africans and a Late Glacial Population Turnover in Europe', *Current Biology* 26: 827–33.

Prag, Key

1995 'The Dead Sea Dolmens: Death and the Landscape', in Stuart Campbell & Anthony Green (eds), *The Archaeology of Death in the Ancient Near East*. Oxbow, Oxford: 75–84.

Prüfer, Kay; Stenzel, Udo; Hofreiter, Michael; Pääbo, Svante; Kelso, Janet & Green, Richard

2010 'Computational Challenges in the Analysis of Ancient DNA', *Genome Biology* 11: R 47.

Quézel, Pierre & Barbero, Marcel

1985 *Carte de la végétation potentielle de la région méditerranéenne orientale*. Centre national de la recherche scientifique, Paris.

Rasmussen, Kaare L.; de la Fuente, Gulliermo A.; Bond, Andrew D.; Mathiesen, Karsten K.; Vera, Sergio D.

2012 'Pottery Firing Temperature: A New Method for Determining the Firing Temperature of Ceramics and Burnt Clay', *Journal of Archaeological Science* 39: 1705–16 <https://doi.org/10.1016/j.jas.2012.01.008>.

Rast, Walter E. & Schaub, R. Thomas

2003   *Bab edh-Dhra: Excavations at the Town Site (1975-1981)*, I: *Text* (Reports of the Expedition to the Dead Sea Plains, Jordan 1). Eisenbraun, Winona Lake.

Read, Dwight W.

2007   *Artifact Classification: A Conceptual and Methodological Approach*. Routledge, New York.

Regev, Johanna; Finkelstein, Israel; Adams, M. J. & Boaretto, Elisabetta

2012   'Wiggle-Matched C14 Chronology of Early Bronze Age Megiddo and the Synchronization of Egyptian and Levantine Chronologies', *Egypt and the Levant* 24: 243-66.

Requejo Pagés, Otilia

2012   'Juan A. Fernandez-Tresguerres Velasco y la actividad arquelogica espanola en Jordania (1987-2011)', in Juan Ramon Muñiz (ed.), *Ad Orientem: Del final del Paleolitico en el norte de Espana a las primeras civilizaciones del Oriente Proximo*. Mensula Ediciones, Oviedo: 367-82.

Rice, Prudence M.

2015   *Pottery Analysis: A Sourcebook*, 2nd edn. University of Chicago Press, Chicago.

Richard, Suzanne

2014   'The Southern Levant (Transjordan) during the Early Bronze Age', in Margreet L. Steiner & Ann E. Killebrew (eds), *The Oxford Handbook of the Archaeology of the Levant, c. 8000-332 BCE*. Oxford University Press, Oxford: 453-83.

Riehl, Simone

2009   'Archaeobotanical Evidence for the Interrelationship of Agricultural Decision-Making and Climate Change in the Ancient Near East', *Quaternary International* 197: 93-114.

Rizzi, Ermanno; Lari, Martina; Gigli, Elena; De Bellis, Gianluca & Caramelli, David

2012   'Ancient DNA Studies: New Perspectives on Old Samples', *Genetics Selection Evolution* 44: 21.

Rohland, Nadine & Hofreiter, Michael

2007   'Ancient DNA Extraction from Bones and Teeth', *Nature Protocols* 2/7: 1756-62.

Roostalu, Urmas; Kutuev, Ildus; Loogväli, Ellen L.; Metspalu, Ene; Tambets, Kristiina; Reidla, Miranda; Khusnutdinova, Elaza K.; Usanga, Esien; Kivisild, Toomas & Villems, Richard

2007   'Origin and Expansion of Haplogroup H, the Dominant Human Mitochondrial DNA Lineage in West Eurasia: The Near Eastern and Caucasian Perspective', *Molecular Biology and Evolution* 24/2: 436-48.

Rosen, Steven A.

1989   'The Analysis of Early Bronze Age Chipped Stone Industries: A Summary Statement', in Pierre de Miroschedji (ed.), *L'urbanisation de la Palestine à l'âge du Bronze ancien: bilan et perspectives des recherches actuelles; actes du colloque d'Emmaüs (20-24 octobre 1986)* (British Archaeological Reports, International Series 527/1). BAR, Oxford: 199-221.

1997   *Lithics after the Stone Age: A Handbook of Stone Tools from the Levant*. AltaMira, Walnut Creek.

2011   'Desert Chronologies and Periodization Systems', in Jaimie L. Lovell & Yorke M. Rowan (eds), *Culture, Chronology and the Chalcolithic: Theory and Transition*. Oxbow, Oxford: 71-83.

Rosen, Steven A. & Gopher, Avi

2003   'Flint Tools from the Survey', in Itzhaq Beit-Arieh (ed.), *Archaeology of Sinai: The Ophir Expedition*. Emery and Claire Yass Publications in Archaeology, Tel Aviv: 184-94.

Rosenberg, Danny & Golani, Amir

2012 'Groundstone Tools of a Copper-Smiths' Community: Understanding Stone-Related Aspects of the Early Bronze Age Site of Ashqelon Barnea', *Journal of Mediterranean Archaeology* 25/1: 27–51.

Rosenberg, Danny; Chasan, Rivka & Brink, Edwin C. M. van den

2016 'Craft Specialization, Production and Exchange in the Chalcolithic of the Southern Levant: Insights from the Study of the Basalt Bowl Assemblage from Namir Road, Tel Aviv, Israel', *Eurasian Prehistory* 13/1–2: 105–28.

Roux, Valentine

2019 *Ceramics and Society: A Technological Approach to Archaeological Assemblages*. Springer, Berlin.

Rowan, Yorke M.

2003 'The Groundstone Assemblage', in Amir Golani (ed.), *Salvage Excavations at the Early Bronze Age Site of Qiryat Ata* (Israel Antiquities Authority Reports 18). Israel Antiquities Authority, Jerusalem: 183–202.

Rowan, Yorke M. & Golden, Jonathan

2009 'The Chalcolithic Period of the Southern Levant: A Synthetic Review', *Journal of World Prehistory* 22: 1–92.

Rowan, Yorke M. & Ilan, David

2007 'The Meaning of Ritual Diversity in the Chalcolithic of the Southern Levant', in David A. Barrowclough & Caroline Malone (eds), *Cult in Context: Reconsidering Ritual in Archaeology*. Oxbow, Oxford: 249–56.

Rowan, Yorke M. & Levy, Thomas E.

1991 'Use Wear Analysis of Chalcolithic Scraper Assemblage from Shiqmim', *Journal of the Israel Prehistoric Society* 24: 112–32.

2011 'Transitions in Macehead Manufacture in the Ancient Levant: A Case Study from Nahal Tillah (Tel Halif Terrace), Israel', in Meredith Chesson (ed.), *Daily Life, Materiality and Complexity in Early Urban Communities of the Southern Levant: Papers in Honor of Walter E. Rast and R. Thomas Schaub*. Eisenbrauns, Winona Lake: 199–218.

Rowan, Yorke M.; Levy, Thomas E.; Alon, David & Goren, Yuval

2006 'Gilat's Ground Stone Assemblage: Stone Fenestrated Stands, Vessels, Palettes and Related Artifacts', in Thomas E. Levy (ed.), *Archaeology, Anthropology and Cult: The Sanctuary at Gilat, Israel*. Equinox, London: 575–684.

Rutter, Graham

2003 'Basaltic-Rock Procurement Systems in the Southern Levant: Case Studies from the Chalcolithic-Early Bronze I and the Late Bronze-Iron Ages' (unpublished doctoral thesis, University of Durham).

Sabatini, Sharon

2019 'Olive Oil in Southern Levant: Rise and Fall of an Economy in the Early Bronze Age', in Elisabetta Gallo (ed.), *Conceptualizing Urban Experiences: Tell es-Sultan and Tall al-Ḥammām Early Bronze Cities across the Jordan; Proceedings of a Workshop Held in Palermo, G. Whitaker Foundation, Villa Malfitano June, 19th 2017* (Rome 'La Sapienza' Studies on the Archaeology of Palestine and Transjordan 13). Sapienza Università di Roma, Rome: 247–63.

Sala, Maura

2008 *L'architettura sacra della Palestina nell'Età del Bronzo Antico I–III* (Contributi e materiali di archeologia orientale 13). Sapienza Università di Roma, Rome.

Sánchez Caro, Jose M. & Calvo Gomez, Jose A.
2015 *La casa de Santiago en Jerusalén: el Instituto Español Bíblico y Arqueológico en Tierra Santa*. Editorial Verbo Divino, Estella.

Savage, Steven H.
2010 'Jordan's Stonehenge: The Endangered Chalcolithic / Early Bronze Age Site at al-Murayghat', *Near Eastern Archaeology* 73/1: 32–46.

Sawyer, Susanna; Krause, Johannes; Guschanski, Katerina; Savolainen, Vincent & Pääbo, Svante
2012 'Temporal Patterns of Nucleotide Misincorporations and DNA Fragmentation in Ancient DNA', *PLoS One* 7: e34131.

Schaub, R. Thomas & Rast, Walter E.
1989 *Bab edh-Dhra': Excavations in the Cemetery, Directed by Paul W. Lapp (1965-1967)* (Reports of the Expedition to the Dead Sea Plains, Jordan 1). Eisenbrauns, Winona Lake.

Schiebel, Vera
2013 'Vegetation and Climate History of the Southern Levant during the Last 30,000 Years Based on Palynological Investigation' (unpublished doctoral dissertation, University of Bonn).

Scott, James C.
2017 *Against the Grain: A Deep History of the Earliest States*. Yale University Press, New Haven.

Seaton, Peta
2008 *Chalcolithic Cult and Risk Management at Teleilat Ghassul: The Area E Sanctuary* (British Archaeological Reports, International Series 1864). Archaeopress, Oxford.

Sebag, Deborah
2005 'The Early Bronze Age Dwellings in the Southern Levant', *Bulletin du Centre de recherche français à Jérusalem* 16: 222–35.

Serventi, Patrizia; Panicucci, Chiara; Bodega, Roberta; De Fanti, Sara; Sarno, Stefano; Alvarez, Manuel F.; Brisighelli, Francesca; Trombetta, Beniamino; Anagnostou, Paolo; Ferri, Gianmarco; Vazzana, Antonino; Delpino, Chiara; Gruppioni, Giorgio; Luiselli, Donata & Cilli, Elisabetta
2018 'Iron Age Italic Population Genetics: The Piceni from Novilara (8th–7th Century BC)', *Annals of Human Biology* 45/1: 34–43.

Shapiro, Beth & Hofreiter, Michael
2014 'A Paleogenomic Perspective on Evolution and Gene Function: New Insights from Ancient DNA', *Science* 343/6169: 1236573.

Shimelmitz, Ron; Barkai, Ran & Gopher, Avi
2000 'A Cananean Blade Workshop at Har Haruvim, Israel', *Tel Aviv* 27: 3–22.

Skoglund, Pontus; Storå, Jan; Götherström, Anders & Jakobsson, Mattias
2014 'Accurate Sex Identification of Ancient Human Remains Using DNA Shotgun Sequencing', *Journal of Archaeological Science* 40: 4477–82.

Sorrel, Philippe & Mathis, Marie
2016 'Mid- to Late-Holocene Coastal Vegetation Patterns in Northern Levant (Tell Sukas, Syria): Olive Tree Cultivation History and Climatic Change', *The Holocene* 26: 858–73.

Stager, Lawrence E.

1985 *The First Fruits of Civilization: In Palestine in the Bronze and Iron Ages; Papers in Honor of Olga Tufnell* (Institute of Archaeology Occasional Papers 11). Institute of Archaeology, London.

1992 'The Periodisation of Palestine from the Neolithic through Early Bronze Times', in Robert W. Ehrich (ed.), *Chronologies in Old World Archaeology*, 3rd edn. University of Chicago, Chicago: 22–60.

Steimer-Herbet, Tara

2004 *Classification des sépultures à superstructure lithique dans le Levant et l'Arabie aux IVe et IIIe millénaires av. J.-C.* (British Archaeological Reports, International Series 1246). Archaeopress, Oxford.

2013 'Dolmen and Tower Tombs (3600–2000 BC)', in Myriam Ababsa (ed.), *Atlas of Jordan: History, Territories and Society*. Institut français du Proche-Orient, Beirut: 119–21.

Steimer-Herbet, Tara; Cousseau, Florian; Haider-Boustani, Maya; Porra-Kuteni, Valérie & Besse, Marie

2020 'Megalithic Art in the Levantine Rift Valley: The Case of the Menjez Megalithic Monuments in the Akka (Northern Lebanon)', *Akkadica* 141: 1–24.

Stiller, Mathias; Knapp, Michael; Stenzel, Udo; Hofreiter, Michael & Meyer, Matthias

2009 'Direct Multiplex Sequencing (DMPS) – A Novel Method for Targeted High-Throughput Sequencing of Ancient and Highly Degraded DNA', *Genome Research* 19: 1843–48.

Tambets, Kristiina; Rootsi, Siiri; Kivisild, Toomas; Help, Hela; Serk, Piia; Loogväli, Eva-Liis; Tolk, Helle V.; Reidla, Maere; Metspalu, Ene; Pliss, Liana; Balanovsky, Oleg; Pshenichnov, Andrey; Balanovska, Elena; Gubina, Marina; Zhadanov, Sergey; Osipova, Ludmila; Damba, Larisa; Voevoda, Mikhail; Kutuev, Ildus; Bermisheva, Marina; Khusnutdinova, Elza; Gusar, Vladislava; Grechanina, Elena; Parik, Jüri; Pennarun, Erwan; Richard, Christelle; Chaventre, Andre; Moisan, Jean-Paul; Barać, Lovorka; Peričić, Marijana; Rudan, Pavao; Terzić, Rifat; Mikerezi, Ilia; Krumina, Astrida; Baumanis, Viesturs; Koziel, Slawomir; Rickards, Olga; De Stefano, Gian Franco; Anagnou, Nicholas; Pappa, Kalliopi I.; Michalodimitrakis, Emmanuel; Ferák, Vladimir; Füredi, Sandor; Komel, Radovan; Beckman, Lars & Villems, Richard

2004 'The Western and Eastern Roots of the Saami—the Story of Genetic "Outliers" Told by Mitochondrial DNA and Y Chromosomes', *American Journal of Human Genetics* 74: 661–82.

Tardi, Alan

2014 'The Culinary Uses of Extra-Virgin Olive Oil', in Claudio Peri (ed.), *The Extra-Virgin Olive Oil HandBook*. Wiley, Chichester: 321–37.

Terral, Jean-Frédéric

2000 'Exploitation and Management of the Olive Tree during Prehistoric Times in Mediterranean France and Spain', *Journal of Archaeological Science* 27: 127–33.

Terral, Jean-Frédéric & Arnold-Simard, Genevieve

1996 'Beginnings of Olive Cultivation in Eastern Spain in Relation to Holocene Bioclimatic Changes', *Quaternary Research* 46: 176–85.

Terral, Jean-Frédéric; Alonso, Natalia; Capdevila, Ramon Buxò; Chatti, Noureddine; Fabre, Laurent; Fiorentino, Girolamo; Marinval, Philippe; Jordà, Guillem Pérez; Pradat, Bénédicte; Rovira, Núria & Alibert, Paul

2004 'Historical Biogeography of Olive Domestication (*Olea europaea* L.) as Revealed by Geometrical Morphometry Applied to Biological and Archaeological Material', *Journal of Biogeography* 31: 63–77.

Thuesen, Ingolf
2009 'From Jericho to Mount Nebo: Results of Recent Excavations of Conder's Circle', *Studies in the History and Archaeology of Jordan* 10: 603–11.

Unger-Hamilton, Romana
1991 'The Microwear Analysis of Scrapers and "Sickle Blades"', in Alison V. G. Betts (ed.), *Excavations at Jawa 1972-1986: Stratigraphy, Pottery, and Other Finds*. University Press of Edinburgh, Edinburgh: 149–53.

Unterländer, Martina; Palstra, Friso; Lazaridis, Iosif; Pilipenko, Aleksandr; Hofmanová, Zuzana; Groß, Melanie; Sell, Christian; Blöcher, Jens; Kirsanow, Karola; Rohland, Nadin; Rieger, Benjamin; Kaiser, Elke; Schier, Wolfram; Pozdniakov, Dimitri; Khokhlov, Aleksandr; Georges, Myriam; Wilde, Sandra; Powell, Adam; Heyer, Evelyne; Currat, Mathias; Reich, David; Samashev, Zainolla; Parzinger, Hermann; Molodin, Vyacheslav I. & Burger, Joachim
2017 'Ancestry and Demography and Descendants of Iron Age Nomads of the Eurasian Steppe', *Nature Communications* 8: 14615.

Vacca, Agnese
2014 'Chronology and Distribution of 3rd Millennium BC Flasks', in Sara Pizzimenti & Licia Romano (eds), *Šime ummiānka* (Contributi e materiali di archeologia orientale 16). Sapienza Università di Roma, Rome: 251–86.

Vaux, Roland de
1955 'La Cinquieme campagne de fouilles a Tell el-Far'ah, pres Naplouse', *Revue biblique* 62: 541–89.

Vigilant, Linda; Pennington, Renee L.; Harpending, Henry; Kocher, Thomas & Wilson, Andrew C.
1989 'Mitochondrial DNA Sequences in Single Hairs from a Southern African Population', *Proceedings of the National Academy of Science of the USA* 86/23: 9350–54.

Wales, Nathan; Andersen, Kenneth; Cappellini, Enrico; Ávila-Arcos, Mària C. & Gilbert, Thomas P.
2014 'Optimization of DNA Recovery and Amplification from Non-Carbonized Archaeobotanical Remains', *PLoS One* 9/1: e86827.

Weinstein-Evron, Mina
1983 'The Paleoecology of the Early Wurm in the Hula Basin, Israel', *Paléorient* 9: 5–19.

Weiss, Ehud
2015 '"Beginnings of Fruit Growing in the Old World" – Two Generations Later', *Israel Journal of Plant Sciences* 62: 75–85.

Wilkinson, T. John; Philip, Graham; Bradbury, Jennie; Dunford, Ruth; Donoghue, D.; Galiatsatos, Nelson; Lawrence, Dan; Ricci, Andrea & Smith, Stephan L.
2014 'Contextualizing Early Urbanization: Settlement Cores, Early States and Agro-pastoral Strategies in the Fertile Crescent during the Fourth and Third Millennia BC', *Journal of World Prehistory* 27: 43–109.

Wright, George Ernest
1937 'The Pottery of Palestine from Earliest Times to the End of the Early Bronze Age', *Eretz-Israel* 5: 37–45.

Wright, Katherine
1992 'A Classification System for Ground Stone Tools from the Prehistoric Levant', *Paléorient* 18: 53–81.

Xavier, Catarina; Eduardoff, Mayra; Bertoglio, Barbara; Amory, Christina; Berger, Cordula; Casas-Vargas, Andrea; Pallua, Johannes & Parson, Walther
2021 'Evaluation of DNA Extraction Methods Developed for Forensic and Ancient DNA Applications Using Bone Samples of Different Age', *Genes (Basel)* 12/2: 146.

Yassine, Khair
1985 'The Dolmens: Construction and Dating Reconsidered', *Bulletin of American School of Oriental Research* 259: 63–69.

Yasuda, Yoshinori
1997 'The Rise and Fall of Olive Cultivation in Northwestern Syria: Palaeoecological Study of Tell Mastuma', *Nichibunken Japan Review: Bulletin of the International Research Center for Japanese Studies* 8: 251–73.

Zeist, Willem van
1980 *Aperçu de la diffusion des végétaux cultivés dans la région méditerranéenne: la mise en place, l'évaluation et la caractérisation de la flore et des végétations circum méditerranéennes.* Naturalia Monspeliensa, Montpellier.

Zeist, Willem van & Bakker-Heeres, Jean A. H
1984 'Archaeobotanical Studies in the Levant. 2. Neolithic and Halaf levels at Ras Shamra', *Palaeohistoria* 26: 151–70.

Zeist, Willem van; Baruch, Uri & Bottema, Sytze
2009 'Holocene Palaeoecology of the Hula Area, Northeastern Israel', in Eva Kaptijn & Lucas P. Petit (eds), *A Timeless Vale: Archaeological and Related Essays on the Jordan Valley.* Leiden University Press, Leiden: 29–64.

Zohary, Daniel & Hopf, Maria (eds)
2000 *Domestication of Plants in the Old World: The Origin and Spread of Cultivated Plants in West Asia, Europe, and the Nile Valley*, 3rd edn. Oxford University Press, Oxford.

Zohary, Daniel & Spiegel-Roy, Pinhas
1975 'Beginnings of Fruit Growing in the Old World', *Science* 187: 319–27.

Zohary, Daniel; Hopf, Maria & Weiss, Ehud
2012 *Domestication of Plants in the Old World: The Origin and Spread of Domesticated Plants in Southwest Asia, Europe, and the Mediterranean Basin*, 4th edn. Oxford University Press, Oxford.

Studies in the Archaeology & History of the Levant & Eastern Mediterranean

All volumes in this series are evaluated by an Editorial Board, strictly on academic grounds, based on reports prepared by referees who have been commissioned by virtue of their specialism in the appropriate field. The Board ensures that the screening is done independently and without conflicts of interest. The definitive texts supplied by authors are also subject to review by the Board before being approved for publication. Further, the volumes are copyedited to conform to the publisher's stylebook and to the best international academic standards in the field.

Title in series

Bassit (Syrie). Fouilles P. Courbin (1971-1984), Volume 2: le tell du XVIe siècle av. J.-C. au VIe siècle ap. J.-C., par Frank Braemer & Pascal Darcque (2022)

Mari Yamasaki, Conceptualizing Bronze Age Seascapes: Concepts of the Sea and Marine Fauna in the Eastern Mediterranean in the Second Millennium BCE (2023)

In Preparation

Households & Collective Buildings in Western Asian Neolithic Societies, ed. by Joaquim Sisa-López de Pablo, Anna Bach-Gómez & Miquel Molist